TROPES OF POLITICS

RHETORIC OF THE HUMAN SCIENCES

General Editors

David J. Depew

Deirdre N. McCloskey

John S. Nelson

John D. Peters

Tropes of Politics

SCIENCE, THEORY, RHETORIC, ACTION

JOHN S. NELSON

THE UNIVERSITY OF WISCONSIN PRESS

The University of Wisconsin Press
2537 Daniels Street
Madison, Wisconsin 53718

3 Henrietta Street
London WC2E 8LU, England

Lines from "Metaphors of Women," from *Antarctic Traveller* by Kathy Pollitt,
copyright © 1981 by Kathy Pollitt. Reprinted by permission of Alfred A. Knopf, Inc.

Library of Congress Cataloging-in-Publication Data
Nelson, John S., 1950–
    Tropes of politics: science, theory, rhetoric, action /
John S. Nelson.
        312 pp.   cm.—(Rhetoric of the human sciences)
        Includes bibliographical references and index.
        ISBN 0-299-15830-6 (alk. paper).
        ISBN 0-299-15834-9 (pbk. : alk. paper)
        1. Political science.   2. Rhetoric—Political aspects.   I. Title.
    II. Series.
JA71.N45   1998
320—DC21   97-36581

For Connie,

who really cares about everyday politics,
some different kinds of inquiry for better action.

CONTENTS

INTRODUCTION

TURNING AND TURNING IN THE WIDENING GYRE

A politics which is presumed to be available to everyone is a relatively new thing in the world. We do not yet know very much about it. Nor have most of us been especially eager to learn.
—Lionel Trilling[1]

Rhetoric must be a bridge, a road; too often it is a wall, an obstacle.
—Jorge Luis Borges[2]

Scholars in the late modern multiversity seem to write more and more, while hearing one another and our students less and less. Fields fragment, disciplines fall apart, inquiries spiral out of mutual reach and drift toward microscopic specializations with little sense of what the others are doing. Yet departments settle into Balkanic warfare to protect positions and budgets. Curricula for liberal education become log-rolling arrangements that leave students with much choice and little coherence. Everywhere the ceremonies of learning suffer from careerist repetition, retaining next to nothing of their inspiriting curiosities and founding aims. The heart and the mind are slowly going out of what might have been the noblest ambition of the second half of the twentieth century: advanced learning in the service of more adequately democratic politics. Or so the litany of complaints has been sounding for at least two decades—and not without urgent if still partial justification.

In this same time, talk of postmodern politics and inquiries has been making a different music. It trumpets multicultural educations and interdisciplinary investigations. It heralds a renewed reflexivity in research, reunification of mind and body in practice, revitalization of public discourses across the academy and throughout the culture. It jazzes up attention to forms and styles, even as it plays down reliance on any singular Method or univocal Truth. The movements and instruments of these postmodern impulses are more self-consciously perspectival and figural than before. They generate many sciences and arts in continuing and sometimes intense conversation with one another, as with the domains that they study. Or so the celebratory version goes but still with a subtle counterpoint of self-criticism and syncopated hesitation.

One of these postmodern movements in learning and community is rhetoric of inquiry, the larger topic of this book. Rhetoric of inquiry explores how scholars persuade. Thus it develops the traditions of the social sciences and humanities to improve current practices of learning. In particular, it appreciates how the learning involves argument, and the argument invokes rhetoric. The rhetoric is neither frill nor fraud, for the most part; rather it is rhetoric in the honorable, sophisticated sense of persuasive dialogue. Hence rhetoric of inquiry is especially eager to learn how we can and should communicate across our old divides of class, discipline, culture, party, and program.

From ritual deliberations to spontaneous demonstrations, people in politics speak and act rhetorically. Everybody knows that, even though our political inquiries have not always made much of it. Perhaps it may be more surprising to learn that all scholars write and teach rhetorically, from logical demonstrations to ethical criticisms. Does anything follow from that fact? Not always, perhaps, but often—and particularly so when scholars from political science and literature to computer science and physics remember the ambition for Unified Science, pretend to practice The Scientific Method, yet find their fields dispersing into many methods and kinds of knowledge. Precisely what follows will depend upon the specific projects and circumstances of each field. Rhetoric of inquiry explores the details.

Without much effort, and with no central orchestration, rhetoric of inquiry is emerging in most departments of the intellect and in many countries. Philosophers who practice it might be startled to find, for instance, that it is arising in sociology too. Students of planning are surprised to see it in psychology. Humanists are amazed that biologists do it at all. Their varied persuasions can in this sense become parts of a single project. To be sure, lawyers cannot directly help physicists run experiments in particle accelerators, but physicists can learn that some of their arguments follow courtroom forms and (like legal arguments) depend on precedent. Anthropologists have no real role in measuring the elasticity of oil supply, but they can teach economists how observations are subtle forms of participation, making supply curves into symbols that shape economic inferences by the economists and other potential targets of anthropological investigation.

Yet rhetoric of inquiry isn't new any more than it is a field unto itself. Rhetoric is arguably the oldest of Western disciplines. Though it began as the study and practice of public persuasion, rhetoric turned gradually with the invention of phonic writing into the appreciation and improvement of argument especially, and communication more generally, in domains beyond the overtly political. The recent turn is to explore how inquiries, scholarly and otherwise, are thoroughly rhetorical. Thus the practices of discovery, conception, invention, or testing in self-avowed sciences are persuasive through and through. Rhetoric is not limited to expression or persuasion of external audiences after the science proper has been completed. By implication, therefore, neither the arts, the humanities, nor the learned professions differ from the natural, social, or formal sciences in their rhetoricity. All these inquiries are alike in that they construct and conduct themselves rhetorically. Each offers a distinctive—yet changing—configuration of rhetorical strategies and devices in comparison with the other fields. Sometimes they share particular rhetorics, sometimes they don't, but always they proceed in rhetorical ways. Rhetoric of inquiry not only studies how but does so within each field, working to improve its conduct and knowledge. There are as many ways to do this as there are arts and artifacts of rhetoric.

To emphasize the rhetoric of scholars is to replace acceptance of reports with scrutiny of reasons. To regard one another's claims as arguments rather than "findings," scholars no longer need doctrines that portray facts as inarguably given. Such philosophies of science neither explain diverse projects of scholarship nor improve the words and deeds of scholars. Rhetorical attention to our researches can resist these epistemologies, preferring better work through greater understanding of the interaction of inquiries with communications. Furthermore it can resist the exclusive concentration on academic inquiries so that it can pursue better thinking, speaking, and acting in all realms of inquiry.

Because rhetoric of inquiry examines the reasoning of scholars in research communities, it studies their devices of inspiration, evidence, speculation, assumption, definition, inference, method, reporting, and criticism. It rejects the old notion that there are ironclad rules for inquiry that stand apart from actual practice. Accordingly it seeks not to distill some single model of Reason, Logic, or Method but to make the many styles of scholarship better aware of themselves and one another. Rhetoric of inquiry achieves little if pursued a priori and apart from substantive research. Working within projects of research, it seeks to make their assumptions more instructive and their operations more persuasive. Working across fields of inquiry, it tries to increase the quality and quantity of collaboration.

Rhetoric of inquiry ties methods to concrete problems, encouraging methodology to become comparative, situating itself in actual researches and exploring their implications for better inquiries. Unlike modernist epistemology, again, it does not seek to become a subject unto itself or an authority over other investigations. Fields may divide into separate conversations with distinct dialects, yet they still share the grammar of our civilization more than they know. Rhetoric of inquiry strives to increase awareness of this happy fact, making the arts and sciences more intelligible to themselves and to others.

At their best, then, rhetorics of inquiry operate in the twilight zone between detailed designs for research and abstract philosophies of inquiry. The ambition is to inform, even to become, the practices of inquiry and their epistemic capacities of self-criticism in every field. With the modern disrepute and eclipse of rhetoric as a discipline, the humanities and social sciences each developed further fragments for appreciating and improving human communication. Consequently rhetorics of inquiry today need to learn not only from rhetoric as a revitalized discipline but from all the humanities and social sciences. The arts and professions have important rhetorical principles to contribute as well. In practice, rhetorics of inquiry turn into politics of inquiry, economics of inquiry, sociologies of inquiry, aesthetics of inquiry, literary criticisms of science, psychologies of research, ecologies of ideas, histories of disciplines, geographies of discovery, and so on.

Rhetorics of inquiry pluralize logics of science. They encompass, embody, and contextualize them in a much richer, more comparative domain of persuasive practices. Thus rhetorics of inquiry resist reduction to abstract epistemologies and philosophies of science. They turn aside from the impulse to singularize Science into an idol of modern culture. As epistemologies, they insist on staying immanent within particular inquiries, contributing to their substances and insights rather than prescribing their methods from afar. As a "field," rhetoric of inquiry teaches how comparing projects of learning can help each improve itself. As a determinedly immanent yet interdisciplinary endeavor, rhetoric of inquiry insists that such comparisons generate no grand transcontextual demarcations between what is Science and what is Not. Instead rhetoric of inquiry plumbs the many important differences and commonalities among inquiries, good and bad. It seeks practical improvements in each.

As an academic movement, rhetoric of inquiry arises in reaction against foundationalisms—especially in epistemology and philosophy of science but also in aesthetics, metaethics, policy science, theology, or any other field that might conceive itself as standing above and apart from practices of inquiry while thinking that it should nonetheless legislate for them in some absolute or at least authoritarian way. As an immanent yet interdisciplinary project, rhetoric of inquiry arises in attraction to the revivals of persuasive and expressive sensibility now discernible throughout the arts, humanities, professions, and sciences. It reflects a renewed concern for the quality of speaking and writing in academic disciplines, and it pursues a postmodern interest in the interaction of media and messages. But mostly, it tries to improve the actual conduct of inquiries—inside and outside the academy—by learning from the diversity of those practices of study that help to make up our world.

Rhetoric emphasizes the quality of speaking and writing, the role of genres and tropes, and the interaction of style and substance. The topics crucial for rhetoric of inquiry include the concepts central to particular projects, methodological practices in specific fields, their educations to initiate new members, and their dynamics of disagreement. The new field examines the exemplars of research, formats of argument, figures of speech, appeals to loyalty, models of data, and metaphors of phenomena that constitute the different disciplines. Such topics are rhetorical. Yet they are also anthropological, political, economical, ethical, historical, philosophical, psychological, sociological, and so forth. Even when analyzing inquiries in a single discipline, scholars diverse in backgrounds and skills can enrich their rhetorical insights.

Accordingly let us begin with definitions broad and diversified. For breadth let us treat *science* as disciplined inquiry; *inquiry* as learned, knowledgeable, truth-oriented rhetoric; and *rhetoric* as stylized persuasion. For diversity, moreover, we should undertake to explore disciplines as (sub)cultures and (political) communities, truths as alignments and tropes, styles as strategies and sensibilities. These can complement—or at least supplement—the conventional Western meanings of disciplines as orders and fields, truths as discoveries and revelations, styles as (mere) ornaments and dispositions. Or, to broach yet another path, rhetoric may be a concern with what is communicated, how, by, and for whom; to what effect; under what circumstances; and with which alternatives. Hence we may well approach rhetoric of inquiry as a concern for every facet of communication in communities of learning.

Argument is more unified than the customary division into academic fields admits, for all fields depend on rhetorics of investigation

Introduction

and persuasion. Yet our styles of argument are more diverse than philosophy of science sometimes implies. Our inquiries rely on a great variety of audiences, topics, tropes, interests, and assumptions. Thus fields are defined by their distinctive styles of language and argument, their own rhetorics. By examining how fields construct and conduct inquiries in rhetorical terms, we can learn how to communicate better across fields. We can also learn how to do better work within any particular field.

The special topic of this book is rhetoric of political inquiry. Thus the late twentieth-century discipline of political science becomes my target. The overarching goal is to acquaint readers with rhetoric of inquiry by doing it in a number of different but important modes. Even within a single discipline such as political science, far more studies and rhetorics thrive than anyone could hope to survey in a single text. My strategy in response is to analyze a diversity of rhetorics in recent inquiries from political science and political action. The desire is to display many devices and dynamics of rhetorical analysis. To keep them in constructive conversation with one another, though, I keep returning to an architectonic inquiry into the eclipse and recovery of articulate argument about politics. In addition, I keep analyzing political tropes of both inquiry and action: hence the title and subtitle of the book.

Trope comes from the ancient Greek word for 'turn', as in a change of direction in space or a change of fortune in the course of events. Each turn traces a figure—of speech (or conception), of experience (or perception), of inquiry (or question), even of conduct (or action). To analyze arguments by their tropes is the main invention of this book.

Thus the first chapter explains seven tropal projects important for analyzing rhetorics of political science and for advancing inquiries into politics. Each remaining chapter then addresses a distinctive set of political studies or practices. Every chapter features a different mix of devices for rhetorical analysis, though enough of them should be deployed in several contexts to give a good sense of how each can work in many ways. Every chapter also follows a separate expositional form, to practice rhetorical analysis in a wide range of the genres available to political analysts and actors.

The first part focuses on figures of inquiry. Chapter 1 offers a programmatic manifesto on doing rhetoric of political inquiry. Next the book ventures an archaeology of political science as perhaps the most presentist of academic disciplines, at least of late. The third chapter offers both an embodiment and an analysis of the genre of the partial confession, as practiced by a number of eminent political scientists since the Second World War. Chapter 4 pursues an apostate's meditation on the tendency of the most argumentative field in the discipline to misplace its proper sense of persuasion. Then the following chapter tells just-so stories of how the discipline's other fields have been turning its argumentative tropes into traps, tokens, and detours of political argument.

The second part moves into myths of action. Chapter 6 enacts a modest rhetorical invention to explore an especially poetic device for making evidence and argument persuasive in politics. The subsequent chapter essays a postmodern refiguration of Aristotle's ancient modes for persuasion in politics or anyplace else, applying it speculatively to liberal ideology in the United States. The eighth chapter presents a poetic experiment in retroping government, politics, and communication for our postmodern times. Chapter 9 provides a playful, partly dialogical deconstruction of deliberation and debate by the U.S. Senate before the Gulf war. And the concluding chapter extends such myth-making into a figural argument about stands and stances as forms of political action for politics moving beyond the twentieth century.

The ambition is far less an integrated argument of any single kind conventional to the academy than a series of experiments in form, style, and analysis that prove themselves pertinent to many a political inquiry and action. Yet the concern throughout is argument, because this is where both our politics and our sciences may grow negligent and unimaginative. Another device meant to remind readers that the book is pursuing a most unconventional set of persuasions is its reliance on aphorisms as modes of inquiry, explanation, and self-irony. Aphorisms from others precede most chapters and subsections. They also spice many paragraphs in between. And throughout I offer a personal voice that is aphoristic at times on its own. The hope is that this can punctuate a strategy of persuasion and inform a style of truth that must turn recurrently into strange terrains of action as well as unfamiliar angles for analysis.

Only the first and last chapters have been published before—in other versions. They are reprinted here with the permission of *Social Epistemology: Approaches, Opportunities, and Priorities in the Rhetoric of Political Inquiry*, 2,1, January–March, 1988, and Taylor & Francis and the *Journal of Politics*, vol. 46:1. "Metaphors of Women," the poem by Katha Pollitt that provides the invaluable template for Chapter 8's experiments in revising tropes of politics and communication, is reprinted here with the permission of Alfred A. Knopf. A few lines of poetry and song appear here with the permission of Random House for the work of W. H. Auden, Stranger Music, Inc. and WB Music

Corp. for a phrase from Leonard Cohen, and Blackwood Music, Inc. and Country Road Music, Inc. for the words of James Taylor.

These reflections benefit from conversations with many colleagues, past and present. Institutionally let me thank the University of Iowa, its Obermann Center for Advanced Studies, and its Project on Rhetoric of Inquiry (POROI) for grants and facilities instrumental to the completion of this book all too many years in germination. Individually let me acknowledge Frank Beer, Arthur Bonfield, Bob Boynton, Marianne Constable, Lane Davis, Booth Fowler, George Graham, John Gunnell, Robert Hariman, Richard Jankowski, Paul Kress, Bill Lewis, Youlika Kotsovolou Masry, Deirdre McCloskey, Benjamin Most, William Panning, Edward Sharp, Ira Strauber, Mary Stuckey, Jim Throgmorton, and Vernon Van Dyke. Their figures and voices gather in these pages like places in the heart, and I have learned from all of them more than I could possibly say. Members of the University of Iowa Rhetoric Seminar and the Triple-I (Illinois, Indiana, Iowa) Seminar on Complex Systems have made helpful comments on earlier drafts. Likewise, the Foundations of Political Theory Workshop on Political Myth, Rhetoric, and Symbolism is a continuing source of inspiration for my inquiries of the kinds offered here. I especially appreciate the encouragement and criticism of these explorations in rhetoric of inquiry by the many doctoral students in POROI's graduate certificate program on rhetorics of inquiry. I have no doubt that they one day will exceed these inquiries in their own excellent terms.

By now, I have been at work more than two decades on rhetoric of inquiry. All that time, one person has been indispensable to the work and to the life that alternately leaps ahead or lags behind it. With love, let every one of these words and ideas be dedicated to her.

PART ONE

FROM FIGURES OF INQUIRY

1 RETURNING PLURALISM TO POLITICAL SCIENCE

A PROGRAMMATIC MANIFESTO FOR RHETORIC OF POLITICAL INQUIRY

Rhetoric of political inquiry promises to improve studies of politics, especially within the discipline of political science. Most political scientists can benefit immensely from better attention to their rhetoric and its roles in their inquiry. In ways far greater than logic of inquiry alone, rhetoric of inquiry arises from within the actual enterprises of research. In degrees much higher than philosophy of science as we have known it in the twentieth century, rhetoric of inquiry enters into the detailed conduct of research on an everyday basis. Rhetoric of inquiry works to provide investigators with greater awareness of the actual practices and diverse principles of science. It also emphasizes the dependence of inquiry on considerations of community and communication. To reap the advantages available from rhetoric of inquiry, consequently, political and other scientists must become their own rhetoricians of inquiry—as well as attending to specialists in the subject. To explain and evidence these claims, this book begins to explore what it can mean to do rhetoric of inquiry in political science.

Throughout, the aim is to clarify approaches, opportunities, and priorities for this endeavor. I begin by tracing briefly the origins of this new enterprise. Then I sketch several of its general concerns and purposes. Rhetoric of inquiry pursues special ties and significance for political inquiry, however, so I also examine its specifically political connections, dimensions, and dynamics. In this chapter I explain seven projects of importance for advancing inquiry into politics. My argument is that this initial agenda for rhetoric of inquiry within political science can make major and, at least in some cases, almost immediate improvements in the disciplined study of politics. The seven projects permit and might eventually require contributions from every part of the discipline. They show how rhetoric of inquiry should be pursued, not only as an occasional focus for specialized research on the rhetoric of political scientists, but also as a continuing aspect of disciplined inquiry into politics. Hence I point in conclusion toward additional approaches and opportunities for doing rhetoric of political inquiry.

Origins

> *Many ideas grow better when transplanted into another mind*
> *than in the one where they sprang up.*
> —Oliver Wendell Holmes Jr.[1]

For a quarter century I have been helping to invent something a little on the order of a new field. It may be located within my home discipline of political science but scarcely more there than within any other organized domains of research. Indeed it pursues homes in all disciplines in order to flourish. Therefore the new "field" is and must remain at once within and throughout—but across—every discipline. It is an *interdisciplinary* field in the deepest and best sense of the word.

I am educated in another oddly interdisciplinary field. Political theory self-consciously straddles the social sciences and humanities.[2] Thus it encourages the graduate student to combine usual curricula in political science with those standard for philosophy, anthropology, law, literature, economics, history, sociology, psychology, and more. That circumstance, plus unusual good fortune in teachers, led me to recognize three peculiarities in these disciplines and their mutual relationships: none gives good accounts of its own inquiries, each does poorer inquiry because of that, and each thinks that its rules or procedures of inquiry come fundamentally from philosophy (and, in some cases, secondarily from mathematics or statistics).

Seeing what I saw, others in political theory, political science, and the many related disciplines argued with the rules then reigning in philosophical epistemology and treatments of science. So did I. Some of the others also sought to restructure actual research in political science or their individual disciplines. So did I. To a lesser and later degree, the same has occurred in disciplines and professions ordinarily even farther afield from political science. And by various routes a growing group is arriving at the perspectives, principles, and practices that we are weaving into a new and interdisciplinary field of inquiries. The time seems opportune, for there are further arrivals virtually every day, and some of the finest talent around appears to be interested in postmodern or post-Western alternatives to authoritarian epistemologies and a priori philosophies of science.[3]

Along the way, I have called this endeavor by a host of names. I began by regarding it as a twilight zone between detailed research design and abstract philosophy of inquiry.[4] Eventually this led me to look for epistemologies of everyday research in political science. But almost immediately, I ran into the rich variety of research practices already evident to me in that discipline alone. On one side, I started to explore the tropes accounting for epistemological disparities among the research practices apparently directed toward the same or closely related subjects.[5] On another, I plumbed anthropology and sociology for better senses of how different situations and topics of research produce contrasting inquiries.[6]

While thinking in terms of a simultaneously epistemological and political theory of practices, I continued to encounter still other domains and directions of research not yet part of political science.[7] That nudged me toward studying the many epistemologies immanent in these largely disconnected projects.[8] Nonetheless it also made me aware of their need for mutual education. Sensitivity to other perspectives and incorporation of alien principles could make these diverse practices of research more accurate, beneficial, and self-critical. Hence I have come to endow such projects of comparative epistemology with an ethos of epistemology as comparison and self-criticism.[9] All these projects and more are converging on what I and others now call *rhetoric of inquiry*.[10]

Purposes

> *Few people even scratch the surface, much less exhaust the
> contemplation of their own experience.*
> —Randolph Bourne[11]

Each field relies on distinctive methods of inquiry and modes of communication, but every field does its work through argument. Fields use various devices of speculation, assumption, definition, evidence, inference, testing, reporting, and criticism. Yet all conduct inquiries through persuading people. In a word, every field is *rhetorical*. The study of rhetorical dimensions in research can improve inquiries within disciplines, communication across them, and education beyond them. These are the purposes of emerging studies in the rhetoric of inquiry.[12]

Because inquiry depends on communication, the rhetoric of inquiry studies how scholars communicate. In particular, it examines the reasoning of scholars in research communities. It rejects the notion that ironclad rules for inquiry can stand apart from actual practices. It seeks not to distill some single model of Reason, Logic, or Method but to make the many styles of scholarship better aware of themselves and one another. Working within continuing projects of research, the rhetoric of inquiry helps to make their assumptions more intelligent and their operations more persuasive. Working across fields of inquiry, it seeks to increase the quality and quantity of collaboration among colleagues. Inside and outside the academy it explores how reason is rhetorical and how better recognition of rhetoric would alter our inquiries.

Rhetoric of inquiry is determinedly interdisciplinary. It stems from a renewed emphasis on persuasion and expression evident throughout the humanities, sciences, arts, and professions.[13] As the term implies, its special virtue is an appreciation of the importance in research of rhetoric. Thus it concerns the quality of speaking and writing in our world, and it attends to interactions of media and messages. It seeks to enter the daily conduct of inquiries of every kind in order that each may understand itself better and learn from related studies.

As an academic movement, rhetoric of inquiry arises in reaction against foundationalism—especially in epistemology and philosophy of science but also in aesthetics, metaethics, policy science, theology, or any other field that tends to regard itself as standing above and apart from practices of inquiry—while thinking that it nonetheless should legislate for them in some absolute or at least authoritarian way.[14] As an interdisciplinary field, rhetoric of inquiry arises in attraction to recent revivals of persuasive and expressive sensibility now discernible throughout the arts, humanities, professions, and sciences. It reflects a renewed concern for the quality of speaking and writing in academic disciplines, and it develops a postmodern interest in the interactions of media and messages. But mostly rhetoric of inquiry tries to improve the actual conduct of inquiries—inside and outside the academy—by learning from the diversity of the many practices of study that help to make our world what it is today.

The purpose is not to replace logic of inquiry but augment it. The goal is to facilitate self-reflection in all studies. Rhetoric of inquiry achieves little if pursued a priori and apart from our actual inquiries. Informally and intermittently it is already part of many kinds of research. The premise is that more systematic attention to it can improve projects individually and link them more effectively. In fact, rhetoric of inquiry thrives on comparisons of projects. These in turn contribute to its rationale as a continuing field of scholarship.

Rhetoric of inquiry also encourages and enables scholars to become more reflexive. It teaches them to examine with care the implications of their substantive arguments and conclusions for their methods of study and modes of inference. Thus it involves the practice and application of the sociology of sociology, the economics of economics, the history of historiography, the psychology of psychology, the anthropology of anthropology, the politics of political science, and the like.[15] Not only does rhetoric of inquiry emphasize such projects of reflection but its approaches to the interaction of inquiry and communication provide especially effective paths for beginning and completing the projects well.

At the level of institutions, rhetoricians of inquiry explore rhetoric in virtually every aspect of scholarship. They recognize as rhetorical, for example, many intellectual divisions among the human sciences. Hence economists favor metaphors different from those of sociologists or psychologists. Political philosophers emphasize styles and topics of argument different from the ones favored by political scientists or political historians. Rhetoricians raise questions about how scholars classify the world and how they reason toward claims of knowledge or recommendations of policy. Rhetoricians study disciplinary boundaries and methodologies as persuasions that alter the beliefs of those who operate professionally within them. Such persuasions come and go, as Thomas Kuhn demonstrated. They serve purposes for their times, and then, with or without public and professional strife, they give way to new persuasions.[16]

In this respect, one aim of rhetoric of inquiry is to remind scientists of the diversity of argumentation in their research. It examines how good work arises apart from (or even in defiance of) preestablished procedures and textbook logics. Moreover it explores how scientists ignore abstract and supposedly universal standards of reason in favor of warrants and backings of particular arguments (to borrow the terminology of Stephen Toulmin).[17] It turns attention away from generalized methodologies and their applications toward particular situations of scholarly communication. Thus it emphasizes the importance of audiences in research, because warrants and backings must be shared if arguments are to have force. Further, it focuses on figurative and even mythic dimensions of inquiry to study the common and often unarticulated characteristics of communities of inquiry.

At the level of individuals, rhetoricians of inquiry study the generation, communication, and reception of scholarship as argument. The quality of scholarly writing reflects the quality of scholarly research, for instance, because the processes that produce them are continuous and interactive. Accordingly rhetoric of inquiry asks how scholars come to speak and write as they do, as well as how their styles influence the conduct and content of their research. It explores how to respond seriously to the recent worries that the professional discourses of academic disciplines in general—and of the human sciences in particular—have become too arcane for the good of the inquiry or the society. It works to keep them from turning too impersonal, condensed, and unargued to foster strong science or too specialized, obscure, and authoritarian to nurture wise policy and intelligent practice.[18]

But the main aim of rhetoric of inquiry is to become integrated into the normal business of scientists and scholars by sensitizing them to good practices of rhetoric. Consequently the interdisciplinary field considers in detail how substantive disciplines diverge from externally dictated norms and how researchers call on reasons specific to individual inquiries. Rhetoric of inquiry intends to replace philosophers of science with rhetoricians of science only insofar as the rhetoricians are the scientists themselves, within programs of substantive research. That is why rhetoric of inquiry arises throughout the social sciences and humanities. It is also why it proceeds by researchers reporting on the importance of rhetoric within their disciplines rather than outsiders telling diverse fields to conform to some overarching norm.

Rhetoric of inquiry can never become an academic discipline in an ordinary sense. Therefore it should never seek to become a subject unto itself or a subject for others only as master legislator. Instead it should serve other inquiries as special parts of each, seeking to penetrate throughout and reach beyond any field of inquiry as practiced. As immanent epistemology, rhetoric of inquiry cannot be severed from work within actual substantive researches. As comparative epistemology, it cannot be divorced from work about and across disparate research projects as they continue to develop.

Thus rhetoric of inquiry addresses how, why, and with what effects inquiry is rhetorical. Rhetoricians of inquiry are already addressing many specific issues, and many more remain to emerge from future work. Even so, three sets of key questions evoke the field's domain:

- What are the rhetorical practices of scientists and scholars? How do they differ from one field and time to another, why, and with what implications?
- How do academic rhetorics relate to nonacademic domains? What are the sources and results of these relationships, and where might they be improved?
- How might increased awareness of rhetoric change inquiry and communication in the academy? Which changes should we cultivate and when?

Although rhetoric of inquiry achieves little if pursued a priori and apart from actual inquiries, it thrives on pursuit in terms of several studies at once. Moreover it can and should cultivate a distinctive body of perspectives, principles, and practices. Consequently it can and should be studied by some people as a distinct—if by no means utterly separate—field. Yet even contributions of that kind should strive to address and improve the substantive inquiries that supply its targets of research.

Thus far I have relied on ordinary understandings of *rhetoric, politics,* and *inquiry.* If I am twisting these categories in any special way, it is mostly away from the highly charged evaluations that sometimes make the first two words express something evil or perverse and the third word something good or neutral. So let us begin with definitions both broad and diversified. For breadth, let us treat rhetoric as stylized communication, inquiry as systematic investigation, and politics as community participation. For diversity, we may approach inquiry as the purposeful exploration of what is, why it is, how it might be otherwise, and how we may know it. We may regard rhetoric as the pointed concern with what is communicated, how, to what effect, and with which alternatives. And we may approach politics as the central project of creating, comprehending, conserving, and criticizing communities.[19] These definitions suggest how closely connected the three can and almost must become, especially for rhetoric of political inquiry. Emphasizing their interdependence encourages us to note, understand, and enhance as many ties as possible among rhetoric, politics, and inquiry.

Politics

> *A new science of politics is needed for a new world.*
> —Alexis de Tocqueville[20]

Like all scholarship, political science is transacted through argument. In turn, argument is rhetorical, not in the cynical sense of empty or manipulative words but in the artistic and political sense of styles or patterns of speech. Yet political scientists have been no more inclined than other scholars to recognize their own strategies of rhetoric. They sometimes act as though adherence to standard forms for reporting research enables them to avoid rhetoric altogether, and they often assume that their modes of argument do not affect their conduct of inquiry.

Thus the main resource neglected by political science and celebrated by rhetoric of inquiry is the capacity for persuasive argument.[21]

As an internal need of the discipline, an ability to argue skillfully is the collective faculty for thinking well about problems of inquiry. As an external need of the discipline, it is the facility for learning from other projects and for teaching them what political scientists have discovered. Change in the world typically includes change in politics. This often mandates change in political inquiry. That in turn requires persistent reflection on the matters, methods, and meanings of political science. As continual attention to the conditions of inquiry, and especially to the quality of argument in research, rhetoric of inquiry is a movement toward self-scrutiny and self-improvement on the part on all disciplines.

Political science stands at the center of this movement, for four reasons. The first form of political science simply was rhetoric, the earliest systematic study of politics on the part of the Sophists. Put the other way around, rhetoric began as political science, and the close connection of the two has held ever since. Speech, persuasion, deception, symbols, and other aspects of rhetoric are too important to politics for the tie to lapse or even loosen to any great degree. The same is true of the place of political processes, strategies, and settings in the study of communication.

A second reason for the prominence of political science is that rhetoric of inquiry persistently comprehends academic disciplines as political systems. Thus it returns epistemology to the significance of politics in the operations of science or scholarship. This ranges from government policy for education and research to everyday politics of professions and university departments. So prominent are various kinds of politics in the conditions and conduct of systematic study that rhetorics of inquiry insistently show an inclination to become politics of inquiry. Hence the issues and methods of political science prove crucial for rhetoric of inquiry.

Appropriately rhetoric of inquiry for political scientists often can and should become self-consciously a study of the politics of political inquiry. As I have already hinted through definitions, one potentially important effect of such reflexivity on the discipline is to challenge recent conceptions of politics—as well as of rhetoric and inquiry. For example, an important point of rhetoric of inquiry as immanent and comparative epistemology is that each of these three activities intertwines its study and practice so thoroughly that neither can proceed adequately without the other. Rhetoric comprehends not only what is communicated but the conditions, processes, effects, improvements, and comparative character of communications. Similarly politics appear in much broader guises than have become common in political science, opening the discipline more fully to important phenomena and issues long ignored.

Such perspectives encourage us to see social sciences as special projects of the humanities and vice versa.[22] In this respect, rhetoric of inquiry is particularly attracted to fields that use both scientific and humanistic methods of study. Accordingly a third reason that political science plays a major role in rhetoric of inquiry is the discipline's rich mixtures of arguments, data, and techniques drawn from diverse humanities and social sciences. Its continuing questions of action, authority, community, law, legitimacy, and representation span the humanities and social sciences. Moreover many of its major programs of research combine methods of the humanities and social sciences.[23]

Examples abound. Formal modelers seek to reproduce processes of voting and legislation, identified independently through humanistically thick descriptions of decision making by voters and legislatures. Organization theorists mesh data from surveys and social observation with depth interviews, archival research, and symbolical interpretations of work environments. Policy analysts inform normative evaluation with statistical studies of policy needs, effects, and processes. Students of public opinion and political ideology increasingly combine survey research and cognitive science with literary interpretation of texts and rhetorical analysis of communication, reasoning, and symbolism. Archival research on foreign policy interacts with computer simulations of decision processes. Analyses of aggregate data about refugees, trade, and flows of information reshape traditionally humanistic studies of human rights, distributive justice, and free speech. Comparative investigators of voting, regulation, and parties in various countries carry on a dialogue with conceptual analysts of authority, democracy, government, power, and rights. Such interactions of diverse issues, methods, and kinds of data make political science a natural laboratory for rhetoric of inquiry.

In this setting, it is not surprising that political scientists are leaders in creating rhetoric of inquiry as a discernible focus of research. This leadership is a fourth reason for the centrality of political inquiry to rhetoric of inquiry. It is evident in the prominence of political scientists whose work pushes toward rhetoric of inquiry, political scientists identified throughout this book as fairly central and self-conscious contributors to date. Lists of less direct or intentional rhetoricians of inquiry among political scientists would be even longer. This situation reflects the special importance of politics for rhetoric, and thus of political science for rhetoric of inquiry. But it signals also that rhetoric of inquiry stands ready to become exceptionally significant for continuing research in political science.

In recognizing how rhetoric is political, we can recover for every human science a neglected appreciation of politics and, consequently, political inquiry. In recognizing how science is rhetorical, we can recover for political science a reflexive capacity to improve our inquiry—and in particular, our argument. To a considerable extent, rhetoric of political inquiry urges and helps political scientists to attend better to what they already know about conducting political inquiry. Rather than promote lessons from afar in the form of logic of inquiry, it identifies familiar objects of concern in concrete contexts of research. From their recurrence and variance it seeks to learn how to do better this time and next.

Problematics

Men are much more apt to agree in what they do than in what they think.
—Johann Wolfgang von Goethe[24]

In summarizing the rhetoric of inquiry, Ellen K. Coughlin has written that "elements of rhetoric . . . are so thoroughly ingrained in scholarly research as to affect every step of the enterprise—how sources are used, how data are interpreted, how findings are communicated."[25] By implication almost no aspect of political inquiry remains irrelevant to the rhetorical scrutiny. To develop rhetoric of political inquiry, then, priorities become all the more important. Seven problematics strike me as especially good places to begin: approved versus underground rhetorics; standards of research; stories of social science; rhetorics of discovery; humanities versus sciences; prose for audiences; and canons of knowledge.

APPROVED VERSUS UNDERGROUND RHETORICS

Within political science as a discipline, the approved and quasi-official rhetorics of political research differ significantly from the informal and usually underground rhetorics of political inquiry. Thus the rhetorics that dominate mainstream journals and methods textbooks diverge widely from the rhetorics that surface in graduate seminars, collaborative inquiries, hallway conversations, and other secluded occasions for talking about how political scientists actually conduct their research. Many political scientists would concede this in general terms. Yet some would deny it altogether, and some others would doubt whether it carries implications important for the content or quality of political science.

Therefore one of the highest priorities for rhetoric of political inquiry must be to document contrasts between approved and underground rhetorics of inquiry within political science. This is probably the main way to release the discipline from continued domination by official slogans of inquiry imported from philosophy of science as a separate and supposedly authoritative study of the logic rules for conducting all rational inquiry. Thus rhetoric of political inquiry should examine the specifics and strategies characteristic of each set or level of rhetorics, both approved and underground. Simultaneously it should assess the comparative advantages of each, perhaps exploring their relationships to the actual conduct and content of the discipline. Further it should consider the repercussions of differences between approved and underground rhetorics for rhetoric of inquiry in general, conceived as epistemology both immanent within particular inquiries and comparative across diverse fields. The book embarks on these tasks.

One major trouble in contrasting approved and underground rhetorics within political science is to secure good examples and statements of the unofficial rhetorics. Seldom do underground rhetorics become countercultural or oppositional rhetorics that proclaim themselves in manifestos or publish themselves in journals outside the mainstream. Instead they are largely private and sometimes surprisingly diffuse. They complement and even correct the publicly accepted ways of thinking, speaking, and writing within and about disciplinary inquiries.

Possibly apocryphal stories and personal anecdotes have been the main kinds of evidence for underground rhetorics of political research. The resonance of such accounts in the everyday experience of political scientists makes these sorts of stories indispensable in explaining the character of underground rhetorics and in persuading political researchers to take them seriously. But casual accounts of these kinds cannot dispel nagging doubts that stem from the discipline's desire for more systematic data. Nor can anecdotes provide texts detailed enough to sustain many kinds of analysis needed in contrasting underground with approved rhetorics of research. By themselves these kinds of evidence offer enough for a decent start but not for an adequate finish. The resources required take time to generate, for only a few sociologists of science have collected similar information for a few other disciplines, and I know of none adaptable to the study of underground rhetorics in political science.[26]

Yet there does exist in political science, as in other social sciences, a scattered body of texts that offer usable, but not utterly direct, access to such underground rhetorics. In the short run, therefore, the main body of evidence about approved and underground rhetorics of political inquiry can come from the essays that a few political scientists have written about how their detailed conduct of inquiry carries through and (sometimes) departs from the discipline's usual assumptions and statements about methods of research.[27] By considering the rhetorical tensions explicit and implicit in these self-accounts of researchers, rhetoricians of political inquiry can transform them into case studies of the partial confessions of political scientists to underground rhetorics of research that fail to surface in the discipline's generally approved talk about the conduct of science.

These texts are few enough to provide a focus for careful treatment of rhetorical details. As far as I know, however, nobody has yet analyzed these fascinating materials in any fashion, let alone with specific attention to issues in rhetoric of inquiry. Rhetoricians can compare these special texts with the works by political scientists that promote the discipline's quasi-official rhetorics of research design and methodology. Rhetoricians also could cast side glances toward similar texts in other human sciences to learn how distinctive the underground rhetorics of political inquiry might be.

STORIES OF SOCIAL SCIENCE

Another priority for rhetoric of political inquiry is to study the interplay of levels of narration in political science.[28] At least three levels deserve attention, and they are demarcated by different subjects: the occurrence of phenomena, the conduct of inquiry, and the communication of research. But does the first mean the events as they really were, as observers would tell them, as participants conceived them, as the researchers (initially) perceived them, or as the researchers (eventually) recounted them in print? Does the second intend the steps of research as they actually transpired, as observers might relate them, as the researchers experienced them in performance, or as the researchers traced them in publication? And does the third invoke the specific patterns of exposition, the general forms of literature, the basic purposes promoted, the precise audiences sought, the particular reactions received, or some other standard referent of rhetoric?

As a topic, the storying of research includes all these perspectives plus issues of their distinction and interaction. From this broad topic rhetoricians of political inquiry may carve particular projects, knowing that anyone can cover only a small part of such a wide territory. These projects can be important precisely because study of the storying of research in political science (or perhaps any other discipline of the social sciences) may sound odd to its practitioners on at least three counts.

First, the previously orthodox contrasts between social science and historiography lead to opposing general theoretical sciences of society to particular idiographic studies of history. The peculiar but unmistakable particularity of narratives accordingly associates them almost exclusively with historiography, or so the Received View of social inquiry would have it. (Actually some stories are exceedingly abstract, general, and formulaic—just as some generalizations are highly concrete, specific, and incipiently narrativistic.) At any rate, official rhetorics of research now encourage few political scientists to think of their findings as stories about politics.[29]

This can pose a real difficulty to the inquiries recommended here, since an obvious result of such a lack of story consciousness in research is that few political scientists explicitly relate their research as stories about politics. Instead they present their fruits of inquiry as descriptions, models, comparisons, theories, explanations of variance, and the like. Implicitly, though, they do story many—if not all—their subjects. That is, political scientists endow their subjects with narrative sequence and significance. In this respect, an initial task for rhetoricians of political inquiry interested in narrative would be to show that political scientists do narrate events. Even when research articles appear merely to report questions, methods, and findings, they strongly imply stories. Further tasks would include the exploration of how, why, with what implications, and to what effects political scientists in general or particular practitioners story their research.

Second, social scientists generally have encouraged themselves to believe that a decisive, continuing difference exists between the "context of discovery" and the "context of justification." Of course, we might say that there are two main contexts of justification, because there may be reason to distinguish the factors or standards that (should) justify the researchers in believing their own conclusions and the ones that (should) justify their colleagues in such belief. Personal belief is more what I target here in writing of the actual conduct of inquiry. On this basis it is easy (but not necessary) to regard most stories of the conduct of inquiry as irrelevant to the methodical presentation of research results—and thus as inappropriate for research reports.

In their relevant respects, moreover, such stories are usually recounted in only a few standard forms. These are affected by what actually occurs in the conduct of inquiry—either as observed by others or as experienced by the researchers themselves. Yet they may be influenced as much by official philosophies of what is supposed to happen in research, conventional practices of what others write about their studies, and educated sensibilities about what others will find persuasive about the researchers' investigations. Here again, some social scientists would have to be shown that narratives of the conduct of inquiry recur significantly in the reporting of research. But rhetoricians of political inquiry would also want to consider what the standard narratives are, when they arise, and how they relate to political science as we have experienced and observed it. What can the stories of research tell us about what political science is and how it proceeds? Rhetoricians of political inquiry also could examine how accounts of inquiry relate to accounts of the (political) phenomena that (purportedly) arise from that inquiry. Do some stories of research show a special affinity for some plots of politics? In what respects? And why might that be?

Third, even when social scientists concede there to be elements of art (that is, rhetoric) in the communication of research to colleagues, the skills and principles involved are so poorly respected, studied, and (dare we say?) practiced that no ready recognition of their specific narrative choices—let alone of their various narrative effects—can be expected. To be sure, a few students of literature have ventured to teach and write in these terms about some products of social science. In programs of composition and schools of education this sometimes occurs under the heading of "writing across the curriculum." But these forays into the literary criticism of social science have been few and confined for the most part to classics, which seldom are typical of the inquiry of their periods, let alone of the research of more recent times. About current political science we could ask what are the overall narratives that express research? When, how, and why are they deployed? And with what effects on whom? How do political scientists try to quarantine this level of narrative from the other two? In what respects do they succeed? In what not? And why?

Let me also note a further complication that cuts across all three levels. Even at the crudest cut, political science surely consists of three rhetorical communities rather than one. Although they interact continually and intensively, these communities remain distinct in important ways. Perhaps their most common names among political scientists are *empirical theory*, *analytical theory*, and *normative theory*. That each term fits its respective community poorly—if at all—is the kind of rhetorical convolution-cum-revelation that rhetoricians of political inquiry can turn into better arguments. Whatever the central level(s) and issues(s) of storying research that rhetoricians of political inquiry choose, however, these will need along the way to give and take some account of the differences and dependencies among these three communities of rhetoric in political science.

Rhetoricians of political inquiry should ask what enhancement of specifically narratival or generally rhetorical self-consciousness might mean for political science.[30] They should pursue these possibilities on any—and across all—of the three levels of narrative in political science. They should pursue such prospects on any and across all of the three communities of political theory. The next chapter begins to do this. To focus on narrative, rather than the whole array of rhetorical dimensions and projects in political science, offers the advantage of resisting the temptation to emphasize political features and principles of rhetoric in regard to the rest of the humanities and social sciences. It should enable rhetoricians of political inquiry to narrow their argumentative responsibilities to manageable amounts, especially in the early going.

STANDARDS OF RESEARCH

Criteria for judging findings, arguments, and other aspects of political inquiry must be identified, selected, defended, and used. This is a domain of political epistemology. Because of the interdependence of rhetorics, politics, and inquiries, all political theory must in some way be epistemological theory—and vice versa. I am inclined to think, moreover, that epistemology is an especially important part of politics in our times—and that politics should become a centrally significant part of our epistemology.[31] Exploring these claims and their implications for political science comprises for rhetoricians of political inquiry a set of issues about the standards of research.

To defend specifically rhetorical and political treatments of knowledge, rhetoricians of political inquiry should engage recent controversies over the features and functions of epistemology. By explicating the rhetorical and political elements of epistemology in theorizing about politics, they should study—and in some cases, they should join—the struggles of style and perspective that permeate projects of inquiry in the humanities and the social sciences alike. Thereby they must display compellingly for political scientists at least some inadequacies of recent philosophies of science for informing political inquiry and action.

In particular, political epistemology examines how reflection on the standards and methods of inquiry can and must be situated squarely within substantive research. By exploring the twilight zones between abstract philosophies of inquiry and specific patterns of argument in political theory, political epistemology can draw detailed lessons for useful interactions between these realms—long related wrongly, when related at all. At least initially, rhetoricians of inquiry need to show in detail how substantive inquiries depart from externally dictated norms. They need to explain how scholars legitimately invoke different reasons that prove persuasive in different contexts. They need to study specifically how individual inquiries can improve their rhetorics and thus their results. Accordingly political epistemologists should study political reasoning by analyzing the rhetorics of actual political arguments—by political theorists and by ordinary actors in politics. The aim is to reveal the rhetorical structures of good argument in order to show how standards for good reasoning operate. These rhetorical structures include the use of linguistic conventions to designate meaning and significance, the creation and application of standards for good reasoning, the invocation of symbols and more explicit comparisons for other entities or contexts, the projection of audiences, the reliance on tropes, and the many other aspects of rhetoric identified by such theorists as Aristotle, Kenneth Burke, and Hayden White.[32]

The case for rhetorical and political epistemology rests in part on the manifest inadequacy of recent logics of inquiry connected with the so-called received view in the philosophy of science. As accounts of learning or persuasion, they are deficient for political studies as well as politics. To date, most so-called philosophies of political science have been limited to the adaptation of abstract principles of philosophy into very general rules for political inquiry. The focus has fallen on logical forms of description, explanation, prediction, and testing. Almost nothing has been said about specific topics of political research. As a result, few implications actually follow from such philosophies of inquiry for detailed methods of political inquiry. This approach has been encouraged by borrowing from a family of philosophies of inquiry too broad to provide day-to-day guidance for studies within political theory and political science. (That is why behavioralism and empiricism in political science must never be identified with—or reduced to—logical positivisms and empiricisms, notwithstanding their many ties to such epistemologies.)

Part of the trouble has been that these philosophies are seriously misleading in their conceptions of inquiry, especially in the humanities and social sciences. In practice, though, that has mattered much less than we might imagine. The larger part of the problem has been that such epistemologies are simply too abstract to connect in any solid, reliable way with specific inquiries into politics. Within political theory and political science such philosophies have had far less chance to produce perverse effects than the critics typically assume. In fact, political theory and political science have lately developed in virtual isolation from any substantive, self-conscious theories of inquiry. As a result, their methods, research designs, and theories of politics have suffered various and sometimes chronic defects.[33]

By contrast, political epistemology is predicated on the notion that apt principles of inquiry do not necessarily (or usually) come before practices of research. Seldom are they so general that they span wide varieties of disciplines. Instead they come from specific programs of scholarship, through internal criticism and comparison with other projects. They are principles that express and direct the basic impulses, procedures, and perspectives of study—whether avowedly humanistic or scientific. Lacking substantive theories of inquiry, recent political science has lacked precisely these principles of study.

A distinctive feature of rhetoric in this regard is that its theoretical questions, categories, and methods are indivisible from its practical limits, tactics, and performances. Modern dichotomies between theory and practice are not central to rhetorical ways of addressing the world. Instead rhetoric spans subject and object, epistemology and ontology, audience and action, academy and polity. It encourages a kind of "practice theory" meant to keep inquiries aware of the contexts of events without sacrificing the capacity to criticize their conventions.

The mistake in most logics of inquiry has been to strive for some fundamental separation from the contexts of concrete inquiry. Thus even the questions raised by such logics—let alone their answers— have been largely beside the point of scientific researches in particular fields. In this sense, many logics of inquiry have become caught up in pseudo-questions. The few scientists who attend much to them have been badly misled about priorities and techniques. Like their philosophical colleagues, they have tended to founder on abstract problems that have no useful answers at the levels posed.[34]

Logics of inquiry must offer contexts through which scholars can (and will be encouraged to) criticize their moves in theory and method. This does not rule out all divisions of labor between disciplinary scholars and philosophers of inquiry. But it does insist on much greater overlap and interdependence than previous views have promoted. This means that epistemologies must stay in intimate touch with the substance of actual projects of inquiry. It also means that scholars—humanistic or scientific—must in some degree remain within range of the perspectives and principles associated with (rhetorical) epistemology.

Although this test is failed by logical positivisms, empiricisms, and the like, it is failed also by their contextualist critics. Such critics have predicated their attacks upon previous philosophies of political inquiry on the same abstract planes originally appropriated by the philosophies criticized. Almost nowhere in this metaliterature of inquiry does the criticism lead into substantive reconstructions of the actual current projects of political research.[35]

Forays into specific examples of research must be the minimum requirement, and even then the main opportunities might be missed. If research projects are to be rethought in the thorough-going fashion produced by good philosophies of inquiry, however, this must not be done from above. The only saving grace of the imperial, dictatorial style of recent epistemologies has been the emptiness of their specific dictates. The needed reconstructions of research must be conducted from within particular programs of research. The would-be epistemologists must be informed by a reasonably full knowledge of the detailed studies within a targeted set of research projects.

The mirror mistake is equally important to avoid. Just as recent epistemologies seldom condescend to the levels of theory and method, so recent designs for substantive research refuse to rise to the levels of epistemological and philosophical reflection. This is certainly not to say that there has been no criticism of political inquiry from within substantive fields. It is rather to notice that such scrutiny falls shy of rethinking the basic assumptions that generate specific inquiries. It is also to observe that such criticisms are informed too little by careful comparisons among scholarly projects. Indeed such reflection hardly has the language (let alone the information) needed for suitably searching attempts to comprehend and criticize its own research results. Finding little help in previous philosophies of inquiry, the average scholar of politics has learned to steer clear of such airy domains when trying to get on with the business of day-to-day research.

That course offers some advantages, but it must fail in the end. In recent political inquiries, as in many of the humanities and social sciences, the result has been an abyss between theories and practices of inquiry. Neither side pays detailed attention to the other. Not even the critics, whose work seems to call for bridging this abyss, have done much to take up the crucial task. For the sake of political inquiry, as well as philosophy of inquiry, though, this is the task that now needs to be started. To do this is to invoke a broad conception of epistemology that specifies itself through interaction with substantive researches of all kinds. Thus rhetorical and political principles of epistemology can come into sharp focus only by fixing sights on actual research projects in political inquiry and elsewhere. In turn, that is why rhetoric of political inquiry moves from defending broad principles of inquiry to refining (not merely applying) them in concrete contexts of current political studies.

The attempt to shape a rhetorical and political epistemology can grow from at least five fairly distinct bodies of inquiry and argument: epistemology and philosophy of inquiry; philosophy of language; literary, rhetorical, and communication theory; political theory; and political science. A further way to evoke how political epistemology approaches standards in research is to sketch how these sources might figure in rhetoric of political inquiry.

Philosophical treatments of epistemology and inquiry serve primarily as targets of criticism, because most have favored the sorts of abstraction from substantive inquiry that rhetoric of political inquiry finds wanting. Nonetheless a small and provocative set of philosophical epistemologies may bear some affinity for the rhetorical and political principles of the new field. The result is that the philosophical works of such scholars as Max Black, Stanley Cavell, Nelson Goodman, Paul Feyerabend, Thomas Kuhn, Hilary Putnam, Richard Rorty, Calvin Schrag, Wilfrid Sellars, and Stephen Toulmin should occupy a special part of the attention of political epistemologists. The point is less to repeat others' (typically trenchant) criticisms of abstractionist epistemology, however, than to develop the rudiments of rhetorical and political epistemology scattered throughout their works. Writings in the modes of these scholars may be especially useful in accounting for the several substantive rationalities most evident within recent studies of society and politics. Exploring recent rhetorics within these philosophies can also afford clues for correcting troubles that beset recent theories of rhetoric.[36]

Sources from the philosophy of language, by contrast, provide more direct support for rhetorical principles of epistemology. Philosophers of language have tried to illuminate the figural resources and limits of language. Their perspectives supplement the traditionally divergent approaches of literary and rhetorical theorists, although both sides have often exaggerated differences of topic and treatment.[37] At any rate, philosophers of language have written a great deal that carries implications for our conceptions of epistemology, its relationship to detailed inquiries and practices, and the principles for its conduct.[38]

A belated renaissance of rhetoric is under way in the domains of speech, communication, and literary theory. The names of useful sources are almost too numerous for a short sampling to suffice. But let me at least mention Wayne Booth, Kenneth Burke, Jacques Derrida, Stanley Fish, Geoffrey Hartman, Michael Leff, and Hayden White. Since the mid-1970s, journals of speech, communication, and rhetoric have published article after article on aspects of the thesis that "rhetoric is epistemic."[39] All these contribute across the board to rhetoric of inquiry, and thus they provide the backdrop for political epistemology in particular.[40]

Because I am a political theorist by education and profession, I am especially sensitive to the rhetorical resources on which this fourth "field" relies. Because I am far from the only political theorist starting to see the promise of rhetorical and political epistemology, identifying and applying those resources offers considerable aid. Too many to mention here have written pieces that contribute in important ways to the principles at the heart of an epistemology that is significantly rhetorical and political. Partly this is symptomatic of the power of epistemic arguments to distract political theorists from politics. Even more, though, it is a result of the special relevance of political theory for shaping rhetorical and political epistemology. In both respects work by political theorists is salient for rhetoric of political inquiry.

We should make sure to acknowledge the social-scientific projects of political science. They are important for political epistemology, because reconstructing various research programs of political science has been one of its prime inspirations and promises to continue as one of its prime occasions. There is little point in listing the political scientists of importance in this regard—for they too are many. The insistence on situating epistemology squarely within concrete contexts of research means that rhetoricians of political inquiry must attend alike to path-finding and path-following scientists, to pioneering and problem-solving projects both. Thus rhetoricians do well to explicate reasons for respecting and improving our political researches as they actually occur.

RHETORICS OF DISCOVERY

One received dichotomy undermined by rhetoric of inquiry is the contrast cultivated between contexts of discovery and contexts of justification. Therefore a high priority for the rhetoric of political inquiry is to investigate rhetorics of discovery and invention in political science. These occur in many contexts and take many forms. Developing Abraham Kaplan's notion of "logics in use," rhetoric of inquiry should insist both that there are multiple logics for initiating inquiry and that these play crucial roles in structuring later rhetorics of investigation and communication.[41]

In political science, rhetorics of discovery involve how to get started on political research. This concern ties directly to studies that rhetoricians of inquiry make of the twilight zone between abstract logics of science and concrete designs in the conduct of inquiry. Rhetorics of discovery also include the teaching rhetorics that introduce students, as beginning practitioners, to professional research in the discipline. Thus rhetorics of discovery and invention intersect the third chapter's concern for approved versus underground rhetorics of political research. Likewise, rhetorics of political discovery encompass our storied sensibilities of proper and improper procedures of political inquiry. Rhetorics of discovery also embrace the beginning beliefs and figures that seldom become fully conscious for researchers until they have finished their inquiries. This can engage Stephen Pepper's "world hypotheses" and "root metaphors," Kenneth Burke's "four master tropes," Northrop Frye's four master plots, and Hayden White's "prefiguration of the phenomenal field" of inquiry by four "tropes of consciousness."[42]

These aspects of rhetorics of discovery appear largely literary in light of current categories, and this encourages rhetoricians of inquiry to assess how various projects in the social sciences relate to fields of the humanities. By defending a rhetorical and political epistemology for the social sciences, rhetoric of inquiry may even be said to display them as research projects of the humanities, especially because rhetoric and philosophy are among the oldest disciplines of the humanities. Thus another priority for rhetoric of political inquiry is to investigate the historical and theoretical development of barriers between the social sciences and the humanities. This should include the reflexive project of addressing the current inclination within rhetoric of inquiry to lead beyond old divides between the two.

HUMANITIES VERSUS SCIENCES

The increased commonality between social sciences and humanities comes as a considerable surprise to veterans of old disputes between scientific and artistic cultures. They remember well how each social science promised to supplant humanistic styles of inquiry in its topics. For some contributors to the behavioral revolution in political science, the new conversations among traditionally humanistic and avowedly scientific projects might appear astonishing and, in some cases, even distressing. But the newly evident convergence does not reflect any diminished dedication of social scientists to rigorous observation and testable theories of human behavior. Instead it expresses a tendency for scientific techniques to develop greater range and complexity in tandem with diverse methods still distinctive of the humanities. This might be how social-scientific disciplines such as political science are coming to acknowledge the propriety of what they call qualitative, as well as quantitative, methods. Many research programs in political science reveal intricate interrelationships among approaches previously segregated as scientific versus humanistic.

This is more than a matter of preserving humanistic concerns in an isolated field of political theory. For one thing, the field's projects of conceptual and institutional analysis, ethics, epistemology, history, and aesthetics may diffuse slowly throughout the rest of the discipline. The interaction of theoretical projects in other fields with the ones central to political theory can promote this. For another, humanistic methods increasingly prove complementary to scientific techniques. The qualitative methods can help scholars of politics argue through the meanings of their research. Such developments surface in the two faces now presented by several fields of the discipline: judicial behavior and public law, comparative politics and area studies, international relations and peace research, political socialization and political education. These show in the aim of policy analysis to meld empirical and normative studies. They also appear in the proclivity of formal theory to elicit normative treatments of federalism, historical studies of parties, rhetorical analyses of movements such as environmentalism, and the convergence of game theory with inquiries into strategy. Later chapters address many of these problematics.

One implication of the surprising interpenetration of political science and various humanities is that political scientists do far more humanistic research than they have recognized.[43] For rhetoric of inquiry this raises fascinating issues about disparities between official rhetorics of research and actual practices or unofficial rhetorics of research. For political science this also poses the intriguing possibility that resources available for research have gone unnoticed.

Another lesson from rhetoric of inquiry is that the qualities of scientific writing reflect the qualities of scientific research, because the processes that produce them are so continuous and interactive as to defy distinction in most practices of inquiry.[44] As Oliver Sacks once observed for *Newsweek*, "I'm not sure science can be, or even should be literature, but I'm very sure it should be prose. The professional journals are quite unreadable, the way the Dow Jones report is."[45] Rhetoric of inquiry begins with issues of logic and method but extends beyond them to encompass as well questions of expression, persuasion, and interpretation. More important, it explores the interdependence of these concerns. Thus it seeks improvements in the conception, conduct, and content of research throughout the human sciences. Hence there emerges from these projects a theme with immediate implications for political scientists: many recent projects in the social sciences and humanities share data, methods, and modes of analysis. Such sharing is not bad for political science, and it can be made even better through rhetoric of political inquiry.

PROSE FOR AUDIENCES

Rhetoric of inquiry emphasizes how scholarly arguments do (or do not) persuade their audiences, both inside and outside the communities in which those arguments arise. Perhaps the most obvious priority for rhetoric of political inquiry is the rhetorical analysis of actual argumentation in political science. Field by field, project by project, book by book, article by article, page by page, sentence by sentence: how does argument in political science in fact proceed? What warrants and backings does it invoke? What assumptions, images, symbols, and tropes does it deploy? How do these affect various audiences—and with what further effects?

The approaches available to such rhetorical analysis are as many and diverse as the discipline of rhetoric has made them.[46] Eventually rhetoric of inquiry needs to invent new modes of rhetorical analysis. But for the time being, there are far more strategies worthwhile than rhetoricians of political inquiry have even begun to use. Political scientists have paid surprisingly little attention to detailed analysis of the arguments made by many of their behavioral and postbehavioral classics.

To see several ways in which rhetoricians of political inquiry might proceed to study the arguments of such texts, we may look at fine examples recently available from the discipline of economics.[47] The same concerns and strategies surface also in the recent prominence of law and literature and legal reasoning as fields of legal studies.[48] Or consider the newly rhetorical ethnography prominent in anthropology.[49] Political science very much needs such rhetorical attention to its own works.

Part One. From Figures of Inquiry

CANONS OF KNOWLEDGE

Here the invocation of "canons of knowledge" is deliberately ambiguous among three kinds of canons. The first is a set of classic texts taken to encompass the crucial or at least the germinal knowledge of a field.[50] As repositories of organizational memory and sources of continuing inspiration, these canons of classics play major roles in most of the dynamics already identified for rhetoric of inquiry. The second is a set of conventions as principles taken to constitute or regulate the generation of knowledge within a field.[51] As standards of research, these conventions are addressed by rhetoric of inquiry in its guise as political epistemology. The third is a set of conventions as beliefs taken to express the basic convictions of a field.[52] As rhetorics of invention and prose for audiences, these presuppositions are susceptible to strategies of rhetorical analysis broached earlier.

Rhetoric of inquiry studies all three canons of knowledge, but it especially explores their interdependence. In political science the first kind is probably the most problematical. On the one hand, "the traditional canon of Western classics of political philosophy" has been undergoing a sustained attack that may well lead to modest restructuring or even thorough reconception.[53] On the other hand, antitraditional science since the Second World War has scarcely begun to produce its own canon of key works. Even though the discipline's canon of classics ancient and modern must surely comprise one of the richest traditions of rhetoric in all the social sciences, the canons of knowledge in political science stand in special need of attention by rhetoricians of political inquiry.

Ends

Watch your own speech, and notice how it is guided by your less
conscious purposes.
—T. S. Eliot[54]

Recent students of rhetoric have begun an intriguing discussion of how rhetoric is epistemic: that is, how it produces, displaces, and shapes knowledge. Their work relates closely to the current criticism of foundationalism in philosophy of science. Yet these endeavors repeatedly run up against at least two barriers to better appreciation and practice of rhetoric. One is a tendency to oppose rhetoric to rationality, with the result that taking rhetoric seriously is mistaken for endorsing radical relativism. The other is a failure to examine rhetoric within contexts of actual inquiry, with the prospect of turning rhetoric back into abstract dictates of philosophy insensitive to real dynamics of research.

The overarching theme of these pages is that rhetoric of inquiry into politics, in particular, can make contributions of special value to overcoming these two barriers. Various projects in political science provide beginnings toward removing both obstacles. Studies of political cognition and opinion have started to get beyond simplistic contrasts between rationality and its utter absence.[55] Increasingly they explore diverse rationalities as reflected in associative networks of beliefs, concepts, and symbols—which is to say, as represented in particular rhetorics.[56] Political investigations of tolerance carry similar implications for attempts to privilege any single perspective as an exclusive standard of rationality.[57] Relatedly studies of political communication, culture, and socialization identify many aspects of political thinking that can be divorced from specific occasions of learning only at the cost of accurate understanding of their character and contents. This can lead toward better appreciation of the political communication, culture, and socialization of political scientists.[58] It also can enhance recognition of their many processes of inquiry within real situations of research.

The book's strategy is to move from figures of inquiry to myths of action. The first part explains rhetoric of inquiry in general, while using it to appreciate aspects of political inquiry in our times. The argument of this part is that a modern disregard for rhetoric displaces and diminishes the arts of argument necessary for disciplinary success. Thus this first chapter tells how rhetoric of inquiry relates to studies and practices of politics. The second chapter considers how the sense of disciplinary history missing from recent work impedes argument now in political science. The third chapter explores how various political scientists compensate through underground rhetorics for what they lack in approved modes of argumentation. Lest self-professed theorists of politics think themselves safe from these troubles, the fourth chapter examines how argumentation suffers in the subfield of political theory. Then the fifth chapter broaches the notion of argumentative tropes, the book's crucial invention, taking advantage of them to confront several traps, tokens, and detours that deplete the discipline's capacity for excellence in argument, inquiry, and action.

The second part articulates such tropal analysis by taking it from studies *about* politics to inquiries *within* politics. The second set of chapters explores how to re(con)figure myths of action for postmodern politics. The sixth chapter uses the inventional device of imaginative etymology to legitimate tropal modes of political evidence and argument. The seventh chapter refigures the ancient rhetoric of ethos, logos, and pathos to come to better tropal terms with liberal ideology in the United States. The eighth chapter deploys poetic tropes and images to reconceive modern government for postmodern times. On the way to a revised appreciation of deliberation in Congress, the ninth chapter shows how the methods of deconstruction are tropal and inventive in important ways. The book concludes with a tropal argument that political ideologies are being supplemented of late by other forms of political action that work very differently.

The emphasis is on tropes of argument—including figures of perception, conception, and action. In ancient Greek, as the preface notes, *tropos* means 'turn'. Figures of speech, experience, and endeavor are the turns that we trace in apprehending the world. They are the movements that we enact when persuading ourselves and others. When these figures become utterly familiar, we take them to be the very characters of our language: we literalize them. To come to terms with the turns taken in and by our arguments, therefore, we often must re-cognize, re-poeticize, even re-animate them. We must re-turn the motion to our figures. We must re-make the dynamics of meaning and doing, which our realisms, literalisms, and other fundamentalisms typically petrify into frozen, lifeless forms. Then we can discern the movements that we make when entering texts and that their words make when entering us.

Several literatures argue the necessity of figuration in language. Contrary to naive or programmatic proclamations of literalism, figures of speech are neither mere ornaments inessential to meaning nor perverse tools of manipulation hostile to reason. Even analytic philosophers of language concede that tropes of speech cannot be translated into literal talk without some loss of meaning. At least some of these philosophers appreciate that the resulting "literalizations" are bound to include irreducible figures of language. The lesson is that tropes are necessary for the expression and creativity of natural languages. They are necessary even in science. Now that the linguistic turn in modern philosophy has rediscovered the indispensability of figures to speech, the rhetorical turn in and beyond analytical philosophy is recognizing the necessity of figures for argument.

The basic idea is this: just as there are figures of speech, so there are figures of imagination and investigation; just as tropes of speech are unavoidable and invaluable, so are tropes of argument; and just as tropes of language may be turned to abuse or advantage, so may tropes of persuasion and inquiry. That is why analysis of tropes such as litotes, chiasmus, or synecdoche can help us comprehend an individual classic or a whole canon, a specific action or an enduring institution.

Even arguments may (and often must) be analyzed tropally—which is to say, in a way, mythically. To see how tropal analysis might fit into mythic analysis, just regard the movements traced by figures as narratives, the traces of events. Then recognize how figures, either stable or dynamic, serve stories as their characters. To analyze tropes within our inquiries is to trace the persuasive contributions made by figures of speech such as metaphor, hyperbole, apostrophe, and oxymoron. By extension, the same can be said and done for figures of consciousness or figures of action: metonymy as a form of argument, prolepsis as a way of reading, or irony as a stance in politics. Tropes *of* scholarly inquiries encompass *maximization* in economics, *regression* in sociology, *decision* in political science, *evolution* in biology, *text* in literary studies, and *event* in historiography. Rhetoric itself relies on tropes: *audience, speaker, occasion,* and so on.

Figures of argument could include many a typical ploy of logic (commutativity of conjunction or associativity of disjunction), many a prominent tactic of rhetoric (including the legitimate use of such "logical fallacies" as appeal to authority or argument to the person), or many a common topic of argument (moving from the particular to the general or vice versa). Mainly, however, figures of inquiry involve dynamics of persuasion that become "paradigmatic" (in Thomas Kuhn's sense) for particular bodies of ongoing studies: linear regression and modeling in some social sciences, root metaphors of organism or mechanism in public law and macrobiology, or figures of equilibrium in classical physics and neoclassical economics. To study literature can be to trace Shakespeare's cagey movement between tropes of persuasion and figures of the forum in *Julius Caesar,* not to mention how Joyce romps through English as a field of blooming, buzzing configurations. To investigate history can be to explore the tropes of government as machine and of politics as representation that informed the American Founders, or to trace the figures of speech and belief that promoted the Reformation and the Renaissance. To study epistemology as argument can be to examine the tropes of academic or everyday reasoning.

Arguments of all kinds revolve around figures of coherence, so it should be no surprise that tropes of argument help to define canons of classic works in various fields. In other words, we may postulate that canons cohere specifically as networks of figuration. Moreover we may anticipate that such classics are classics in part precisely for their figural influence. Thus each classic distinguishes itself from others in the same canon by contributing figuration that commentators and other users of the canon find inspiring or useful. And a particular set of classics seems to go together because they share important dimensions or commitments or devices of figuration. Thus these tropes of persuasion configure the canon as a whole, insofar as it is a whole. They shape a canon's fields of experience, inspire its turns of interpretation, and inform its modes of inference.

Tropes of argument are the epistemic and political foundations of all inquiries, all communities. This is to say that tropes of argument are mythic. Turns of argument are comparable to the turns of plot or event in a narrative; figures of argument are comparable to the figures or characters whose actions comprise a story. Networks of these tropes constitute whole, distinctive fields of argument: paradigms of inquiry, platforms of politics, styles of life. Because all tropes are irreducibly symbolic, tropes of argument fit well a conception of myths as symbolic stories of the whole. Thus to analyze inquiries or practices for their tropes of argument is to conduct a kind of mythic analysis.

Yet tropal analysis can also be regarded as a kind of ideological analysis. This is a good way to understand the dynamics of what Michael Calvin McGee has called "ideographs."[59] As logics of ideas, ideologies are more overtly argumentative than narratival. Yet tropes are where the symbols and stories implicit in every argument begin to emerge. As a mythic mode, tropal analysis helps us to appreciate how arguments are symbols and stories, because they are figures and turns. Tropal analysis can display a political argument for free trade as a symbolic solution for an economic problem.[60] Or tropal analysis can appreciate the same argument as one of many stories about that coolly archetypal character, Economic Man.[61] As an ideological mode, however, tropal analysis can turn around such insights to re-cognize cultural symbols, stories, and other objects as constellations of argument. We can analyze a building as a complex of architectural arguments, each deploying several telling tropes.[62] We can analyze a revolution as clash of political arguments, again each founded on characteristic figures.[63] Thus tropal analysis of argument is where the mythic and the ideological intersect, interact.

The trick is keep the tropes specific and numerous. Then they can tell volumes. Kenneth Burke argued that there are "four master tropes," at least for our times: metaphor, metonymy, synecdoche, and irony.[64] Yet he also acknowledged that each of these master tropes tends to blend into the others when scrutinized only in principle, just for its general dynamics. If that is true for a repertoire of four tropes, imagine how much greater the trouble becomes when we work with only two—as in

Roman Jakobson's pitting of metaphor against metonymy or Richard Brown's contrast between metaphor and irony.[65] Even worse are the analytical philosophers, such as Max Black, for they diminish metaphor to figural language (of any and every kind) by contrast with literal language.[66] For tropes to stay individuated, for their turns to differ in telling detail, not even four are enough. And if four are insufficient, how inadequate must two or one remain?

Even George Kennedy, a superb rhetorical critic, tends to neglect tropes other than metaphor. Probing the rhetoric of the New Testament, his second of only two index entries for *tropes* turns out to address metaphors exclusively, beyond the eleven other entries for *metaphor*. The effect is to collapse all tropes into metaphor. This reinforces a foolishly general contrast between literal and figural language. It tends to empty tropal analysis of specificity, and that mostly serves the misbegotten prejudices of literalists and other modernists.

How Kennedy slips into this diminution of tropes is telling. With Aristotle, Kennedy divides the theory of style into two parts. Lexis, or diction, involves the choice of words. Then synthesis, or composition, combines words into phrases and larger units. Following the classical rhetoricians, Kennedy regards tropes as single words, whereas he treats figures as phrases. This leaves tropes a set of moves in diction, whereas figures are a branch of composition. Then Kennedy can persuade himself to feature metaphor as the purest form of figural language.

Kennedy's excuse for detailed attention to differences in tropes becomes that "figures in the abstract do not have single definable effects; the impact has to be determined from the context." This is true enough, as is the point that many tropes "are primarily devices of emphasis which call attention to a phrase within a sentence; some, like rhetorical question, help to maintain audience contact." The danger, though, is an overdone contextualism that keeps us from good comparisons and telling generalizations about separate tropes. When we know little or nothing about specific turns, we fail to differentiate them in our studies. Yet our diverse figures are still at work when we inquire, whether we recognize them or not. Different figures make for different politics, in turn making tropal analysis indispensable for facing the nagging but glorious multiplicity and contestability of "the political."

Kennedy is too good a classical rhetorician to omit all mention of other tropes, and he says with some justification that "the most studied aspect of composition is the use of figures, both figures of speech and figures of thought."[67] The rhetorical tradition knows more about tropes than do modern philosophy, modernist linguistics, and epistemic theories of literature. This is primarily because it knows more tropes in detail—many more. Rhetorical handbooks are full of figures, differentiated one from another in ways helpfully precise. Two outstanding examples are Richard Lanham's *Handlist of Rhetorical Terms* and Arthur Quinn's *Figures of Speech*.[68] This is no surprise, because rhetoricians long have inventoried tropes as crucial devices of persuasion.

Yet even the rhetorical handbooks are not enough. Partly this is because their definitions of particular tropes often conflict with one another. Partly, too, it is because their definitions seldom receive the ample illustrations needed to communicate tropal uses and dynamics in detail. Mostly, though, rhetorical handbooks are not enough because they rarely extend their lists of turns beyond the traditional moves acknowledged in antiquity. Few modern, let alone postmodern or post-Western, turns get noticed.

Recent times generate many new and distinctive tropes to add to the traditional rosters. In no small part, these stem from the late and postmodern modes of inquiry that reach beyond classical rhetorics. Sometimes we define classical tropes in terms that might be regarded as tropes in their own right. Thus scholars attempt to specify the turn of metaphor as identification or even representation. When this works, the effect is to translate classical turns into modern terms. There need be nothing perverse about that. Nevertheless we do well to notice how the later terms often designate different turns, ones especially prominent and important from modern times onward. In addition to identification and representation, the candidates for more recent tropes are manifold: imbrication, deconstruction, evacuation, and so on. Reach into figures of action, and we may add almost any "speech act" and most other forms of action as well: participation, authorization, play, regimentation, institution, constitution, projection, sublimation, and so forth.

We owe to tropal deconstructionists like Paul de Man and Jacques Derrida the recent turns to much more nuanced and individuated analysis of tropes.[69] To see their work tweaked toward constructive analysis of political theory, read William Corlett's *Community Without Unity*. Or examine Diane Rubenstein's provocative essays. Michael Shapiro's work sometimes takes deconstructive turns.[70]

To stay with politics, perhaps the best fulfillment of the promise of tropes for rhetorical invention (as substantive political invention) is Michael Pollan's *Second Nature*. Pollan tropes gardening, lawn care, and forestry for a fine reworking of environmental politics and ethics. "A tree in a garden, as my maple taught me, is also a trope," explains

Pollan. "But imagine: a trope that gives real shade."[71] The larger lesson is that no tropes are mere, and few are words only, let alone single ones. Not all give shade where it is wanted, but any trope well turned can cast a considerable shadow within our inquiries and actions as well as our texts. Some of the best tropes even light the way to new sources of insight. So, our literalism and positivism notwithstanding, do we still trope the light fantastic in these late-unto-post yet still strangely modern times.

In the end, rhetoric of political inquiry should strive to improve research and action by teaching people engaged in studying or practicing politics to learn from their own inquiries. Especially they should learn how their rationality and inquiry are thoroughly rhetorical, truly tropal, intensely political. As ensuing chapters show, this can be an exciting prospect. To know more about our tropes of science, education, and politics is to gain practical means to improve our inquiries and our actions.

2

RETURNING HISTORY TO POLITICAL SCIENCE

A DISCIPLINARY ARCHAEOLOGY OF AMNESIA IN POLITICAL ARGUMENT

"Discipline" may be identified neither with an institution nor with an apparatus; it is a type of power, a modality for its exercise, comprising a whole set of instruments, techniques, procedures, levels of application, targets; it is a "physics" or an "anatomy" of power, a technology.
—Michel Foucault[1]

To discipline in the modern sense is to encourage an exclusive concentration on control of the present situation. It is to control through making the modalities of control omnipresent. Positively this makes control present to all—establishing its overwhelming *presence* through the modern charisma identified by Max Weber. Negatively this makes all present to control—establishing their total surveillance by devices on the order of the panopticon proposed by Jeremy Bentham. To discipline in the modern sense is to control through making subjects of control one dimensional. Positively this is to control by monopolizing all incentive—obliging all completely through presents, gifts, debts. Negatively this is to control by removing all freedom—making all pre-sent, given, fixed. To discipline in this modern sense is to control through rendering all completely present, here and now. So I read Michel Foucault to imply in his exploration of the birth of the modern prison.

As Foucault's account may suggest, presentism stems directly from dynamics that characterize modernist discipline. (Modernist disciplines differ radically from traditional disciplines such as rhetoric.) Though Foucault concentrated on modern control of the body through surveillance and punishment, his treatment of discipline also proves apt for the professionalized fields of the late modern academy. Reading narrowly, most interpreters of Foucault's writing on discipline miss the many precise analogies between modern features of surveillance and modern philosophies or methodologies of science.[2] Likewise, they miss the fascinating implications for comprehending practices of the late modern social sciences. For example, divisions and subdivisions of the (third) section of Foucault's *Discipline and Punish* devoted specifically to discipline beg to be read into modern epistemology, as the very labels convey. Let me pair these parenthetically with potentially apt analogies from the late modern multiversity.[3]

1. Docile Bodies:
    (1) The art of distributions
        [1] Enclosures (offices and boundaries)
        [2] Partitions (majors and specializations)
        [3] Functional sites (classrooms and libraries)
        [4] Ranks for units (professorial ranks and reputational ratings)
    (2) The control of activity
        [1] Timetables (class schedules and convention calendars)
        [2] Temporal elaborations of the act (teaching and publishing)
        [3] Correlations of the body and the gesture (lectures and paper presentations)
        [4] Body-object articulations (paper guidelines and style manuals)
        [5] Exhaustive uses (all-nighters and committees)
    (3) The organization of geneses
        [1] Divisions of duration into successive or parallel segments, each ending at a specific time (class periods and convention panels)
        [2] Organizations of these elements by an analytical plan (curricula and tables of contents)
        [3] Finalizations and fixes for these temporal segments, ending each in an examination (courses and semesters).
        [4] Lists for series of series (college catalogues and research annuals or review essays)
    (4) The composition of forces
        [1] Individual bodies as elements to place, move, and articulate (enrollments and full-time equivalents)
        [2] Machines as chronological series to form a composite time carefully measured (credit hours and time-allocation reports)

[3] Precise systems of command (provosts, deans, chairs or heads, professors, teaching assistants)
2. The Means of Correct Training
   (1) Hierarchical observations (proctors and laboratories)
   (2) Normalizing judgments (grading and refereeing)
   (3) Examinations (enough said)
3. Panopticism
   (1) Functional inversions of the disciplines—from negative protection to positive provision (from critical thinking and liberating arts to professional training and job-placement networks)
   (2) Swarmings of disciplinary mechanisms (evaluate and number everything from teaching to service)
   (3) State controls of the mechanisms of discipline (state or federal agencies and grants)

These are merely proposals, of course, playful exercises in imagination for author and reader alike. Such categories and the associated claims are similar to many in the literatures of anti-or postfoundationalism in the history and philosophy of science.[4] At this level Foucault's notion of modern discipline becomes closely comparable to the philosophy and history of science produced, for example, by Paul Feyerabend.[5] Here I propose to explore the modernism of academic disciplines and their related presentism as a challenge to the resources for history available through rhetoric of inquiry. Throughout, of course, I pay special attention to the modernist rhetoric of discipline in political science.

Disciplines

If we fail to see that we live in the same world that Homer lived in, then we not only misunderstand Homer; we misunderstand ourselves. The past is our definition. We may strive, with good reason, to escape it, or to escape what is bad in it, but we will escape it only by adding something better to it.
—Wendell Berry[6]

Not all disciplines are thoroughly modernist, to be sure, but many disciplines—academic and otherwise—are becoming so. As Foucault observed, "Many disciplinary methods had long been in existence—in monasteries, armies, workshops. But in the course of the seventeenth and eighteenth centuries the disciplines became general formulas of domination."[7] Thomas Kuhn's portraits of the natural sciences as paradigms of dogma and presentism bear a striking resemblance to Foucault's models of modernist discipline. Some philosophers and historians accuse Kuhn of caricature, especially through his notion of normal science, but the value of that art lies in exaggerating to evoke crucial truths. That actual sciences depart somewhat from the modernist models of Foucault and Kuhn seems the result, moreover, of features retained from other models of discipline that we often collect under the category of tradition. Among its recent advocates, four favorites are especially persuasive to me: Hannah Arendt, Wendell Berry, Edward Shils, and Garry Wills.[8] (Through all these treatments, of course, run the arguments of Max Weber about the disenchantment of the Western civilization and its decline from charismatic freedom to institutionalization, legalization, rationalization, and the iron cage of bureaucratic control.[9])

We know older disciplines of agriculture, music, poetry, politics, self-defense, storytelling, and many other endeavors. By contrast with the modernist models these could be called classical or traditional disciplines. Many are now reviving, perhaps signs of the postmodern times, and they depart markedly from both the negative and positive versions of modernist discipline indicted by Foucault:

> There are two images, then, of discipline. At one extreme, the discipline-blockade, the enclosed institution, established on the edges of society, turned inwards towards negative functions: arresting evil, breaking communications, suspending time. At the other extreme, with panopticism, is the discipline-mechanism: a functional mechanism that must improve the exercise of power by making it lighter, more rapid, more effective a design of subtle coercion for a society to come.[10]

Foucault held that "the movement from one project to the other, from a schema of exceptional discipline to one of a generalized surveillance, rests on a historical transformation: the gradual extension of the mechanisms of discipline throughout the seventeenth and eighteenth centuries, their spread throughout the whole social body, the formation of what might be called in general the disciplinary society."[11]

The traditional disciplines escape both these extremes of modernism. Consequently the traditional concerns for patient craft, personal place, and proper diversity nourish far greater respect for their pasts than can be found among modernist disciplines. Modernist disciplines promise continual progress and practice a mass production that de-means most products and producers. Classical disciplines, by contrast, pursue high standards and promote a critical conservation that re-deems most works and workers. Modernist disciplines tout capacities for self-creation, self-criticism, and self-control. Instead classical disciplines promote the very self-history that I recommend here as a limit or substitute for the modern ambition to self-control.

For several centuries, modernist ambition and control have come to dominate classical caution and order. As Berry argues, "Disciplines, typically, degenerate into professions, professions into careers."[12] But the need is not simply to restore classical disciplines, any more than it is to liberate modern disciplines from classical constraints. Instead the need is to wed the two. Where they join successfully, one result is to augment modern capacities for creation and criticism with greater capabilities for comprehension and conservation.[13] Another is to curb the tendency of modernist disciplines to sink into the faddish nihilism of oxymoronic "traditions of the new."[14] As Philip Rieff put the classical criticism of modernist discipline,

> You cannot maintain a true tradition of breakthroughs; "the tradition of the new" does not exist—no more than can a world of celibates. We are first born to our parents, however then we learn to dishonor them, and their satisfactions in us, so to claim some rebirth. There is no traditioning except in the re-cognized authority of the old. There is no honor without a sense of the past; every genius is indebted to it, beyond quits.[15]

A third result is to pit the presentist impulse of modernist disciplines against the antiquarian bent of classical traditions, transcending both to produce more sophisticated sciences—especially of human society.

Focusing on my home discipline of political science, let us explore these possibilities by addressing three key questions about disciplinary history: what it is, how to do it, and why to do it. The answers involve three theses about disciplines: what they are, how they improve, and why they need rhetoric of inquiry.[16] In turn, these theses generate three proposals for the history and rhetoric of inquiry. MY FIRST PROPOSAL IS THAT WE PRACTICE RHETORIC OF INQUIRY AS DISCIPLINARY HISTORY AND VICE VERSA. I do not suggest that either endeavor subsume the other, only that they should overlap—a lot. BY IMPLICATION, MY SECOND PROPOSAL IS THAT WE PURSUE HISTORY OF INQUIRY MORE AS HISTORY WITHIN DISCIPLINES THAN AS A SEPARATE FIELD OF HISTORY. This is to say that intellectual history and history of science are better practiced as parts of substantive inquiries than solely as professional specialties, even though the specialties should con-

tinue to encourage historical comparisons across fields. AND MY THIRD
PROPOSAL IS THAT WE PROMOTE PHILOSOPHY OF HISTORY AS RHETORIC OF
INQUIRY, TO REUNITE ITS CRITICAL AND SPECULATIVE PROJECTS WITH
EACH OTHER—AS WITH THE DESCRIPTIVE AND EXPLANATORY PROJECTS
OF PROFESSIONAL HISTORIOGRAPHY. Already, exercises in rhetoric of in-
quiry tend to reveal that none of these four projects of historiography
can proceed well without reliance on the other three.

Presentations

> *Correct discipline, given enough time, gradually removes one's*
> *self from one's line of sight. One works to better purpose then*
> *and makes fewer mistakes, because at last one sees where one is.*
> *Two human possibilities of the highest order thus come into reach:*
> *what one wants can become the same as what one has, and one's*
> *knowledge can cause respect for what one knows.*
> —Michel Foucault[17]

What better way to support these proposals than to
do a little rhetoric of inquiry as disciplinary history? Rhetoric of inquiry encourages practitioners to emphasize their own disciplines, so
it makes sense for me to target the history of political science. Yet
rhetoric of inquiry also urges comparison across fields, so let me attend as well to other disciplinary histories—especially in the social sciences. I have little direct training for the role of historian, even in political science, so my account is more a schematic sketch than a full
narrative evocation of diverse events. But it deploys evidence from
documentary and oral sources, as befits historiography. It conjoins impulses both critical and monumental, as suits philosophy of history.
And it accents the standing (ethos) of the speaker, as enjoined by
rhetoric of inquiry.

From the aspects of my standing already evident, you may conclude that I study political science as an insider, though not as an ordinary member of the discipline. Coming from a marginal subfield,[18]
and doing rhetoric of inquiry, I have advantages in yoking the understanding of an insider to the overstanding of an outsider.[19] Moreover
the domination of my subfield by projects of intellectual history requires them of me.

Beyond such general preparations, however, I bring to this essay
specific experiences pertinent to its key issues. Thanks to Neil de
Marchi and the National Science Foundation, I enjoyed two semesters
of graduate study in a unique seminar at Duke University on the his-

tory of the social sciences. Courtesy of several conferences and conventions, I have conducted useful conversations with numerous historians of science and most specialists in the history of political theory. Leading up to this essay in particular, I have discussed its arguments with all but a few of the twenty or so political scientists who might count as internal historians of my home discipline.[20] At several conferences, likewise, I have talked intensively with historians of economics, statistics, history, sociology, and psychology.[21] I have even enjoyed the pleasure of considering these ideas for several days with the philosopher Richard J. Bernstein, surely the most prominent (and perhaps the only) external historian of latter-day political science.[22]

Rhetoric encourages the recognition that every advantage can be its own disadvantage and vice versa. Recommending this perspective on the unconventional character of this study and its author, let me essay some schematic fragments toward the practice of disciplinary history as rhetoric of inquiry—with my special attention to political science leavened by occasional comparisons to other disciplines.

Histories

> *Our past is not merely something to depart from; it is to*
> *commune with, to speak with. . . . Remove this sense of*
> *continuity, and we are left with the thoughtless present tense of*
> *machines.*
> —Wendell Berry[23]

Present political science in any way you please, and still you are not likely to find another discipline more dedicated to ignoring its own history. Why do political scientists know so little history of their discipline? Because they learn little as initiates and use little in their later work. Why do they learn and use their history so little? Because they think it irrelevant to their work. Why do they think it irrelevant? Because they mistake its content and potential. Why do they mistake its content and potential? Because they know it so little. Why do political scientists know their history so little . . . ? The circle song goes on and on.

Assail this vicious circle anywhere you please, and still you will not find it easy to escape the presentism of such modernist disciplines. POLITICAL SCIENCE SELDOM PRACTICES SELF-HISTORY OF ANY KIND. It produces few sustained accounts of its accomplishments and ambitions, let alone its failures or frustrations. (It inspires professional historians to fewer still.) The last book to bill itself as a sheerly descriptive history of the discipline—and still receive significant attention—appeared several decades ago.[24] Political science consigns the very category of historical investigation to "political theory," for decades the subfield of least prestige and fewest practitioners.[25] And there the history of political science receives least priority, beneath even the history of politics.

In political science the rhetoric of history is often a rhetoric of sneer and dismissal. Political scientists seek better data, impose more rigorous methods, ask more general questions, and provide more theoretical answers than can mere historians. But the worst is that, for political science, there is simply no rhetoric of self-history. The discipline scarcely notices the possibility, rating it beneath talk as well as contempt. The field lacks even the sad tradition of textbook history that Kuhn criticized so tellingly in natural sciences[26]—save for the brief history of research approaches that may occasionally grace an introductory text on methods.[27] Graduate studies used to begin with a course on the history, scope, and method of political science, yet even that has disappeared from most programs, supplanted by courses on research design and statistics.

Not everyone in the discipline of political science might seem to share my sense of its presentism. John Dryzek and Stephen Leonard go so far as to say that "in political science more than elsewhere there is an essential link between disciplinary history and the actual practice of inquiry" so that "political science has multiple histories."[28] Yet what Dryzek and Leonard actually argue in detail is that political science needs disciplinary history in order to do its present work well. Though they mention a few examples of admittedly "cursory" Whig history by the likes of William Riker, they do little to show that the discipline even tries to detail "multiple histories." Instead their essay strongly suggests the contrary, concluding that "what remains [for political scientists] is to write histories that would sort out the lessons of the past in a way that future practitioners—and publics—might find useful."[29]

Kuhn decried the rhetoric of internal histories of science as simplistic strings of discovery: stories of one triumph after another, presenting current orthodoxy as the pinnacle of past progress.[30] But students of political science seldom learn any disciplinary history, beyond a frazzled thread sometimes showing in courses on philosophy of science—themselves an endangered species within the discipline. In fact, students cannot even count on reading Kuhn's brief classic: once the source of many a rough analogy to political science, it has left no classroom successor.[31] Alone of the social sciences, political science celebrates no founders, ignoring most of its modern originators and disparaging most of its ancient ones.[32] Its only prominent place for self-history occurs in the obligatory reviews of relevant literature that begin most journal articles in the sciences, but even these are to be brief, confined to a few issues, and focused on recent research.[33]

There are, however, several species of disciplinary history in political science. The catch is that they seldom present themselves as such, which may be warranted by their specific purposes but which helps to prevent the discipline from developing a conscious practice and rhetoric of self-history. A sketch for a history of the history of political science—if I may say it that way—probably should stress that the most numerous and important of the discipline's full-fledged histories have attempted to transform political science in fundamental ways. Presumably because the descriptive and explanatory histories favored by professional historians say little of significance to political science, the discipline instead inclines toward works that combine the critical (epistemic) and speculative (prophetic) projects that characterize philosophies of history. These are the programmatic histories by David Easton, John Gunnell, William Riker, and others—some of them partial confessions, as we see Chapter 3.[34] Perhaps the same could be said, on a much smaller scale, of the genre of presidential addresses to the American Political Science Association.

Such transformational histories are arguments for launching new projects, reviving old ones, and eliminating those with too little rigor of method or importance to politics. These works tend to obscure their own character as disciplinary histories. Sometimes they pass off their conventionally historical parts as literature reviews in support of particular problem definitions. Then they solve the target problems by discovering new courses of investigation for the discipline. Potential revolutions are described and defended in the same breath, typically as the obvious response to a technical problem. A good case in point is Gunnell's devastating criticism of most disciplinary inquiry, presented first in the guise of an undergraduate text on the canonical tradition in political theory.[35] More often, transformational histories pose plans for perfecting the discipline—through demolishing an old project here and building a new endeavor there. The usual result is bad feeling, bad history, empty promises, and movement in unexpected directions. Good illustrations are the two "revolutions" proclaimed with mixed success by Easton—first for systems theory to complete behavioralism and then for policy research to carry forward postbehavioralism.[36]

In practice, therefore, transformational histories reach toward a reunification of the critical and speculative projects that analytical philosophers ascribe to separate compartments in philosophy of history. Contrary to analytical claims of logical incoherence, these histories proceed from felt need and familiarity with the disciplinary situation. Furthermore they proceed across the usual boundaries between philosophy of history and historiography. We might conjecture, accordingly, that modernist and presentist disciplines are precisely those that can and must revive ties between such modernist compartments of history. This agrees with other theoretical considerations common to the philosophy of history and rhetoric of inquiry.[37]

At decent intervals in political science, disciplinary histories also are performed as epistemology. Here again the work of Gunnell, the discipline's preeminent historian, comes to mind, but there are a number of other examples.[38] Again there is a strong implicit argument against segregating the epistemic and substantive projects of history, after the fashion of analytical philosophies of history. Moreover both epistemic and transformational histories carry forward current substantive issues of political science—in ways seldom evident in the external histories of any discipline. This, plus the paucity of internal histories in the (external) mode of mere reconstruction, suggests that the way to improve the historical consciousness of presentist disciplines lies more through internal than external history. The largely alienated descriptions and explanations of professional historiography do not speak compellingly to practitioners of the subject disciplines.

Indeed the attempt from afar that historians of the intellect and the sciences typically make to talk at or about the work of disciplinary practitioners is apt to repeat the mistake that characterizes logicians of inquiry. The posture of external historians is seldom as arrogant as the prescriptive stance of abstracted epistemologists. Yet the external historians must make judgments, and most good ones will carry repercussions for current questions in the target discipline's studies. Can the historian pretend to judge well above the fray, fraught as it must be with crucial details as well as passionate convictions? The histories attractive to political scientists are those that seem to say something important about pressing issues of political science. And the most direct way to produce such histories is internally, engaging actual work ongoing in particular projects and fields. Let the professional historian then act as the committed rhetorician who, like "the stranger" studied by Georg Simmel, "comes to stay."[39]

Political science provides as close an approximation as anyone should want to a discipline proceeding purely in the present. Yet even it manages to conduct some self-history, though seldom in ways conscious or direct. It remains to be seen whether such presentism is workable or wise. It also remains to be shown whether any keener and more effective awareness of disciplinary history can be achieved. Two analysts of the enterprise of disciplinary history argue that "one form of reaction and, sometimes, consolation consists in the re-historicization of a field. In retrospect, hitherto neglected and hidden alternatives to the mainstream of scientific developments become visible and attempts are made to re-interpret the cognitive identity of a discipline or even to re-invent it as a whole as has been the case with anthropology." When this happens, "the semantics used to describe the development of disciplines has changed: the narrative of quasi-natural growth has in most cases been replaced by the vocabulary of political conflict in which the decadent 'anciens regimes' of established theory traditions are overthrown by a coup d'état or a scientific revolution."[40]

As a political scientist, I can acknowledge a few advantages in normalizing research and streamlining curricula. Still I am inclined to suspect related disadvantages in argument, wondering how to identify and evaluate them.[41] As a political theorist, I can know some of what might go wrong with self-history, because my subfield is beginning to confront misconceptions of its past. Still I may imagine corrected conceptions, striving to attain and disseminate them.[42] Yet it is as a rhetorician of political inquiry that I can tell best the troubles with presentism in political science, for then I can study the full impact of presentism on the organization of argument in the discipline, comparing it to other fields and times.

Traditions

> *If . . . one of the functions of tradition is to convey a sense of our*
> *perennial nature and of the necessities and values that are the*
> *foundation of our life, then it follows that, without a live*
> *tradition, we are necessarily the prey of fashion.*
> —Wendell Berry[43]

As implied by the prevalence of modernist disciplines in the academy, the larger trouble is that presentism is far from unique to political science. In this respect, political science is special only in the extremity of its penchant to discipline and present. The other social sciences and many of the natural sciences follow close behind in their disregard for practicing self-history, especially as part of their substantive research.[44] Wolf Lepenies and Peter Weingart note that "the humanities could almost be defined as those disciplines in which the reconstruction of a disciplinary past inextricably belongs to the core of the discipline."[45] Otherwise, the fields of the late modern university have—at least until recently—gravitated toward the presentism of modernist disciplines.

Focusing on abstracted issues of philosophy and ideology, external historians of inquiry have tended to acknowledge only description, explanation, and legitimation as major functions of disciplinary histories. From perspectives internal and rhetorical, however, we can recognize that disciplinary histories serve many purposes important to the conduct of substantive inquiries. Disciplinary histories justify new fields or subfields. They communicate paradigms across fields and subfields, they transfer resources throughout fields, and they promote revolutions in established fields. They initiate new practitioners, and they help experienced practitioners to take stock of their situations for inquiry and instruction. Thus they help to cull old boundaries and projects. They educate outsiders as consumers, supporters, and critics.

Consequently the potential exists for a small boom in disciplinary histories, both internal and external. As our two external historians observe, "In the human and the social sciences the growing interest in the disciplinary past has many reasons: these are different from discipline to discipline and from one national scientific culture to the other."[46] Nevertheless we may identify some common sources:

> Among these are a new idea of the process of scientific
> developments where a thinking in discontinuities has become
> prevalent; the re-structuring of sub-disciplines and specialties
> in various sciences which have to be justified not only by
> systematic reasons or external demands but also through
> historical reasoning; last but not least the changes in the self-
> image of several disciplines which are most obvious perhaps in
> the behavioral and social sciences and which are closely
> connected to the processes of social change which occurred in
> all industrialized countries since the 1960s.[47]

For external historians to contribute best, they need to perform more like rhetoricians of inquiry in the role as practitioners of the field. They need to explicate and articulate their implicit commitments of theory and value, joining disciplinary controversies rather than pretending merely to mop up afterward. For internal historians to contribute best, moreover, they too need to model themselves more on rhetoricians. In their case, however, the need is to develop the capacity for comparison across fields—as shared also with the professional, external historians.

To endow modernist disciplines with the resources and proclivities for self-history does not come easily. To propose specifically that political scientists, along with rhetoricians and historians, should do the history of political science far more than before is to accept the challenge of disciplinary self-history as a rhetorical and political challenge. As Max Weber might have suggested, it is to provide a drill for the long hard boring of the long hard boards needed for altering the complexes of power that are the modernist discipline. As rhetoric of inquiry implies, the trick is to do history of political science as part of doing political science itself. Good things may come to those who practice self-history. Hence the next three chapters offer modest and sometimes playful exercises in such rhetorical self-history for the modernist discipline of political science.

3

TURNING UNDERGROUND
INTO APPROVED
RHETORICS

A PARTIAL CONFESSION
FROM A SCIENTIZING
DISCIPLINE

Academic disciplines are institutionalized practices of inquiry. Necessarily they come complete with all the dynamics of personal and political relationships common to institutions. The details differ from one discipline, place, and time to the next. Across all disciplines, though, such general dynamics are integral to science and scholarship. They do not merely cover inquiry, as the corrupting but protecting crust comes to coat an aging cheese; they create and permeate inquiry, as the bacteria throughout help to produce the taste and texture of the cheese.

To show that all disciplines are rhetorical requires no more than showing how they are personal, institutional, and therefore political. In general terms this is so easy that it almost accomplishes itself. The principle has only to be announced for us to recognize its validity. But its significance is another matter. Some theorists (such as Stanley Fish) are tempted to dismiss this as a truism that could never carry significant implications for the study—let alone the conduct—of our inquiry.[1] It is, they maintain, like learning that you have always spoken prose: true but with no practical consequences.

Taming the claim in this way is a good strategy for those who least want to face the consequences. Yet arguments in principle against according importance to the recognition of rhetoric in research proceed by the same respect for context that characterizes the rhetorical turn. Because situations differ, as both rhetoricians and these critics insist, recognizing rhetoric need not change conduct in any specific way, for good or ill. From this the critics infer correctly that recognizing rhetoric carries no necessary or universal implications for inquiry. Their mistake is to equate no *necessary* implications with no *actual* implications. Whether and what consequences occur must differ from one circumstance to the next. Only by inspecting particular situations can we tell the actual or potential effects of coming to terms with specific rhetoricities of research.

Tip O'Neill said that "all politics is local," and surely every discipline lives a local existence. To evoke a proper ambition for political action and knowledge, Michael Walzer quotes W. H. Auden: "A poet's hope: / to be like some valley cheese / local, but prized elsewhere."[2] Guided by the same goal, rhetorical practices and knowledge stem from specific situations, but they may aspire to more general (though neither necessary nor universal) relevance. Rhetoric of inquiry can hope to achieve this significance through comparing disciplines, projects, and situations—rather than postulating some uniform setting for research. This is why rhetoricians of inquiry value communication across fields, by others as well as themselves. Yet it is also why rhetoricians of inquiry must attend with care to the seemingly idiosyncratic details of particular projects, controversies, and silences in research.

More specifically, it is why much rhetoric of inquiry already is and always should be done as an integral part of substantive research in every field. Otherwise, the very rhetoric of rhetoric becomes too fixed, formulaic, and insensitive to stay insightful. Rhetoricians of inquiry have special reason to remember the oldest truth of any craft: without excellence of detail, excellence of vision must remain unknown.

In this respect, my main reason as a rhetorician of inquiry for focusing on the social sciences is simply that their details are the ones I know best. As a social scientist, moreover, I have a strong interest in discovering whatever rhetorical analysis can show about how to understand and improve inquiry in my major fields of study. At this early time, though, rhetoricians of inquiry have at least four other reasons to emphasize research in the social sciences. These say why you should care about rhetorics of social inquiry, even if you intend never to become a social scientist—or at least, any more of one than necessary for attending to rhetorics in other inquiries.

First, the social sciences include many of our most extreme examples of willful oblivion to rhetoric in research. Unlike the arts, humanities, and professions, the social sciences have insistently denied and ignored their own rhetoricity. Even so, sheer oblivion to the rhetoricity of a field's own inquiries is probably greatest now in the mathematical, natural, and technological sciences. Unlike these latter fields, however, the social sciences have developed almost directly from the older discipline of rhetoric. Retaining many of its phenomena and even some of its methods, the social sciences would find themselves reminded of their rhetoricity at every turn, were they not willfully to cultivate and enforce oblivion to it.[3] For rhetoric of inquiry to prove valid and useful, it must successfully confront the main modes of resistance to recognizing how inquiries are appropriately rhetorical. Because the resistance is strongest where the stress is most persistent and acute yet where oblivion persists nonetheless, the social sciences become our best arenas for exploring the resistance to rhetoricity.

Second, the social sciences stand, in the short and middle runs, to gain the most from greater sophistication about rhetoric. On one hand, early studies in rhetoric of inquiry suggest that ignorance of rhetoric causes more trouble for argument and theory in the social sciences than elsewhere.[4] On the other hand, recent concerns of the social sciences imply that knowledge of rhetoric carries more relevance for method and substance in the social sciences than anywhere but in the humanities.[5] Greater awareness of rhetoric in the humanities lets us forget that the social sciences are just as much its substantive successors. The social sciences have inherited so many perspectives and questions from rhetoric that we might even describe them collectively as a continuation of the older discipline by other names and means.[6] As this chapter reflects, in fact, specifically rhetorical problematics are beginning to reemerge on many frontiers of social research—after decades of mere neglect or outright repression.[7] If so, though, these new incarnations remain sadly unaware of themselves as rhetoric. Consequently rhetoric of inquiry speaks with special directness and sophistication to many phenomena and techniques at the heart of current research in the social sciences.

Third, the social sciences provide new means and problematics for analyzing rhetoric. Furthermore these means and problematics are among those most urgently needed by rhetoricians of inquiry. Challenges to the rhetorical analysis of inquiry reach beyond the arenas and resources assumed by early paradigms of rhetoric.[8] As new forms and methods for studying dynamics of rhetoric, the social sciences stand ready to teach rhetoricians much about the practices of rhetoric in various inquiries. Moreover an underused advantage of centering studies of rhetoric in departments of communication is the enrichment of rhetorical theory with social-scientific investigations of organizational, interpersonal, political, small-group, and other branches of what we sometimes call *communication science*. Theories of argumentation and persuasion stand to benefit greatly from such research. For example, rhetoricians need to inform their studies of inquiry with what psychologists know about social cognition.[9] Similarly rhetoricians can learn about tropes of language and argument from economists as well as literary theorists.[10] And rhetoricians of inquiry in particular should learn from political scientists about the politics of disciplines.[11] Therefore the social sciences speak with special directness and sophistication to many of the phenomena and techniques at the heart of current research in rhetoric of inquiry.

Fourth, the social sciences continue to become ever more important and controversial in public affairs. Arguments over public policy fuse issues of the natural and social sciences in ways that challenge our capacities for rhetorical analysis of both.[12] There is also reason to think that the rhetorical relevance of the social sciences to everyday affairs of government, business, and most other spheres of society is continually increasing. The resulting reliance of society on rhetorics from the social sciences makes the comprehension and improvement of their rhetorics into a high priority.

Let me hasten to add that other considerations can turn attention to inquiries beyond the social sciences. For instance, the rhetorical analysis of mathematics, statistics, and physics could claim a high priority because of the general prestige of each discipline and the false reputation that they share for purifying their studies of all rhetorical complications.[13] At this time, rhetoricians might emphasize biology and geology because of their exceptional ferment, their internal diversities of reasoning, or their special significance for social issues.[14] Artificial intelligence and cognitive science might merit rhetorical treatment as linked fields early in formation.[15] American studies, global studies, African American studies, and women's studies deserve rhetorical examination for their exceptionally politicized projects and for their attempts to cut across the grain of current disciplines.[16] Yet these and related reasons to target work outside the social sciences can seldom promise the substantive effects that rhetoric of inquiry should make in social theory. Nor do other targets offer the detailed lessons that attention to social inquiry should produce for rhetorical theory.

This said, the next point is plainly that I am less a generic social scientist than a specifically political scientist. My discipline borrows so much from others that it remains less limiting than most research situations.[17] Yet the issues, texts, and theories that I know best are the ones that surface in political science. So let me frame a problematic for rhetoric of inquiry that is now highly important for political science. Because it is one that focuses on the willful incapacity of political scientists to recognize their own rhetoricity, I suspect that aspects of the same problematic may surface significantly in other disciplines, especially in the social sciences. Like the fine valley cheese, therefore, my ambition is for this particular inquiry into the rhetoric of political research to say something important to political scientists and perhaps to others as well.

Approved versus Underground Rhetorics

I apologize to the reader for the personal focus of this account. Writing it is uncomfortable, because we are trained to write with cold impersonal logic. But that is a professionally sanctioned fib. The "I" is an important part of the research experience; an honest narrative cannot fail to include it.
—James A. Stimson[18]

Stimson's remark appears in an unusual forum. He was asked to reflect on how he came to conceive and conduct a good inquiry into political beliefs of the 1972 electorate in the United States.[19] Officially, as Stimson knows, "cold impersonal logic" is for political scientists the guarantee—not the antithesis—of honesty. Unofficially, as Stimson implies, many political scientists recognize such logic as nothing more or less than an aspect of the rhetorics approved for most professional publishing in the discipline. In fact, the "professionally sanctioned fib" is a feature of official and semiofficial rhetorics throughout the social sciences. And it is far from the only feature of such approved rhetorics in disciplinary research. They encompass the entirety of conversation considered fully respectable among researchers: from genres of publication to tropes of method, from conventions of observation to strategies of argument, and from models of explanation to prefigurations of the phenomenal field.

In a mood of unmasking, there is a temptation to call most of these standard locutions *fibs*, because they often present research in terms that researchers concede in other contexts to be misleading or even mistaken. But that need not make them mistaken or misleading in their original contexts, and so they should generally be taken for what social scientists ascribe to others as *conventions*.[20] Because they are conventions that express or enforce strategies of speaking and writing, we may recognize them as conventions of rhetoric.[21]

Such rhetorical conventions of research are highly diverse in origin, meaning, and effect. The one identified by Stimson is a generic convention of the research article as a sheer report—a positive, impersonal building block of knowledge. It stems from assuming that all personal aspects of inquiry can and must remain confined to a nonlogical context of discovery, by contrast with the strictly logical context of justification in which the research is reported to other scientists. Insistence on impersonality virtually requires the passive voice of that last phrase. The genre presumes that reality—not merely some scientist—speaks to the research community through the inquiry as conducted and reported. The impersonal delivery helps the article count as a contribution to some hypothetico-deductive science that melds largely separate moments of logical and empirical inquiry into well-tested theories that have survived repeated attempts at falsification.[22]

In this case, as Stimson intimates, most practitioners know at some vague level that personality affects even the most scientific of inquiries.[23] Yet they take utterly impersonal research to be the ideal: even if its complete achievement proves impossible, the effort to achieve it should improve the quality of inquiry actually conducted.[24] When that is not so, however, the convention becomes mistaken and misleading in its prime context. And when approved conventions become chronically mistaken and misleading, researchers often generate unapproved, underground rhetorics in trying to keep their inquiries on track.

Like other social sciences, political science appropriated many of its approved rhetorics from philosophers of science who preached logical positivism and empiricism.[25] Approved statistics are the other main source of quasi-official rhetorics in political science. Even though statistics began as figures from or about the state, political science gets most of its statistical methods—and rhetorics—from other sciences of society.[26] Both sources tend to produce chronically poor rhetorics of political inquiry. In turn, these approved but inadequate rhetorics contribute to poor studies of politics. Rhetorically, though, we need to notice that complaints against such research get lodged at different levels, generating separate strategies of response. Let me distinguish two that might otherwise become conflated.

One current trouble with the rhetorics approved for political science is that they encourage the discipline to concentrate on poor problems and procedures.[27] Resistance to this mainstream agenda of research accounts for attempts to create alternatives to the approved rhetorics of research. Thus some comparativists, institutionalists, interpretivists, Marxists, and others have dissented from the discipline's mainstream rhetorics of research since World War II.[28] The dissenters propose contrary agendas and rhetorics of inquiry. So far they remain marginal to the discipline, but their intended corrections are overt: visible, vocal, and sometimes strident. Advocates of these alternatives cultivate their own arenas of discourse such as special panels, conferences, and journals. Moreover the mainstream targets of these alternatives address them directly—if rarely—in forums more central to the discipline. Therefore approved rhetorics that seem chronically inadequate can occasion programmatic attempts to create *alternate rhetorics* of research.

A distinct trouble with rhetorics approved by and for political science is that few fit how most political scientists actually conduct their inquiry.[29] What political scientists do differs immensely from what they say, because their approved rhetorics miss so much about basic realities of their research.[30] Such official rhetorics imply that routine and sometimes necessary steps of research are always invalid and therefore absent: mining the data, for example.[31] They always insist on including steps that are often superfluous or misleading, such as tests of statistical significance.[32] They misunderstand the character and implications of other commonly made moves, for instance, confusing the specification of formal models with their testing.[33] And so on. Much of the discipline's official preaching simply cannot be practiced in any way that is decently literal or direct, let alone in any mode suited to the problems and procedures currently in the mainstream of political science.[34]

One result is that much research in political science is far better than political scientists can tell officially, almost no matter how hard they try.[35] If their research is not to degenerate, however, political scientists must nonetheless be telling one another many things largely unsayable by approved rhetorics. That is, they must have other rhetorics for addressing what the official rhetorics misconstrue or miss altogether. Moreover they must have other occasions for communicating what the official forums discourage. These occasions and rhetorics must enable decent research contrary to approved categories, but they must do so without discrediting the official locutions. Therefore approved rhetorics that appear chronically inadequate can prompt informal efforts to sustain *underground rhetorics* of research.

Alternate rhetorics seek to supplant the rhetorics approved at present; underground rhetorics try to complement or even rescue them. Alternate rhetorics aspire to accounts of inquiry that are comprehensive and coherent; underground rhetorics provide accounts that are partial and fragmentary. Alternate rhetorics project new paradigms; underground rhetorics protect established ones.[36] Of course, some underground rhetorics eventually get articulated into alternate rhetorics.

Let me emphasize, though, that the contrast is practical and rhetorical—rather than logical and philosophical. Logically and philosophically, most rhetorics now approved by political science are hypothetico-deductive. At that level, consequently, rhetorics of abduction and induction are equally offensive to the discipline. Thus the approved rhetorics of political science reject the self-consciously abductive talk related to clinical work in psychiatry, interpretation of symbols in psychohistory, and participant observation in anthropology. Political science treats such talk as an alternate rhetoric.[37] Yet the same approved rhetorics accept or at least overlook the merely inductive or haphazardly abductive discourse connected with many area studies, taking it to be an underground rhetoric.[38]

Approved rhetorics that practitioners perceive to be insufficient for understanding or conducting useful research can provoke alternate and underground rhetorics simultaneously. In political science, at least, the two often intertwine. The discipline's approved rhetorics celebrate the pursuit of "empirical generalizations" that transcend the limits of particular polities, cultures, and times. But its underground lore is a rhetoric insistent on the peril of such generalization across contexts. Thus major works of "comparative politics" continue to feature "case studies" that emphasize single countries, societies, and periods. Moreover some critics of the comparativist rhetoric now approved by political science advocate an alternate rhetoric of "thick description," to establish instead a general methodology of area and case studies.[39]

Within political science as a discipline the approved and quasi-official rhetorics of political research differ significantly from the underground and usually informal rhetorics of political inquiry. Thus the rhetorics that dominate mainstream journals and methods textbooks diverge widely from the rhetorics that surface in graduate seminars, collaborative inquiries, hallway conversations, and other secluded occasions for talking about how political scientists actually do their studies. Though some political scientists would deny this altogether, many would concede it in general terms. Yet most would doubt that it carries implications important for the content or quality of political inquiries. In the rest of this chapter, I dispute that impression and suggest some of its consequences for the substance of political science.

Confession

There is no refuge from confession but suicide; and suicide is confession.
—Daniel Webster[40]

Little has been written about disparities between the actual practices of political science and the approved rhetorics for political inquiry. But even less has been published about differences between the discipline's official rhetorics and its underground guidelines. For the contrast between approved and underground rhetorics to prove useful, we need persuasive ways to demonstrate it and trace its consequences. To document the existence and effect of the contrast in political research could involve analyzing instances of the disparities and interactions between these two sets of rhetorics. Thus I propose a series of case studies to cover the various arenas of political inquiry significant for the contrast between approved and underground rhetorics of research.

To target and conduct such studies implies a rhetorical conception of political science as a discipline. Accordingly let me essay a map of some rhetorical arenas and genres prominent in the discipline. The purpose of this little diagram, which appears in Figure 3.1, is to distinguish several forums, genres, and subgenres of communication among political scientists that bear on contrasts and interactions between approved and underground rhetorics.

There is no hierarchical order from most to least important or the like. As far as possible, however, I have paired the contrasts. Each pair implies a mirroring, a complementarity, a compensation: each form or forum of underground rhetoric stands roughly across from the kind of approved rhetoric that it most often or directly addresses. I take these to be the main, but by no means the only, practical relationships through which the discipline's underground rhetorics seek to correct or offset its approved rhetorics.

Approved rhetorics concentrate in	*Underground rhetorics appear in*
Philosophies of (social) science	Private conversations (hallways, offices,
Approaches textbooks	telephones, etc.)
Methods textbooks	Partial confessions:
Statistics textbooks	Stories of research processes
Articles on methods and statistics	New projects by old leaders
Association style manual	Field notes and working notes
Research reports	Research popularizations
Research controversies	Research collaborations
Book chapters	Prefaces and acknowledgments
Association reports	Independent conferences
Convention panels	Convention roundtables
Association politics	Association administration
Department administration	Department politics
Graduate core seminars	Advanced graduate seminars
Undergraduate courses	Research help for Ph.D. students
Oral history of the discipline	Popular or research interviews

Figure 3.1. Approved versus Underground Rhetoric

Although the figure includes genres especially significant for the field's political learning of late, it is far from complete. For one thing, it omits the manifesto and other genres central to alternate rhetorics. For another, it misses the complication of many interactions between the two broad kinds of rhetorics within—rather than across—the sorts of situations and structures evoked in these comparisons. Therefore private conversations surely include approved rhetorics, even as they produce special concentrations of underground rhetorics.

Mindful of these and many other analytical perils in genre theory, let me emphasize that the figure is highly tentative and admittedly restrictive. It only begins to clarify the status of the underground rhetorics in political science. In fact, further study might show that approved rhetorics dominate a few of the occasions where I expect underground rhetorics to concentrate. Figure 3.1 is designed to initiate research on such rhetorics, and it cannot pretend to express anything more than the most preliminary of conclusions about the rhetorical realities of political science. Nor can the figure claim to diagram other disciplines. Even for other rhetorical issues of political science, a graphic depiction that turns solely on the contrast between approved and underground rhetorics is likely to distort the discipline beyond recognition or usefulness.

Fuller analysis of such a comparison would examine the conventions, strategies, and other features that characterize each form of rhetoric on both sides of the grand divide. Then we would be able to assess the comparative advantages of approved and underground rhetorics to the current conduct and content of the discipline. Moreover this might let us demonstrate some categorical repercussions of the contrast already claimed for rhetoric of inquiry. But such analysis would also require rhetorical standards for deciding at least some present needs of political knowledge, and therefore of political action, necessitating in turn a much more complicated analysis than I can mount here.

Furthermore any of these projects would put the cart before the horse, because the first challenge is to figure out how to study the contrast as sketched. To conduct case studies that feature rhetorical analysis seems relatively straightforward for approved rhetorics. Thus we could examine features of rhetoric common to introductory texts on approaches, methods, and statistics of political inquiry. Then we could extend the study to book chapters and journal articles on advanced statistics for political research. Practitioners of the discipline would readily recognize these as several distinct but related genres of argument. Yet they might be surprised at the internal incoherence of approved rhetorics in prominent instances of these texts:

for example, the common but uncritical combination of research rhetorics from naive verificationism ("empirical generalization" and "direct versus indirect observation"), crude operationism ("real versus nominal definitions"), naive falsificationism ("rejecting the null hypothesis" and "critical tests"), sophisticated falsificationism ("specifying the model" and "avoiding ad hoc hypotheses"), or even incipient contextualism ("identifying the boundary conditions"). Moreover they could be discouraged by the reminder of the many roads often recommended for methodological reasons but seldom taken in substantive research: for instance, "analyzing the residuals" in linear regression. In the end, perhaps, they should be appalled at the persistence of the resulting oxymorons ("pretheoretical frameworks" and "political behavior") and redundancies ("statistical generalization" and "empirical evidence").

To characterize even the approved rhetorics of political science is a considerable challenge, because the discipline lacks a history of overtly authoritative statements on the order of the manual of style promulgated by the American Psychological Association.[41] In fact, only recently has the American Political Science Association established a distinctive manual of style for the discipline, and this on a scale far less ambitious (or presumptuous) than its predecessors in psychology. Nonetheless textbooks on methods of political research provide specific examples and statements of the approved rhetorics that are: (1) widely taught, (2) mutually consistent, and (3) consonant with other quasi-official expressions of the approved rhetorics of political research.[42] Working from such textbooks, analysis of approved rhetorics could identify several key features, examining their roles in the conduct of the discipline.

The main trouble in contrasting approved and underground rhetorics within political science, though, is to secure good articulations of the underground rhetorics. The challenge, in a word, is to get political science to *confess* its underground rhetorics—despite the considerable resistance to acknowledging or analyzing them that remains entailed by their underground status. Lest the concept of underground rhetorics or the task of investigating them seem a contradiction in terms, let us recall with Webster—and Sigmund Freud—that confession is virtually inescapable. Though the difficulties in studying them are many, even underground rhetorics remain susceptible to systematic scrutiny. And as the obstacles to knowing and improving them increase, so also do the potential rewards to political science and rhetoric of inquiry.

My crude map of the contrast between approved and underground rhetorics of political research suggests that underground rhetorics manifest themselves in many ways to practitioners—and potentially to rhetoricians. Each type of manifestation could occasion studies of underground rhetorics, though some types seem more promising than others. Because underground rhetorics crowd into the crevices and aporias of approved rhetorics, the study of underground rhetorics should become easier as approved rhetorics yield more omissions or troubles. Yet as these anomalies, convolutions, or gaps increase, the resulting prominence of underground rhetorics makes them less distinct from approved rhetorics. This is when underground rhetorics sometimes become approved or when they sometimes turn into alternate rhetorics. At any rate, different crevices and aporias require different techniques of rhetorical analysis.

Surely underground rhetorics of research invite study by various forms of social-scientific inquiry: recording graduate seminars and hallway conversations for detailed study of their research rhetorics, observing research projects as a participant or regular onlooker, comparing the official classification of disciplinary fields with the categories and work patterns of specific departments, and so forth. Another approach would be to call on the recollections of political scientists through depth interviews with them.[43] In general terms these approaches have been the province of the new social studies of science that range across anthropology, history, philosophy, rhetoric, and sociology.[44] A recurrent trouble to anticipate with many of these techniques is that the sheer presence of observers, recorders, and the like might tend to increase reliance on approved rhetorics—at the expense of opportunities to study underground rhetorics. Nonetheless turning such methods to the exploration of those contrasting rhetorics seems worthwhile.

Still another set of approaches is more literary. Thus critics or rhetoricians could analyze field notes and working notes, the prefaces and acknowledgments in books, or good popularizations of research. All are promising sources of underground rhetorics, because all involve speaking directly to the practical challenges faced by one or another project of inquiry. These literary approaches offer the advantage of less effect on the objects of study—or less immediate effect, at any rate, because the results might eventually legitimate some underground rhetorics or increase official vigilance against others.

A more lasting advantage of the literary approaches is the potential for greater confidence in deconstructions of rhetoric wrought with relative care. By contrast, psychoanalytic approaches emphasize the potential for greater frequency of revealing lacunae, slips, and the like in rhetoric constructed less reflectively. Either way, though, the rhetorician of inquiry must use techniques of deconstruction precisely because of the proclivity of underground rhetorics to appear in the aporias of approved rhetorics.[45]

A few historians, rhetoricians, sociologists, and contributors to the interdisciplinary field of literature and science have already begun to analyze field and laboratory notes for their rhetorics. Something similar to the contrast between approved and underground rhetorics seems a largely unstated premise of many such efforts. None of these studies known to me addresses political science, unfortunately, but explicit recognition and investigation of the contrast could produce implications for exploring the contrast in that discipline as well. This should be especially true of the discipline's increasing collaborations on a large scale—as in the collection of data about elections, public opinion, international relations, democratization, political advertising buys, and more. Even so, the potential for such rhetorical analysis of notes will remain severely limited in political science as long as it continues to disdain the experimentalist and naturalist tradition of keeping notebooks about research in progress.

Among political scientists, disparities between claims in the body of a book and rhetorics in its preface or acknowledgments are a standing source of jokes. Indeed my sense of underground rhetorics owes almost as much to reading prefaces as to talking privately with other political scientists. Especially striking is the contrast between prefaces or acknowledgments (on the one hand) and introductions or conclusions (on the other). For obvious reasons, approved rhetorics of political science seem to cluster in the introductions and conclusions. Comparing rhetorics across the two sets of occasions therefore ought to prove exceptionally revealing for the study of underground rhetorics of political inquiry.[46] I have little notion of whether this pattern might hold in other social sciences or in other regions of the academy, but it is a possibility worth investigating.

By contrast, my expectation that popularizations often manifest underground rhetorics stems mostly from reading about disciplines other than political science. Through interviews, observations, and other modes of research, good popularizers reach well into the informal and unapproved regions of inquiry. Because popularizations typically address a general public (rightly) taken to have a special interest in "the human side of science," they display a generic interest in many issues for rhetoric of inquiry—with the contrast between approved and underground rhetorics no exception to that rule. Perhaps I should say *popularization* with some hesitation, because the term is sometimes taken to demean its referents, whereas I respect them as

works of journalism and science for nonspecialists. As a great popular-
izer has said about rhetoric, science, and popularizations,

> The rhetoric is not ornament—science is, among other things,
> a running argument in which resolution or consensus is cause
> not for satisfaction but for restlessness to move on. Further,
> almost without exception, scientists who have been effective
> popularizers have written about the field that encloses their
> own work. To be effective, this sort of popularization must be
> the natural extension of the scientist's daily activity, which
> includes persuading himself and then others that he is not
> wrong about his latest particular finding.[47]

Thus popularizations testify powerfully to the crucial importance of
rhetoric in the substance of inquiry.

In my opinion, political science has yet to generate or perhaps even
deserve the excellent kinds of creative popularization that some other
disciplines enjoy from the likes of Isaac Asimov, Jeremy Bernstein,
Henry Cooper, Stephen Jay Gould, Horace Freeland Judson, Berton
Rouechè, Robert J. Samuelson, Lewis Thomas, and those who write
for publications such as *Scientific American.* I suppose that two of the
more prominent popularizers of political science are David Broder
and Garry Wills. But neither is generally known for that aspect of his
work, and both attend to apparent results rather than actual dynamics
of political inquiry. Consequently popularizations are a more promising source for information about the underground rhetorics of most
other disciplines than they are for political science.

We should not find it difficult to imagine other studies as well. For
instance, there might be advantages in experimenting with situations
for collaborative research that differ in their rhetorical needs or conditions. Presumably such inquiries could be structured as studies of
communication within small groups. Indeed data already generated
from small-group experiments on problem solving might also prove
revealing in this connection. And as with so many other subjects, the
more we learn about underground rhetorics of research, the greater
will become our resources for knowing how to study them further.

What if we were to take more seriously still the notion that underground rhetorics of inquiry reveal themselves through forms of confession? To me this suggests yet another set of manifestations, one that
coheres as a distinct genre of argument in political science. It figures
prominently in recent research, but it has not previously been recognized as a distinct genre. Or, more precisely, its peculiar ties to ap-

proved, alternate, and underground rhetorics lead insistently to its confusion with a genre usually considered crucial to approved rhetorics.

I do not claim that political scientists sustain a vital genre of direct, self-conscious confessions. If they existed, presumably they would criticize approved practices or rhetorics as errors that require recanting. There is nothing impossible about this in principle, still the discipline in fact gives me not so much as a single clear case, let alone a continuing genre, that would qualify as confessional in this sense. Insofar as it has generated any overt or comprehensive impulse toward confessions of this kind, they appear mostly in the manifestos for alternate rhetorics, where new programs for research sweep away attention to underground rhetorics in the old programs. And in general, the high value that the sciences attribute to constructive criticisms, proposals, and especially results seems likely to discourage confessions at once systematic and straightforward. Yet only such comprehensive confessions would detail departures from approved rhetorics but without turning any incipient recognition of underground rhetorics into grist for some alternate rhetoric.

Perhaps there have been a few comprehensive confessions that despair equally of approved and alternate rhetorics for political science: something approaching a pox on every house in town. This might be preliminary to renouncing the whole discipline, or at least its interest in science. Even these confessions might leave underground rhetorics in the dark, unremarked as inconsequential adjustments beneath contempt. Yet they may instead explicate underground rhetorics, either as signs of corruption or as devices insufficient for salvation. The simple fact, however, is that no such confessions have come yet to my attention, though I read the literatures of political science where they would be most likely to appear.

In my experience, the main candidates turn out to be attacks by those who were never really a part of what passes for scientific studies of politics and who thus lambaste its epistemic rhetorics from outside.[48] Whatever their merits, such criticisms are polar opposites of research confessions. Because their claims rest on grounds of abstract logic and epistemology, such critics tend to ignore the details of actual inquiry in political science. That disqualifies such criticisms as an important source for the study of underground rhetorics in political science, and it leads most political scientists to ignore them as well.

There is nonetheless at least one general kind of confession practiced by political scientists. Moreover it attracts some of the discipline's most distinguished members. It persists—so far—in two subgenres that differ considerably in their ends and means. Each is a widely scattered set of texts that offers usable, though indirect, access to underground rhetorics of political science. But both are recognizable as research confessions. Together they comprise a genre of the *partial confession*.

Propriety

> *Explaining is generally half-confessing.*
> —Marquess of Halifax[49]

All confessions are partial in significant respects. Aside from obvious limits on the motivations, occasions, and self-understandings needed for confession, mere limits of memory leave every confession seriously incomplete. So crucial to confession are the constraints of memory that St. Augustine's famous *Confessions* become by their end some of the West's most impressive reflections on memory and time.[50] Asking colleagues about details in their conduct of research only a few months earlier repeatedly identifies matters that they cannot remember at all, let alone correctly. Of course, we recognize similar phenomena in the testimony of officials tangled in misdeeds. Even in their cases, however, the plea that they "do not recollect" specifics is often plausible. After all, research on social and political cognition shows that people retain only the relatively general impressions that they form at the time of an event, for such judgments enable them to cast aside the details.[51]

But that comparison should remind us of a further complication: what we do remember has been reconstructed, and those reconstructions are informed or even motivated by what we believe in general to be the actual or appropriate ways to act in such situations. Thus we have every reason to expect that our memories, as reconstructions, are biased toward approved rhetorics of inquiry. This need not preempt memories of underground rhetorics or actions in accord with them— especially from unusually skillful researchers, whom we might expect to be exceptionally attentive to the actual nuances of their inquiry. Yet it probably restricts the memory of underground rhetorics still further. Certainly it gives us greater confidence in confessions based on field notes or research diaries that record the revealing minutiae that later or less tutored memories might otherwise miss.

All these limits surface readily in the research confessions of other disciplines. Surely the most notorious of my time has been *The Double*

Helix, in which James Watson confesses how he and Francis Crick set out to win a Nobel Prize for discovering the structure of DNA.[52] Given the success of their pursuit, Watson acknowledges and even glories in the selfish motivations, personality conflicts, institutional scheming, and other unsavory sides of inquiry omitted or obscured by the official rhetorics of biology. As usual in modern science, the book counts as a confession not so much because it admits mistakes (of inquiry or morality) as because it concedes (and celebrates) how scientists depart in practice from the conduct projected by their approved rhetorics. Thus the whole analysis implies the existence of underground rhetorics, and Watson explicates several elements of them.

When I report that political science lacks full-fledged research confessions, therefore, I am saying something more than that the discipline fails to depart from its approved rhetorics of scientific progress. The Watson book is a such story of scientific discovery and progress. As such, it can be and has been approved according to the official rhetorics of biology. Yet it is no less a research confession, because it specifies the importance of many underground realities and rhetorics of biology. What political science lacks is direct, self-conscious attempts of that kind.

Even a little reading between the lines, however, suffices to identify still more offensive interpretations and schemes that Watson's surface account slides past. And numerous commentators have said as much. Other commentators point out that Watson was in no position to know significant parts of the DNA story, parts that change the plot and implications greatly when noted. Still others disagree with his memory on issues that range from incidental to crucial. Whatever the detailed truth about *The Double Helix*, we entertain such arguments because they appeal to limits of confession and memory familiar from immense personal and social experience. This makes the twofold consensus on that book all the more remarkable: *of course*, it manifests the many constraints on memory and confession; *still* it remains extraordinarily valid and valuable as a source of insights into the actual conduct of inquiry.

To talk then of partial confessions is to imply some special incompleteness beyond the limitations virtually inevitable for all confessions about research or anything else. Thus partial confessions lack the direct, self-conscious dedication to revealing unsavory events that marks unqualified confessions. In this sense, they might be called *half-confessions*. But they *are* confessions, in a more specific and even intentional way than the usual explanations, which the Marquess of Halifax acutely described by that same term. Though the confessional implications of most explanations help to generate the inevitability of confession noticed by Webster, and though they help to justify several other targets of attention for rhetoricians who study underground rhetorics of research, these quasi-confessional features fall far short of the concentrated revelations provided by partial confessions as a genre of writing in political science—and perhaps elsewhere.

In particular, instances of partial confession go categorically beyond ordinary explanations in acknowledging the ends, means, mistakes, and other moments of research officially driven underground. Some partial confessions flirt in a semiconscious but sustained fashion with saying more than intended about underground rhetorics. Other such confessions carefully limit their revelations to small sugar-coated doses palatable enough to many who need the medicine but who would refuse large straight doses as sour and dangerous. Both kinds of incompletion exceed the characteristic gaps in full-voiced confessions about research. But neither devolves utterly into the impersonal modes of approved rhetorics or turns entirely into the confrontational styles of alternate rhetorics.

Political science currently includes at least two subgenres of partial confession. One is the detailed recollection by respected professionals of how they happened to produce particular pieces of research. Let me name that the *research story.* The other is the stock-taking recollection by distinguished professionals of what a particular project has accomplished and how it now needs to take a major new turn that will at last produce what it supposedly sought all along. Let me call that the *research turn.* Semi-intentionally and semidirectly, each confesses to a previous and perhaps continuing reliance on underground rhetorics of political research.

The research story is a subgenre in all social sciences, I think, and many other disciplines as well. Typically the authors are highly reputed for their technical competence in some established or newly fashionable kind of inquiry. Usually they compose research stories in response to an invitation to recount in detail how they performed some inquiry or produced some publication regarded as a good example of that kind of research. Their charge is to put flesh on the bones of approved methods and rhetorics of inquiry, often so that students can improve their sense of the practical conduct of such research. The subgenre assumes that methods texts and other media for approved rhetorics of research convey neither the mundane details nor the human drama that fill the everyday lives of disciplinary practitioners, make the difference between good and mediocre studies, and keep researchers excited about their work.

For political scientists, prominent examples of the research story appear in the first three chapters of *An Introduction to Models in the Social Sciences* by Charles Lave and James March; the appendix of *Home Style* by Richard Fenno; *The Research Process in Political Science*, edited by W. Phillips Shively; *Missing Elements in Political Inquiry*, edited by Judith A. Gillespie and Dina A. Zinnes; *Strategies of Political Inquiry*, edited by Elinor Ostrom; and "workshop" articles in the *American Journal of Political Science*.[53] Many political scientists also read such research stories from sociology as those in *Sociologists at Work*, edited by Phillip E. Hammond; the appendix to *The Sociological Imagination* by C. Wright Mills; and *The Research Experience*, edited by M. Patricia Golden.[54] Perhaps they are starting to read the research stories by economists that appear in the *Journal of Economic Literature*. And so on.

In such stories of research, practitioners write about how their detailed conduct of inquiry carries through and (sometimes) departs from the discipline's usual assumptions and statements about methods of research. Even though the people who commission and write such stories usually presume that they fill out approved rhetorics of research, the actual accounts often wander (only half aware) into the same locutions that surface insistently in graduate seminars, lunchtime conversations, and other occasions for underground rhetorics. In addition, simply to detail approved rhetorics can be (however unwittingly) to clarify the existence and character of the aporias that deconstruct into underground rhetorics. The texts themselves suggest that the authors seldom intend to confess their underground rhetorics. Nonetheless the encouragement to reflect on their actual steps in research often leads the authors to recover unapproved rhetorics of research.

Such stories of research are not easy for political scientists, at least, to write. A few years ago I participated in a group of highly able colleagues whose discussions had gravitated toward surprising aspects of the ways in which good practitioners of political science actually conduct their work. Many of the participants are known for exceptional creativity and reflexivity in their research. Perhaps as a consequence, members decided to assign themselves the task of producing five-to-ten-page descriptions of how they start particular inquiries. Members agreed that they would simply attempt to summarize how they had actually begun a particular project already completed or well underway. When the group reconvened several months later, several frustrated members professed themselves stymied by the task. Those who had products expressed uncertainty bordering on anxiety that they had somehow failed to capture in prose the crucial elements of their research conduct. In addition, the products were astonishingly

diverse in content and style. And though most of us judged each prod-
uct to have considerable merit, none of us believed that more than
one or two had actually accomplished the assignment. More than
that, there was virtually no agreement on which products had succeeded in those modest terms. When many political scientists agree
that such accounts achieve surprising insights, therefore, those research stories deserve careful analysis.

By considering the rhetorical tensions explicit and implicit in these
accounts by researchers, rhetoricians of inquiry can study such partial
confessions as jumbles of direct and indirect invocations of underground rhetorics. So far as I know, nobody has yet analyzed these fascinating materials for any aspect of their rhetorics, let alone their erup-
tions of underground talk. The targeted texts are few enough and
short enough to provide a focus for careful treatment of rhetorical details. Still they are numerous and diverse enough to afford a ground
for generalizations. Rhetoricians especially ought to compare such research stories to the approved summaries of research in the texts on
approaches, methods, and statistics. For these promote the discipline's quasi-official rhetorics of research design and methodology.
And because the subgenre appears also in other social sciences, rhetoricians should compare these stories of political research with similar
texts in other disciplines. This could spotlight distinctive features of
underground rhetorics of political inquiry, and it could improve our
sense of their consequences for the current and improved studies of
politics.

The research turn has played an exceptionally significant role in political science for at least two decades. I do not know whether it is a
subgenre in disciplines other than political science, but there are
strong reasons to anticipate instances of it elsewhere. Like research
stories, research turns are usually articles or chapters rather than
books. Also like research stories, such turns often appear as invited
essays, though they typically seem to have deeper sources in theoretical cogitations over many years. Indeed the research turn often proposes striking changes in the target discipline's theories or methods.
Unlike research stories, therefore, such turns seldom cluster in collections; their initial appearances, at least, are far more likely to be in one
of the discipline's major journals.

My favorite research turns in political science are "The New Revolution in Political Science" by David Easton, "Clouds, Clocks, and the
Study of Politics" by Gabriel Almond and Stephen Genco, "Prebehavioralism in Political Science" by John Wahlke, "Political Theory and
the Art of Heresthetics" by William Riker, and "Toward Theories of

Data" by Christopher Achen.[55] As political scientists can recognize immediately, prominent figures in the discipline produce most research turns. Moreover each is associated strongly with a particular project of inquiry. Often the author was a key founder of the project, and this is crucial to the character of the subgenre.

Often the project has fared so well that the author has been honored as president of a regional or national association in the discipline. Indeed a sizable proportion of the research turns known to me were presented as presidential addresses to the American Political Science Association, then published in the discipline's central journal. Although this might be one reason that this subgenre has gone unacknowledged among political scientists, who do recognize presidential addresses as a genre, I should add that only a small proportion of presidential addresses are research turns and that virtually no other presidential addresses bring underground rhetorics to the surface of disciplinary attention. Thus the issue here is the subgenre of the research turn, not the genre of presidential addresses.

An instance of this subgenre typically presents itself as a recapitulation of the author's main research project up to the present, and most of the authors present themselves as continuing trustees of their traditions of research. Sometimes their summaries emphasize the failures, frustrations, or insufficiencies of the project; more often their accounts stress the project's achievements. In either event, though, the essay then turns to future needs for research—consistent with the project's original purposes and its progress to this point.

Or so the author says directly. Yet the rest of a research turn causes the careful reader to pause. Characteristically the proposals for further research diverge radically from recent directions taken by the project, and they may even seem to repudiate its initial program as well. On the surface such a text insists that these proposals are the next logical steps in the project. Or it maintains that the proposals return a straying project to its founding and proper pursuits. Yet the details intimate much greater problems with the entire project than the text announces directly, and the proposals imply much greater departures from it than the text claims explicitly.

Thus Riker displayed his "heresthetics" as a good complement to the "positive political theory" of rational choice that he had helped to establish. But Riker's express story of the development of rational choice theory implies that it has reached a virtual dead end. In suggesting why, he noted how it has come to rely on what I would call underground rhetorics. Similarly Riker took pains to distinguish his new concern of heresthetics from the old, typically despised discipline of rhetoric. Yet his description implicitly assimilates it to rhetoric, rightly comprehended, and that description indicates how it should articulate some aspects of the same underground rhetorics previously acknowledged.

In much the same vein, Achen celebrates achievements of methods and statistics prominent in postwar political science. But his summary suggests between the lines that these are really failures and that much of the work using them is worthless. He too notes in passing how such "successes" have depended on underground moves. Likewise he calls for increasing efforts to invent specifically political statistics. But the specifics of his proposal concede that aptly political statistics remain almost nonexistent, that they would differ dramatically from current mainstays of the discipline, and that they would have to encompass and legitimate some rhetorics now kept underground.

Easton and Wahlke might seem opposite cases. Each would excoriate practitioners of his project for betraying its crucial elements so early and thoroughly that a new beginning is now needed in order to get the project back on track. Even more than the implicit self-criticisms in the research turns of Riker and Achen, these explicit criticisms by Easton and Wahlke identify modes of reliance on underground rhetorics of research that compensate for obvious deficiencies of the projects as recently practiced and approved. (Remember, though, that these remain implicit as *self*-criticisms, because they blame others for betraying the original project: therefore these sorts of research turns are partial as confessions in ways closely related to the previous examples.) By the time each author has articulated his criticisms, however, he has implicitly discredited not only the alleged betrayals but also the original projects that they have been said to betray. Moreover the subsequent proposals for renewal almost unmistakably—though never avowedly—reinforce the inference that the main troubles have been with the author's initial project. That is what they implicitly repudiate, as much as the later "betrayals." In the end, the research turns make these betrayals come to seem sadly consistent with the original project, with the discredit falling to both as one.

Why do these authors leave their explosive arguments between the lines? Why do these texts pretend to a continuity with previous work that their details typically belie? Through brief correspondence and conversation with such authors, and especially through an extensive analysis of such texts, I am inclined to infer that these confessions remain partial for two reasons—usually intermingled. To varying degrees the authors fail to recognize how far they are moving toward criticizing or even repudiating their past projects. And to the extent that they do understand this, the authors worry that their arguments—that is, their confessions—would have no good effects if presented straightforwardly. The authors seem to appreciate how threatening a late confession from a senior leader can be to the rest of the tribe. Therefore they protect the tribe and their status in it by portraying their criticisms as praise and their departures as continuities.

The results are surely a species of partial confession. And its generic acuity about the reliance of established projects on underground rhetorics renders it excellent grist for rhetoricians of inquiry. As a partial confession of underground rhetorics, the research turn depends on the old maxim that it takes one to know one. Thus it affords a prime occasion for distinguished practitioners of inquiry to see and say what underground arrangements have been compensating for evident deficiencies of the approved arrangements for research. Best of all, rhetorically, it works to accomplish this confession in partial ways that protect its practitioners through both displacement and indirection. At least in political science, this makes the research turn—like the research story—a key target for analyzing underground rhetorics of inquiry.

Decorum

> *None but the well-bred man knows how to confess a fault, or*
> *acknowledge himself in an error.*
> —Benjamin Franklin[56]

In distinguishing forms and forums for the study of underground rhetorics of research, I have emphasized thus far the advantages to rhetoricians of inquiry. But what are the advantages to political scientists? More generally, why expect awareness and analysis of underground rhetorics to have good effects on any discipline? As I insisted at the outset, answers to the last question must differ from one discipline and time to another. Therefore let me summarize several advantages available to political science in particular, suggesting them as a first list of general possibilities (only) for other disciplines—especially in the social sciences.

First, underground rhetorics are among the main ways in which political scientists respect many kinds of evidence different from the few sanctioned by the discipline's approved rhetorics of research. Accordingly to recognize and articulate underground rhetorics could help political scientists to legitimate and develop new kinds of evidence. Their acknowledgment in underground rhetorics suggests that political scientists already need them, but their consignment to the underground prevents political scientists from refining them directly or assessing their relationships to approved species of evidence.

One easy example is the underground reliance of political scientists on the data of *Verstehen,* Max Weber's term for the self-understandings available to members of a practice. As citizens and sometimes as political activists, political scientists often rely on explicating their tacit or conventional knowledge as members of a particular polity in generating and evaluating other evidence about that polity. To address this unapproved reliance on Verstehen evidence could enable political scientists to use it more critically and appropriately.

Second, underground rhetorics are major domains for several kinds of arguments that political scientists seldom confess but often make—to themselves and to one another. Here again the study of underground rhetorics could aid political scientists in legitimating and improving their reliance on these repressed modes of argument. One is the argument from personal experience: "That just doesn't fit what I know firsthand." Another is the appeal to imaginative etymology: "As the structure of the word suggests, *irony* dominates the politics of iron ages conceived as times of terrible trouble." A third is the invocation of an anecdote: "My model is illustrated by the well-known story about Lincoln as a lawyer." In my experience these and many other arguments appear often and persuasively in the underground talk of political scientists, though seldom in their publications. The failure of such arguments to receive disciplinary recognition and approval does not eliminate or minimize them so much as it limits unduly their quality and use. Repression of these arguments also deadens the discipline's prose.

Third, underground rhetorics include or provoke new strategies, tactics, and tools of research that could benefit political scientists. I have already mentioned a couple of potentially useful tools implied by the discipline's underground rhetorics: field notes, research diaries, and imaginative etymologies. I suspect that the discipline stands to gain also from largely repressed strategies of thought experimentation that seem practiced sporadically, despite their lack of official recognition or approval. And I would guess that these possibilities barely begin to penetrate the discipline's underground resources.

Fourth, attention to underground rhetorics should enable political scientists to discover gaps and other troubles of inference now hidden by underground—and therefore largely uncriticized—connections. If Achen, Easton, Riker, and Wahlke are right to imply that many mainstream inquiries suffer disabling troubles, yet these projects continue to limp along, their underground rhetorics might be largely responsible. Until the crutches are noticed, chances are scant that the disabilities will be spotted, let alone repaired.

Fifth, the same critical attention to underground rhetorics can, where desirable, prepare the ground for earlier and better consideration of alternate rhetorics. Moreover it can help to clarify when alternate rhetorics ought to replace approved rhetorics and when the approved rhetorics should instead be adjusted. Surely both contribute to the prominence of underground rhetorics in partial confessions on the order of research turns. And I have already suggested how an insider's sensitivity to underground rhetorics of political science could make some outsiders' cases for alternate rhetorics more accurate— and thus more persuasive to insiders and outsiders alike.

Benjamin Franklin suggests that skillful confession is a mark of great quality in individuals. For many of the same reasons, skillful consideration of their underground rhetorics is a mark of high quality in disciplines. That is how political science and other fields can learn well to confess their faults, acknowledge themselves in error, and strive for improvement.

4 OVERTURNING ARGUMENT IN POLITICAL SCIENCE

AN APOSTATE MEDITATION ON DISAPPOINTMENTS OF POLITICAL THEORY

When is a meandering about the nature of things . . . the
work of a genuine philosopher, and when is it the babble of
an isolated and perhaps deranged spirit . . . ?
—Amelie Oksenberg Rorty[1]

What follows is as much a meditation as an argument. It considers possible natures and futures of political inquiry. To do that it tours possible pasts and presents of political science. Along the way, it features the discipline's rhetorics of theory, argument, and action. In the end, it strives to produce less a program than a set of insights and a proposal for political invention. Altogether this meditation shows the urgent need of political science for political argument.

If a recommendation results from these musings, it would be that we practice political argument as reasoning designed to persuade us of particular claims about what or why various politics are as they are, as well as how they might well be otherwise. Thus I suggest that political science be pursued as disciplined political argument. Yet I caution against the presentism of academic disciplines, and I warn against any move to (mis)take political argument for the whole of political inquiry. Likewise, I propose that political theory be practiced as political rhetoric. But I parse *rhetoric* in unusual, though not unprecedented, ways. Throughout I explain how social sciences might be re(con)figured as projects within the humanities or the very politics we analyze, even as I play with possible contrasts among political and social sciences of politics.

Detachment

*Some meditations are intended to effect a radical transformation
in the reader and his world. Everything in the reader's life is
affected by his transformation: his embodiment, his friendships,
his practical and political life.*
—Amelie Oksenberg Rorty[2]

At least since the turn of the century, mainstreams of American political inquiry have repeatedly proclaimed a need for arguing adequate theories of government and politics. This quest has changed the face of political science several times over. Nonetheless theory remains little understood, let alone attained. (As subsequent chapters explain, much the same can be said of argument.)

At the end of the twentieth century, the evident result is that many projects of political science have become perplexed about politics and themselves. As later chapters show, recent political sciences tend to substitute devices of assumption and method for adequate, persuasive argumentation. Thus they generate peculiar notions of theory, method, models, logic, testing, evidence, objectivity, and other supposed parts of scientific inquiry.[3] Because they generate few viable kinds of theory or inventive rhetorics of political action, however, they rely on conventional wisdom for key questions about politics. They force new phenomena into old and ill-fitting concepts, or they virtually disregard politics and government in favor of issues generated by statistical methods and newspaper headlines. Even when good work is done, and it often is, political science has trouble recognizing and developing it.

The effect is less an advance over ordinary political argument than a displacement of it. As a discipline, political science wants to be relevant to current politics but fears revising concepts and methods to do so. Gradually and inadvertently, political science is saying less to actual politics. Not even the recurrent celebrations of policy studies seem capable of stopping the alienation of political science from politics—its nominal topic of inquiry.[4]

Humanistic scholars of politics used to complain about the substantive insignificance of much of what the avowedly scientific discipline does.[5] The criticism has faded but is no less true, and perhaps just as much for the self-professed humanists as the scientists. It holds even more emphatically for studies of government.[6] Political science appropriates much from other fields but seldom acquits the intellectual responsibilities of borrowing.[7] Like many other academic disciplines, political science fragments itself into tiny compartments that seldom manage constructive communication with one another, let alone with alien disciplines or more worldly endeavors.[8] Like other social sciences, it shrugs off whole domains of phenomena and methods, only to borrow some of them back in oblique and often unproductive ways.[9] Aspiration to focus on the political behavior and the rational choice of individuals continues to lead the discipline to rid itself of much of its content: action, education, governance, institutions, law, strategy, and values.

As public law has become judicial behavior, for instance, political science has tried with some success to jettison substantive inquiries into law. It cedes to law schools large parts of such subjects as administrative law, constitutional law, and jurisprudence. It leaves legal reasoning to the philosophers and rhetoricians. Similarly what had been a subfield of public administration is being pushed part way out of political science, toward establishment as a more practically oriented discipline. While public administration is being replaced by studies of public policy and political organization, it suffers an uneasy and often imposed alliance with the rest of political science—in order to maintain enrollments of graduate students through masters' programs in public affairs. The field of international relations is booming these days but in important part by constructing itself as an interdisciplinary field where most of the scholarly action occurs outside political science conventions and curricula.

The same could be said of the constricted subfield of political theory—to which historical, normative, and speculative theories of politics are consigned because of their status as humanistic rather than social-scientific projects. Political theory is flourishing beyond the often unwelcoming orbits of political science. Disciplines such as law, history, literature, geography, sociology, and communication percolate happily with the sorts of enterprises that used to define the field of political theory—and still seem central to most conceptions and thus most studies of politics. Yet modeling has largely replaced theorizing as the respectable mode for making scientific sense of politics. In mainstream journals, publication space for avowed theory has contracted dramatically in the last three decades. Perhaps in response, so few of the self-identified theorists orient themselves positively to political science that the second most prestigious journal in the discipline has failed repeatedly in attempts to solicit more submissions from the field of political theory. At the same time, the graduate curricula of fewer and fewer departments of political science provide—let alone require—courses in the history, scope, and methods of the discipline. The implication seems to be that political science has no philosophical and historical heritage of knowledge worth conserving. Only the methods of the moment really count, along with a highly selective range of findings that define "holes in the literature" for directing further research.

To note such developments is not necessarily to deplore them. On balance, some may be good. Surely other self-professed sciences display various of these features. For example, many seem dedicated to ignoring their own histories of inquiry. Still political science stands out for its eagerness to abandon so much plainly political and governmental territory to other fields. What was once billed as the master science now shows no signs of intellectual imperialism. It even apologizes for serving the substantive aims of civic education. As political science detaches itself from politics and government, perhaps we should detach ourselves from the ideas of science, theory, and argument that produce such alienation from politics. Then we may hope to reinvent some of the ambitions, devices, and practices that can make our inquiries into politics meaningful and effective.

Skepticism

> *In contrast to such revolutionary meditations, analytic meditations bring the self to a new understanding but leave everything else—especially practical and political life—as it had been.*
> —Amelie Oksenberg Rorty[10]

How have these things happened? What should we do about them? Many attempts at scientific and humanistic theories of politics suffer two defects. Formally they fail to treat theories as arguments about politics. Substantively they fail to face inadequacies of liberal democratic representation as the hegemonic starting point for research. Both failures are shared by most attempts at political theory—whether normative, speculative, historical, or analytical. And the failure to face inadequacies of liberal democratic theory is shared also by many political practices in America, as when claims to policy "mandates" are based on elections unable by their very structures to communicate voter preferences about policy.[11]

SYSTEMS THEORIES

Despite its ambitions, the behavioral revolution generated little theory of politics, American or otherwise. Its three main projects were systems theory, empirical theory, and democratic theory. They are best identified in terms of founding fathers such as David Easton and Karl Deutsch, Gabriel Almond and Heinz Eulau, or Robert Dahl and Charles Lindblom. Yet the systems and empirical theories of the behavioralists lack both theoretical form and political substance. Instead they come implicitly to rely on conventional wisdom or personal ideology. Usually they echo tenets of democratic theories, which represent issues and convictions long dominant in American life. By contrast, the rational choice revolution is generating lots of theory but far less supporting evidence in terms of the actual politics in America or elsewhere. Hence political science cannot justify esoteric terminologies and methodologies by the usual route of claiming insight much superior to the commonplace. After a suitable lag, it mostly repeats public opinions in reformulated language with somewhat diminished diversity of political viewpoints.

Behavioralism and rational choice work have intended to endow political science with true theory. Both have given political science important new understandings of the crafts of political inquiry, yet both have left the discipline's substantive theories of politics pretty much as before. Both have been offering refinements of liberal democratic representation. Whatever the merits of that body of theory, neither its behavioral nor its rational choice versions provide any bold departure from the alleged bankruptcies of earlier political theories. Should we say that behavioralism and public or social choice have been failed by their theorists?

At the more philosophical levels, the main theorists of political science as a behavioral discipline were David Easton, Karl Deutsch, and the followers of Talcott Parsons. Their systems theories should be credited with attending to governance, which attracted little notice from previous empirical and democratic theories. The systems theorists could turn to governance because they practiced much less methodological individualism than they preached and far less than other behavioralists such as Dahl. Nevertheless many theories of systems and functions were misguidedly, if loosely, begotten in the Euclidean image of axiomatic systems. With little content, and less argumentative mooring, they seldom managed to be more than "conceptual frameworks," which is to say not theories at all.[12] Those who tried to test such "theories" had to endow them with political substance. This led to ad hoc hypothesizing, which tended to import conventional ideas of pluralism and liberal democracy into the "theories" and the "results" of testing them.[13]

Although widely lauded, these theorists were seldom emulated, even at the time. Today their work is little taught and less imitated. Parsons, the most substantive of the three but also the interloper as a sociologist, was the only one to begin anything approaching a school of research. His work, located mostly within the subfield of comparative politics, hardly survived a decade, at least in the United States. Indeed none of these systems theories is now remembered in much more than an occasional term, such as *ascription* or *feedback*. Is this progress? Do we stand on their shoulders to see better than before? Have we no need to acknowledge them, because it would only confuse our students or ourselves? Do we treat their work as a false start or even as a dead end? Is amnesia one of our norms of scholarship?

Systems theories did contribute the impoverished ideal of theories as strictly analytic sets of propositions, to be tested by deducing empirical claims narrow enough for addressing with data. Political scientists seldom pursue this ideal with conviction and vigor, but it still influences some work. It encourages scholars to replace their theories with "models" or "perspectives," similar in some respects to the earlier conceptual frameworks.[14] It also encourages ad hoc hypothesizing and importing opinions from the public realm. Thus its actual legacy is not a substantive vision of politics but a subtle revision of ordinary political claims. In short, most systems theory did little to meet the argumentative needs of political science—or even of behavioralism.

EMPIRICAL THEORIES

In fact, the notion of empirical political theory was invented to legitimate the actual substantive work of most political scientists. The behavioral revolution reinforced the discipline's dedication to seeking theories of politics, but the Easton and Deutsch brand of theory failed to generate a substantive agenda for research. The examples of substantive theories about politics can range widely—from the work of William Riker and other rational choice theorists on federalism to the writings of Michael Walzer and other normative theorists on just wars, from the arguments of Herbert Simon and other cognitive theorists on decision schemas to the useful inquiries of Richard Merelman and other behavioral theorists on political socialization. More often that not, however, available technologies and research programs have proceeded without substantive theories. To save the discipline from failure in its own terms, many political scientists simply branded the results of their research as theory. As empiricists who disdained speculation and prescription, these political scientists then could term their work *empirical theory*.

Along the way, the discipline tried to explain how its "findings" were "theory laden." Having renounced all political inquiry before behavioralism as "hyperfactualism" and "barefoot empiricism," the behavioralists had to be different—that is, theoretical. Weaned from "traditionalism" by visions of universal laws and deductive systems, the empiricists had virtually nothing in their actual research to justify their inquiry as "theoretical"—that is, "scientific." Hence they sought a loosely inductive counterpart to the diffusely deductive approach of systems theory. By contrast, they promoted "cumulation," "middle-range theories," and "empirical generalizations." Eventually they decided that regression equations or models can count as theories. As the formal theorists of rational choice point out, however, these moves make scientific explanation and theoretical understanding into correlation mongering. Then "explanation" becomes merely the variance accounted for statistically, and "understanding" is the goodness of fit between the regression equations and the observations—regardless of the actual contribution to our comprehension of government or politics.

This wing of the behavioralist movement had been adamant about methodological individualism and direct observation: fully scientific explanations must be in terms of the immediately accessible behavior of individuals, presumably people.[15] But again the actual research of the empiricists has posed a problem for their self-conception.[16] Empiricist explanations no more focus on the surface behavior of individual human beings than empiricist research generates ironclad laws of politics.[17]

The ideal of empirical theory was empirical generalization through a rigorously comparative political science. In research, if not always in teaching or graduate field examinations, all political science would become comparative politics. No longer would that remain a subfield of the discipline. Nor would it continue to feature area studies, which depend on immersion in the details of individual cultures or polities. Almost by definition, area studies were incapable of comparative rigor. This core of the old subfield would either fade away or be expelled. Like other unwelcome projects in political science, it would depart the discipline for such relatively unscientific fields as anthropology and history. In fact, area studies have not disappeared from political science, though they have mushroomed in the interdisciplinary modes of international and comparative studies. (As comparativists like to note, moreover, a good third of the discipline remains the area study called American politics.) Good comparativists know well that the immense need for knowledge of cultural particulars is a great barrier to generalizing across countries or regions. It can and should be done, yet its actual practices legitimate few empiricist conceptions of science and theory.[18]

The ideal of empirical generalizations as steps toward or even as substitutes for full-fledged theories has not been posed coherently, let alone practiced competently. It even fails to make sense of empiricist practices, though they suffer from its influence.[19] When the results of research are reckoned, and "cumulation" means making good sense out of complicated collections of "findings," then the troubles of empirical theory in providing substantive patterns for understanding politics become too evident to belabor. Off the record, of course, many of its practitioners confess as much. Empirical research provides political science with methodologies and technologies of inquiry, as well as some of its theoretical figures, and these structure much of the discipline's everyday activity. Yet empiricists have been no more successful than systems theorists in providing the discipline of political science with substantive theories of government and politics.

RESEARCH PRACTICES

Genuine theories generate questions for research. Because systems and empirical theorists fail for the most part to produce substantive theories, they fail to meet this disciplinary need. Whence come the substantive questions for inquiry? In political science, research topics come mostly from filling holes in the literature and addressing current issues in politics. Not even rational choice theories escape these dispositions, because they share the liberal democratic theoretical presuppositions of American behavioralism and journalism.

To justify political inquiry as filling a hole in some research literature is to signal empiricism without self-critical theorizing. Hole filling is predicated on applying a new method to phenomena thus far unstudied with it. When methods define issues, political science suffers from what Sheldon Wolin effectively lambasted as "methodism."[20] Then the discipline tends to become largely irrelevant to government and politics, because it gets caught up in questions of research technique and epistemology instead.[21]

When phenomena determine issues, political science still needs a source of phenomena. So it tends to depend on popular discourse about current events, and it shifts from hole filling to headline chasing. Because it is principally an American discipline, its topics come mostly from surface self-understandings of American politics.[22] And because these stress liberal democracy and pluralist representation,

political scientists emphasize issues of democracy and representation.[23] Thus political scientists take research questions from the current popular controversies over those topics. Scholarship takes time,
of course, so the findings are not always current when they finally appear. But when regulation is an issue in American politics, it becomes
an issue in political science. Where overload of government is a political claim, it is eventually a topic of disciplinary research. If growth in
government is a political worry, it subsequently becomes a concern of
political inquiry.[24]

What is wrong with this? Might it rebut the accusations that political science seldom addresses significant issues of government and
politics? Perhaps it calls into question the scientific status of the discipline, for lacking the theories needed by a science to generate an internal agenda of substantive issues for research. By itself, though, this
would not keep political science from giving objective, technically
competent answers to current questions of politics. Even if this were
to undermine the discipline's credentials as a science, perhaps the
cost would be small by comparison with the public good. In short,
there is a good deal to be said in favor of following the headlines, then
filling in the holes left by earlier research.

Unfortunately there are at least three potent objections to how the
discipline appropriates public issues for academic inquiry. First, political science tends to misconstrue issues of government as matters
of politics. As my examples suggest, public discourse in the United
States often turns on questions of government: regulation, overload,
growth, and so forth. But to say the least, government is hard to
comprehend strictly in terms of individual behavior, as the discipline
commits itself to doing. Though no less collective than government,
politics is easier to (mis)conceive as a mere aggregation of individual
decisions and deeds. Nor do research methods common among empiricists relate well to problems of governing. Hence political science
is ill equipped to answer many questions posed in political debate,
whether in the United States or elsewhere. Worse, the discipline is
often unable to recognize that its results do not tellingly relate to the
purported issues. How far can survey research and budget statistics
take us toward specifying advantages and disadvantages of multilat-
eral action in foreign and military affairs, telecommunications regulation, or welfare reform—let alone "eliminating the IRS as we know
it" or deploying new antiballistic missiles? In the end, little of political science successfully addresses significant issues of government.

Second, political science picks up the popular preoccupation with
transitory questions. For instance, elections are notorious for turning

on trumped up, impermanent, and misleading issues.[25] Quemoy and Matsu, anyone? How about that missile gap? And those were only the infamous issues of 1960. Yet election issues dominate political talk in the United States. When political science takes issues uncritically from electoral discussions, it trivializes itself rather than instructing the debate. The argument is not that political science should ignore the surrounding politics. But unless it learns to listen to current affairs through the intelligent ears of substantive theories, its attention to issues of the day is prone to be more misguided than on target. The discipline stands to be mesmerized by campaigns and their pseudo-issues, even as the main phenomena of the times go too long unrecognized and unresearched.

Third, political science often yokes itself to dubious assumptions implicit in the ordinary language of talk about politics. Political scientists take pride in developing technical, scientific terminology. But if politicians start talking globally about "growth in government," many political scientists clamor to investigate it as a single coherent phenomenon—because that is how politicians discuss it. Too few political scientists ask whether there is a single such thing as "growth in government," let alone what its components and dynamics might be. Instead empiricists (especially) rush to say where it is present and what causes it. Hence they sacrifice the chance to improve on the conventional wisdom.

Put more broadly, political science uncritically presumes the (liberal democratic) ideology that structures most talk about politics in the United States and many other advanced industrial countries. ·Do Americans sometimes seem to identify politics with elections? So do political scientists. Do Americans reduce all government to mechanisms of representation and regulation? So do political scientists. Do Americans equate elections and legislatures with popular instruments of political accountability? So do political scientists. Time and again, political scientists base inquiry on liberal democratic theories drawn uncritically from public discourse:

> If one reflects on what we study when we study American government, one comes to the conclusion that democratic theory is the perspective which guides our research. How would one explain the huge research commitment to the study of elections if we did not believe (with democratic theory) that elections make a difference? How would one explain the research on and continuing interest in representation? How would one understand the almost total lack of interest in the

> organization of the executive branch of government? In
> general, how would one explain the almost total emphasis on
> the "input" side of governing and politics?[26]

Almost despite itself, recent political science reveals over and over that this popular theory of American politics is too wide of the mark to serve most research (or political) purposes worth serving. Indeed the discipline's recurrent calls for more and better theorizing typically begin by disputing the accuracy of something suspiciously like liberal democratic theory, sometimes calling it *classical democratic theory.*

The one substantive theory central to political science has been pluralism after the fashion of Robert Dahl and Charles Lindblom.[27] The concerns of rational choice theory stay mostly within this orbit.[28] It is the one prominent source of theorizing truly internal to political science. Insofar as Easton, Deutsch, Eulau, Almond, Riker, and company have actually dealt in substantive accounts of politics, this is the theory they and their colleagues use. From the first, therefore, tenets of democratic pluralism have guided the program of comparative research instigated by Almond and Sidney Verba through their study of civic culture.[29] Yet this is simply a set of variations on the liberal democratic theory prominently embedded in our political practices and headlines—though it is only one among several such theories encoded in present practices by their architects, and it misses almost entirely the further politics generated within those practices.

Vague attacks on "classical democratic theory" are enough to keep political scientists persuaded that they relentlessly criticize and correct—rather than unreflectively appropriate—popular political theory. But what they discredit as classical democratic theory is more pronounced in (only a few of) America's aspirations than in its many self-descriptions. As dissenters have insisted, political science and American opinion embrace much the same framework of government and politics.[30] This is why political science can take its issues from everyday discourse without generating much political conflict within the discipline. As Robert Dahl has intimated, his pluralism comes close to the Madisonian constitution for American politics. This is also why Dahl's theory did not exactly start a distinct school of research: few stand out by disciplinary identity as students of Dahl because virtually all political scientists accept most of his tenets without question.

Much may be said for such theory. Beyond the usual points, let me stress how shrewd Dahl in particular was to turn attention toward such issues as who governs.[31] This allowed him to combine a public affairs focus on questions of government with a behavioralist insistence on studying individuals. His methods also took advantage of behavioralist inclinations to substitute verbal expressions in interviews for actual behaviors in politics. Typical of the political science to follow, this research avoided most substantive and strategic issues of government and politics, prompting Hannah Arendt to dismiss most of the discipline by muttering that perhaps the key questions of the times do not include who governs.

Yet the pluralist versions of liberal democratic theory are not so superb as guides to government and politics in the United States—let alone elsewhere—that they should stand unchallenged and unaugmented. Their manifest deficiencies should produce a strenuous search for other theories. The point is less that another theory must be better overall than that good inquiries into politics need at least several substantive theories about actions that are not only liberal and democratic but also republican, feminist, environmentalist, electronic, and more.[32]

Similar reservations may hold for humanistic, interpretive, and traditional theories. On the whole, they seem little more relevant to current troubles and opportunities than are the discipline's supposedly scientific theories. As Michael Walzer says, "Political argument has always co-existed with deep theory; the distance between them, the degree of linkage varies over time. Today, however, the relation of the two is peculiarly uncertain. None of the standard theories accounts for our everyday experience."[33] Although humanists criticize political science for its methodism and pluralism, they fail to supply persuasive substitutes in the form of plausibly argued theories and rhetorics for current politics.[34] Moreover too much of their work remains largely irrelevant to the rest of political science, even when the humanistic theorists strive for relevance. For example, conceptual and normative theorists write relentlessly about representation but with few further insights and fewer discernible effects on empirical inquiries.[35] Such a failure of effect may trace mostly to the discipline's behavioralism and empiricism. Yet it may also reflect flaws in more traditional political inquiries.

Accordingly let us not overemphasize past mistakes. As Sturgeon's Law would have it, 90 percent of political science might be awful, but 90 percent of nearly everything is awful.[36] The moral is not that there is a lot of bad or mediocre work in political science or that salvation lies just around the corner, if only the correct corner could be found. Instead the lesson is that political inquiry can be significantly better than it has been. Indeed the means and signs of real improvements already abound. These involve later developments in political science. They indicate that both the scientistic and the humanistic projects of the discipline are ready for more substantive theories of government and politics. For a time, let me take the two sides for granted in order to explore what they might be able to do for political science. This may end in transcending the dichotomy, pushing the discipline toward a multiplicity of enterprises that cut across the old divide between the arts and humanities on one side and the sciences on the other.[37]

Reflection

> *Though speaking to himself, the ascensional meditation's author speaks to be overheard, but his monologue and his conversation have the same voice and language. He is Everyman, marking the signposts of his journey for others to follow. Guide rather than director, he does not manipulate the stages of the reader's self-realization. The reflective reader will find the light of nature within himself: it is in him already, awaiting the turn of his attention.*
> —Amelie Oksenberg Rorty[38]

What may it mean to pursue a science of politics? For a century the standard assumption has been that there would be (at most) one such thing. It would include various fields and projects of research. But these would be united by topics (government and politics), procedures (observation, measurement, testing), and goals (facts, laws, theories). Master keys have been sought in many features: method, theory, logic, testing, evidence, or objectivity. But even before the Vienna Circle conceived of Unified Science, people seeking political science presumed that it would have a single—if exceedingly simple, general, subtle, or abstract—form. They assumed that sciences are separated by topics or subjects rather than forms, procedures, or goals. And they took for granted that target phenomena appear to the scientists in reliable (if only tentative) packets. Given the fundaments of science and politics, political scientists need only apply the standard forms, procedures, and goals to given topics and observed occurrences. However hard the task, at least those undertaking it could be confident of the shape of their success: a disciplined study of politics, with the same form and surety of knowledge as any other science.

In mirror reversal, the scholars who oppose specific aspirations to a science of politics often object to the very idea of any science of politics (or even society). Such critics agree that Science occurs only if strict conditions are met: not for them the laxity of a mere family resemblance. They even concede the claims of physics, chemistry, and a few other disciplines to the mantle of Science. Nevertheless they deny the possibility of a (natural) science of politics.

There have been two main camps of such critics. Both hold that all sciences of nature are formally unified, unifiable, or unifiable in principle. The single-science camp contends that, because there can never be a natural science of politics, political studies can never be scientific. The split-science camp insists that there is a second sort of science: different in form from natural science yet fully deserving the accolade of science. Although the split-science camp admits the impossibility of a natural science of politics, it holds out for the possibility or even the actuality of a distinctively social (cultural, historical, hermeneutical) science of politics. But both camps of critics agree with the original advocates of political science that there may be only one science of politics or none. And although the three sets of disputants evidently know fairly few details about natural sciences, the three agree that all natural sciences share a single form.

Typically the two-science camp borrows categories from the German *Methodenstreiten:* explanation versus understanding, natural sciences versus cultural sciences, and so on. Anglo-American philosophy evokes the two sorts of science by such distinctions as hard versus soft, empirical versus hermeneutical, and nomothetic versus idiographic. The two kinds of science are supposed to interest themselves (respectively) in causes versus reasons, motions versus actions, and observation versus participation. These dichotomies do not divide domains of science in ways fully identical or even parallel to one another, of course, nor are they very precise. Instead they are roughly equivalent to usual separations between the sciences and the humanities.

They pose a possibility of two sciences of politics—different in form yet equally scientific. Perhaps we should recognize a natural science of politics and a social science of politics.[39] Or if we accept the strong desire of self-professed social scientists to emulate natural science, we could distinguish between a social science of politics and a specifically political science. Then we would regard society as a realm of externally stimulated and regulated behavior, whereas we would treat politics as an arena of internally inspired and individuated action. A social science of politics would study the causes, rules, roles, drives, objects, characteristics, environments, processes, and systems of politics plus their maintenance. By contrast, a specifically political science would study the reasons, principles, actions, motives, subjects, characters, contexts, histories, and institutions of politics as well as their mistakes. A social science of politics would investigate the (social) conditions for politics; a specifically political science would investigate the dynamics of politics proper.

In recent work the mainstream projects closest to a specifically political science may be formal theories, including those about rational choice and social comparison.[40] These address issues of strategy and purpose central to political action. They even study processes of political argument, persuasion, and rhetoric.[41] Outside the mainstream, the idea of a specifically political science has been more popular, especially in calls to study political action rather than behavior.[42] An example is the current interest in hermeneutics, which likewise leads to special concern for political language and argument.[43] A two-science approach could even come from the likes of Hannah Arendt, who insisted that politics is conceptually and practically irreducible to society. Social processes are deterministic and can be comprehended by a natural science of society. By contrast, the heart of politics is freedom, the heart of freedom is action, and the heart of action is speech.[44] Because the study of speech is rhetoric, this or some close relative could be pursued as a specifically political science.[45] These are attractive approaches, not least because they lead to treating political theory as political rhetoric and to emphasizing political argument. Moreover they imply many paths to a specifically political science.

Even so, the two-science camp resists the idea of many sciences of politics. Neither rational choice theorists, hermeneuticists, nor Arendtians recognize the possibility of several political sciences.[46] Positioned to applaud multiplicity, the two-science camp instead restores an old division between the sciences and the humanities. Before accepting this grand dichotomy, let us look further. Do separations between a social science of politics and a specifically political science promote improvements in political inquiry? Do they provoke parallel splits between a political science of society and a specifically social science? How well do deep separations of politics from society serve our studies? If we grant these units, then why not others such as economy, psyche, or culture? If there are reasons for recognizing two sciences of politics, then why not more?

Consider, however, that there are many reasons to resist the idea of two sciences for politics. This idea clings to much of what has been behind the dictatorial ideal of Unified Science. Thus such a proposal depends on dubious dichotomies: between analytic and synthetic as well as empirical versus normative. It tends to forget the need for critical assessment of the sets of topics drawn initially from common sense. It needlessly valorizes some inquiries as science while denying that name to others as plausible, with the result that it reduces the quality of scholarly argument on both sides.[47] It even repeats the opposition of scientific theory to traditional theory. Supposedly scientific theory focuses on the social conditions of political action: sometimes simply correlated with political acts, usually policies, but also said to cause or even supplant them. Purportedly traditional theory presents itself as necessary to human dignity and responsibility, as well as political comprehension and motivation. Here we go again. . . .

If we are to acknowledge two sciences of politics, then why not many? Consider the sciences of biology. Some seem physical (anatomy or mechanics), some appear chemical (genetics or physiology), some might be behavioral (ethology or cybernetics). None transcends the others or reduces to them. Why rule this out for studies of politics? Just as talk of a unitary and singular form of Science seems less helpful than harmful in comprehending the natural sciences, the same may well hold for the social sciences. Might this imply also that to segregate the social sciences from the humanities is obsolescent, perhaps even obnoxious in principle?

Further exploration of this possibility leads into reflections on the history, sociology, and rhetoric of scholarship in general. That could take us far from specifically political inquiry. Let us instead explore a road already said to run toward political science as political argument. Rational choice theorists often present their brand of work as the route to the scientific study of politics. When a chief architect of rational choice theory reflected on its main promises and problems, however, he strongly suggested that there is room and need for multiple sciences of government and politics. Indeed he even seemed to acknowledge inquiries into political argument and rhetoric as a crucial part of political science as a discipline.

Recognition

> The mind's ability to free itself from error depends on the will's
> capacity to suspend judgments it had once affirmed. But the
> movement from error to truth is discontinuous. The distance
> separating the author-guide from the reader-meditator that is so
> distinctive of penitential meditations reflects this discontinuity:
> the movement to truth requires a clearing of old rubbish to
> prepare the ground for a new foundation.
> —Amelie Oksenberg Rorty[48]

So far I have said little of analytical theories. They appear more recently than systems, empirical, and pluralist theories.

88

Some ally with analytical philosophy, especially that by John Rawls and Robert Nozick.[49] Some incline toward cognitive science, after the fashions of Herbert Simon and James March.[50] Some appeal to formal logics and mathematics, as in the work of G. R. Boynton.[51] But the formal theories most prominent in political science tie to economics: positive political theory; theories of rational, public, and social choice; and political economy.[52] Rational choice theorists often make criticisms of the "empirical theory" pursued by behavioralists that resemble the ones broached here. In many respects, the ambition of rational choice practitioners has been to achieve the theory that has eluded earlier projects of behavioralism. Thus the rational choice conception of proper theory is formal—usually axiomatic, in the mode of microeconomics.

Although diverse, analytical theories share rhetorical features.[53] Here let me record their gradual discovery that *political theory is political argument is political rhetoric.* The articulate case in point is William Riker, examined in greater detail in other chapters. He emphasized positive political theory, that is, rational choice theory, but much of his reasoning applies to other analytical projects as well. Most formal theories conceive themselves as axiomatic, nomothetic, or hypothetico-deductive. Riker even wrote that only analytical projects merit the name of *political theory.*[54] But this claim can be set aside to examine his summary of past studies and his program for future work, for these converge with my reflections on the need for a rhetorical turn in political theory.

The history of analytical or formal theory is not entirely happy. Especially its economic and philosophic branches produce troubles for themselves by featuring patently false axioms about human individuals.[55] Because true claims can be "deduced" from false premises, analytical theorists say that anything goes for premises, as long as they generate hypotheses that withstand empirical testing. Because analytical theorists display more interest in producing theories and models than in testing hypotheses, however, this situation fails to defend the actual practice of analytical theory at any level beyond heuristics. Worse, the virtue of analytical theory is rigorous deduction, which is to preserve truth in moving from premises to hypotheses. What use is this, though, when there is no truth to preserve, because some premises are false?

Yet many analytical theorists cling to their dubious assumptions. Why? Inspecting formal theories and talking with analytical theorists lead me to suspect that they cite heuristics and testing less out of conviction than convenience or even self-deception. Rational choice theorists in particular suffer three difficulties in facing up to the evident falsity of their presuppositions. Seldom do they really believe their assumptions to be false. Seldom do they have any sense of how to replace presumably false assumptions with ones potentially true. Seldom do they understand the rhetorical dynamics of their own theorizing.

Many analytical theorists display deep needs to regard humans as basically "rational."[56] Call this a respect for humankind or a refusal to face human diversity and perversity; call it an aesthetic sensibility or a cultural commitment; call it what you will. For all their talk about the truth of premises being beside the point of scientific tests for predictions deduced from the premises, many formal theorists care more for the premises than for any predictions or tests. Some assume this rationality as a bedrock conviction; some assert it without good warrant; and some research its presence, absence, or degree. Yet most presume such rationality to be a unitary thing—like "intelligence" or "government growth." Just as some researchers pose poor questions about the sheer presence, absence, or degree of democracy in a polity, so analytical theorists often frame poor issues of citizens' rationality.[57]

The evidence of everyday lives and all the social sciences seems overwhelming that people act according to various principles. Either people often act nonrationally, or they act according to diverse plural rationalities.[58] Strong evidence to this effect sometimes spurs formal theorists to retreat to "bounded rationality," as Herbert Simon termed it, but this usually results only in replacing a singular rationality with such synonyms such as *consistent, maximizing, optimizing,* or even *satisficing behavior.*[59] (Satisficing may be implicitly plural, with individuals calculating in different ways as well as to different ends. Partly for this reason, it attracts little more than lip service in economics or in the rational choice regions of sociology and political science.) Committed metaphysically to Rationality, analytical theorists tend to explain (away) every divergent act or institution as somehow based on (self-interested and successful) calculation of effects. This result is ironic for theorists who celebrate falsification by empirical testing as the mark of science. By the standards of formal theory itself, concepts such as rationality and self-interest become crude acts of faith, not sophisticated categories for science.

Formal theorists, furthermore, are reluctant to cope with multiple motivations, which might push inquiries into less elegant modes. At the least, it would make them learn new logics and mathematics in order to address higher orders of political complexity. Beyond that, it should mandate more creative and extensive efforts to evidence formal claims. For it would expose the data typically cited by political scientists as poor tests of claims complicated by diverse principles of action.[60] A survey of analytical theorizing discloses little testing of accepted or acceptable sorts. Typically theorists offer exemplary data rather than systematic tests. This makes them mildly notorious among empiricists in political science. Often analytical inquiries deploy data to establish parameters or otherwise fill in the details of their theoretical claims, which are not tested in any sense accepted by the analytical theorists or by political scientists generally.[61] Contrary to the conventional wisdom, I would argue that such specification of theories actually can become a kind of testing. Though seldom applauded, it is more and more widely practiced in political science.[62]

To generalize this is to note a third shortcoming: analytical theories seldom comprehend their own dynamics of argumentation. This is lamentable precisely because of the past achievements and future promise of formal theories, notwithstanding their present defects.[63] Analytical theorists cling to their enterprise because they sense its worth. Yet they have not been good at seeing or saying how they actually produce persuasive studies of government, politics, or even economies.[64]

That is why rational choice theory turns so much of late to game theory, which I would portray as a village of halfway houses on the route to fully rhetorical inquiries into political, economic, and other strategies. Riker's culminating account of formal theory shows that it stems from interest in strategy as much as in rationality. As strategy theory, however, it faces several challenges. It seldom

- Recognizes the actual uncertainties under which human decisions are made
- Studies the real substance of values informing human decisions
- Accounts for the sources of those values
- Addresses how human interactions make individual choices contingent on the acts of others
- Comprehends the actual dynamics of persuasion and decision by individuals or groups
- Sees the significance of the cultures, organizations, and other entities not decomposable without remainder into individual humans
- Takes adequate account of human time and historicity

All these are familiar complaints. The point is not that analytical theory is failing to address these concerns, but rather that its various attempts are leading it toward better appreciation of the importance of argument and rhetoric for political theory. Riker, for example, addressed at least five of these defects in proposing to complement analytical theory with what he called *heresthetic* and almost everybody else terms *rhetoric*.

Riker coined heresthetic to name a sort of study of the strategy of decision. I take *action* to encompass more than *decision*, but Riker posed no barrier to such a heresthetic in this bolder sense. He did, however, separate heresthetic from rhetoric, "since the rhetorical tradition from the beginning emphasized persuasion by eloquence rather than persuasion by argument." Shifting ground, he also wrote that "rhetoric is persuasion" but that heresthetic tries "to structure the situation so that the actor wins, regardless of whether or not the other participants are persuaded."[65] Riker argued the difference was to be evident in dilemmas:

> Rhetorically, the dilemma-maker succeeds because he convinces the auditors that, if his opponent cannot resolve the dilemma, then the opponent's position is intellectually weak. Hence the dilemma is a device for persuasion. Heresthetically, the dilemma-maker succeeds because he forces his opponent into a choice of alternatives such that, whichever alternative is chosen, the opponent will alienate some of his supporters.[66]

Somehow dilemma mongering is not rhetoric?

Accordingly Riker's examples turn on strategies that win or lose because of coalitional dynamics.[67] His assumption that strategies and dynamics of coalitions do not involve persuasion is debatable. But his idea that rhetoric involves only persuasion or speech, by contrast with action, is simply wrong. It owes more to commonly accepted caricatures of rhetoric than to historically defensible conceptions. Riker's examples place heresthetic well within the realm of rhetoric, and at least some of his actors would have regarded their heresthetical moves as rhetorical. As Riker noted, rhetoric since the Sophists has been reduced (by its foes) to *eloquence* or *ornamentation*. Although no one identifies any heresthetic as such before Riker, his examples suggest that it was part of the rhetorics for which the Sophists remain famous. Indeed these could be termed the first systematic inquiries into politics.[68] Just as Sophistic concerns for argument and persuasion were excised by Aristotle to confine rhetoric to topics (and not even tropes, given to poetics), so were Sophistic interests in strategy and action eliminated by moderns to limit rhetoric to language and speech.[69]

History is full of reasons not to restrict rhetoric to persuasion. Riker featured the setting of deliberative assemblies for understanding the domain of rhetoric, saying that this political limitation of the Greeks and Romans kept them from recognizing heresthetic as a separate branch of knowledge. Yet the original situation of rhetoric could as easily explain why it includes heresthetic. In deliberative assemblies, attempts "to structure the situation so that the actor wins" typically are and must be done through rhetoric in Riker's sense. Consider his example of the Lincoln-Douglas debates.[70] A rhetorician could easily recast his account of Lincoln's strategy for splitting the Democratic Party in terms of different audiences for the debates. Then Lincoln would be said to take advantage of these disparate audiences in order to persuade one (which one would depend on the response by Douglas) that Douglas did not support its main interests. Indeed rhetoricians do analyze these debates in terms much like Riker's.[71] In the end, Riker himself acceded to the term, entitling his last book, on the campaign to ratify the U.S. Constitution, *The Strategy of Rhetoric.*[72]

What turns on keeping heresthetic within rhetoric is recognition of the importance of rhetoric and argument for substantive theories of politics. Read as a turn to rhetoric, Riker's story of positive theory makes the moral clear. Of course, there are times to distinguish action from speech, and in various ways. In politics, though, deeds and words intertwine so insistently that we cannot long analyze them separately. As Riker and game theorists would agree, political scientists should attend broadly to strategies of action—including rhetorical concerns for arguments, tactics, and standards of political or scientific speech.

Ascension

> *Ascensional meditations move the reader relatively smoothly, without reversals or turmoil, to a new mode of existence. . . . The author of an ascensional meditation moves to self-realization through exhortation and admonition, celebration and prayer, but he does not suffer the dark night of the soul. Metaphors of light and illumination, clarity and precision of vision, are used, with strongly heuristic intent.*
> —Amelie Oksenberg Rorty[73]

Political inquiry urgently needs better sensitivity to rhetoric in both politics and inquiry. At a minimum, political sciences can benefit from seeing themselves as political argument. Then the theorizing would become an enterprise of advancing and contesting reasons for whether to accept or reject claims to political truth. Far too often, as the next chapter relates, political scientists are substituting models, statistics, exemplars, and principles for adequate argumentation. The discipline portrays theorizing as sheer stipulation of premises followed by mere deduction of hypotheses, rather than as making cases for explanations of political occurrences. Or it pursues theorizing as performance of regressions and reporting of findings rather than presenting the reasons and evidence to persuade colleagues of contentions about politics. The discipline needs to see theories as networks of arguments far more than as axiomatic systems or empirical generalizations. It needs to remember that persuasive arguments define what can count as evidence more often and appropriately than ready data or methods produce valid conclusions.

Without substantive theories at least somewhat independent of everyday politics, the discipline limps through its political arguments displaced and denatured from relevant political discourse. Without its own theories, the discipline cannot generate the independent questions needed to improve its capacity to speak to actual politics. Translated into political science, vital arguments are truncated, trivialized, and otherwise travestied. Then political science tends to become political argument without the passion and discipline of directly political speech or action. To think rhetorically is the first step toward revitalizing the play of political argument in political science.

Consider evidence. For most political scientists reflections on evidence turn immediately into questions of method. By its Greek root, a method is a path or way toward some destination, however well known in advance of reaching it. For ancient Greeks, the destination of inquiry would be a theory or set of arguments. For recent political scientists, the destination is often a fact or set of data. In a sense, political scientists often seek to stop on the path and reach only part way to the proper goal of theory. Thus political science often confuses the means with the ends, and it inclines to hypostatize the means, treating the data as simply given by the method. "The myth of the given" remains a practical, unironized reality of the discipline.[74]

This puts a premium on the selection and performance of methods. Then they—not theories or arguments or evidence—guarantee the facts, the "findings." Hence we might speak of "the method of the given" in political science. Somehow the method is to ensure the accuracy and propriety of data. Either the method is to produce "direct observations" of the world, or it is to regulate and warrant "indirect observations" of reality.[75] In this respect, political science remains a mostly empiricist discipline. It acts as though data can methodically and validly project reality for scientists to report. More genuinely theoretical disciplines, by contrast, know that evidence only works in and through arguments—and then to project positions for debate among those scientists. Lacking theories and disinclined to argue, political science forces itself to rely almost exclusively on methods, that is, research designs and statistics.

That methods are the subject of some of the loosest talk in the discipline should not obscure their pivotal role. In the rhetorics of recent political science, methods range from using a particular mode of statistical analysis to designing strategies for the generation of data, concepts, theories, or even hypotheses. Although systematically kept separate from assessment of normative implications, and awkwardly (if at all) invoked in enterprises of problem selection, method has become an amazingly broad and flexible category for current political scientists. It spans emulation of exemplars and testing of theories, selection of statistics, and execution of approaches. If few political scientists use the word in all these ways at every opportunity, still it remains remarkable how many political scientists use it in most of these ways on numerous occasions. Usually method is reconstructed as a set of rules to be applied as rigorously as possible, because the rules must carry exceptional evaluative weight and do extraordinary rhetorical work. In particular, methods are to define and deliver the *objectivity* sought by political scientists.

Whether political scientists practice their methods in such a way is another matter. And we should ask also about the related ideas of rules, rigor, and objectivity. Few of us continue to preach ridiculous aims of achieving scrupulous science through rigorous adherence to The Scientific Method, whatever that might be. Yet the ideas linger in textbooks of "political analysis" meant to introduce students to the discipline's approaches to politics and principles of research design. But the exposition is becoming halfhearted—a recitation of ritual phrases with only honorific ties to the realities of political research.

Political scientists know that methods are tricky business. This is one reason that they learn and (to a surprising extent) practice methodology as a separate field. Some journals even give manuscripts two reviews, one on substance and the other on method. Some think this the only realistic way to respect the discipline's proliferation of methods. To be sure, innovative methods sometimes get confused with sophisticated methodology, as though new paths were necessarily better than old or pathbreakers were bound to know well and wisely where they are going. Yet the main trouble here is a drastic separation of method from substance.

Political science is hardly alone in having a journal that specializes in method.[76] Most social sciences have passed through a period of prizing new methods almost for their own sake. Then methodism or even methodolatry is obvious. But now political science has joined most other social sciences in trying (with mixed success) to reassert in research and publication the primacy of substance—and therefore, potentially, the importance of theory as argument. A few journals have (but do not always execute) a policy of rejecting manuscripts with no substantive contribution to political science—no matter how dazzling their methods.

Still political science needs methods tailored specifically to its topics. Because method and substance depend on each other, disciplines may have distinctive methods as well as subject matters. In fact, the task is to make them mutually appropriate. Yet a chronic source of poor studies about politics is reliance on statistics (or similar elements of method) from other disciplines. Too often, the worry is, these fail to fit issues and data of political science well enough to enable rigorous arguments about theories or findings. Methodism, as uncritical use of given methods, can discourage the methodological inquiries needed for better substantive studies of politics. In this respect, the discipline could use more methodology, in order to generate appropriate statistics and other elements of method.[77]

Mostly, though, political science needs better and more innovative argumentation. Now we political scientists tend to *report* that economic conditions explain a large part of the variance in American voting from one election to another. The need is more for us to *argue* that economic conditions are (or are not) central to American elections in *a specific set of ways*. We need to develop *theories* of elections and of voting as sets of arguments that articulate and test positions about these issues. Such a theory would define concepts, specify indicators, articulate evidence, defend findings, permit inferences, and so on. It would also *explain* why the phenomena are as it finds them, why its concepts take their particular forms, why its data evidence some contentions but not others, why its accounts are better than those of competing theories, why its positions are pertinent to politics, and so forth. Moreover it would anticipate reasonable objections and respond constructively by defending and refining its positions.[78] Therefore it would generate issues for further inquiry because its explanations would suggest other questions, refinements, applications, and competitors.

If such theories were the aim of political inquiry, we could use methods more intelligently. Then theories as arguments would contribute contextual criteria for what data is relevant, how, and why. Instead of processing data and reporting findings, we would assess evidence through arguments. Then we could jettison the phrase "empirical research" as a redundancy. Eventually we might even renounce the concept of empirical theory. The term might appear broad-minded in recognizing other projects as theoretical, but actually it reserves the mantle of science and academic respectability for empiric*ist* pursuits. For it implies that some sorts of theory—the normative, speculative, or even analytical—are bound to lack empirical content, when in fact they would cease to be theories, because then they would cease to make arguments. Actually they invoke different kinds of evidence, which are no less empirical or potentially respectable for falling outside the usual kinds of survey or aggregate data. Notwithstanding what the methods texts sometimes say, in fact, these other kinds of evidence often carry the burden of persuasion in arguments throughout the social sciences.[79]

In this connection, political scientists also would do well to reconceive falsification. Contrary to interpretations of Karl Popper still dominant in the discipline, falsification does not afford criteria for being a theory or testing one so much as it insists on reasonable arguments for any claims advanced.[80] To treat theory as argument—and therefore as rhetoric—is not to abandon scientific constraints of testing theories before a community of skeptical colleagues. It is to reinforce them, realistically and rigorously. It is to recognize the rhetorical structures of academic disciplines as institutions to provide audiences for good argument and norms for effective criticism.[81] The point is not that other branches of political theory have been better supported than empirical theory but that every theory must be evidenced. When we fail to inquire argumentatively, we lack *any* valid conception of evidence.

Good notions of evidence accommodate diverse kinds of data. We must overcome the idea that "humanistic" theories need be less reliable than systems, empirical, or analytical theories. Why frown on normative or humanistic theories as "interpretive?" *All* theories need evidence, *all* evidence is argumentative, therefore *all* theories are interpretive and normative. (As already intimated, it is hard to imagine how any brand of theory could be more normative than rational choice theory.) Humanistic theories may deal expertly in political evidence, even though they depart from mainstream methods and data. Harold Lasswell and Robert Lane used to conduct telling clinical and psychoanalytic inquiries into politics, yet few political scientists today show any respect for their kinds of evidence.[82] Through argument let us assess—not dismiss—diverse sorts of evidence.[83]

Historians, anthropologists, and sociologists of science observe that aesthetic criteria such as elegance and rhetorical figures such as metaphor and metonymy play a major role in theoretical sciences. This is a way of making the rhetorical point that evidence ties intimately and inextricably to emotion, experience, imagination, introspection, narration, authority, and the like. Sometimes these are the aspects of evidence, argument, or inquiry most prominent in humanistic theory. But they cannot be absent from other, avowedly more scientific, theories of politics. Conversely good humanistic theory neither could nor does lack any trace of the kinds of evidence prominent in good scientific theories of politics. Theorists must *judge* the propriety of methods, the meaning of data, the selection of evidence, and the merit of arguments. The apt and actual criteria of judgment amount to principles of interpretation. They must be personal and communal, but they need not be prejudiced or otherwise perverse.

Reconstruction

> *What distinguishes Us philosophers from Them lunatics is that we . . . are beset among friends; we are caught in a moment of doubt or elation; we read; we struggle to interpret; we write; we answer our friends' objections. We are reviewed by strangers whose preoccupations are quite different from our own; their perspectives reveal presuppositions hidden to ourselves and our friends. We talk and we struggle, our thoughts critically responsive to what we see and hear, all of us together.*
> —Amelie Oksenberg Rorty[84]

Meditation on political science can expose many disappointments of political theory in particular and political inquiry in general. It can display a discipline inadequate at some forms of theory and alienated from many others. It can identify infatuations of method and failures of argument. It might provoke doubts about our languages of politics and inquiry. And it stands to reveal uncritical reliance on conventional views of public affairs, even as it is apt to encounter inquiries unduly distant from actual government and politics.

It also can disclose an academic profession insufficiently aware of its own governance and internal politics. Officially the discipline acknowledges only a narrow range of the "humanistic" and "scientific" reasoning that actually persuades its practitioners. Nor does it study the *political* processes by which the discipline comes to accept or reject different kinds of logic and evidence.[85] For a generation or more, the discipline has divided itself internally between scientific and humanistic modes of inquiry. But do we understand the *government* processes by which the discipline organizes its scholarship? In this sense, too,

98

Part One. From Figures of Inquiry

rhetorics of inquiry need to become politics of inquiry. In this sense, political science could benefit from encouraging political inquiry into itself. Among other moves from the repertoire of rhetoric of inquiry, the discipline would do well to include a political science of political science.

There are many ways to separate "sciences" from other modes of disciplined inquiry.[86] No single criterion can suffice to demarcate, explain, or improve what we call political science. But old divides between scientific and humanistic theories make less sense with each passing day of scholarly endeavor.[87] If we would deemphasize debates about demarcations and legitimations of science, there is every reason to think that we could pursue our diverse but interdependent inquiries more effectively than before. Perhaps the social sciences should be reconstructed as projects of the humanities, intersecting and diverging in ways foreshadowed by projects now prominent in our research (but straddling established disciplines).[88] Some cultural studies could be argued to demonstrate the usefulness of reconfiguring some enterprises of the humanities as social sciences. The purpose would not be to renounce the special methods of the humanities or the social sciences. Nor would it be to reject all the theories already started in disciplines such as political science. Instead it would be to augment our resources both methodologically and theoretically—that is, argumentatively. The aim would be to revitalize our awareness and resources of rhetoric, which is to say, our many facilities for reasoned communication with one another.

We need good minds to generate and to appreciate unconventional theories and evidence. Yet these good minds need better rhetorics of inquiry to sensitize them to what we really think, speak, write, and do in our political inquiries. Then we can intelligently investigate ways to improve our performances. When we cannot rely uncritically on data or methods, we must rely—communally and critically—on ourselves. Neither self-professed scientists nor other scholars reflect often on their rhetoric or its repercussions for political inquiry. Consciously or not, however, science and scholarship are conducted through argument—or they have no chance of being conducted well. In turn, argument is constructed through rhetoric. Because rhetoric is a political science and practice, rhetorics of inquiry are at least partly politics of inquiry. By their strategic paths we may appreciate the importance of political argument in political science. And along the way we may overcome at least some of our past disappointments of political theory.

5 RETURNING ARGUMENT TO POLITICAL INQUIRY

A MYTHIC NARRATION OF MODELS, STATISTICS, AND OTHER TROPES

A story is what remains when you leave out most of the action.
—Russell Hoban[1]

There is truth to Hoban's definition, and it tells volumes about the stories of politics promoted by political science in the second half of the twentieth century. They leave out most of the action. Because politics is action, and principally so, this is troubling in itself.[2] But it is compounded by the disposition of the discipline also to leave out most of the argument. When you explain action by featuring only a small part of it, the arguments that justify the focus become crucial. Omit them overmuch, and political inquiry tends to become incapacitated.

Inquiry too can be a kind of action. Telling its tales is bound to be partial, so Hoban's caution no doubt holds as well for the story to come. Yet this account of argument and rhetoric in political science is intended to be sympathetic rather than one-sided.[3] It recounts the recent career in political science of models, statistics, exemplars, and principles. It treats them not as mere enemies but as potential tropes of intelligent inquiry into politics. More specifically and properly, they are *tropes of argument* about politics. Like all figures, though, they can be misconceived and misused. In political science, they have become tokens more than tropes of argument, replacements rather than resources for substantive studies of politics. Here I tell how these tropes of political inquiry have come to be abused widely and unawares. Hence my story explains how RECENT POLITICAL SCIENCE IS WHAT REMAINS OF POLITICAL INQUIRY WHEN YOU LEAVE OUT MOST OF THE ARGUMENT. But my tale also relates how these tropes, understood

Part One. From Figures of Inquiry

and used well, can be valuable and virtually necessary figures for political inquiry.

Accordingly my story portrays models, statistics, and other tropes of politics as more the victims than the villains of recent political science. At worst, this can be truly a tragedy, with the seeds of self-destruction planted in the protagonist by those very virtues that lead us to lament the final fall. At best, it might be a comedy, with the seeds of self-awareness brought to bloom by those very devices that help us to produce the present trouble. In its comic aspect, this tale points toward a conceivable reconciliation of conflicting methods and contending factions of political inquiry. It can reveal their common figures and grounds of political argument. It can show how what often function now to befuddle inference and bemuse understanding could serve as apt tropes of improved inquiries. Thus it can point out ways to turn recent losses of explanatory power into future gains. It can suggest how to transform our debilitating perplexities into promising problematics. Then a redirected discipline may hope to turn them into fruitful solutions. In conclusion, it can even hint of enhancements in the discipline's overall capacity for inquiry. Just so, let us learn some of the tales in the larger story of political science.

How Political Science Lost Its Arguments

> *I dislike arguments of any kind. They are always vulgar, and*
> *often convincing.*
> —Oscar Wilde[4]

Whatever happened to argument in political science? In a word, it was lost. In a phrase, it has been gradually but largely misplaced—and therefore displaced—in the aftermath of the behavioral and rational choice "revolutions." This does not put the proposition as precisely as required for many purposes, but it will suffice for those at hand. For the aim at the moment is to tell in general terms how the loss has occurred, how it has been little detected or lamented, how it nonetheless cripples political inquiry, and how it might be overcome.

But you may doubt from the outset that such a crime—either of commission or omission—could have been perpetrated against any "political science" worthy of the name. Controversy and (therefore) argument seem to be the life's blood—if not the true calling—of academic disciplines. How could any field of inquiry lose its capacity, sensibility, or even proclivity for argumentation? With politics often defined as 'contest', 'struggle', or 'controversy over goods and values', is it even conceivable that studies of politics could cultivate an absence of argument and the resulting controversy? Actually I do not believe my home discipline to be the only one to suffer such a loss of late. It certainly has company in the other social sciences and perhaps even in some of the humanities. But that is a tale for another time.[5] For now, read on, and you shall see how political science has diminished itself radically—yet not irrevocably—in every one of these respects.

The self-declared behavioral revolution ·was a sort of social movement within the academic discipline of political science. It was meant to liberate the discipline from liabilities of older inquiries into politics. Hence it rejected traditional analysis of laws and institutions as trivial description, evaluative prescription, or unjustified speculation. Many stories are still told of its ambitions, achievements, failures, and followers.[6] The same can be said of the closely connected turns to rational, social, and public choice.[7] But here I tell of their tragic aspiration to render political argument at once rigorous, vigorous, and ample. Along the way, as in many another Faust tale, political science seems to have sold its soul for success, only to find that synonymous with failure. Increasingly it has sacrificed significance to rigor, only to become sloppy as well as insignificant.[8] Similarly it has formalized and mechanized argument, only to conflate explanations with correlations, assumptions with findings, tests with specifications, and arguments with methods.

Just so, many intertwined tales make up the story of how political science lost its arguments. Drawing on accounts of protagonists in each, let me reconstruct three episodes from the many already detailed elsewhere. For the most part, my contribution is simply to tell them all as parts of the same story of disciplinized inquiry into politics.

Significantly each episode embodies many of the same structural ironies. Seeking short, straight, swift routes from their wilderness of chaotic history and human individuality to the great city of science and theory, political scientists pursue rigorously restricted means. These are thought to promise many quick and safe trips to the metropolis. But actually, none reaches more than part way to the original destination. Some travelers understand this at the outset; some do not. But while a few rediscover it along the way, far more gradually forget the first goal in favor of the frequent rewards and satisfying simplicities of retracing familiar routes. With more traffic, the paths take on the appearance of transporting travelers all the way to the city. With so many way stations and talking places, they may seem to be streets of the city itself. With personal experience in erecting edifices or paving paths, moreover, some travelers even settle into dreams of working on the city's main street. All around their bustle, of course, lies the wilderness of unexplained occurrences: more walled off from the city than before but easily seen by lifted eyes.

The Behavior Vanishes

Our actions are like rhyme games: we fill out the rest of the lines
with whatever motives for the actions we please.
—La Rochefoucauld[9]

Behavioralism began as a commitment to the scientific study of politics. Through logical positivism and empiricism it conceived this study as "behavioral science." That is, it would become the theoretical, quantitative, and empirical study of the directly observable behavior of persons in politics. Previous studies were pervaded by hyperfactualism, barefoot empiricism, normative manipulation, and pontificating about governmental or other institutions. In their place, behavioralism would create and test truly scientific theories about the real units of any and all politics: behaviors by individuals. The theories would be nomothetical or hypothetico-deductive instruments for discovering new facts, predicting future events, and explaining established ones. As such, they would stay strictly separable from any models of behavior used to operationalize, test, or express the results of research. To execute this program, behavioralism turned political science toward kinds of data, models, statistics, exemplars, and principles already purporting to suit the study of individual behaviors. These came mainly from psychology, with later assistance from sociology and economics.

Of course, psychology was more interested in attitudes and other mental phenomena than behaviors in some "directly observable" sense. To make matters worse, behavioral requirements of direct observation were both scientifically mistaken and philosophically incoherent.[10] And perhaps worst of all, the behavioralist conception of theory was equally confused and incorrect.[11] The result was considerable incompatibility between the principles or assumptions of behavioralism on the one side and its other tropes of argument plus its technologies of research on the other. Soon behavioralism was burying not only its principles but also its argumentative sensibilities beneath an avalanche of election and related studies. These were fostered at first by borrowed data and statistics, but soon they were sustained by new data and different kinds of statistics—largely refinements of linear regression analysis. Thus behaviors became opinions or (at best) decisions; theories became regressions or (at best) models; and the new tropes, technologies, findings, and examples of research created further applications for themselves. But who wants to argue with success?

Evidently the answer is that the earliest succeeders and fiercest defenders of the original principles want to contest such success. For them, a triumph heedless of the inspiriting principles seems hollow and perverse. Thus political science has a virtual tradition of presidents of the professional association declaring that the founding dream has been betrayed. Time and again, presidential addresses seem to recall colleagues to first principles in yet a further reorientation of the discipline. One founder of behavioralism urged a return to America's Enlightenment norms in studying politics and a recovery of the ontological base lost by behavioralism.[12] Another heralded an era of postbehavioralism.[13] Although still other cases could be cited, the most pertinent is John Wahlke's discovery that the behavioral revolution has been betrayed.[14]

Wahlke notices how the purportedly behavioral political science, which is to become more scientific by restricting itself to the external movements of bodies, instead comes to be dominated by attitudinal and mentalistic concepts. He complains that variables cannot be directly observed or empirically established. Nor does he recognize inquiry in these terms as adequately theoretical, in behavioral or any other legitimate terms. Indeed he maintains that the survey research that dominates behavioral studies of politics cannot begin to meet behavioral standards of science. What, then, is political science to do? It must recognize that it has only been prebehavioral to date and that it now needs a truly behavioral matrix of inquiry. This can come from applying sociobiology and psychophysiology to politics, he holds. The resulting biopolitics would use ethological principles as working hypotheses to inform research and psychophysiological techniques to conduct it.

The first lesson is that Wahlke is right about recent political science: the behavior vanishes from self-professed behavioral sciences. (The cognitive revolution in psychology resulted in part from a similar recognition about the consequences of behaviorism in that discipline.) As the next section emphasizes, this happens mostly when the behavioral tropes supplant rather than support argument. Sadly the second lesson is that subsequent paradigms of superbehavioral research are well on the way to repeating such a debacle. To date, ethology in particular and sociobiology in general have proceeded mostly by using previous principles of human action to redescribe animal behavior. Then they circle (viciously) back to reconceive human behavior in the allegedly biological categories supposedly derived from animal studies. Hence it is hard to portray these inquiries in anything like the intended sense as rigorously—let alone justifiably—behavioral.[15]

Furthermore the biopolitics performed thus far unfortunately have followed Wahlke's call to use the principles rather than the (purported) methods of ethology. Yet ethology would be behavioral far less for its principles than its methods, especially the "direct observation" of individuals. In fact, biopolitics mostly ignore individual behaviors in favor of speculative adaptations of sociobiology or general commentaries on human nature. Again the behavior vanishes. Wahlke himself claims that political scientists should attend to ethology because it reveals (1) the normality of war; (2) the dependence of war on cooperation, groups, and acceptance of authority; (3) the subsistence of polities as pseudo-societies or pseudo-species in a biological sense; (4) the universality of political bonding; and (5) the dependence of government on cooperation, groups, and acceptance of authority. These are hardly insights unique or even original to ethology. Virtually all can be found in the writings of Karl Marx, Saint Augustine, or Aristotle.[16]

In sum, various biopolitics seem to include (but not be exhausted by) one more set of behavioralist attempts to rescue dubious principles of scientific method, under the guise of detailed studies of politics. Repeating the pattern of behavioralism, these can convince themselves of success as a substantive paradigm or field mostly because they pursue what should be tropes of argument as though those simply were arguments: complete, persuasive, and progressive. For the insular audiences of scholars sympathetic to biopolitics, of course, the favored principles, exemplars, models, and statistics indeed are the arguments: basically adequate, if not unassailable. This same moral emerges from fables of other latter-day legacies of behavioralism, as the next story suggests.

The Regression of Political Science

Statistics [are] figures used as arguments.
—Leonard Louis Levinson[17]

Most political inquiries after the behavioral revolution have proceeded as though they were the epitome (or perhaps the parody?) of Thomas Kuhn's "normal science." If not by full-fledged disciplinary matrixes, most studies are conducted within and according to what could be called *research literatures*. These include exemplary cases of research, on which other studies are modeled—albeit loosely. Such exemplars usually inspire far more by innovations of method than by inventions of argument, expansions of subject, or alterations of theory. Conversely each research literature is usually conceded a distinctive domain of (potential) subjects. Similarly each is typically if tacitly characterized by a set of principles. Together these comprise the special perspectives of the literature. Such perspectives are more diffuse and far less directly at issue in concrete research than are any specific theories in the literature.

Within a research literature, political scientists sometimes seek to ape or articulate exemplars in the manner described by Kuhn.[19] They sometimes try to solve puzzles as well. Most often, however, they work at recognizing and filling "holes" in the literature. By far the most common justification offered for individual projects of research in political science is simply that nobody has studied a specific political phenomenon in this way before—and here are the findings. Indeed many purported solutions to such puzzles as apparently contradictory findings actually attempt little more than to fill an alleged hole in the neighborhood of the seeming clash. Another frequent justification of political research is the chance to try some refinement of method, in the hope that it might be applied more substantively in later research—presumably by others. This sounds somewhat like research organized around exemplars, except that Kuhn's exemplars provide substantive as well as methodological inspiration for inquiries modeled after them.

Research oriented to filling holes in a literature of inquiry is the most prominent part of political science because it is practiced as though it were the least problematical part of political science. This is because it seldom seems more challenging than the routine application of standard forms of multivariate regression to conveniently collectible sets of data not already so analyzed. In this role, linear regression has become the single most important trope of recent political science. But it has also become the single most common substitute for genuine argumentation in political science. As such, it is the main heritage of behavioralism in political science.

Regression began as a figure of argument sometimes suited to eliciting patterns from large sets of data that meet fairly exacting requirements. Regression can be done in myriad permutations, and most statistical techniques prominent in political science are forms if it. Some requirements tended to make regression pertinent to behavioralism's emphasis on the study of individuals. Thereafter it quickly became something akin to an all-purpose medium of inquiry. This much is widely agreed upon in political science, where regression is sometimes the occasion of good-humored jokes about the discipline. As the use of regression has grown, however, so have the pretensions of its practitioners—sometimes self-consciously but often not.

The proliferation of regression has greatly reduced the ability of some of its users to distinguish between correlations and explanations, between models and theories, or even between evidence and theories. Practitioners of regression talk unfortunately in terms of "explaining the variance" in their data when they are merely measuring correlations between their dependent and independent variables. Abstractly they know that moving from correlation to causation or to other modalities of explanation requires skilled argument. But in research they short-circuit the complications of argument. They report the results of regression analysis as though these were the best argument for their substantive conclusions—rather than some evidence available for weaving into an argumentative evaluation of their contentions. Thus they make a useful trope of argument into a pernicious token of argument. Here are the sheer facts as found through regression analysis: you may take them or leave them, but you need not ask nor give arguments about them. Instead you should go out and regress your own results—presumably about some other hole in the literature.

Theories are networks of arguments.[20] If individual arguments are replaced by regressions, can the conflation of theories with regressions be far behind? Expressing the practice of many political scientists, one sophisticated exponent of multivariate regression asserts that "a political theory . . . is a multivariate hypothesis about a political event." He speaks further for the mainstream of the discipline in declaring that such a hypothesis is best addressed scientifically as a regression equation. And this too he terms "a political theory."[21] In such a political science, what room remains for rigorous, vigorous, ample argumentation? With the reduction of theories to regression, the highest and most complicated levels of inference are laid low, if not made easy.

The cult of regression can also overwhelm the nature and function of models in political research. On the one hand, modeling has long been methodologically precarious in political science, partly the result of its shaky philosophical status in the logical positivisms and empiricisms behind many principles of behavioralism.[22] On the other hand, modeling has been developed as one of the main steps away from sheer correlating and toward substantive theorizing. Formalized and mathematicized, some models have even become further tropes of argument in political science. At best, however, overreliance on regression assimilates modeling to that hoary figure of political science: the conceptual framework. This is supposed to be a decently complicated set of concepts that profess from the outset their own insufficiency for scientific explanation and justification.[23] As political scientists gradually came to recognize, though, this purported step toward genuine theory actually worked to preempt adequate explanations at almost every turn. At worst, the substitution of regression for argument in political inquiry tends to pull modeling all the way down to the level of grab-bag correlation. Then political scientists dump lots of variables into an equation to see what happens when their measurements are run against each other. As the field's specialists in statistics keep trying to teach their colleagues, this is a good way to generate diagrams in which profusions of factors somehow produce large but little differentiated effects. This is when merely statistical significance, created by high numbers of cases, tends to chase out substantive significance.[24] Again this tends to diminish not just the precision but the very disposition of argumentation.

There are enough tricks important in regression to make graduate education necessary, but they are not so many or so difficult as to restrict its practice much further than that. The real troubles with regression are to know what it can accomplish (which is often less and otherwise than many political scientists think) and to recognize when it should not be used (which is fundamentally more than most political scientists think). Another sophisticated practitioner of regression has recently reassessed its proper conditions and conclusions in use. This methodologist demonstrates that many of its common applications by political scientists are statistically—which is to say inferentially and argumentatively—unwarranted. The implication is that most behavioral inquiries conducted in political science are so fundamentally defective as to be worthless or even pernicious in their pretensions to coherence, let alone defensibility. Their argumentative inadequacy is so great that this respected methodologist insists on the need for new (and unprecedented) theories of specifically political data. In the face of the cult of regression, this political scientist shies away from the clear implications of his own case against it. (This is something I detailed in Chapter 3.) But in the end, his is a brief on behalf of recovering regression and other statistics as appropriate parts of political argument rather than as replacements for it.[25] Otherwise, the moral is that political science will continue to regress.

How Rational Choice Theory Got Its Paradoxes

> *The irrational is not necessarily unreasonable.*
> —Lewis Namier[26]

Modeling has already been mentioned as one of the main modes of resistance to the regression of political science. Lately a prominent contributor to this alternate trope has been what is usually known as *rational choice theory*. (Some advocates call it *positive political theory* or simply *political theory*—not for short but to emphasize their deductivist view of theory.[27]) Rational choice theory itself is best conceived as only one branch of formal theories of politics. It is distinguished from other branches by its substantive presuppositions about politics. Others argue—and the advocates themselves sometimes concede—that these assumptions are highly unrealistic in regard to politics. But that has not kept rational choice theory from becoming the prime mover of formal analysis in political science.

For a capsule presentation of formal analysis generally, let me borrow an excellent summary from a colleague who practices it: "Formal analysis is distinguished as a mode of inquiry by the kind of theory to which it aspires and by the means it employs in developing it." There are three standard steps. "First, the observed entities and their relations are translated into an appropriate representation." This is called *mapping*. "Second, accepted principles are used to draw implications concerning the representation." Mathematical representations are thought to facilitate this. "Third, these implications are translated back into statements about the original phenomena, a process called 'inverse mapping.'" Similarly formal theory in political science has three main goals. "The first is the discovery of principles that account for our empirical generalizations. . . . The second is the use of such principles to generate new hypotheses." The third is "to lend coherence to what we know."[28]

In these terms, rational choice theory is distinguished from other formal theories by its representations, or maps, of politics. It suits behavioralism not only in its deductivist view of theory but also in its individualist view of behavior. It represents politics as the result of individuals' rational choices. "It represents individuals as preference orderings (or real-valued utility functions) with respect to alternate actions available. And it states that individuals choose the actions that rank highest in their preference orderings (or for which their utility functions are maximized)." Although avowedly directed at (strategic) actions or (purposeful) decisions rather than (caused) behaviors, inattention to the sources and substances of preferences leads most rational choice theory to repeat the behavioralist principle of staying on the observable surface of human events. Yet it requires some specification of preferences in order to operate. So in practice, rational choice theory usually accepts "the principle of self-interest, which ascribes a particular content to individuals' preference orderings."[29] In addition, it typically assumes conditions of (virtually) complete knowledge or negligible information costs.

Given what ordinary people, let alone political scientists, think they know about politics, every one of these assumptions would seem to be either generally wrong or at least severely limited in potential application.[30] But the deductivist view of theory rescues rational choice theory from this shaky start by declaring that false premises are fine— so long as they produce predictions that prove true. Hence rational choice theory defends its assumptions as useful instruments for exploring politics. Its predictions must meet the test of reality or experience: keep those that do, discard those that do not. Of course, the assumptions themselves are prized partly for their formal elegance but also for their tacit ties to particular views and values of liberal democracy.[31] Even so, the fundamental doubtfulness of the principles of rational choice theory make it especially important to discipline their every use by details of actual, careful argument—that is, to remember that such principles are never more than tropes of political argument.

To say this is to suggest how much it is a stricture forgotten in recent political science. The result has been a series of paradoxes within and about rational choice theory. Directly or indirectly, many practitioners acknowledge these paradoxes. Some—such as the particular paradox of voting or the more general paradox of Arrow—are intrinsic to the axioms of the theory. Of course, these are produced by the substantive principles assumed by the theory. But others are produced by comparing its predictions to evidence about politics. Thus the (fortunate) infrequency with which the paradox of voting occurs in actual voting calls into question whether rational choice theory can claim to be a theory of politics. The same goes for the erratic and relatively infrequent appearances of free riding, which rational choice theory anticipates around almost every corner. Similarly the insistent demonstration by rational choice modelers that voting in large elections must be irrational for individual voters is (happily) at apparent odds with actual turnout of voters. To practitioners, rational choice theory and its predictions seem sound, yet the contradictory facts seem valid. Arguably rational choice research involves many such anomalies.

If the principles and models of rational choice theory were tropes of argument, these results would encourage their reconsideration and modification. For many proponents, however, this means taking both sets of paradoxes as puzzles for further research. This in turn means tinkering with details of particular models while refusing to reassess their premises. To be sure, many opponents make the mirror mistake of taking at least the second class of paradoxes as decisive refutations of the entire domain of theory. The trouble is not that either proponents or opponents are bound to be wrong; it is that neither side engages in the detailed argumentative analysis needed to discover more adequately what to make of the results thus far.

If that were to remain the case, then the critics would deserve to prevail, because the practitioners of rational choice theory often (but far from always) fail their own standard of successful prediction. As already shown, the critics do deserve to be taken seriously, for they have lodged several significant complaints. Rational choice theory fails to recognize the actual uncertainty under which human decisions are made, fails to study the actual content of preferences or values informing human actions, fails to account for the sources of preferences, fails to address how human interaction makes individual choices contingent on the actions of others, and fails to detail the actual processes of decision by individuals or groups.[32] Sometimes these criticisms are expressed as a failure to consider the contexts of human affairs. At other times they are advanced as a failure to take history or time itself into account.[33] In this sense, rational choice theory in political science has defined AN ACTION AS WHAT REMAINS WHEN YOU LEAVE OUT MOST OF THE STORY. Hence all this tends to slip back toward a study of mere behavior.

But there is no reason to recommend a categorical choice between uncritical pursuit of rational choice theory and supercritical rejection of it. The heroes of the story of how rational choice got its paradoxes are the scholars who turn to addressing deficiencies of the kinds just listed by offering additional ideas articulated in careful and sometimes complicated arguments. They have begun to explore such amendments or complements to rational choice theory as the costs of information and the effects of uncertainty, the contents and sources of preferences, the effects of interaction, the processes of social decision, even the character or operation of rationality.[34] In doing so they manage to return to treating models of rational choice as true tropes of argument: as figures of analysis and evidence rather than as fudges for them.

Tropes, Traps, Tokens, and Detours

> *What therefore is truth? A mobile army of metaphors,*
> *metonymies, anthropomorphisms: in short a sum of human*
> *relations which became poetically and rhetorically intensified,*
> *metamorphosed, adorned, and after long usage seem to a nation*
> *fixed, canonic and binding; truths are illusions of which one has*
> *forgotten that they are illusions.*
> —Friedrich Nietzsche[35]

How could any academic discipline long lose its disposition to argument? At least three stories later, my answer should be even more evident than before: disciplines can turn desirable tropes of argument into detrimental substitutes for argument. This is to say that disciplinary tropes of argument can become traps, tokens, or detours of argument. To explain what this means, how it can happen, and how to prevent or redress it, let me turn more directly to the notion of tropes or figures of argument.

Let me caution, though, that no initial presentation of this idea can do more than evoke its implications and justifications. For one thing, it projects theories of argument radically different from those implicit in the usual discussions of deduction and induction.[36] For another, it partakes of complicated and unconventional networks of notions about language, inquiry, and even politics.[37] Here neither set of connections can be adequately developed, let alone decently defended. Nonetheless the concept can be broached so that further discussion can contribute to its development and defense.

The basic idea is this: just as there are figures of speech, so there are figures of argument; just as tropes of speech are unavoidable, so are tropes of argument; and just as figures of speech may be turned to abuse or advantage, so may tropes of argument. Of late, several massive, intersecting literatures argue the necessity of figuration in language. Contrary to naive or programmatic proclamations of literalism, figures of speech are neither mere ornaments inessential to meaning nor perverse tools of manipulation hostile to reason. Rather such tropes are necessary for linguistic expression and creativity.[38] Furthermore they are specifically needed for scientific expression and creativity.[39] Just as the linguistic turn in the human sciences has rediscovered the indispensability of figures to speech, so their rhetorical turn must be ready to recognize the necessity of figures in argument.

This idea depends on realizing that, in ways important to argument and inquiry, the medium is or at least shapes the message. Rationalists conceive good arguments to order all the relevant or available evidence so as to reach a sound conclusion. As literalists, they believe in a single, general, and—ideally—formal discipline of logic that can discern and construct sound arguments. Grudgingly they concede the need for compromises such as ellipsis and enthymeme, because life is short and resources are limited. What they fail to appreciate, however, is the sense in which AN ARGUMENT IS WHAT REMAINS WHEN YOU LEAVE OUT MOST OF THE EVIDENCE. In other words, the art of argumentation is to discover, endow, and deploy logics in a world of limits—to our knowledge, time, intelligence, imaginations, emotions, and more. In our world, the art of argument is to order and convey information by presenting it in terms of positions, particularly relevant evidence, and pertinent criticisms. Whether the aim is persuasion, inquiry, or otherwise, argument therefore proceeds by tropes.

To date, there has been some study of argumentative tropes, both in academic affairs and everyday life.[40] The kinds or levels of tropes identified thus far are largely different from the ones at issue in my stories of how political science lost its arguments. Epistemically, at least, the "world hypotheses" of Stephen Pepper and the "prefigurations of the phenomenal field" analyzed by Hayden White are more fundamental, but also more diffuse, than the sorts of tropes in my stories: models, statistics, exemplars, and principles. By contrast, the "metaphors we live by," as elaborated in the work of George Lakoff and Mark Johnson, are sometimes more precise but almost always more ambiguous in their implications.[41] Yet this might only be to say that different tropes need to be distinguished in addressing distinct issues and domains of argument. Were the arguments and stories at hand articulated, they would surely find room for talk about these other types of tropes, not to mention a more extensive presentation of the tropes identified in the preceding stories.

Still there is a signal advantage of recognizing these particular tropes of argument—in political inquiry and elsewhere. They suggest more directly than many other tropes how academic arguments often go wrong or even go away. Plainly this is where tokens, detours, and traps enter the picture.

The three preceding stories told how tropes can come to replace argument rather than mediate it. The presentation of a principle, emulation of an exemplar, citation of a statistic, or mention of a model can short-circuit and otherwise substitute for arguments. Then the trope is a mere *token of argument:* a way of avoiding evidence and reasons rather than a potentially helpful selection and communication of them. There are many motivations for transforming figures of argument into flights from argument: inadequacies of understanding, desires to win rather than learn, disputes too deep and personal to be addressed for a while, differences in perspective too gaping to be transcended at the time, and so on. But the key point is that tropes of argument are not primarily, normally, or properly (mere) tokens of argument. I do not mean to suggest that every instance of the substitution of tokens for tropes is bad, even in academia. In some cases we may even concede that tokenism in argument serves urgent personal, academic, or even intellectual needs. Any politician is apt to know that tokenism can be better in some situations than articulation with a seemingly inevitable confrontation to follow. (This is one way in which any argumentation, no matter how scholarly, must remain rhetorical and political.) Still I do mean to say that the difference between tropes and tokens of argument can help to explain such trends as the recent decline of argumentation in political science.

The other two travesties of argumentative tropes appear less prominently in my just-so stories of political science. Yet they are likely to be no less evident in the events that those stories portray. When tropes are twisted to perverse advantage in argument, we may say that they have been transformed into *detours of argument*. Then the intent or effect is manipulation—more than outright suppression—of argument. Because the literalist would say that all tropes of argument are detours at best, the distinction of argumentative detours from tropes is especially important to sustain. But because books of formal and informal logic are full of examples of perverse—and not merely mistaken—reasoning, and because that topic is another essay in itself, here I shall simply assert the difference.[42] No less than tokens, of course, detours of argument are motivated by diverse considerations and may sometimes be justified in rhetorical or political terms. Yet no more than tokens are detours to be identified with tropes, which form the very fabric of all argumentation, even though the particular tropes may differ dramatically across domains of inquiry and action.

By insisting that tropes of argument are not reducible to tokens or detours of argument, I am simply articulating the point that argument cannot avoid figures—and should derive real advantages from them. In other words, figures of argument are as vulnerable to abuse and prone to misuse as figures of speech. By contrast, I introduce the notion of argumentative traps to emphasize that tropes of argument are never without limits and costs. Even apt figures of speech are able to serve us well precisely because they shape our thinking, speaking, and acting. Any such shaping, however, also constrains and directs arguers away from thoughts, words, and deeds that might well be pertinent and perhaps even appropriate in the circumstances. As the circumstances change, moreover, the shapes (with their constraints and directions) seldom change precisely apace. So the lesson is not just that perfection is impossible in argumentative tropes but that even the best tropes are in some respect *mis*tropes.[43]

Perhaps the main manifestation of this effect is in the tendency of tropes to become *traps of argument*.[44] Many theorists of rational choice might be described as trapped by their tropes. The models, principles, exemplars, and even statistics for rational choice theory serve their scholars well in many ways. Yet they still restrict the abilities of these scholars to shift to other figures of argument more favorable for addressing aspects of politics poorly appreciated by the several versions of rational choice theory. As summarized earlier, the figures of argument favored by rational choice theory slight or distort aspects of politics important for its concerns about politics. The moral before was about how in some ways this can and should be avoided. The lesson here is about how in other ways it cannot.

More generally, the ways in which argumentative tropes also can and almost must be traps relates to the troubles in communicating across paradigms that figure so prominently in the writings of Thomas Kuhn and Paul Feyerabend.[45] As Feyerabend's injunction to pluralize paradigms suggests, a good response to the tendency of tropes to become traps is to produce more (diverse) tropes, capable of criticizing one another.[46] To cultivate illusions of avoiding all figures of argument is mainly to increase the rigidity, credulity, and dishonesty that are inclined to creep into any body of argument after a while. The real—if surely uncertain—protection against argumentative traps is to proliferate argumentative tropes and turn them on one another. Then they can afford effective ways to make and to break those spells of order that we call arguments. (Much the same can be said for the spells of order that we call politics.) And in the end, this is what many of our stories show about inquiry and politics. Just so.

PART TWO

TO MYTHS OF ACTION

---

6 TURNING POLITICS INTO WORDS

A RHETORICAL INVENTION OF EVIDENCE AND ARGUMENT

Words are the source of misunderstandings.
—Antoine de Saint-Exupéry[1]

Of all human inventions, is any more suspect than words? Not in the late modern sciences: positivists and constructivists, behaviorists and formalists, modelers and experimenters, surveyors and analyzers, hypothesizers and ethnographers, engineers and clinicians, empiricists and even theorists—all proclaim the dangers of words. To be sure, words might be required as labels for the concepts indispensable in science, considered as systematic inquiry. But late modern scientists accept this only as a regrettable concession to necessity. According to the modern credo, good scientists never relax their vigilance against the subtle traps set by language. They know that words can be false, fuzzy, vague, equivocal, ambiguous, misleading, and otherwise bound to trouble the unwary.

Oh, there might be a few late modern sciences of words. The linguists claim already to tame words and grammars into behaviors and rules. The semioticians might someday manage a genuine science of signs, to corral our unruly mustangs of meaning. And if the historians prove themselves capable of science, then perhaps the etymologists and the philologists might eventually achieve testable truths about the temporal trajectories of words and their uses.

But make no mistake: these prospective sciences share the modern dedication to eternal vigilance against the poetic and rhetorical power of words. Their main justification, by modern standards, is to expose and explain such power—so that scientists and possibly others can eliminate or repair the inevitably perverse effects of language on their work. "Keep our inference from the pollutions of language," they urge. And by extension: "Spare our substance the perversions of style!"

In the late modern academy, we celebrate the distrust of language as the beginning of method. Method, we know, is what makes any inquiry reliable, testable, truthful, progressive. And scientific method, the methodology textbooks tell us, must start in *conceptualization:* careful specification of the meaning(s) of key terms. Precision at the outset can help us to exclude unwanted meanings. We stipulate the sense intended, then specify the operations for measuring the concept that results; we might even name it anew, coining some neologism. (Never mind that to specify the definitions and operations is to express them in still other words, which themselves cannot receive such special treatment—upon pain of an infinite regress. Nor should we worry that any new word can label intelligibly only to the extent that scientists can and do translate it into some existing terms.) Though there is no escape from language when we face communication among scientists, let alone politicos or ordinary people, still there is real protection in the rigorous articulation of terms encouraged by such procedures.

This methodological protection must be especially urgent for the sciences of society, because they address objects embedded intrinsically in language. Social phenomena come already laden with words, because many happen in speech and the rest appear in social situations sculpted of language. To resist the siren songs of meaning in ordinary words, therefore, late modern scientists of society must be even more vigilant and clever than their counterparts in the purely natural or formal sciences. Thus social scientists must know well their words but only as puritans must know well their sins: to escape them where possible and, where not, to minimize and repent of their damage. Indeed social scientists must study the polysemy of words to combat their invidious effects on the souls of our sciences, but social scientists may not rejoice in the slippery richness of language.

Only humanists and literati would revel in the playful nuances or historical dimensions of words. Sometimes such people seem to study the same subjects. But social scientists know that these critics, novelists, playwrights, and poets lack rigor in their procedures of inquiry and communication. Always the two camps must share entanglement in words, because social scientists too must write and talk, but proper scientists know that humanists and "writers" are unsystematic in their evidence—if, indeed, they may be said to deal in evidence at all. Words are the last place a modern scientist would look for good evidence about social phenomena.

Or are they? Contrary to the conventional wisdom, the arguments of social scientists rely often and crucially on evidence from several kinds of disciplined play with the meanings of words. Even in the most rigorous modes imaginable, I would argue, the conceptualization and operationalization of the social sciences involve the play of meanings. This first kind of dependence on words must remain a case for another occasion, but some of my colleagues in the social sciences might think the point a modest concession at most. The official purpose of conceptualization, after all, is to confine the play of meanings to one step in the scientific method—limiting the perverse powers of words to a single separate context where they can receive special scrutiny.

More remarkable, perhaps, is the reliance of some work throughout the social sciences on arguments from etymology. Then the histories of word usage become evidence for various claims about human action. Thus histories of *participation* and *voting* can figure into social-scientific arguments about how to explain the turnout patterns in an election, how to describe the political mobilizations of a populace, or how to the measure the economic conditions for a revolution. But, again, a staunch social scientist might minimize the significance of the point. Express turns to etymology as historical evidence are not now prominent in the social sciences, I must admit, save for the small subfields devoted directly to historical and normative questions. By marginalizing these subfields, furthermore, modernist social sciences strive to make them the exceptions that prove the recent rule: that words and meanings make bad evidence, deserving suspicion rather than respect.

Yet social scientists cannot dismiss or minimize the importance of a third kind of word evidence in their inquiry. Though it offends outrageously the official modernist canons of evidence, this play with the powers of words contributes mightily to persuading social scientists (plus politicians, judges, lawyers, the laity, and the like) to accept some of their most prominent arguments. Nearly unnoticed, such power plays with language even help to secure allegiance to several of the presently paradigmatic styles of research in the social sciences. Shared with the humanities, such evidence seems all the harder to legitimate because it is more imaginative than historical. Its historical warrants are often weak and always peripheral to its success. On striking occasions it even defies historical usages to persuade instead by configuring large bodies of data and reasons in useful ways. This is the type of evidence we may call *imaginative etymology*. My adventurous thesis is that imaginative, or poetic, etymology is a legitimate form of evidence and a valuable trope of argument—in the social sciences as well as the humanities. Imaginative etymology puts the postmodern power of myth and poetry into historical persuasion throughout the human sciences.

Words, Words Everywhere, and Many a Meaning to Each

The best explanation of a word is often that which is suggested by its derivation. . . . There are cases, in which more knowledge of more value may be conveyed by the history of a word, than by the history of a campaign.
—Samuel Taylor Coleridge[2]

Dictionaries treat etymologies as exercises in history. What we regard as an ordinary etymology, therefore, is a document-able account of linguistic change. It tells the derivation of a word or its evolution in meaning. By contrast, an imaginative etymology invents a plausible account of a concept crucial to some substantive argument. To recognize imaginative etymologies as devices of argument is useful but not enough: we also must acknowledge them as potentially valid evidence. And to do that requires an exercise in the poetics—as well as the rhetorics—of argumentation.

Imaginative etymologies often stem from poetic inspection of a word's apparent structure or elements. If iron ages are situations of terrible trouble, perhaps *iron-y* is a figure of language and life espe-cially fit for coping with troubled times.[3] If a *com-promise* is a 'promise with', 'promise-in-common', or 'promise shared',[4] perhaps a *comm-unity* is a 'unity with', 'unity-through-commonality', or 'unity-with-respect-to-what-we-share'.[5] These imaginative etymologies readily give rise (or at least give voice) to provocative, useful theories of irony, compromise, and community—not only as words but also as phenom-ena. Historical etymologists would tell us that only the middle etymol-ogy of compromise is a factually defensible derivation. (At any rate, this is what they say at the moment: the judgments of historical etymologists have been known to change, depending on new textual evidence and new imaginative connections.) By strict historical stan-dards, the other two "etymologies" are made up, imaginary, false. Yet all three contribute to good arguments in several fields. Imaginative etymologies need not be mere mistakes of history; they can be valid devices of argument.

Rhetoricians of inquiry focus on what actually persuades specific audiences, especially in the academy. Thus Deirdre McCloskey shows that many an economist's argument depends more on appeals usually classified as literary than on considerations generally regarded as scien-tific in some harder sense.[6] The point is not to discredit economists; it is to invalidate their inaccurate scientistic contrast between literary and scientific arguments. More sensitive to their actual dynamics of argument, economists can learn better how to improve their inquiries.[7]

Not to renounce but to improve our uses of imaginative etymology: this is the main reason to recognize its poetic importance in arguments throughout the social sciences. To be sure, it has seldom been noticed as such by writers or readers in the humanities, let alone in the social sciences. Were it acknowledged, however, more than a few analysts of argument would misclassify it as a fallacy—perhaps calling it *false etymology*. Thus John Ciardi, that grumpy lover of words, used to boil with outrage about the "spook etymologists" who derive their meanings from spurious, pseudo-etymological fabrications of word histories.

Some philosophers of evidence might deny even "true etymology" a respectable role in substantive argument, at least in arguments about so-called empirical questions. Dismissing matters of etymology as merely semantic or conceptual rather than empirical, these standard setters would condemn invocations of historical etymology as commissions of "the etymological fallacy." And some social scientists would extend this fallacy to cover any use of etymology in addressing warrants for their technical concepts. Surely, they would say, the histories of ordinary words are largely irrelevant to the uses of technical concepts with stipulated meanings—even if these share the same name. If the goal of conceptualization is to avoid confusing new definitions with old meanings, what strange conception of evidence would let old usages test our applications of newly operationalized categories?

These accusations against etymology depend on the philosophical dichotomy between the logical or conceptual (form or reasons) and the empirical or substantive (evidence or contents). After Ludwig Wittgenstein and W. V. O. Quine, however, we have ample reasons for rejecting this dichotomy.[8] After the structuralists, moreover, we should know better than to treat any terms as meaningful in complete separation from their contexts: words mean in networks of discourse rather than as atoms of speech.[9] And if that were not enough, we also have the several "new histories" in political theory, literature, and other domains—telling us how speech paradigms construct the social objects and meanings of their disparate times.[10]

In all these endeavors, there has been a concern (often unaware and unsystematic but important in the details) to escape a homogenizing (Hegelian) preoccupation of intellectual history with "perennial issues" and patterns of "continuity versus innovation." In place of the history of ideas, the new historians study paradigms of language, epistemes of concepts, and discourses of rhetoric. They are interested in how ways of thinking, talking, and acting cohere.[11] Some study as well how they appear and disappear. Some of these new historians turn overtly poetic, favoring the "archaeology of knowledge" or the "genealogy of discourse" over the (old) history of (high, elite) ideas.[12] The new historicism in literary studies is more prosaic, arising to counteract the New Critical and deconstructive concentration exclusively on the text. It restores context, and it often entangles with reader-response criticism—with the historical ambition to appreciate how texts are read when published. Even the most cleverly conceptualized and operationalized of inquiries, then, must reckon with the rhetorical conditions of their technical terms—which can be useful only if connected intelligibly to their antecedents and implications. Whether imaginative or historical, tropal or narratival, this intelligibility is a must.

Furthermore social scientists need to rethink the notion that they can stipulate new or narrowed meanings for technical terms in order to cast off earlier meanings as though they were old baggage or clothes to be discarded once and for all. As J. L. Austin wrote, "A word never—well, hardly ever—shakes off its etymology and its formation. In spite of all changes in and extensions of and additions to its meanings, and indeed rather pervading and governing them, there will persist the old idea."[13] The fine philosopher-poet of ordinary language and mundane history for the communities of our times has been Stanley Cavell.[14]

No doubt this is easier for most late modern scholars to accept for historical than for imaginative, poetic etymologies. But it is true for both and in much the same way. In fact, the two kinds of etymology often serve substantive arguments in precisely the same way. In telling rhetorical terms, they are primarily devices of invention, meaning that etymologies of both kinds project structures of inference and argument.

Please note, though, that figures of invention must not be reduced to heuristics in some objectivist sense. They are not mere devices of discovery that contribute no evidence toward justifying the resulting claims. (This parallels the positivist contrast between contexts of discovery and contexts of justification, another dichotomy that we have good reasons to reject.[15]) On the contrary, tropes of invention become intrinsic to the evidence and reasons for whatever the positions argued. Moreover this is precisely what imaginative etymologies often do for good arguments in the humanities, the social sciences, and politics.

Presented as derivations capable of summary in a sentence or two, imaginative etymologies comprise a kind of evidence. Higher-and-harder-than-thou critics are perfectly prepared, of course, to agree that most arguments in the social sciences—let alone the humanities—are soft and confused. The critics sneer that many social scientists substitute silly word games of one kind or another for the proper proofs and solid evidence of true Science. Perhaps the most provocative thing about the thesis, therefore, is its insistence that imaginative etymology often is good evidence, even in the highest and hardest of the social sciences.

EVIDENCE AS AN EXAMPLE

A pedagogical example of imaginative etymology as evidence might be a treatment of evidence itself. Social scientists generally talk as though evidence were mere data, simply a set of facts. Once I wanted some students to understand instead how evidence is information arranged persuasively within an argument. The resulting discussion pushes at the limits of imaginative etymology, because it plays on unrelated etymologies of three or four words rather than one. Etymologically, please notice, *evidence* is e-vidence, from *evidere* in Latin. As the *Oxford English Dictionary* says, evidence is an outseeing, a seeing out—that is, a making to appear. (The German *aussehen* works much the same way.) Thus the *OED* begins its inventory of meanings:

I. To be in evidence, to be present.
   1. The quality or condition of being evident; clearness, evidentness; *in evidence*: actually present; prominent, conspicuous.
   2. Manifestation; display (obsolete).
II. That which manifests or makes evident.
   3. An appearance from which inferences may be drawn; an indication, mark, sign, token, trace.
   4. Examples, instance.
   5. Ground for belief, testimony or facts tending to prove or disprove any conclusion.
III. Legal uses of 5.
   6. Information, whether in the form of personal testimony, the language of documents, or the production of materials objects, that is given in a legal investigation, to establish the fact or point in question.

So far we have something on the order of historical etymology, and we can note from the *OED* that the English word arises in the Reformation and changes in the eighteenth century (with Lord Shaftesbury) to a more specifically scientific usage.

This illuminates the status of evidence in postmodern sciences, because it encourages us to focus on rhetorical questions of audience and setting: making to appear to whom, where, when, and so on. Already we are reaching beyond historical into imaginative etymology, but this is where the real fun begins. Next we can remember that, by Nietzschean and Heideggerian etymology, which always seems poetic and imaginative to me, *myth* means much the same: a making present, a making to appear. Because we see already that myths are symbolic stories that present whole accounts of events, we can recognize that evidence works in similar ways—not as isolated facts but as parts of persuasive accounts.[16]

Moreover we can notice a nominal resemblance of evidence to *events* and *evince*. Late modern sciences often seek to endow evidence with the ethos of the events themselves speaking, so that we can simply hear and see the facts of any matter adequately evidenced. This is exactly the province of evincing: just as we say that the professor evinces a fine knowledge of physics, we may say that the historical evidence evinces a compelling case for some hypothesis about pricing or party realignment.

Evince comes from *ex vincere*, literally 'out of' or 'from conquering'. *Conviction* has the same root, so that it suggests 'conquering with'. By contrast, rhetorical *persuasion* stems from *suadere*, with an unmistakable implication of 'sweetening'. The point from imaginative etymology, as you can anticipate, is that late modern sciences treat evidence as something that is to conquer us. Evincing too means to make manifest, to show plainly, compellingly. "Though it has lost its original English meaning of conquering, it now means 'to show beyond a doubt' and, in that sense, some trace of conquering remains."[17] Then the argument from imaginative etymology becomes that we should return evidence to its mythic sense of presentation and its rhetorical sense of persuasion, turning away from its latter-day confusion with evincing. Rather than conquering by sheer data, evidence should mean our seeing out of information and our making of it to appear (in arguments) to others or even to ourselves.

INFORMATION AS AN INSTANCE

A related example of imaginative etymology as good evidence is the very notion of information just invoked. Thanks to cybernetics and cognitive science, we are beginning to reassess the late modern sense of *information*. From the origins of the information revolution a century or more ago, people have worked to regard information as raw content that is capable of representation in diverse forms with no alteration in substance or meaning. Thus the language of media came to dominate our talk about information: senders, messages, channels, receivers, and so forth. Oddly the information was the unformed data, to be conveyed with minimum distortion from one place or person to another. Once collected and communicated, the information could be analyzed in various ways to ascertain its significance. But the information was separate from its form and its significance.

This perspective permitted immense leaps in our technologies of information and communication. It also taught us about its limitations. We learned that there can be no information without communication or mediation, because information is intrinsically a sharing of sorts. (Of course, that is why evidence should be seen as a communal construction with arguments rather than a conquering imposition of given facts.) Yet we learned also that there can be no communication without what has been regarded as distortion, because such sharing must span differences by coordinating rather than negating them. For a long time we regarded such distortion narrowly, as a mere loss of information. But of late we are coming to reassess it in broader terms as translation, implying a possible enrichment of information. No longer is information raw data or mere content; rather it is the stylized content that emerges from us and enters into us, forming us from without and within.

Accordingly we are learning that there is no communication without analysis of information. To convey or transmit information from sender to receiver, we must analyze the information sent according to the very characteristics that make the receiver different from the sender. And this implies that there can be no analysis of information without some concern for its meaning or significance. Therefore the earlier ideal of unanalyzed or unformed information—the notion of data fully separable from their forms of communication—yields to a sense of information as content both formed and forming. From the artificial intelligence work in the two Cambridges to the computer innovations in California and Japan, we are starting to appreciate how *information* is 'in-formed' and 'in-forming'. Marshall McLuhan, the Media Lab, and many others have come in diverse ways to much the same insight: media are not wholly external to messages; instead each interpenetrates the other.[18] Thus form is in in-form-ation, intrinsic to it, and we are formed through and through by the information that enters into us to structure our awareness and action. I find little in the historical etymology of information to warrant this imaginative reading, but there is much in our practices and problems of information to recommend it. The poetic etymology is more insightful and even persuasive about our politics and histories.

Imaginative etymology succeeds as evidence when it contributes to persuasive arrays of information. As evidence, imaginative etymology not only adds (content) to our information but (re)forms, (re)orders what we knew already. Now, because of this additional information, we must know differently—and we must hope to know better—than before.

NEOLOGISMS AS ILLUSTRATIONS

This even happens at another frontier of imaginative etymology: when it becomes the intentional invention of etymology for a new word. The social sciences have yet to equal the formal and natural sciences in this endeavor, but interesting examples do arise from time to time. A personal favorite is the meditation by Raymond Williams on implications of "distant seeing" in the word manufactured—complete with etymology—to name that central implement of late modern cultures, *television.*[19]

Another case is William Riker's clever etymological justification for coining the awkward word *heresthetics,* in order to avoid association with what ought to be termed *rhetorics.*[20] Riker's understandable fear seems to have been that his implicit apostasy in turning from the Hard Science of rational choice, which he helped to found, to the Soft Art of rhetoric could devastate his credibility among political scientists.[21] So he labored mightily to generate an etymology for the construction of heresthetics—to show how it is behavioral rather than persuasive, a matter of lasting structure rather than ephemeral speech. Gainsaid by his own examples, the invented etymology became Riker's main (if to me unpersuasive) evidence for heresthetics as separate from rhetorics. His gambit seems to be succeeding, yet some game theorists now edging into heresthetics are able to recognize their efforts as rhetorics, and Riker himself finally embraced the term.[22]

Other invented etymologies serve the inventors even better. Easy examples are Sigmund Freud's poetic etymology stipulated for the *id* and the one Hannah Arendt provided for *totalitarianism.*[23] Such efforts hint that, to succeed as evidence, any etymology—imaginative or historical—must make persuasive ties throughout a field of information. It must fit rather than contradict the rest of a text; it must configure rather than cross-cut the pattern of an archive; it must connect rather than disrupt the entries in a database.

Not Just Data but Reality

> *Of course the issues [of culture and society] could not all be*
> *understood simply by analysis of the words. On the contrary,*
> *most . . . persisted within and beyond the linguistic analysis. Yet*
> *many of these issues, I found, could not really be thought*
> *through, and some of them, I believe, cannot even be focused*
> *unless we are conscious of the words as elements of the problems.*
> —Raymond Williams[24]

Because it works best as evidence when it makes myriad connections to other evidence, imaginative etymology readily becomes as well a trope of argument. Like models and statistics in the social sciences, the argumentative trope of imaginative etymology pre- or configures whole logics of persuasion. Historical etymology can work in the same way.

A humanities example is Marlena Corcoran's philological argument about Immanuel Kant's *Critique of Judgment*.[25] Kant's German word for judgment is *Urteilskraft*. Corcoran explains that *Teil* is 'part'. But whereas *Ur* is originary in some contexts, here it combines with Teil to form *Urteil*, as dealing and as dividing into parts. Indeed *einteilen* means to divide or to categorize. Corcoran observes that Kant's movement is from lower parts to higher, as in the Roman law he knew so well. This sets up a striking contrast between such dealing or dividing and Kant's word for reason, *Vernunft*, which means grasping. Thus when Kant suggests that our aesthetic judgment proceeds through application of the "law of specification" to nature, he follows the logic and language of Roman law. The harmony between nature and the judging subject asserted by Kant as a "fortunate coincidence" seems redolent to Corcoran of the "Fortunate Fall" for Christians, and so Kant's subject has (even is?) a divine and mystical heart of irrationality coordinated in judgment with nature.

Here the point is less Corcoran's virtuosity of reading than her way of configuring a major problematic of Kant's *Critique*. She provides many persuasive connections between the specifics of her etymologies and the diverse details of the text. (The paper offers a profusion of ties beyond those summarized here.) Assuming that Corcoran is right (as a matter of history in word meanings) to set aside the originary sense of Ur, then we could readily imagine enriching her reading still further by turning it into avowedly imaginative etymology. We could invoke the originary sense of Ur (as in *Urmyth*) to configure a coordinated set of connections between the node of dividing versus grasping and the node of the fortunate fall from grace in the Garden of Eden. Then we might comprehend still better Kant's (and Heidegger's Kantian) arguments about (aesthetic) judgment as the origin of human attunement to the world.

At this point, though, the game gets bigger than single arguments or particular texts. How the issues grow becomes evident when we turn to Raymond Williams and his "vocabulary of key words." Corcoran shows how any etymological evidence depends on connections throughout texts or arguments, with each connection a confirmation of sorts. These ties pattern our reading of the whole text. Likewise, they offer standards and procedures for the whole of an argument, working in the same manner as models or statistics to provide and validate the overall shape or figure of the argument. That is why they are *tropes of argument*—in much the same sense that metaphors, oxymorons, and hyperboles are tropes (or figures) of speech. The tropal arguments of one era are the literal or positive or historical arguments of another period. And, likewise, the historical arguments of one time are the poetic or mythic or imaginative figures that inform another epoch.

What the Williams book on *Key Words* shows is how etymologies may configure substantive arguments about events, societies, institutions, and the other issues addressed by various of the human sciences. The Williams etymologies for key words explicate ties among structural and operational details throughout late modern societies. Defining *culture, myth, representation, society,* and other important concepts, Williams coordinated manifold data, information, instances, specifics, stories, theories, and other elements of argument about those societies. The results are patterns of telling detail, figured as etymological evidence and configuring his arguments as etymological. Williams advanced these patterns as abductive figures of inference about his (largely Marxian) issues concerning modern civilization. Each etymology evokes scores of ties to familiar phenomena in modern societies, and together the set of etymologies provides an exceptionally persuasive argument for a set of positions that usually leave me, at least, in some disagreement. Much the same thing, though with less explicit attention to etymology, is accomplished by William Connolly in his analysis of several "essentially contested concepts" as *The Terms of Political Discourse.*[26]

Because the Williams and Connolly coordinations of meanings with etymologies are feats of political theory, and thus imagination, their books underscore a crucial lesson: ALL EXTENSIVE ETYMOLOGIES MUST BE IMAGINATIVE. In addition, they suggest that one practical standard for what to count as "extensive" is whether an etymology pursues issues beyond the histories of words considered mostly as ends in themselves. Albeit in historical and humanistic veins, the Williams and Connolly tomes illustrate how etymologies can achieve larger ambitions. This is the same set of lessons long ago suggested by Giambattista Vico, and his work merits rereading in this context.[27] Yet it is equally a set of lessons as recent as today's news analysis, as Lawrence Weschler has demonstrated in his imaginative-etymology-as-political-history of the Solidarity movement in Poland.[28]

We can recognize imaginative etymology in past arguments that remain famous and influential. An obvious political example is how Thomas Hobbes invoked imaginative etymology to braid together several reasons for complete obedience to the Sovereign. Hobbes maintained that the Sovereign's author-ity to command obedience derives from the meaning of *author-izing* as 'author-ing'. The subjects, or so claimed Hobbes, have "authored" the Sovereign—thus author-izing its acts. This means that the subjects are the ultimate authors of the Sovereign's acts, which is to say that the Sovereign's acts are deeds of the subjects themselves. Therefore the subjects can disobey the acts of the Sovereign only by disobeying themselves. Such self-contradiction is a morally obnoxious and impermissible move, concluded Hobbes. The lesson is not that this conceptual dance is debatable in logic and in history, as surely it is. Rather we can learn from this instance that (1) Hobbes presented his case for absolute obedience through an etymology invented to tell the meaning of authority, and (2) his etymology aptly configures an argument plausible within his larger theories of political power and obligation.

The Center Cannot Hold

> *Concepts, like individuals, have their histories and are just as incapable of withstanding the ravages of time as are individuals. But in and through all this they retain a kind of homesickness for the scenes of their childhood.*
> —Soren Kierkegaard[29]

Imaginative etymology is especially prominent these days in the social and political criticism produced by deconstructivists. Their deconstructions often show how apparent meaning and evidence could be contradicted by etymological meaning and evidence, as generated through historical research *or* imaginative connection. A skillful example is Michael J. Shapiro's etymological deconstruction of sociological and political arguments by James Q. Wilson about criminal investigation and punishment.[30] Enlarging imaginatively on the historical etymology of *tasks* as 'taxings' (from the Latin *taxo* and *taxare*) as 'fixed payments to a king or feudal superior', Shapiro argues that Wilson's avowed program of replacing top-down administration fails because of its thorough implication in contrary figures—not only of speech but especially of argument.

Shapiro is a political deconstructivist with a negative, mostly Foucauldian mission to scoff at hierarchy and sneer at domination. In some cases, however, the deconstructive moment can lead into something of a reconstruction—which also becomes configured by etymology. A particularly apt example is William Corlett's book *Community Without Unity*.[31] By evidence and figures of etymology, some historical and most imaginative, he first disassembles the principles of political community advanced by many moderns, revealing immense troubles of evidence and reasoning within recent texts. Some followers of Foucault evoke textual and cultural contradictions as objects for snickering. This is because they can imagine no reprieve from our dilemmas of domination. Many neo-Marxists, such as Williams, explicate contradictions to give hope that our structures of domination must collapse of their own dynamics. But Corlett writes more in the style of Derrida than Foucault or Marx. Accordingly he turns out to be less interested in social or textual contradictions as such. He emphasizes political ironies, oxymorons, aporias, and the other poetic figures of incongruity, dispersion, and extravagance. These he traces in various texts and practices. Having done such deconstruction, he then joins it to the historical etymology of community as *com-munare* or 'with giving'—that is, giving together. He ends with imaginative ties of etymology to such Derridean dynamics as *the supplement* and *extravagance*. The result is a playful and persuasive case for reading overtly contrary theories and practices of community to support his Derridean ideals more than their own professed principles.

Were this a book in itself, rather than one among several chapters about poetic politics, I would be tempted to argue that the current turn to literary and political deconstruction arises in important part from our growing awareness that evidence and reasoning cannot stay bifurcated into synthetic and analytic compartments. To me, this is a major lesson of Jacques Derrida's strictures against Western logicist penchants for dichotomies and dualisms.[32]

More adventurously still, I would explain that such arguments take some of their main justifications from imaginative etymologies. Indeed a proclivity for this kind of argument distinguishes a whole family of dissenters from the Western project of controlling and dominating nature through skillful representation of it.[33] The shared technique is to repoeticize our languages, our arguments, our worlds. A host of aphorisms testifies to this imaginatively etymological approach; browsing just a few pages in the *Oxford Book of Aphorisms* suffices to suggest that this ambition is an enduring legacy of the last couple of centuries, as we have moved into high and late modern times:

Ralph Waldo Emerson: "All Language is fossil poetry."
Georg Christoph Lichtenberg: "Most of our expressions are metaphorical—the philosophy of our forefathers lies hidden in them."
Charles Baudelaire: "The immense profundity of thought contained in commonplace turns of phrase—holes burrowed by generations of ants."
Thomas Carlyle: "The coldest word was once a glowing new metaphor."[34]

Thus the rationales and tactics of genealogy in Nietzsche, Foucault, and others depend more than a little on the persuasive power of etymologies, imaginative even more than historical.

At this level imaginative etymology leads into what Paul Hernadi and Katherine Hayles call the "erotics of argumentation."[35] As a prime topic in the rhetoric of evidence, this explores how our dispositions of desire inform our senses of the adequacy of arguments. Thus imaginative etymologies play on and to our aesthetics of image, rhythm, voice, and resonance. These tie more readily to our senses of myth and poetry than our ideas of history or science. Yet no efforts, modern or otherwise, can eliminate these tropes of argument and aesthetics of desire from our histories and sciences of society. Nor does our ignoring their dynamics improve the arguments of us human scientists. One value of imaginative etymology is to turn such ignorance, embarrassment, and outrage into positive but playful modes of study. Thus a little imagination suffices to turn Michael Walzer's ruminations on the origins of *citizenship* into an inventive rhetoric of citizenship that configures and defends policy positions on current issues through etymological appeals.[36] Or, in a different vein, the tropal imagination of Hayden White can turn the cultural etymology of Michel Foucault toward a better sense of the dynamics of social inquiry.[37]

The Play's the Thing

> *As men abound in copiousness of language, so they become more wise, or more mad, than ordinary.*
> —Thomas Hobbes[38]

For us, the most important thing to stress about imaginative etymology is its insistence on *poetic play*. As an exploration of the powers of words, etymological evidence and argument require a keen sense of the inter*play* of meanings and connections. They seek to di*splay* our spheres of activity as languages, as vocabularies, as myths, as fields of terminology and mutual implication. Especially they encourage us to *play* with the aesthetic possibilities of our information, particularly as we configure it into inferences and it configures us into characters in the ongoing *plays* of our lives.

Through this emphasis on play, we can recognize that imaginative etymology may take several forms, many of them evident in the examples already provided. These forms also may be regarded as distinct dynamics or strategies of any etymology with an imaginative twist:

PLAY POETICALLY WITH THE COMPONENTS OF A WORD—as in *community* and *re-presentation* (Pitkin and Redner).[39]

PLAY POETICALLY WITH THE IMPLICITLY ETYMOLOGICAL, TROPAL, OR HISTORICAL CONFIGURATIONS OF ARGUMENT—as in logical, psychological, and social *con-straints* suggesting webs of belief or networks of meaning rather than fully axiomatic systems or merely causal links (see the treatment of Philip Converse that follows).

PLAY POETICALLY WITH MISTAKEN DECONSTRUCTIONS—as in *community* and *iron-y* (see earlier discussion of Corlett).

PLAY POETICALLY WITH HISTORICAL CONTEXTS—so that *citizenship* (not a Greek but a Roman concept, partly republican and partly imperial) fits mass republics better than participatory democracies, or so that revolutions as *re-volvings* have an aspiration to recover or return to past conditions (see discussions of Arendt and Williams).[40]

PLAY POETICALLY WITH OTHER FORMS OF THE ROOT—for example, *rationality* as 'rationing' to understand economistic conceptions of reason and choice, or *authority* as 'author-ing' as 'author-izing' (Hobbes); or authority as 'augmentation' as 'tradition' (Arendt) and therefore as 'nurturance' (Richard Sennett).[41]

PLAY POETICALLY WITH NOMINALLY SIMILAR WORDS THAT HAVE DIFFERENT ROOTS—*evidence* and *evince*, for example, or reasoned judgment as 'grasping' (Vernunft) and reasoned adjustment as 'dividing' (Corcoran on Urteilskraft).

Sometimes imaginative etymology might be confused with the persuasive definition and persuasive naming well known to the social sciences, as in the notorious "statistical tests of significance," which routinely get mistaken by social scientists (let alone others) for guarantors of substantive significance when they only concern inferential properties of different sample sizes.[42] But the playful dynamics of imaginative etymology move in opposite directions, seeking to display the erotics and aesthetics of argumentation rather than to exploit them covertly.

Playful exploration of meaning connections can enable imaginative etymology to improve our understanding of work throughout the historical arts and sciences. Such connections can surface, for example, in our parsing of arguments among the political scientists who study elections. These scholars depend for evidence on configuring elections as events of *voting* and *representation*. Their terms get etymologized historically and imaginatively as *voicing* and *re-presentation*, despite findings that insistently question whether elections do—or even could—fulfill mandates of voicing and re-presentation. Much the same emphasis on re-presentation also holds for the economists who study agency theories of rational choice in corporations and for the epistemologists who pose modeling accounts of the knowledge generated by various sciences.

The main reason to become more conscious of our reliance on such connections is to make them and evaluate them better. Within the social sciences a good case in point is the pioneering work by Philip Converse on political ideologies as mass belief systems.[43] Unaware of the subtle ties of meaning encouraged by imaginative etymology, Converse portrayed belief systems as constrained logically, psychologically, socially. For all its difficulties, the Converse argument continues to exert immense influence on political psychology and public opinion research. Current interest in modeling beliefs in n-dimensional space makes sense mainly in terms of the Converse assumptions.

The key trouble with the Converse scheme, many critics agree, is its inability to comprehend how belief systems change step by step—that is, how people learn. This trouble remains with the n-dimensional mapping of beliefs, because it includes no substantive conception of the connections among beliefs that would enable us to trace how changes in a belief should and do induce changes in others. A good solution to that problem, though, lies in Converse's figure of *constraint*. This word projects powerful etymological echoes of 'drawing together', as in the 'straining with one another' of strands in a web. Visualizing beliefs as nodes in a network lets changing tensions among the strands explain how changes in one node become communicated in specific ways to other nodes. It even encourages us to understand how the nodes or beliefs themselves are intersections of the connecting strands (of experience or thought) rather than a separate kind of entity. This permits us to eliminate the perplexing (modernist) dichotomy that continues to bedevil accounts of belief systems: a strange contrast between the many different nodes of content (the synthetic beliefs) and the formal connection of those nodes into a single system through a small set of logical ties (the analytic operators such as *and, or, unless*, and *implies*). It also helps us to overcome the unworkable barrier against inferential ties between the two main kinds of beliefs quarantined by modernists: facts and values.

We get all this through a little poetry of sorts. Indeed I would argue that the imagery of cognitive networks or webs of belief implicit in the Converse talk of constraint explains why his early work persuaded so many of his colleagues. If so, a telling irony is how such network notions have come to the fore in supplanting some of the conclusions and methodology generated by Converse and *n*-dimensional modelers.[44] These are the substantive kinds of contributions awaiting the human scientists who pursue imaginative etymology as a type of evidence and a trope of argument. The same goes for other resources in the rhetoric and history of inquiry when pursued as intrinsic aspects of any human science.

7 TURNING IDEOLOGIES INTO MYTHS

A POSTMODERN ESSAY IN POLITICAL AND RHETORICAL ANALYSIS

That's how it goes, everybody knows.
—Leonard Cohen[1]

Everybody knows that our talk about argument is vividly figural. Everybody knows that our ordinary language about neat, sharp, pretty, hard, slippery, forceful, evasive, and various other kinds of common arguments is a zoo—maybe even an ark—of colorful (if less than literal) evocations of the human talent for reasoning in public. And everybody knows that our academic discourse about grounds, foundations, fields, roots, branches, spaces, places, claims, warrants, backings, constructions, deconstructions, questions, issues, positions, links, turns, and literally all other terms of argumentation is a magician's trunk of tropes. The puns, images, symbols, associations, inversions, and myriad other operations seem never to cease. Until we speak. Or write. And then we forget. Even the scholars. That's how it goes.

Everybody knows, likewise, that our practice of argument is fully figural, thoroughly tropal. Otherwise we could not argue very well. Everybody knows at some level of performance and craft—if not exactly consciousness—that every argument turns on tropes. And everybody knows in some glimmering way that the tropes are not only of language (in some limited sense such as figures of speech) but therefore also of awareness, evidence, specification, criticism, and action.[2] At least Nietzsche knew.[3] And what Nietzsche knew, can we help but learn anew?[4]

Lately both the practitioners and analysts of political argument have become mightily impressed with its rhetorical, its symbolic, and especially its mythic dimensions. We learn how Bill Clinton, George Bush, and many other campaigners play with erratic results on political myths.[5] We learn how Ronald Reagan's success as the Great Communicator comes from his mastery of movies and myths, which is to say pretty much the same thing in two different words.[6] We learn similar things about the politics of Martin Luther King Jr. and Jesse Jackson. We learn that this is the general unto deconstructive rule of American politics in media times.[7] We even learn how American political history is mainly a texture of myths.[8] And we learn the same for the politics of culture in other late unto postmodern societies.[9]

As this essay shows, or at least suggests, that's how it goes when we reach for ways to appreciate (practically) or analyze (rhetorically) the tropal dynamics of argument in politics—and probably elsewhere as well. At any rate, that's how it goes when we want to come to good terms with tropes of argument. Then we resist faulting them as defects or dismissing them as distractions from the real substance of politics. Instead we learn to listen to tropes of argument as integral, defining features of our politics. For we learn, whatever our aspirations, that we cannot have decent politics without arguments, any more than we can have decent arguments without tropes.

Analogy

> Though analogy is often misleading, it is the least misleading
> thing we have.
> —Samuel Butler (the younger)[10]

Even arguments may (and often must) be analyzed tropally—which is to say, mythically. To see how tropal analysis might fit into mythic analysis and thence into rhetorical analysis, let me sketch just one of the possible strategies for political argumentation. Please permit me to present this strategy as a radical updating of Aristotle, putting his *Rhetoric* and *Poetics* back together.[11] And allow me to offer a general outline first, followed by illustrative details about U.S. politics.

If our schemes of analysis were to become specifically tropal, poetic, and mythic, then how might they figure in late and postmodern practices of rhetoric? Rhetoricians realize that to analyze a political argument of mass persuasion is necessarily to synopsize it. Even when much longer and more articulate than the argument, an analysis must channel and limit the argument's functioning as rhetoric. As poetry teaches us, a paraphrase or translation is never the same and seldom as good as the original. As deconstruction shows us, though, an analysis sometimes can exceed the original target in inventiveness, intelligence, and quality. Although it rarely has the aim or result of outshining its target and inspiration, rhetorical analysis usually tries nonetheless to make an original contribution to the issue (and to the audience) addressed.

In this respect, at least, I am inclined to suspect that Aristotle and his classical colleagues got it backward when defining rhetoric as loose and elliptical argument—by contrast with logic or dialectic as rigorous and complete argument. Precisely because of their analytical rigor, logic and dialectic are elliptical, whereas rhetorics and poetics are capable of completion precisely because of their practicality. As Ludwig Wittgenstein suggested, any philosophical analysis points toward an infinity of relevant things that it has not said.[12] Thus it evokes the inexhaustible susceptibility to further analysis of any objectified reality. A rhetorical analysis, by contrast, is a practical reality in its own right. Typically, therefore, it is complete as a presentation, perhaps the main kind of completeness possible for human endeavors. In other words, rhetorics and poetics can be complete existentially—in performance and experience. Accordingly they operate *by implication*, in the expansive and symbolic sense. Thus they evoke, invoke, provoke, and even revoke our reasons or meanings in ways that logic and dialectic typically cannot—if abiding by their admittedly impossible ambitions for analytical rigor.

Analysis of possible arguments and counterarguments can take many forms, because different purposes can imply diverse kinds and parts of argument. Accordingly Aristotle distinguished three modes of "proof"—ethos, logos, and pathos—and these serve well as a classic scheme of rhetorical analysis. Unfortunately Aristotle tended to sunder poetics from rhetorics, whereas (as Kenneth Burke has suggested) we need to meld them.[13] To evoke a sense of argument more adequate for rhetorics in our time, therefore, let me reconceive Aristotle's modes somewhat. Then let me augment them with a fourth mode of mythos, to encompass the concerns of poetics featured by preclassical and postmodern cultures. I have been arguing, after all, that rhetorics require the moment of mythos in order to appreciate mass persuasion.

But let me caution that these four topics of rhetorical analysis are not mutually exclusive, and their boundaries are hard to draw. Like Kenneth Burke's "Four Master Tropes," these topics gradually lead into one another, the more enthusiasm and subtlety that goes into analyzing them—or into using them for analyzing a particular argument. Unlike tidy philosophers, adventurous rhetoricians regard this as an advantage, not a defect. Their general aim is to comprehend, conserve, criticize, or create political arguments-in-action, so anything able to lead them throughout the whole of an argument or an action can be a big help.[14]

Ethos

The underlying meaning of Greek ethos *was* personal disposition. . . . *Gradually the meaning broadened out to* trait, character, *and then* custom, *or in the plural* manners *or* morals.
—John Ayto[15]

Ethos features the speaker's standing with the audience and—by extension—the relationships between the speaker and the audience, or within the community of speakers and listeners. It points toward the ancient category of goodness. Modern cultures tend to reduce ethos to mere atmospherics or tonalities on the one side or to sheer questions of credibility on the other side. But a postmodern appreciation of ethos might regard rationalities as ties, exchanges, and other interactions among members of a community. And definitely it would recognize that rhetorics move within their specific practices from ethos to ethics—that is, to moralities and their sustaining cultures.[16]

Within the late modern model of communication, the element most comparable to ethos is pretext: what comes before the message communicated and generates it. To treat ethos as pretext can capture much of the classical concern for motivation: what moves the speaker to talk as she does, when and where she does? But to reduce ethos to pretext would be to miss the (important republican) concern of ethos for character: who is the speaker for this audience, why, and with what plausible alternatives; what other characters does the speaker invoke; and how do they interact?[17]

Furthermore the concerns of motivation and character can encompass the audiences as well as the speakers. About a modern passive audience of mere listeners or spectators, ethos asks how the speakers construct motives for their audiences, who the audiences are for respective speakers, and how speakers might provoke other motives or identities for their audiences.[18] For the postmodern participatory audiences of potential democrats or even republicans, ethos also can inquire how an audience constructs its speakers as actors, itself as a community of interactors, and the community as sources or possibilities.

All this implies, in addition, that the audience must be made or cultivated. They are communities woven from diverse individuals. This might be done primarily by speakers or by some members of the audience. Yet this suggests in turn that the audience consists of other actual and potential speakers. Each of them, too, generates an ethos. Accordingly the widest and best sense of ethos encompasses the full texture of relationships comprising the public. From the margins of such an arena, ethos has the modern aspect and meaning of a 'pervasive spirit', 'subtle tone', or 'diffuse atmosphere' that characterizes the gathering as a whole and almost from outside. Within the sustained interactions of such a public, however, ethos has the ancient aspect and meaning of the 'patterns of practice' or the 'norms of conduct' that characterize the community in (inter)action. In this way ethos embraces or becomes ethics as the patterns of appropriate practice, the norms of good conduct, and the community's interest in improving them.[19]

As Wayne Booth argues eloquently throughout *The Company We Keep*, rhetorical criticism often should be ethical criticism. Even in literary studies, however, critical ethicists such as Booth and John Gardner have had to struggle long and hard to gain an academic hearing for this modest contention.[20] Worse, as Booth and others are wont to admit, the struggle has taken a toll on the quality of ethical criticism. It often devotes more attention to justifying itself as an enterprise than to doing its job well, and contributors have lacked the vigorous public of other practitioners that helps the whole body of work get better faster. To argue as much would be the work of another essay altogether, but I would say the same about the quantity and quality of ethical criticism for late modern politics.

Logos

> Greek logos *had a remarkably wide spread of meaning, ranging*
> *from* speech, saying *to* reason, reckoning, calculation,
> *and* ratio.
> —John Ayto[21]

If late modern analysts of argument nervously skirt ethos and ethical criticism, we have already seen that they try to award hegemony to a narrow range of logos and logical criticism. Logos emphasizes the speaker's reasons and evidence as shared with the audience through rigorous dialectic. It strives toward the ancient category of truth. The modern impulse is to deify logos as singular Logic and to methodize dialectic as analytical rationality. But a postmodern appreciation of logos might regard rationalities as institutional networks of topics and tropes for argumentation. And certainly it would concede that rhetorics move within their specific practices from logos to logics—that is, to rationales and their enabling institutions.[22]

At least implicitly, analytical philosophy identifies logos with logic in some formal deductive vein. In more general terms, however, the late modern category loosely equivalent to logos would be text: what comes as the message and communicates it. One of the strangest things about late modern philosophy is its effort to bifurcate logic and information, so that logic becomes the strict and undistorting medium for various data or messages. Etymologically and rhetorically—that is, etymopoetically—though, it makes better sense to move logic back toward its older meaning as 'the structure or study of meaning'. Then a rhetorical analysis focused on logos would explore the structure of any text's meaning as an argument—which is to say, as a pattern of means to ends or reasons to judgments.

Consequently the philosophical terms for interpreting logos can be refigured to accommodate its connections with ethos, pathos, and mythos. A useful updating of Aristotle on logos is Stephen Toulmin's three-part scheme of claims, warrants, and backings.[23] A claim performs one or another of the rhetorical moves that begins an interaction. There are hundreds of kinds of claims pertinent to our politics alone, and rights are just one of them. But already we have glimpsed how diverse and multiplicitous even rights claims can be when regarded rhetorically. A rhetorician's responsibility typically begins with appreciating the meanings of claims in use by particular persons in specific publics. A warrant is what permits us to make a claim, and our political talk often turns to these "licenses of inference," as Toulmin terms them. Then a backing is what we invoke to support a warrant or its relevance to the claim.

Toulmin's examples typify analytical philosophy, even though his flexible logic does not. They are dry, trivial, and largely outside the dynamics of actual argumentation in public. In being brief, I can do only a little better, but at least my example can move into the twilight commonplace in politics, where modern dimensions of logic, fact, value, imagination, history, will, or emotion can scarcely be separated without doing violence to any argument. If I claim that we should raise taxes to pay for our standard of living, you might ask why. In reply, I might warrant my claim by responding that we should not burden our children with debts when we can afford to pay our own way. But you might resist further. And I might back this warrant with evidence that debts between generations probably harm many public relationships, with explanations that only a modest belt tightening would suffice to save us from deficit financing, with prognostications that such stringency is now unlikely to produce a deep recession, and so on. Thereafter, of course, you might well criticize at any and every one of these levels—posing questions and counterarguments of various kinds. To Toulmin's threesome, then, a rhetorician might well add a fourth level or moment: claims, warrants, backings, and *criticisms*.

Whatever our scheme for analyzing logos rhetorically, we should take care not to identify argument with reasoning and thence with logic in the narrow sense now dominant within the academy. The first move is fine, but the second can undo the main gains available through skillful rhetorical analysis. It could bar ethos, pathos, and mythos from real recognition as modes of reasoning. One big lesson of decent rhetorical analysis for political argument is that ethical, "pathical," and mythical appeals are just as reasonable (in general) as logical appeals. Another is that logical reasoning seldom, if ever, proceeds far or well without reasoning also from ethos, pathos, and mythos—as intrinsic aspects of the resulting political argument.

Pathos

> *Pathos inheres in the audience and may be defined as the emotional reactions the hearers undergo as the orator "plays upon their feelings."*
> —George Kennedy[24]

During the modern hegemony of logos, pathos has suffered even greater denigration than ethos. "That was a pathetic argument," we sneer in late modern English, meaning that the argument has failed in every respect to persuade us—and seemed to have been uttered in sheer desperation besides. Just four sentences ago, in fact, I had to invent a new adjectival form for pathos just to avoid reinforcing your modern prejudice against arguments that appeal to feelings, settings, or symbols. Only mythos rivals pathos in this regard, and my use of *mythical* in the same sentence probably made you suspicious of what I was saying, even if *pathical* did not. (*Pathic* and *mythic* could work too, but *pathological* and *mythological* have been preempted for other uses.)

Pathos targets the speaker's invocation of emotion, imagination, and volition to evoke particular feelings from the audience. It drives toward the ancient category of beauty. Modern philosophies tend to make pathos liminal or subliminal, banishing the feeling to the hazy horizons of experience—as far as possible from the central site of rationality. But a postmodern appreciation of pathos might regard rationalities as de-centered or multicentered complexes of diverse passions and images. And unquestionably it would acknowledge that rhetorics move within their specific practices from pathos to pathics (there I go again!)—that is, to styles and their resulting sensitivities or sensibilities.[25]

A late modern category roughly similar to pathos is context: what comes with the message and surrounds it. To see why, consider the modern pathology of pathos. In recent literary theory, the "pathetic fallacy" is said to occur when a writer uses parallels between "inner states of mind or being" and "outer settings or conditions."[26] "It was a dark and stormy night," writes a no-talent Snoopy, to signal that his character is in distress or turmoil. Telltale weather is only one of the many forbidden delights condemned under the heading of this alleged fallacy. In fact, my favorite novel about rhetoric—Robert Pirsig's *Zen and the Art of Motorcycle Maintenance*—would have to be sent back to the shop for repairs so extensive that we would probably never read it again, were all its commissions of the pathetic fallacy somehow to be removed.[27] Such (mythic or postmodern?) fiction is not "realistic" or "sophisticated" enough for the late modern critics, who would hold all serious literature to a special, sometimes idiosyncratic standard of historical and psychological versimilitude.

Nevertheless rhetoricians interested in political arguments pay close attention to the emotions evoked or invoked by each arguer. They inventory every image and symbol, comparing their implications with one another and with other modes of argumentation. Likewise, rhetoricians will plumb symbolic and emotional details of our settings for speech-in-action. These include the immediate physical surroundings for the speaker and the audience, but they also include the historical and emotional backdrops for what is said and done. And rhetoricians take special care to notice how the speech might invoke still other settings for the audience. Finally, rhetoricians explore the commitments evoked or invoked by the argument in question. For the modern world, emotion and volition are our main modes of dedication to almost everything other than what we regard as narrowly logical or strictly experiential. For the modern world, Goethe got it right in saying that "passions are vices or virtues in their highest powers."[28]

Pathos should prove exceptionally significant for political action and argument in our times. As the study and practice of settings for speech-in-action, pathos can encompass the structures and dynamics of publics. As the analysis of public commitments, furthermore, pathos can include the sources and issues of political mobilization, social-

ization, obligation, and revolution. All these are prominent features—
not to say pathologies—of late and postmodern politics.

Mythos

*Myths are poetry, but a special kind of poetry—the poetry men
live by.*
—Lee C. McDonald[29]

Even late modern people know that pathos meets
mythos at sites of ritual, symbol, and tradition. For the postmodern
rhetorician, mythos further concerns the speaker's origination, narration, and figuration. Accordingly it leads toward the ancient category
of friendship, which the ancient Greeks considered a political good
beyond justice. Modern terminologies dismiss myths as mere falsehoods or debunk them as sheer superstitions—always suffered by the
audience or somebody other than the speaker. But a postmodern appreciation of mythos might regard rationalities as webs of tropes and
stories. And surely it would affirm that rhetorics move within their
specific practice from mythos to mythics—that is, to symbols and
their articulating stories.[30]

For rhetoricians of a postmodern orientation, at least, mythic analysis could include something on the order of Aristotle's topics. These
are the places (topoi) of argument, in the sense of spaces or patterns
created by persuasive moves often repeated across different contexts
in regard to more or less the same set of issues. (The modern everyday usage of *topics* shifts the focus from repetition of persuasive
moves to persistence of concerns, making the word synonymous with
issues or subjects of study, discussion, etc.) Aristotle's twenty-eight
topics include how we define terms, address parts of an issue one at a
time, identify potential alternatives, argue to consequences, and induce to conclusions. A latter-day list might include Aristotle's topics
and many more. Certainly what Aristotle regarded as special topics
have proliferated in late and postmodern times. What topics does a
public argument articulate and how? What topics does an arguer re-
press and why? Often these are things that rhetoricians of liberty
need to know.

The usual mythic synonym for topic is *theme*. This underscores the
close connection between myth and music. *Mythos* connotes the musi-
cal or poetic tale, sung or recited aloud. In this way it urges rhetoricians to analyze arguments less exclusively as "lines" of reasoning—
sadly the standard translation for Aristotle's topoi. Beyond sequences

of claims, warrants, backings, and criticisms let us fathom arguments as fields, patterns, or worlds that mean little until we dwell in them (or deconstruct them) as wholes.[31]

Mythic analysis has a special interest in our common places of argument. Aristotle defined these as the universal topics common to all bodies of argument. If the rhetorical tradition may be regarded as the republican tradition, however, postmodern rhetoricians would do better to regard commonplaces as the distinctive topics that help to define whole branches of inquiry or conversation.[32] Dividing phenomena into dependent and independent variables is a commonplace of empiricism in social science, just as separating events into stimulus and response is a commonplace of behaviorism in psychology. Likewise, dividing activists into moderates and extremists is a commonplace of liberals, just as the interaction between substructure and superstructure is a topic characteristic of orthodox Marxists. Distinguishing between public spaces and private realms has been a commonplace of republicanism. It often gets conflated with the commonplace liberal contrast between the public (government) sector and the private (business) sector. A fully rhetorized, postmodern republicanism would reconceive publics precisely as commonplaces.

If topics are a commonplace of myth-taking, then the same goes for tropes, stories, and styles. To analyze tropes in argument is to trace the persuasive contributions made by figures of speech such as metaphor, hyperbole, and oxymoron. By extension, the same can be said and done for figures of consciousness or action: metonymy as a form of argument, prolepsis as a way of reading, even irony as a stance toward politics. Beyond Aristotle, though, lies a bolder mode of analysis that targets tropes of argument: maximization in economics, regression in sociology, decision in democratism, or tradition in conservatism. Analysis of myth (what I like to call *myth-taking*) pursues the tropes deployed or avoided by political arguments and actions.

Myths are not just beliefs or systems of belief, let alone false ones. Instead myths are stories, tales, narratives. Therefore myth analysis attends carefully to the plots, characters, settings, deeds, and consequences of arguments-in-action. These are not always explicit within political arguments; and modern argumentation, especially, tends to efface its reliance on narratival persuasion. Nevertheless many a concept, reason, fact, or question makes little sense aside from an inspiriting story. In addition, the rhetorical concerns for character (ethos) and setting (pathos) testify that many arguments unfold in practice and are experienced at the time as narratives, even if this receives no express acknowledgment within the argument. If nothing else, a decently reflexive sense of its own dynamics impels rhetorical analysis toward matters of myth.

Stories are rhythms established among plots, characters, symbols, and similar components.[33] Thus mythos explores arguments as rhythms established among considerations of ethos, logos, pathos, and mythos itself. These rhythms are what we often call *styles*. Notoriously subtle, slippery, and evanescent, styles are to methods what themes are to theses. Shaw defined style in the singular as "effectiveness of assertion"; Swift as "proper words in proper places." Schopenhauer linked mythos to ethos in noting how "style is the physiognomy of the mind, and a safer index to character than the face." Yet the best link to argumentative myths (and tropes in particular) is Oppenheimer's:

> It is style which complements affirmation with limitation and with humility; it is style which makes it possible to act effectively, but not absolutely; it is style which enables us to find harmony between the pursuits of ends essential to us, and the regard for the views, the sensibilities, the aspirations of others; it is style which is the deference that action pays to uncertainty; it is above all style through which power defers to reason.[34]

So myth analysis also offers a sense of the styles practiced or opposed in political arguments.

In contexts of American political argument, this fits beautifully with what I have come to regard as the distinctively republican interest in political styles. As spaces of action, publics simply are sustained styles of conduct. As architectures of memory, public spaces configure acoustics, monuments, perspectives, and patterns of movement conducive to their distinctive liberties, tragedies, and other stories. These are some of the reasons that one of my favorite political theorists, Hannah Arendt, found the metaphor of "public space" so pleasing.[35] Postmodern culture has begun to relearn how politics are styles, but it still tends to aestheticize this lesson, leaving the sense of style far too slick, superficial, and merely fashionable. Mythos can endow rhetoric and republicanism with a vital and permeating sensibility of publics and politics as potentially virtuous styles of speech-in-action.[36]

In this sense mythos as a rhetorical and political mode of analysis implies ways to articulate one of Arendt's most provocative but least comprehended insights: that we in the West fail to understand political freedom as public action because we have no name or notion of "doing beauty."[37] Unable to articulate this insight, Arendt remained one of the theorists who excoriated mass society and mass persuasion as the material and mechanism for manufacturing kinds of totalitarianism. We forget what publics are and why we need them, she argued, and we do so because we have never understood publics as places for doing beauty. By contrast, the specifically tropal moment of mythos lets us appreciate how mass publics can become, in Arendt's sense, authentic publics.

As already noted, late modernists routinely charge any project of purposeful myth-making with "aestheticism" or "romanticism." How sentimental, self-indulgent, or manipulative to presume to make myths for ourselves, let alone for others! Either we succumb to the absurdity and narcissism of art for art's sake alone, or we surrender to the cynicism of style as a surrogate for substance.[38] Between the lines, though, these accusations acknowledge that a tropal sense of style-in-action is a capacity to appreciate mass publics as mythic actors and arenas.

For these reasons the best late modern category to relate to mythos is subtext: what comes in the message and supplements it. Subtexts share the subtlety and pervasiveness of themes in music or poetry. The modern model of communication is a conduit for undistorted transmission of messages from senders to receivers, all within a larger context. But notice that this lacks an obvious place for subtexts, though the model knows precisely where to position pretexts, texts, and contexts. Should the text that we diagram as within—or at least, on its way to—the receiver be regarded as the subtext rather than the "retext"? No, because subtexts are located as much within the sender, the message, and the medium as they are within the receiver. Moreover the social or cultural context is equally vital to telling subtexts. In fact, subtexts are specifically what senders, receivers, messages, and media share with their contexts. Modern communication cannot encompass subtexts precisely because its resolute literalism leaves no room for figures, symbols—in short, tropes. Neither subtext nor mythos fits any place in particular within the modern paradigms of communication and representation. And this turn to tropes arguably makes mythos the most distinctively postmodern, perhaps post-Western, of our four main modes of rhetorical analysis.

Consequently mythos is especially good for dispelling the modern hegemony of the conduit paradigm of communication, something that continues to bedevil studies of mass politics and persuasion in late and postmodern times. Because it fits no specific boxes or categories of modernity, mythos disperses the tight boundaries around modern messages, media, and communicators. In that very facility lies our best hope for disseminating publics throughout postmodern life, to overcome the near despair of many late modernists for our prospects of genuine liberty.

Example

Example is the school of mankind, and they will learn at no other.
—Edmund Burke[39]

Aristotle identified two general modes of persuasion. One is the enthymeme—the target of my rhetorical scheme of ethos, logos, pathos, and mythos. (It has dominated almost every theory of political rhetoric from Aristotle onward, and so it dominates this essay as well.) But the other is the example. To elaborate this argument for recognizing tropes of political argument, let me exemplify its potential by becoming a bit more ample in identifying tropes of argument from American liberalism.

Most accounts of U.S. politics characterize liberalism as the mainstream ideology.[40] To analyze liberal discourse in the United States, then, is to appreciate in important (but not exclusive) ways liberal rhetorics as distinctive sets of argumentative tropes. Several are easy to identify:

Liberal Tropes of Argument (for example)
Representation
Hypotheticals
Original Positions, States of Nature
Universalism
Cause/Effect

To say that these are tropes of argument for liberalism in America is to say that they define far more than defend liberalism as a coherent style of argument in politics. It is also to say that each makes a common and important move in liberal persuasion. And it is to say that liberalism neither does nor could do much to defend such argumentative moves. Thus when critics challenge John Locke or Abraham Lincoln or Franklin Roosevelt or John Rawls on their wont in argument to derive natural rights from original hypothetical positions, none of them has had (or needed) much to say in response. Such tropes are "fundamental" to liberalism as political argument.[41]

Something similar holds for the related tropes of consciousness that together characterize liberalism, among them,

Liberal Tropes of Consciousness (for example)
Visuality
Dichotomy
Identity
Irony

Visuality and dichotomy, especially, have come in for immense discussion in connection with the place of liberalism as the preeminent ideology of specifically modern politics.[42] Liberal democracy, especially, wants political bodies and actors to be fully visible in their identities.[43]

To explore these tropes in use is to consider their interactions with a number of linguistic figures long recognized to pervade liberal talk in the United States—including metaphors (corporations as individuals), metonymies (Clinton administration), synecdoches (Washington), oxymorons (military intelligence), euphemisms (revenue enhancement), and the like. Especially it is to distinguish between the academic uses of such tropes and their appearances within ordinary politics in the United States. Likewise, it is to examine how these tropal dynamics interact with what some might count as the political topics that characterize liberal rhetorics:

Liberal Topics (for example)
Issues
Distinctions
Communication
Information
Freedom
Rights
Trust

To understand liberal argumentation in this scheme would be to notice how these can function as Aristotelian topics of argument (only?) in tandem with liberal tropes of argument. It might also be to appreciate how American politics are bringing topical and tropal liberalisms into increasing conflict, but that must remain an argument for another place.

Under the rhetorical category of mythos, of course, the analysis of liberal discourse would include particular attention to narrative levels of liberal argumentation. These are the characters, scenes, and plots that figure prominently in American discourse about politics:

Liberal Characters (for instance)
Individuals, persons
Peoples, nations

Sovereigns, governors, diplomats
Politicians, activists
Interests, factions, parties
Fanatics, agitators, extremists
Institutions, organizations

Liberal Scenes (for instance)
Frontiers
States
Legislatures
Campaigns
Lobbies
Interviews
Inner sanctums (Oval office)

Liberal Plots (for instance)
Responsibility
Opportunity
Commemoration
Crisis

Again the emphasis would fall on their interaction with other dimensions of tropes and topics in liberal argument.

But the most adventurous and intriguing connection is the last: a tropal and mythic analysis of liberal argument in America must encompass comparisons to other ideologies of politics. Later Table 8.1 projects how this might proceed in detail. The candidates for comparison surely include republicanism, conservatism, socialism, and democratism. Again there is a substantive promise to repay the trouble, for initial work in these veins (*Habits of the Heart*, for example) shows how the narratival dynamics of political discourse in the United States often depart from liberal tropes and myths.[44] Sometimes they promote political persuasions that remain more republican than liberal in their predominant styles of political argumentation. And other times America's democratism seems to work tropally against the grain of its liberalism. Exploring such possibilities is the set of tropal tasks to come, for rhetorical analysis that reaches beyond Aristotle's enthymemes and examples to our political world and its argumentative figures and myths.

8 TURNING GOVERNMENTS EVERY WHICH WAY BUT LOOSE

A POETIC EXPERIMENT IN POLITICS AND COMMUNICATION

Poets are the unacknowledged legislators of the world.
—Percy Bysshe Shelley[1]

Many metaphors and other tropes inform our words of politics and communication. In turn, these words configure our acts and institutions of political communication. *Political* says 'pertaining to the polis'. The ancient Greek city-state originated much of our political language by organizing communities as polarizations, alignments that rally people into persuasive poles or positions akin to the standards for deploying strategies on the battlefield.[2] *Communication* virtually says 'community'—making it the kind of common, shared, reciprocal giving that modern people since John Locke have understood as a sending of messages through media to separate receivers.[3] This takes the ideas that first occurred (in)to some people and re-presents them in(to) other people. We in the modern West have learned the resulting tropal harmonics of mediation or middle grounds and of alignment or commonality. We know that they can counterbalance the tropal dissonance between shared, preestablished standards on one side and polarizing separations on another.

Such figural dynamics have been prominent features of modern communication within and about politics. We name the *mass media* for their supposed mediation among individuals and for their transmissions between citizens and governments. Mediation is the dynamic of the modern model of communication (see Figure 8.1). Political discourse as we practice it tends to oscillate between polarizing talk of classes, interests, and parties on the one side and converging talk of mainstreams, common grounds, and shared values on the other. Over and over, we populate our political worlds with distinct, even

150

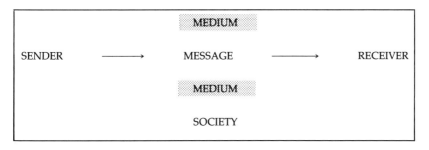

Figure 8.1. Modern Model of Communication

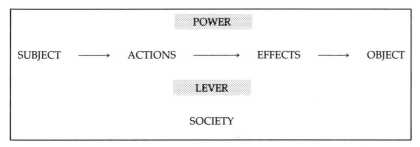

Figure 8.2. Modern Model of Power

distant things that either develop strong connections (and draw closer to one another) or pull further apart (as their ties atrophe and disappear). Then we imagine the spaces between these entities as fields of (inter)action, and we treat the connections as channels of communication, levers of power, or both (see Figure 8.2).

So we learn in figure and fact how politics can be communication and communication can be politics. Yet we also learn how the two should differ enough for *political communication* to escape redundancy (in one direction) and oxymoron (in the other).

The very language shared by scholars of politics and communication with politicians, journalists, and citizens assumes liberal democracies to be machines of political re-presentation and modern communication. They enact the modern model of representation (see Figure 8.3). The senders are the private individuals and institutions whose ideas or interests become communicated to the public officials and institutions. The communication is a process of re-presentation: what first became present in the private arena of civil society gets transmitted through elections, parties, interests groups, bureaucracies, media, and other channels of communication in order to be re-presented in the public arena of government. In the liberal model of political representation,

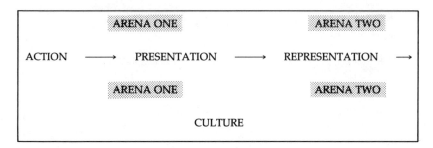

Figure 8.3. Modern Model of Representation

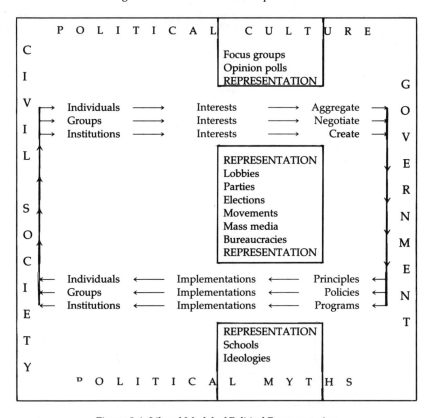

Figure 8.4. Liberal Model of Political Representation

this is how citizens tell officials what to do (see Figure 8.4). The liberal machine of political communication provides for feedback by transmitting government messages of principle and policy back to the people in civil society. Experiencing government programs, citizens then adjust their interests and ideas for a new round of communication.

Yet we have reason to recognize that these tropes for modern times are not always adequate to the electronic and other politics emerging in our turn into a new century and millennium. Murray Edelman, one of the premier scholars of political communication, argues that social changes proceed from art to politics.[4] Likewise, Shelley proclaimed poets as the people who rewrite our world, political and otherwise. In part, this is because poets prefigure and re(con)figure our experience. They invent the tropes, sounds, images, meanings, and rhythms that inform our lives. To explore how the recently emerging modes of politics and communication might be transforming our lives, let us pursue an exercise in poetry for refiguring our politics. We may take as our template a brief poem that suggests how new or anticipated conditions might reform political tropes for postmodern or even post-Western times.

Female Metaphors

What if the moon
was never a beautiful woman?
Call it a shark shearing across black water.
An ear. A drum in a desert.
A window. A bone shoe.

What if the sea
was discovered to have no womb?
Let it be clouds, blue as the day they were born.
A ceremony of bells and questions.

What if a woman
is not the moon or the sea?
Say map of the air. Say green parabola.
Lichen and the stone that feeds it.
No rain. Rain.
Katha Pollitt[5]

Pollitt's "Metaphors of Women" prompts us to recognize how all our language, all our life, is poetically, powerfully, irremediably figural. As Pollitt recognizes, all metaphors cannot help but work backward as well as forward, so that a woman is for us the moon and the sea, even as the moon and the sea are womanly.[6] Because the modern conceit is that governments are men and machines, we also configure men and machines as governors. Thus rationality governs every liberal (economic) man, and a carburetor governs fuel use in cars. Does *governs* mean much the same in both phrases? Well, the liberalism of rational choice theories does configure men as choice machines. . . .

Shuttling back and forth in this fashion, the figures become networks of associations that reach in additional directions—until, after a fashion, they encompass entire cultures. The same holistic dynamics of these constitutive tropes tend to endow new configurations with the aura of natural forms.

In modern times we imagine that these figures are simply waiting to be *found* by new and better inquires than before: "What if the sea was *discovered* to have no womb?" Accepted figures thus appear always already given, or at least available. And trying new forms often means reconfiguring history as we have known it: "What if the moon was *never* a beautiful woman?" When one complex of figures replaces another, the mythic result can seem Orwellian, because experiences within the resulting network of symbols often imply that the eliminated figures never existed, never functioned as part of our world: today Oceania wars with Eurasia, but tomorrow Oceania has always been at war with Eastasia.

These constitutive dynamics are why we sometimes find it hard to invent new figures and symbols for our worlds and selves: established tropes configure our activities so thoroughly that we cannot imagine, let alone live, alternatives. As Thomas Kuhn observed for scientific paradigms, themselves equally figural, seldom does a proliferation of anomalies prove enough by itself to displace a matrix of disciplinary worldviews and research programs.[7] There must be some alternative to reconfigure scientific imagination and inquiry, before the practitioners of the old paradigm have adequate reason to abandon it for a new one.

In late modern liberal democracies, the study and the practice of political communication are proliferating anomalies. Caught in the old terms and inadequate tropes of modern civilization, however, we can hope to do little more than arrange our actions and observations as dilemmas or paradoxes. In the figural looms that simply are our modern cultures, there are few pure re-presentations of people to polity, or polity to people, yet there are fewer still unbridgeable gaps between individuals and institutions than our re-presentational sciences of politics imply. There are no undistorted messages between senders and receivers, of the kind that our late modern theorists of communication must postulate as ideals, yet there are many informative exchanges among political actors and audiences. For such reasons, more than a few issues of the social sciences appear (in figural perspective) as interesting errors. They are less practical problems in search of solutions than pseudo-problems in need of dissolutions.

So we have been learning in this series of forays into the figural troubles of modern civilization, with special reference to politics and communication. Here we may take a few further, perhaps erratic steps beyond our earlier efforts, again offering less an argument to stand on its own than a network of experiments meant to augment the possibilities beginning to emerge in our times. Elsewhere I have emphasized the drive of modern (especially liberal democratic) politics and communication to achieve representation. And I have recommended that we recognize the political and epistemic trick of such representation as *re*presenting there and then what first presented itself here and now. That can lead into explorations of (opinion) *publics* and (mass) *media* that turn away from modern liberalisms toward postmodern feminisms, environmentalisms, even republicanisms. This time let us turn us in a different direction, exploring how to refigure modern notions of government and the state.

Modern ideologies—liberalism, socialism, and even some species of conservatism—all imagine a state or government as a human machine for powering and regulating the (other) humans who comprise the society supervised by the government. Typically these ideologies configure government as the functional equivalent of a (male) human who operates by mechanical (or physical) force to control the conduct of ordinary citizens. Symbolically such governments tower above ordinary citizens to oversee their various interactions: note the eye high on the pyramid of American government featured by the dollar bill. Thus governments provide rules and surveillance to keep order among the populace.[8]

As with the original illustration for the Leviathan projected by Thomas Hobbes, the modern Machine Man writ large is often taken to be a huge structure built of common people who look Lilliputian in comparison with the (sovereign) state they constitute. This is only a half-step from the computers, robots, bionic people, and cybernetic organisms (cyborgs) that populate science fiction, military strategy, even feminist theory late in modern times.[9] As Stewart Brand writes, "If humans are most distinguished from other organisms by the elaborateness of their communications, then the coming of new levels of world communications implies the arrival of something more than human. Cyborg civilization, maybe, or a cognitive planet." "Politics, even more than usual," he concludes, "is lagging well behind the process."[10] Yet there are ways in which cyborg imagery itself is lagging well behind the process.

The imagery of a Machine Man helps to make persuasive the modern notion that governments process citizen claims neutrally, expertly, and responsively while embodying or representing the sensibilities of those citizens. Likewise, it evokes the strength presumably needed to enforce decisions when more than a few individuals might be expected to dissent: the "power to keep them all in awe" asserted by Hobbes for his Sovereign and made by Max Weber into the principle that a modern nation-state must monopolize the means of legitimate violence. The Machine Man of modern government stands tall and far seeing in the center of every society.

When mass media and multinational corporations rival nation-states as centers of twenty-first-century power, however, we may have to wonder whether societies or powers remain *centered*. We have to wonder harder when we discern how internally complicated and fractured such operations turn out to be. When global economies, transnational organizations, and regional ecologies configure our lives, we have to wonder whether even the most modern of governments were ever much like those machines or men designed to regiment the affairs of ordinary folk. And the wonder grows when we learn how such regimes, structures, and organizations are simply sets of smaller practices that stitch together our endeavors in ways never recognized by the modern figures of Men and Machines.

When Europe 1992 turns in centuries of prickly patriotism for new dynamics of production, trade, identity, and bureaucracy, we must wonder whether we need better figures for governments of the next century and millennium. When the mighty (if ramshackle) government of the Soviet Union disappears in a matter of months, we may permit ourselves to muse about whether Hobbes was right to envision the modern state as an all-or-nothing proposition of domination by some gigantic Machine Man. And when we notice how the disintegration of the USSR is yielding handfuls of new-old ethnic and territorial governments, dancing the intricate and sometimes bloody waltzes of regional confederacy and ethnic alliance, we might let ourselves ponder whether modern images of government must themselves yield to handfuls of new-old figures for fathoming how we adjust and adjudicate human efforts across diverse spheres of activity.

For at least a moment, therefore, let us wonder what might happen if we set aside modern images of government and the state. What if the government was never a machine or a man? Need we change the cognitions and actions that issue from these webs of modern figuration, as Pollitt encourages where Western women are concerned? Then let us play the game of figures more purposefully, more inventively, than before. Hinting at how our words are the seeds of our deeds, the Pollitt poem provokes us to reconceive the places, turns, tales, and forms for our increasingly postmodern politics. Properly, inevitably, this is the place of myth.

Mything Words

*All the chemical and energy activities in a body (or a society)
have a word for their sum action—"metabolism"—but there's no
equivalent word for the sum of communications in a system. The
lack of a word signals a deeper ignorance. We don't know what
constitutes healthy communications.*

—Stewart Brand[11]

Myth is the word that Brand needs, that we all need,
for *the sum action of communications in a system.* Myth is the overall, permeating pattern of communication in those humanly given systems
called *cultures* and *subcultures.* Accordingly *an individual myth is a symbolic story of the whole*—the whole system, thing, person, practice, polity, culture, or the like. Thus any culture or subculture is a mythos—a
body or network of interrelated stories that share characters, settings,
plots, symbols, rhythms, styles, and so on. And a society is bound
then to be a complex of mythoi that support and criticize one another
in turn.

Many an analyst has noted in this connection that the American media may be regarded as textures of intertwined myths. Of late, for example, they tell how

The world is a texture of problems and happenings, both to be ap-
prehended as events—THE MYTH OF ACTIVITY.[12]

Events are separate dramas or stories—THE MYTH OF NARRATIVITY.[13]

What makes an event important is its novelty, its newness—THE
MYTH OF MODERNITY.[14]

Truth, facts, and therefore news must be objective and unitary—
THE MYTH OF OBJECTIVITY.[15]

News is primarily a matter of politics—THE MYTH OF POLITICALITY.[16]

Politics is primarily a matter of individual actors—THE MYTH OF PER-
SONALITY.[17]

Politics is secondarily a matter of issues—THE MYTH OF RATION-
ALITY.[18]

U.S. politics turn on presidents and elections—THE MYTH OF THE
PRESIDENCY.[19]

The presidency is primarily a matter of "tactics and polls and
staging"—THE MYTH OF STRATEGY.[20]

Elections send messages mandated from the people to the politicians—THE MYTH OF REPRESENTATION.[21]

To distill these myths, I offer them as propositions. But the American
media enact them as stories about presidents, polls, and citizens.[22]

In one way or another, of course, commentators typically take such myths to be mistakes or falsehoods perpetrated by the news media. Until recently, in fact, academic theories of news have been little more than complaints against the alleged professional slant and ideological bias in the American news media. But nothing could be further from my own meaning in talking about media myths. Analysts must not prejudge the acuity, accuracy, or adequacy of any myth. Instead they must examine any myth in ample contexts of its own and other cultures (which is to say, in part, in terms of other myths) before they hazard any judgments about its truthfulness. Moreover they must remember that truth is not always the most important test of a myth, political or otherwise.

In these terms myths are at once the most prominent and neglected features of our political landscape.[23] We readily spot and dispute the political myths of others, to be sure, but we seldom appreciate our own for what they are—even when they differ little from the very tales we debunk beyond ourselves. Within the mythoi of modernity, the bodies of Western myths that have configured our cultures and politics for half a millennium or more, we continue to scorn myths as mistaken beliefs that somehow become widely held. Because modern stories of consistency suggest that minimally rational people cannot simultaneously hold convictions that they know (or even believe) to be contradictory, the modern mythos of antimyth implies that our own myths go unrecognized out of logical necessity—until the nearly inevitable discrediting leaves them no longer among our current beliefs. The notion that we could be sane, let alone sage, to study and improve—rather than debunk and overcome—our own myths (except in retrospect) remains an anathema within modern civilization. In fact, the idea that we could do so intelligently while keeping some of the myths studied intact as myths is for narrowly modern cultures an abomination. Yet that is precisely what we scholars of political communication and cognition can and should do, especially now.

Unfortunately, many who study the politics of mass communication seem to miss this point, over and over. We might say that practitioners of mass communication include more than a few who understand it fairly well, though (as groups) our filmmakers and songmeisters probably have done better overall in this century than our journalists and television programmers. But these are the people who dance the light fantastic of figuration directly, unapologetically, with verve and skill. For the most part, modern scholars—particularly modern scientists—do not. Instead they attack the myths of others, ignore their own, and pretend that they partake of practically none. A bigger mistake would be hard to imagine. Even at the humble level of prepositions, let alone at the sophisticated levels of concepts and theories, our languages are far too figural to reward abstinence from engaging this music of the night.[24] To re(con)figure government and other aspects of political communication is to play purposefully with our resources of myth.

Some of our best work is starting to explore how the individualist assumption that cognition precedes communication is no more valid or helpful than the holist postulate that communication precedes cognition. When we understand cognition in terms of schemas and associative networks generated in human interaction, we are ready to recognize such schemas and networks as the structures or webs of symbols that we call myths.[25] When we acknowledge that media can transmit messages from senders to receivers only where the senders and receivers already share the multitude of messages that just are the media, we are primed to appreciate how "the effects" of any individuated communication depend on "the effects" of prior communications. This means reconceiving the very idea of communication or media effects until it features the systemic communicational milieus that we now know to term myths.[26] And when we comprehend the manifold studies that imply why the location of people in abstracted spaces of beliefs, values, opinions, or attitudes seldom can give a good sense of who they are and how they act in politics or any other places, except interviews conducted by strangers, we are ripe to apprehend that any culture's recurrent scripts for personal identity and political action are exactly what we have long branded as myths.[27]

In short, myth is the word that we need in order to evoke the conditions and consequences of political cognition and communication. Myths are the metacommunications of culture and thus of politics. *Metabolisms* are immanent to bodies. They are not external monitors or outside programs for a body's internal dynamics; rather they are inside regulators that simply are the systems of interactions among body parts—conceived chemically, mechanically, and otherwise. Likewise, myths are immanent to persons and cultures. They are not outside governors or external determinants of a person's internal cognitions or a culture's internal communications; instead they are inside regulators that simply are the systems of interactions among mental and cultural structures—whether conceived intellectually, institutionally, behaviorally, or otherwise. As metabolism permeates the body biological, so does myth permeate the body political. Thus myths are the varying but pervasive subtexts of all political communication.

Immersing Myths

You're in the myth now, you know, completely in the myth.
—Poul Anderson[28]

One way to pose current troubles in coming to terms with political communication is to consider how its figuration is thoroughly liberal. For years scholars have acknowledged liberalism as the mainstream or the hegemonic ideology of America. But scholars are not accustomed to confronting such liberalism in mythic terms. Then it shares the stage somewhat more generously with competing and collaborating networks of symbols and stories—such as republicanism, conservatism, socialism, and democratism. To provoke mythic considerations of these ideologies, let me offer a map table to evoke this mythic terrain of American politics. To articulate Table 8.1 would require a book of its own. Suffice it to say here that any such table can enable us to define by comparison and that this is a particularly apt way to conduct many tropal experiments.

Comparison is often the best strategy for myths, especially when outright narration is not practical. By labeling the major tropes or figures of American liberalism, Table 8.1 lets us highlight a few of the images and dynamics that configure American politics as representation—and thus as communication. To get beyond the hegemony of government as a Machine Man, as the table helps us to recognize, we need to augment our figures of representation, trust, consent, sovereignty, rights and institutions, persons, fear, morality, privacy, issues, negotiation, visuality, and more. We need alternatives or at least additions for some of our political situations.[29] Some needed tropes may come from extant, largely modern ideologies such as republicanism, conservatism, socialism, and democratism. But others, as the final chapter suggests, must come from political stands and stances yet to become prominent or even promulgated. Inventing alternatives and complements to existing figures of government and politics just *is* myth-making, pure and complex.

The advantage of a mythic emphasis on the admittedly intellectual construct of liberalism is that it directly engages the rhetoric of media, politicians, and scholars alike. These realms have important differences, but they often play out in terms of speech-in-action within our institutions configured liberally.[30] Moreover the language of liberalism readily puts us inside the problematics of political communication that most perplex our inquiry. Given what we know about their significance in advanced industrial politics, how can we imagine the media

Table 8.1. Tropes of Ideology

Political Ideology	Liberalism	Republicanism	Conservatism	Socialism	Democratism
Pervasive Political Purpose and Dynamic	Archetrope of REPRESENTATION	Archetrope of INVENTION	Archetrope of GOVERNANCE	Archetrope of SERVICE	Archetrope of PARTICIPATION
Mode of Political and Personal Ties	Intertrope of TRUST	Intertrope of RESPONSIBILITY	Intertrope of RESPECT	Intertrope of WELFARE	Intertrope of EXCHANGE
Measure for Action by Ordinary Members	Undertrope of CONSENT	Undertrope of EMULATION	Undertrope of DEFERENCE	Undertrope of ASSOCIATION	Undertrope of INTERACTION
Model of Political and Personal Ambition	Overtrope of SOVEREIGNTY	Overtrope of LEADERSHIP	Overtrope of REGULATION	Overtrope of POWER	Overtrope of CHOICE
Sources of Targets of Personal or Political Thought and Action	Prototrope of RIGHTS AND INSTITUTIONS	Prototrope of JUDGMENTS AND GESTURES	Prototrope of RITES AND TRADITIONS	Prototrope of REASONS AND ORGANIZATIONS	Prototrope of PRINCIPLES AND PEOPLES
Primordial Identity of the Individual	Pretrope of THE PERSON	Pretrope of THE CITIZEN	Pretrope of THE PLACE OR ROLE	Pretrope of THE COMRADE	Pretrope of THE HUMAN
Ground or Foundation for Politics and Backing for Argument	Metatrope of STATES OF NATURE	Metatrope of LESSONS OF HISTORY	Metatrope of PATTERNS OF PRACTICE	Metatrope of NEEDS OF CLASSES	Metatrope of DECISIONS OF VOTERS
Characteristic Principle of Action	Subtrope of FEAR	Subtrope of VIGILANCE	Subtrope of SUSPICION	Subtrope of ENVY	Subtrope of INTEREST
Standards and Styles of Communal Memory	Retrotrope of MORALS	Retrotrope of VIRTUES	Retrotrope of MORES	Retrotrope of ETHICS	Retrotrope of COMMUNITIES
Place to Enjoy Most of the Highest Goods	Topotrope of PRIVATE	Topotrope of PUBLIC	Topotrope of FAMILY	Topotrope of SOCIETY	Topotrope of POLITY
Keys to Decision and Explanation	Paratrope of ISSUES	Paratrope of CHARACTERS	Paratrope of STATIONS	Paratrope of CLASSES	Paratrope of VOICES
Norm for Reflection and Distribution	Intratrope of NEGOTIATION	Intratrope of DELIBERATION	Intratrope of DEMONSTRATION	Intratrope of ADMINISTRATION	Intratrope of PERFORMANCE
Tenor and Dynamic of Cultural Figuration	Hypertrope of VISUALITY	Hypertrope of ORALITY	Hypertrope of CONFORMITY	Hypertrope of VISUALITY	Hypertrope of PROXIMITY

as merely "mediations" between peoples and polities? Given what we know about how little citizens remember in the way of detailed data about politics and government, let alone how erratically they speak on such matters, how can we continue to write (and in the singular!) about "informed public opinion"? Given what we know about the methods of elections, surveys, focus groups, and censuses, how can we still speak of mandates, attitudes, individuals, and enumerations? Given what we know about latter-day developments in the specifically "civil" societies created by modern politics, how can we resist the movement to substitute language about late modern "mass" societies, with all their overtones of totalitarian control and quiescence? Yet—given what we know about the diverse construction, destruction, and negotiation of meaning by the "masses" themselves—how can we keep using such totalitarian terms? Given what we know about the many kinds and boundaries of publics in any liberal democratic society, how can we maintain the old terminology of public versus private? Yet—given what we know about the languages and mind-sets of citizens in all liberal democratic societies so far—how can we abandon such categories as irrelevant to political reality?[31] If nothing else, intentional immersion in the mythos of liberalism lets us convert these perplexities into problematics for our poetic research.

Measuring Humans

> They say that only mathematics can make sense of the physical world. Well, only poetry and music can make sense of the human world, because humans are the least rational of the animals and how else shall we symbolize their madness?
> —Poul Anderson[32]

Another way to configure our current mythic troubles of political communication is by sketching a comparison of the three main approaches among scholars. These conceptions and practices of mass communication raise troubling issues for recent theorists of democracy. For related reasons these notions do the same for recent theorists of rhetoric. And a similar situation is fast developing for scientists of political cognition. None of these projects is coming to adequate terms with the rhetorical and communal dynamics of myth, especially in conceiving new problematics for inquiry. This is unfortunate, because myth analysis proffers many advantages to the vigilant study of mass communication. But more than that, it is perverse, because myth-making provides crucial requirements for the virtuous practice of mass communication.

Recent theories of democracy favor small homogeneous communities in orderly dialogues on the way to public consensus. Or they evoke large polyglot societies in carnival confusion on the way to market rationality. For the communalists, mass communication means hordes of Kmarts and Wal-Marts, or Hitlers and Lenins, or crowds and consumers. These masses or mass makers trample the green congenial groves long nurtured for quietly logical conversation. For the pluralists, mass communication implies tyrannies of stupid states or big businesses or single-minded movements to regiment the free, colorful bazaars shrewdly constructed for richly commercial exchange.

Recent theorists of rhetoric love a few heroic individuals whose words might resound through the ages. Or they prize the many practical people whose native talk might become the material genius of history. For elitists, mass communication means loosing the great power of words over ordinary mortals from its proper sense of responsibility to great values or virtues. Or it suggests undistinguished speech smothering the vital and necessarily individual power of thought. For populists, mass communication connotes charismatic talk of freeing the great power of people by turning them away from communal standards and restraints. Or it denotes mistaking the patterns of pseudo-argument and action (imposed from above) for the genuinely common resources of rhetoric (generated from below).

Recent scientists of political cognition target atomic, anonymous individuals to explore elementary processes of thinking and interaction. Or they arrange small-group experiments to identify social dynamics of problem solving. Or they generate computer programs to simulate the knowledge and calculations of expert communities and individual types. For social psychologists, mass communication involves constructing and activating individual impressions and traits. Thus it serves as a recurrent but variant stimulus to personal schemas and particular responses. For students of artificial intelligence, mass communication includes creating associative networks, structuring social information, and producing political cognitions. Accordingly it functions as a permeating but instigating culture for both individual and community operations. Scientists of political cognition so far attend little to relationships between their individuals and small groups on the one side and the actual institutions and practices of politics on the other, but their assumptions seem conventionally representational and democratic.[33] Therefore their concerns for mass communication echo the distrust and denigration characteristic of most recent theories of democracy.

The point is that such conceptions of mass communication relate poorly to our actual practices and possibilities, especially in American politics. All three sets of studies suggest this insistently, though the lesson remains largely lost on the students. Worse, our experiences with mass communication mostly imply a set of political practices with a (distinctively liberal) language of self-understanding at war with their own tactics, activities, internal tales, and external results. These talk of themselves as "media" that "represent" the "government" to the "public," and vice versa. And all three sets of scholars frame their research in the same terms. But the actual practices depart markedly from this framework, and we can tell this from accounts of practitioners and students alike, even though neither group yet recognizes as much.

Consequently the best that late modern analysts are able to do with *mass communication* is to deplore our "spirals of silence" or deploy our categories of "ideology." The spirals of silence are real and revealing enough. But they have yet to prompt needed reconceptions of *public, opinion, mass, communication,* and the like.[34] Likewise, the resulting "critiques of ideology" help in some ways, and I would not have us do without them, but they still miss many dynamics and resources of myth. Worse, "ideology critique" perpetuates the late modern monomania that sees all "mass publics" as protototalitarian movements, regardless of their differences in historical genesis and trajectory. In turn, this makes all mass communication into an exercise in the (proto)totalitarian mobilization of atomized individuals—standing already lonely in the crowd or, as consumers, at least incipiently so. Because they leave us with no way to approve any mass communication, the ideological approaches yield us no way to criticize most mass communications intelligently.[35]

In terms at once historical and mythic, we could tell the tale of our political communication as a failure of the political principles and forms of modern government. From their gradual beginnings four or more centuries ago, modern states and politics have defined themselves less by their actual practices than by their avowed principles. Popular consent, national sovereignty, political representation, governmental regulation, personal interests, human rights, economic rationality, and related ideals are among the distinguishing marks of modern politics. So thoroughly do these norms shape modern questions and answers about community affairs that we heirs of modernity have trouble recognizing how our practices depart more and more from such principles.

To be sure, we castigate particular regimes, institutions, or situations for gross violations of modern norms. We denounce apartheid, imperialism, and military dictatorship for failing to meet minimum tests of legitimate governance; we fear Balkanization, terrorism, and civil war for failing to yield any effective governance at all. Yet these kinds of judgments obscure our more pervasive departures from modern principles of politics—because they implicitly normalize consent, sovereignty, representation, and the rest. Even the most negative of our pronouncements about present conditions treat these principles as the proper features for our governments. And the most pervasive of our comments portray them as the usual practices in our politics.

The point is not that such judgments err in their own terms but that they take the absence of consent, sovereignty, and so on to be exceptional and objectionable conditions on the modern scene. If outlaw governments or obnoxious politics offend by failing to respect consent, achieve sovereignty, provide representation, or the like, then our other governments and our ordinary politics surely succeed for the most part in observing these modern principles. At a minimum, we assume, there exist some paradigms (if not paragons) of modern politics—presumably inclining the United States of America. Moreover their main successes and failures plainly occur in the modern terms of consent, sovereignty, representation, and so forth. Where we fail to find these, we say that the real politics are perverse, nonexistent, or misunderstood: consent suffers corruption, sovereignty reaches limits, or representation goes unrecognized. In principle, therefore, we believe that most of our practices of government and politics are modern—or aspire to be. And we take *consent, sovereignty, representation, regulation, rights,* and the like to implicate plausible accounts of how our politics generally work: when they go well, when not, and why.

Perhaps these principles once made decent sense of modern politics and gave adequate direction to modern governments. In meanings specific to a number of earlier contexts, I am inclined to think that they did.[36] But our late modern conceptions of consent, sovereignty, and such have been abstracted far beyond those original contexts. This abstraction is itself a pervasive modern impulse (if not imperative), so I do not say that it violates the earlier meanings—only that it transmutes them. No doubt the results are sometimes to fit these concepts better to our conditions and occurrences later in modern times. But more often, I suspect, the changes leave modern principles increasingly confused or empty. No longer do they make good sense of our governments or give apt direction to our politics.

The abstraction aggravates and dramatizes troubles long festering in these modern concepts and principles. How can we construe *consent* in the mass societies of late modernity? What can *sovereignty* mean in a world of multinational states and corporations? What sense can it make for a politics routinely to celebrate the rights of individuals but to secure them through the rights of groups? Why can studies that show political representation as impractical, incoherent, or nonexistent present themselves insistently as paeans to representative government?

People oriented to posing such questions spot such contradictions and consternations of modern politics almost everywhere around us. They proliferate with each passing year. But most of us normalize modern principles too completely to notice how poorly they account for present politics. We simply "know" that our activities and institutions are modern. Thus we seldom see how little our governments work as modern governments or how much modern politics are no longer our politics.

Reconfigured mythically, postmodern communication and politics would imagine their very elements in different terms. These would undo our nearly exclusive reliance on the modern model of communication as mediation as representation as politicking in regard to government. By trying to perform and interpret our practices as consensual, sovereign, or representational, we keep twisting them back toward modern shapes. This does make the markers of modern government more apt than they might be otherwise, yet it also confuses more than it improves our conditions.

Dueling Myths

> *What I feel upon us is a gigantic conflict of . . . mystiques—a conflict so deep-going that human beings and whole civilizations are turning themselves willy-nilly into archetypes and reenacting immemorially ancient myths—for only myth and music can even hint at such truths.*
> —Poul Anderson[37]

So we slip largely unknowing into postmodern, even post-Western worlds. The atrocities and disasters of late modernity tell us that something might have gone desperately awry.[38] Totalitarianism, nuclear weapons, genocide, world wars, propaganda, environmental destruction, resource depletion: the litany of late modern troubles can depress us too much for the details to sustain our attention.[39] But why attend to them anyway, when modern principles leave us little constructive to do or say? Politically is there a bigger mythic question of the moment?

Modern maps of consent and governance, in particular, give scant guidance to postmodern politics. This is because modern spaces of consent and governance resolutely enforce dimensions of *above* or *below* and *outside* or *inside* that relate poorly to postmodern conditions and institutions for politics. Consent from below empowers governance from above. Power from outside produces and even controls changes inside.

The prime (mis)understanding of politics and government ties to the liberal, Archimedean ideal of power as leverage: standing far enough apart from something to move it as a whole and in control. The mythically obvious remedies for perversions of such power are to "stand beside" the other—not above or below—and to remove the oppressive boundaries between outside(rs) and inside(rs) by eliminating one or the other. Thus Marxians imagined that the properly socialist state would work itself out of a job as the outside supervisor of human development. First, it would step down from on high to stand beside ordinary citizens in a socialist democracy, and then it would wither away. This would put people into a condition of such intimate association that there would be no need for political mediation between them. With the medium withering away, sender and receiver can achieve, then, the ultimate for communion or community in sheer social unity, the apotheosis of modern communication.

Much the same goes for conceptual and practical perplexities in liberal attempts to construe power as influence: witness the famous fate of counterfactual inconclusiveness that befell Robert Dahl's definition of power in terms of one person's ability to get another to do something that the other would not have done otherwise.[40] Troubles with saying "who governs?" (in) America also arise from problematics of leverage, because they run directly into the practical limit that there is no (extracommunal) place to stand outside the society allegedly being leveraged. When we try to identify and to draw lines between the insiders who wield power and the outsiders manipulated by it, we learn that any boundaries soon waiver into others and then still others—in infinite regress—figuratively ad nauseam for the liberal literalists about individuals and institutions.

American federalists try to avoid such mythic difficulties by transforming the leverage figure into other tropes about countervailing authorities or powers. When they embody these other figures in stories about institutions that check and balance one another with regularity, they anticipate the artificial intelligence paradigm of governance as homeostatic regulation (summarized later), but then they also have to take their equilibria in such forms as "The Deadlock of Democracy."

When they don't, there seems little difference between their paradigm and that of liberal leverage: now we merely define a system of two (or more) levers, instead of one.

As mentioned, our political practices and sciences give us many reasons to doubt that such ideals ought to inform the normal practices of fully modern politics. Yet when we condemn obvious departures from modern principles of government and politics, whether in fact or norm, we miss how our mythic understandings in these terms remain aspects of our cultural realities. And when we try to discern fully figured alternatives already in practice, we tend to treat such ideals as accomplishments.

Here the easy example is the late liberal model of governance suggested by work on cybernetics and artificial intelligence. This replaces the classical liberal notion of control with routine monitoring for system variance unto failure. The governor (as on an engine to keep a car going 65 miles an hour) pursues homeostatis, regulating the system by producing adjustments to some prescribed equilibrium. How the equilibrium gets set and changed, though, remains outside the system of governance. Liberals would call it a question for private citizens, who are supposed to tell the government what to do. Intriguing and useful as this figure is, then, it remains within the liberal orbit.

There are four challenges of political myth-making for our times: to recognize modern myths as myths, transform them into new myths more adequate to our changed circumstances, augment them with further myths needed for the times ahead, and especially to remember that all these—including the ones we ourselves adopt, adapt, and create—remain myths. Specialists in political communication face four specific tasks in meeting these challenges. We need to come to terms with how the media aren't media, how representatives don't and can't represent, and how government doesn't govern. Moreover we should strive to replace mere attitudes and opinions with more articulated, argumentative dynamics as targets of attention by scholars, reporters, and politicians alike. We must work to understand the diverse kinds of masses and publics capable of making and living postmodern and post-Western myths. At the other end of the channel between sender and receiver, we need to reconceive the diverse kinds of governments that actually figure in political communication. The rhetorical trouble so far, we might say, is that all masses have been created equal (or at least treated equal) and that all publics have been homogenized, then condensed into one. Mythically, however, neither masses nor publics are homogeneous (let alone singular)—and our rhetorics need to learn what this means.

How can we meet these challenges? A creative emphasis on myth can be carried forward critically and inventively through attention to our four moments of rhetoric: ethos, logos, pathos, and mythos. The first three are classical and the last more recent as a rhetorical interest.[41] Here we can pursue these through attention to topics, tropes, stories, and styles. To rework modern government, then, we should reconceive the central, sovereign, ruling state through inventing different topics, new tropes, original stories, and strange styles of political communication.

Rhetorically topics are places. And our new places for political communication may be marginal, interstitial, and dispersed in comparison to the modern state. I suspect that they might even be proliferated and disseminated as many kinds of publics and issues. Imagine the media as an octopus with tentacles that intrude and connect almost everywhere, or even as the fluids that flow into or float most vessels in our oceans of political culture and cultural politics (see Figure 8.5).

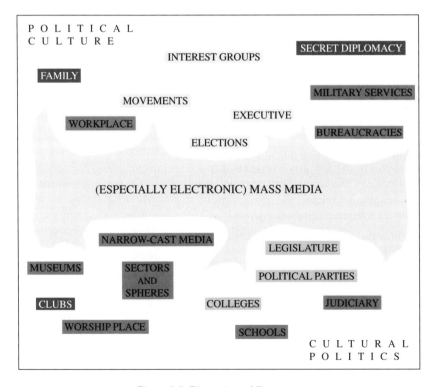

Figure 8.5. Disseminated Democracy

At a minimum, though, the media would need to become self-transforming places, as environmentalists now understand population niches to be.[42]

Tropes are the figures we have been investigating throughout this essay. More generally, they are turns, moves, or dynamics—whether in awareness, language, or argument. They trace figures in space. They even define specific spaces with their moves. Yet turns also happen in and on places, of course, so that tropes and topics connect intimately. Hence we need new images of governments and states. But we might benefit as well from new configurations in place of states and governments. Hence the next section begins to flirt with a few.

STORIES ARE EVENTS FOR CHARACTERS IN SETTINGS, as Kenneth Burke might say. Modern sciences often seem to destroy societies and perhaps to destroy them in the process. As rhetoric of inquiry may demonstrate, however, the dimension of narrative is more persistent than the mythos of modernity recognizes—and stories remain, at least implicitly, as important aspects for even the most scientistic of texts.[43] The mythic attention to story suggests that one good way to get beyond political perplexities of modern communication is, literally and literarily, to *characterize* political institutions and actors in ways other than as the modern state, the Machine and Man writ large as the liberal Sovereign.

And styles are the forms-with-content that virtually comprise the actual conduct of many politics. Modern liberalism configures politics as sets of mere styles in the conduct of truly substantive government. Then governments are the containers, the vessels, while politics are the fluids and ephemeral machinations that flow around and through them. Or governments are the relatively fixed structures, with politics the less solid functions and effects. By contrast, modern conservatism stylizes the government itself—treating states as textures of illusion or myth. In this dimension, too, there are many promising resources for restyling government in order to re(con)figure political communication.

Strange Attractors

It is indeed disturbing to find oneself in a foreign myth.
—Poul Anderson[44]

Discomfort with liberal figures of governance is a practical part of our present situations. Self-professed conservatives fret about ungovernable claims and movements overloading the capacity of a central state to manage them. On the ideological left, the worries tend toward an abdication of state responsibility in ignoring social problems.[45] Both sides insist on the representational truism that the government is us consenters, so that these are personal as well as political troubles. "As citizens in a democracy, we have been the authors of the situation we are in, and we won't begin to find our way out of it until we begin to demand a style of governance that emphasizes both accountability and steadfast commitment to long-term goals," says *The New Yorker*'s "Talk of the Town."[46] In part, these troubles result from deficiencies in our liberal myths for politics and communication. In part, they produce those deficiencies. And in some ways, they simply are the deficiencies. One way or another, nonetheless, we need to generate further figures—postliberal figures—to enhance the present play of alternatives.

A particularly intriguing possibility to scholars of political communication is bound to be Jean Baudrillard's notion of seduction, because it stems from his meditations on mass media and American politics in particular.[47] Murray Edelman's persuasive reading of Baudrillard and Guy Debord leads to the "political spectacle" that leaves us with little hope of improvement or even transformation.[48] Yet surely we ought to go further in provoking other figures before resigning ourselves to such a recommendation.

Far more than committing ourselves intellectually or politically to some single alternative, we need to play with possibilities. Let us invent new images from old; let us generate strange places from familiar settings. Let us entertain figures foreign to our myths of modernity, along with stories alien to modern lives. We may find surprising fits—and starts and failures and futures in such expressly poetic politics.

Inventing figures of government might not be the easiest thing for us to do, especially for specialists in politics and communication whose disciplines have been constituted by modern liberalism. Constituted as a classical discipline instead, rhetoric often makes (Greek) *mimesis* or (Roman) *imitatio* a path into invention. This is the mode long known to Anglo-American students of Latin. To learn good rhythms of English—let alone of Latin—prose, the student copies long sections from the works of Caesar and Cicero. Gradually such exercises cultivate in the student such a thorough feeling for their Latinate sentences that later phrases originating with the student in English pay unconscious tribute to this training. In much the same fashion, gener-

ations of would-be essayists and novelists have reproduced their inspirations word by word. Then they have moved on to mimic the styles
of their models as writers. These traditions suggest that we might try
to invent better figures of government by adopting the discipline of
congenial forms already devoted to inventing useful figures or images
for our times. Modeling our work on theirs, we might adapt these figures to characterizing anew the media and governments and other
parts of political communication in our times.

Such a strategy puts a premium on selecting good models, and this
is where Pollitt's poem reenters the story. Borrowing its form, we
might try to walk with Hanna Pitkin beyond familiar modern ruminations on the Machiavellian politics of realist or republican hardball by
projecting another version of the Pollitt poem to wonder "What if
Fortuna was never a beautiful woman?"[49] Or we might, as the chapter's title suggests, try tropal alterations that target government. Ponder how intelligible and provocative even a minimally changed edition
can be:

> What if the government
> was never a machine or a man?
> Call it a shark shearing across black water.
> An ear. A drum in a desert.
> A window. A bone shoe.
>
> What if the public
> was discovered to have no voice?
> Let it be clouds, blue as the day they were born.
> A ceremony of bells and questions.
>
> What if a people
> is not a government or a public?
> Say map of the air. Say green parabola.
> Lichen and the stone that feeds it.
> No rain. Rain.

For government, though, we may hope to do even better with a language less oriented to objects, to nouns and adjectives. Look at what
only a few more verbs, a little more activity, can accomplish:

> What if the government
> was never a machine or a man?
> Call it a seduction among strangers.
> An eye. A drum in a forest.
> A movie. A blue sky.

What if the public
was discovered to have no voice?
Let it be dreams, still as the night of their deed.
A ritual of polls and mandates.

What if a people
neither governs nor speaks?
Say rides with the storm. Say spirals unwinding.
Acting and the stage that plays it.
No change. Change.

As the preceding sections explain, continuing inquiries into political communication in our electronic polities and postmodern societies yield strong reasons to displace the conventional modern metaphors featured in the first two lines for each of the three stanzas. The hope is that fresher, more mysterious metaphors in the finishing lines of each stanza might provoke better senses of how postmodern politics already proceed or post-Western politics could be enacted. Let them be more activating, more accurate, more apt than the tropes they might try to supplant.

What if we turn to the Western politics of boundaries, especially the late modern mania for sovereign divisions of nationalist politics? Then we might enter the territory of "Border Figures."

What if the border
was never a dividing line?
Call it a question awaiting many answers.
A c(h)ord. A vein in a body.
A shadow. An ink spill.

What if the edge
was discovered to have no end?
Let it be turns, deft as the rivers we run.
A rollercoaster of gains and losses.

What if a border
is not the stop or the start?
Say tale of the tape. Say strange curriculum.
Whispers and the tongue that shapes them.
No fringe. Friend.

This game of political invention is great to play. Once you get into Pollitt's provocative rhythm, the tropes tumble out nearly on their own.

As I finish this chapter, I am teaching a course on environmental action and persuasion. We have just discussed Aldo Leopold's "The

174

Land Ethic" and now are reading Michael Pollan on trees and tropes
and garden tours.[50] How could I resist regaling the class with "Garden
Grounds"?

> What if the land
> was never a biblical garden?
> Call it a lab keeping us in the test tube.
> An ethic. A peel on an apple.
> A goddess. A gravity well.
>
> What if the plant
> was detected to have no root?
> Let it be words, deep as ideas on a page.
> A branching of probes and symbols.
>
> What if a garden
> is not the land or the plant?
> Say tour of the year. Or lawn run riotous.
> Image and the eye that needs it.
> Left brain. Right.

The ruminations that preface these experiments in refiguration suggest at least a few of the meanings and reasons for playing around
with such adaptations of the Pollitt poem. One way to end these experiments would be to explicate my poor poems, yet it is well known
among practitioners of poetry and other figural literature that this responsibility falls more effectively to readers than to authors.

Instead let me end by reporting that I recently began an advanced
course on postmodern politics and communication with this very exercise in re(con)figuring modern government and politics. Because the
exercise started the term, the students had minimal priming from
their erstwhile instructor. Given only the Pollitt poem, my two steps
in rewriting it, and the mandate to use it as a model for reimagining
modern politics, the class surprised me with a host of provocative
possibilities.

One poem of postmodern possibilities for politics came from a
second-year graduate student fascinated by feminist re-visions of
power:

> What if power
> was never an apple pie?
> Call it dough rising.
> A hand. A river roaring through canyons.
> A horizon. Hammer and nails.

What if ruling
was discovered to have no fist?
Let it be a story, retold by many voices.
A ceremony of washing feet.

What if power
is not a pie or a fist?
Say green branch budding. Say multiplication.
Daily bread and the children fed by it.
No force. Force.

A second rewriting of Pollitt enabled a sophomore to express some common frustrations about how we construct our political spectacle:

What if politics
never led to conflict?
Never a slanderous accusation ending in denial.
No hype. A boring media event.
A sideshow. Back-page news.

What if candidates
weren't dragged down by labels?
Let them be judged by their qualities and values.
Men/women of integrity and trustworthiness.

What if political conflict
was recognized as garbage?
Call them spineless. Say there's no set agenda.
Figureheads and the bureaucracy that runs the
    show.
No politics. Anarchy.

A third offering came from a junior environmentalist, and several other poems mined much the same vein:

What if the earth
was never a mother?
Call it a ball bouncing through space.
A severed toe. A moment of silence.
A floor. A dirty napkin.

What if the earth
was discovered to be a battered child?
Let him be lost and abandoned, wandering in the
    dark.
A mind full of questions erased before asking.

> What if the earth
> is not a mother or her child?
> Say empty page. Say dented sphere.
> Father fast fun and run.
> No life. Life.

Another junior targeted the modern American mythology of elections and mandates:

> What if an election
> did never decide the winner?
> Call it pacification of closed minds.
> A Greek lesson. A poll.
> A cat flaunting. Dan's hairdye.

> What if the purpose
> was never founded in virtue?
> Let it be self-anointment, pursuit of happiness.
> To consecrate by unction and truth.

> What if the majority
> does not choose by evident intent?
> Say token placebo. Say Lucy and a football.
> Scarecrow in a rock garden.
> Choice. No Choice.

A sophomore's political poem made similar concerns even more plaintive:

> What if an election
> was never the will of the people?
> Call it an exclusionary club.
> An ivory tower. A barrier.
> A dividing wall.

> What if a vote
> was discovered to carry no weight?
> Let it be an unheard voice.
> Unheeded bells and whistles.

> What if representative government
> is gained neither by votes nor an election?
> Say undemocratic. Say utopia.
> Say family and the heritage that feeds it.
> No change. Change.

Somewhat in the spirit of Susan Sontag's plaintive cries against the capacity of social metaphor to turn cancerous,[51] a senior wondered:

What if Lady Liberty
was never a beautiful woman?
Call her guardian of the gates of hell.
A statue. A buoy in a bay.
A wall. Nothing.

What if this land
was discovered to have no milk and honey?
Let it be a desert, dry as the sand that fills it.
A queue of confusion and questions.

What if America
is neither justice nor opportunity?
Say desolation. Isolation.
Revolution and the hunger that feeds it.
No peace. Peace.

If government as a shark shearing across black water is not enough of the libertarian politics so popular on college campuses for more than a decade, a senior asked:

What if the government
was never a caring friend?
Call it a hustler sneaking around a pool hall.
A hood. A con artist.
A thief. A liar.

What if this body politic
was found to have no heart?
Let it be a leech, hungry as could be.
A session of doubt and controversy.

What if the government
is not a hustler or a leech?
Say failing corporation. A dying species.
A scavenger feeding off the sick and dead.
No money. Money.

Relatedly a junior challenged the Weberian model of mass organization for our times:

> What if bureaucracy
> was never a decision tree?
> Call it Atlas without arms.
> A mask. A decaying body.
> A broken glass. A thorn.
>
> What if bureaucrats
> were discovered to have no faces?
> Let them be death, the eternal ending of dreams un-
> realized.
> A procession of worn, cold feet.
>
> What if bureaucracy
> is neither tree or mystery?
> Say elaborate sewer system. Say infant crying.
> Communion of demon-flesh.
> No creation. Creation.

Likewise, a first-year graduate student offered "Metonyms of Love," useful to read also as better metaphors of communication:

> What if sharing
> was never a giving birth?
> Call it a word of solitude and certainty,
> So buried in its night that it is barely audible to itself.
> A word of refusal. A bond of silence.
> The silence of bond. A sacrifice.
>
> What if creation
> was discovered to have no womb?
> Let it be the empty space of a missing tome,
> between one book and the next,
> linking only one of the two.
> A battle with every shadow, taking them to our-
> selves.
>
> What if a mother
> is not sharing or creation?
> Say map of the air. Say green parabola.
> Lichen and the stone that feeds it.
> No rain. Rain.

And one senior even took on the whole mythos of modernity, history, and science:

What if the new
was not an edge, was not cutting?
Call it Indian Summer. A lost ball in high weeds.
A match. A young jay.

What if our theories
were not explored by pioneers in frontier
    singularity?
Let them be rivers fed by streams.
Frames in a gallery. Birds on a line.

What if the latest idea
is not cutting edge or frontier?
Say hand clapping silently.
Molecricket and ant. Weeds of the ricefield.
Rain. No rain.

These are only ten out of four times that many generated in a few minutes by one class. But surely they suggest that the challenge of inventing better figures of government and political communication is not beyond our abilities. And now it is your turn.

9 TURNING DELIBERATIONS INTO DEBATES

A DIALOGICAL DECONSTRUCTION OF SENATE RITUALS OF COMITY

*How much the Druids . . . left behind: kissing under the
mistletoe, throwing spilled salt over your shoulder,
gargoyles as a civilized alternative to displaying the
severed heads of your enemies above your roof, even calling
two weeks a fortnight, since the Druids measured time by
nights rather than days. Druids never wrote anything
down, perhaps as an aid to memory. They often spoke in
triads, since three was their sacred number.*
—Ramsey Campbell[1]

Some analysts—often anthropologists—emphasize ties between myths and rituals to the point that they virtually reduce myth to "the spoken correlative of the acted rite, the thing done."[2] Although sometimes overdone by its enthusiasts, such "ritual-dominant" treatments of myth can be "a helpful corrective to the earlier view that myth was primarily or exclusively a verbal or literary phenomenon."[3] Here the project is to repoeticize the ties between myth and ritual in order to revitalize our understanding of some staid rituals in the politics of the United States.

In particular, let us change from an established conclusion to an explorable possibility the nostrum of the Myth and Ritual School that "myth regarded as a statement in words 'says' the same thing as ritual regarded as a statement in action."[4] To do this, let us reverse the usual direction for reading this claim, so that we move from ritual to myth even more than the other way around. For then we can produce what rhetoricians would do well to recognize as a first-rate mode of mythical and analytical invention. To compound the rhetorical interest in such a move, let us notice that the invention in this case can proceed through a playful dialogical deconstruction of rituals into tropes.

Greater mythic and tropal attention to political rituals especially commends itself as a way to overcome the modern prejudice that myths are simply mistakes—either former truths now outdated or errors all along.

Whoa! Wait a minute! you interject. How did we go so fast from ritual and myth to rhetoric? you wonder. Isn't rhetoric about argument in particular or talk in general? What do myths—let alone rituals—have to do with arguments? Aren't myths stories rather than arguments? And why connect ritual as repetitive action with rhetoric as strategic talk or argument? What can we gain by moving quickly among these very different things, especially in connection with politics?

A great deal, I would answer—except that I should not concede the presupposition (common in our times) that ritual, myth, and rhetoric are three different things that ordinarily have little to do with one another. In one of the few books specifically about political myth, Henry Tudor has explained that "myth is a common but neglected type of political argument."[5] And in a series of popular columns, Roland Barthes showed how we argue politically with gestures, posters, faces, films, and other mythic devices.[6] So it may not be as odd as it sounds to propose a bit of reflection on *how we argue politically with rituals,* particularly because I suggest that we learn to read rituals as myths.

Here I am punning on *with,* and I try to make good on the puns later in the essay. We argue politically with rituals in the sense of wielding them as devices of argument. As myths, such rituals serve our political arguments as topics or themes, as tropes or figures, as plots or genres, and so on. We argue politically *with* rituals by using them as media of argument: persuading *through* rituals, we might call this. In addition, we argue politically with rituals by developing them as fields or forums of argument: persuading *within* rituals, we might say. And finally, all three of these dynamics for reading rituals as myths as arguments depend on a fourth dynamic of pitting some myths (or their elements) against others in mythic criticism. In late and postmodern conditions, at least, this is a matter of "arguing with rituals" in the sense of disputing or criticizing some aspects of rituals with others. The criticism opens enough distance between present rituals and their commonplace myths to create a field for further readings of those rituals—readings at once mythic and argumentative. Thus we argue with our rituals as myths in order to separate mythic words and deeds somewhat in the fashion of the Myth and Ritual School of myth criticism.

Attention to rites, rituals, and other dimensions of conduct can commend itself to us in contrast with the modern inclination to separate thought from action or theory from practice.[7] Thus modern treatments tend to equate myths and beliefs—where the beliefs become conceived as analytically separate and substantially independent from whatever behavior might issue from the believers. These same modern treatments tend to equate myths and mistakes (as beliefs we can know to be false).[8] To the contrary, the emphasis on actual practice steps around the modern prejudice that myths are subtly or spectacularly mistaken beliefs, because it features the meaning (implicit) in sustained patterns of behavior. Then the behavior is not so much true or false as it is simply there, intriguing in its strange but inescapable reality. Attunement to ritual can enable analysts of myth to turn from the modern epistemic interest in (evidencing or explaining) a myth's falsehood to the late modern interpretive challenge of (explicating or enhancing) a myth's meaning.

To be sure, the Myth and Ritual School typically fails to take full advantage of this difference in orientation. Insistently it targets behavioral patterns that it displays initially as bizarre unto irrational—until we learn from the analyst to interpret them in terms of some old, obscure, or alien beliefs that we modern people can now reconstruct. These beliefs formed the myths that helped to originate those mysterious routines, which somehow persist into the present day. These myths help to make sense of the otherwise weird rites, rituals, and traditions that either characterize other cultures or linger largely unnoticed within our practices. At the same time, however, such beliefs almost always betray their implausibility. Only if you were to believe these (plainly false) things, could you or would you do those (previously inexplicable) deeds, go through those (otherwise arbitrary) motions, and so forth. Or so the Myth and Ritual School implies.

Why do we kiss under the mistletoe? All unknowing, we follow the superstitions of the Druids, who believed mistletoe to bless new love in its proper season.[9] Why do some people throw spilled salt over their shoulders? Yes, they learned the habit ritualistically, unaware of its original meaning. But still they are aping the Druids, who believed in spreading misfortune and putting it immediately behind them. Why do the preachers, professors, and other public speakers of Britain and the United States favor three principles, particulars, or examples at a time? Presumably Druid rites of three-speaking have worked to rhythm our oratory for many centuries—to the point where the oratory can exploit such resources for an established style as elective affinity and prefigured memory.[10] For most of us, the Druid reasons for talking in terms of threes are "mere myths," lost in the mists of history. Yet the archaeologist and the paleoanthropologist can tease Druid beliefs from various artifacts, helping us to make sense of Druid rites and present rituals of three-speaking. And without this help our traditions would remain odd, unexplained, even unjustified in our midst—if ever we happened to take thought and notice them. So reasons the Myth and Ritual School.

Mis-Stake

> *One definition of a ritual would be: a circumstance in which images fall into an order that makes deep sense. One definition of television would be: an unsuccessful ritual; or a ritual that works only for the priests.*
> —George W. S. Trow[11]

Some members of the Myth and Ritual School balk even at the conceptual distinction between myths and rituals. But ours have been modern times—when words and deeds, prescriptions and performances, accounts and actualities are kept separate in concept because they so often seem distanced in experience. Starting thus with the distinction, modern analysis moves to specify the relationship. We should recognize as well that to characterize the rituals as "related" to (their) myths is not to imply some connection given in a reality that endures apart from (our) myths. No such relationships can be inscribed in nature—divinely, materially, or otherwise. Nor can any be (pre)established, apart from human invention and interpretation. Such relationships are instead artifacts—or, better, dynamics—of the myths themselves. Again etymology is revealing: mythos in ancient Greek writing means a 'tale uttered by the mouth', specifically a 'relating'.[12] And today we have all the more reason to understand relatings as recountings. This is to say, as accounts or narratives or stories—and therefore potentially as myths.[13] Even conceived as separable from the myths, of course, the rituals are themselves discursive—encouraging us to regard them also as sources of their own relationships to myths: a disposition that grows stronger as we move past the modern dichotomies such as myth versus ritual.

Most practitioners read myths as rituals. They use (the meanings of) rituals as guides for interpreting (the meanings of) myths rather than the other way around. And thus they treat particular myths as the verbal forms, accompaniments, or residues of specific rituals—which they regard as activities instead of stories (or even words). Want to understand enduring American stories of climbing the corporate ladder or of thanking God for abundant provisions? Then read them, respectively, in terms of the rites of business organization (dressing for success, doing the first assignment, navigating a staff meeting, surviving the company picnic) or the rituals of holiday dining (dividing the labor, grouping by age, eating before football, reheating the leftovers).

Thus the myth analyst can focus elusive patterns of story through the lens of accessible ritual. Presumably the analyst equally could clarify patterns of ritual practice with help from accounts in mythic narratives, but the ritual-dominant analyst rarely features moves in that direction. First comes the myth, as a set of symbols (capable of being) included in a story—but where the symbolism remains unusually debatable. Then the analyst identifies a plausible candidate for the ritual source (or association) of the myth. And thereafter the analyst explicates the ritual and the myth in tandem—to show how they depend on each other in practice, manifest the same structure, fulfill the same function, or otherwise cohere. Yet almost always the analyst interprets the myth in terms of the ritual, taking the (interpreted) ritual as the nexus and template of meaning for (interpreting) the myth.

On this account, the rituals can persist and reproduce themselves so successfully precisely because their actions easily (or at least eventually) separate from their beliefs. Often this happens even for the words. The mythic chants and incantations—the blessings, curses, invocations, charms, and all the rest—that originally accompanied the physical motions become lost, while the physical movements remain. The movements get staked out or nailed down—because they are behavioral or material—whereas the ephemeral, evanescent words blow loose, change responsively as situations change, or simply evaporate. Then we learn no words to join with throwing salt over the shoulder or kissing under the mistletoe. In other cases we do remember words, but they sound to us like nonsense poems or nursery rhymes—always just on the verge of making sense without ever quite doing so.[14] Or we may have literalized the verbal formulae, retaining ready access to conventional meanings while losing the "original" (poetic or historical) meanings. Hence the (behavioral) rituals become mistakenly fixed or fixed in mistaken ways, whereas the (verbal) myths evolve more freely and rapidly, metamorphosing into later myths or sciences.

Notice, however, the modern complications in inferring from ritual to myth when we assume the modern gap between words and deeds. And note how the complication becomes convolution and even consternation when we acknowledge the mutual suspicion unto revulsion between thought and action characteristic of some brands of modernism (especially late and perhaps even post). This is a reason for wary care in the inference from ritual to myth, and it is a reason for inferring equally from myth to ritual. More than that, it is a requirement for sophistication in identifying bodies of ritual and myth to match with one another. But most of all, it is a mandate for distrust of the myth/ritual contrast as a specifically and lamentably modern remnant—the close equivalent of modern dichotomies between word and deed, thought and action, mind and body, culture and nature, and so on and so forth.

Rarely do analysts—from the Myth and Ritual School or any other approach—read rituals as myths; rarely do they generate or invent the myth from the ritual. Analysts often extrapolate the (alleged) meanings of a myth (already identified) from some (arguably) associated ritual, but seldom do they explicate (or extrapolate?) the myth itself from a set of rituals. Furthermore the few analysts who do feature the move primarily from rituals to myths tend to be iconographers rather than mythographers. They regard rites or other ritual(ized) objects as mythic images supercharged with symbolic significance—often, though not always, religious (or dogmatically ideological) at root. Then they deemphasize verbal symbolism and the tropal dynamics of words in favor of visual imagery and the pictorial implications of sights. This can reify words into objects, arrest gestures into statues, and generally transmute active figures into passive sights.[15]

The Myth and Ritual School, by contrast, tends to assume that its target myths and rituals already have separated from each other. It takes the myths and related rituals to diverge as thoughts can distance themselves from actions or words from deeds. Consequently the school's readings of rituals in terms of (but seldom as) myths imply that the myths and perhaps even the rituals have been riddled (in both senses) with mistakes.

Myth-Take

A man who never makes mistakes has long since ceased to do anything new. A man who is always making mistakes is a doomed man with swollen ambitions. But he who judiciously salts success with mistake is the rapid learner.
—Donald Kingsbury[16]

Accordingly the school works to supply the (verbal) myths that can make sense of the (physical) rituals. Sometimes it turns to verbal sources largely separate from the behavioral rituals to explicate stories or beliefs that might make sense of the deeds repeated. Even with such independent guidance, however, the school must read the (target) rituals as performances of the (explanatory) myths. This gives us confidence that each myth fits with its rituals. In more than a few cases, though, the school's virtuoso analysts read the meanings—and therefore myths—directly from the rituals. What story or pattern does the ritual enact? ask these analysts. The more complicated the ritual, and the more adequately its details appear in the putative myth, the more persuasive the reading.

The reading of rituals as myths proceeds abductively. Attention shuttles between particulars of the ritual and details of the analyst's reading—under development as the related myth. The very separation of belief from action that enables and necessitates reading rituals this way implies that they might become corrupted, diverging in transmission from the behavioral details that fit with the meanings of the ritual as originally practiced. On the one hand, this suggests that a reading becomes more reliable as the details of the ritual that it explains become more complicated—and therefore as inventing alternate readings becomes more difficult. But on the other hand, this abductive procedure admits that the analyst may need at times to "correct" the ritual itself (as well as the reading, the myth). Thus the analyst might postulate that some of the ritual's current details have been lost or modified from the early "original" pattern of conduct clarified by the myth.

Why not, then, read our own (present) rituals, rites, or other regularities of conduct as myths? This approach can be especially promising when there might seem something odd about how the ritual proceeds, how its words match its acts, or the like. But the reading of rituals as myths should generate insights even where we do not start with a sense of tension between the ritual as performed and its related beliefs, verbal accounts, occasions or effects, and the like. To be sure, the myth inference here risks the movement from myth analysis to myth-making that I like to term *myth-taking*. Yet that seems an inevitable and acceptable aspect of the rhetorical invention we pursue when reading rituals as myths.

Unfortunately the Myth and Ritual School seldom takes this step or even prepares us for it. Rather the school typically sets aside current rites, rituals, and other patterns of behavior that (seem to) make sense without resort to odd beliefs from days gone by or ways still obscure. Rarely does it take current activities as candidates for interpretation by—or as—myths. Thus does a promising approach lose much of its potential for learning about our own myths by reading them from present rites, rituals, and routinized conduct of various kinds. Notwithstanding the school's neglect of present rituals, we can easily imagine how to walk this road not taken.

To judge from work by various members of the Myth and Ritual School, the situation most congenial for reading our own rituals as myths is when we have long performed an activity unreflectively, then stop to take stock of it. If our first thoughts about its meaning or rationale generate no plausible account that readily fits conventional wisdom, we might take it to need the amplification of some original myth. When an activity is familiar and produces few problems for us, though, we take its reasons to need no quotation marks for alerting any unwary readers that defective beliefs might be at work.

Surely, we might say, the current newspaper rite of printing issue summaries shortly before elections serves the needs of readers. We take the readers to be citizens, who seek representation as constituents, and who therefore are potential electors. Surely they need and want to know the positions of the major candidates. Any candidate, after all, is a putative leader and potential official; one or another of the candidates will soon be our political representative. Surely political officials should represent our positions (as citizens) on the issues? Well, then, we need inquire no further about the rationality of this newspaper rite: it makes obvious sense as a device for political representation in our democracy. But is it part of our mythos of representation or democracy? you want to ask. Well, maybe, but why have recourse to talk about myths when our conduct is so clear in meaning, familiar in defense, and rational in belief? Only when we want to contradict such conventional wisdom would we have reason to speak of myths. So if someone were to detail persuasively how newspaper information about electoral issues misleads more than it informs, or how elections seldom concern issues anyway, then might we agree on a need to read the newspaper rite of issue summaries as (part of) some myth? Perhaps, but surely it is simpler and just plain saner to concede that few arrangements do work perfectly—or need to work perfectly in order to deserve their usual names and descriptions. Surely we need not invoke some arcane myth to make sense of these familiar patterns of political conduct?

As it happens, of course, I am inclined to argue in detail that we have strong reasons for persuasive arguments against the "simple rationality" of newspaper issue summaries for elections. Mercifully, though, I am content to leave such arguments to another occasion.[17] The point here is that we have ample reasons to read our rites and rituals as myths, even when we do not take them to stem from mistaken beliefs.

De-Liberation

> *The flow of words became formalized, condensed, blunt, then*
> *slowly, in a back and forth ritual, was forged into poetry.*
> —Donald Kingsbury[18]

One candidate for political mythhood almost independent of its ritual enactment is something that we may term the *myth of Senate deliberation.* This myth might seem to present exactly the kind of tension between words and deeds that could encourage us to (re)read the ritual as a symbolic story significantly different from the one usually propagated in summaries of the Senate at work. As separate from the ritual itself, the myth of Senate deliberation suggests that the U.S. Senate accomplishes its work primarily through a sustained flow of discourse back and forth among senators, usually on the floor of the Senate. Let us explore, therefore, how reading the ritual of Senate deliberation as a republican myth of Senate deliberation can reconfigure the verbal account that (myth-takingly) informs much commentary on the Senate by journalists, academicians, citizens, and even politicians.

According to the verbal myth, encouraged by the Founders' sense of legislatures, U.S. Senate deliberation gradually enlightens the participants and leads them to agreements—occasionally consensual and usually wise—on what to do about the public issues of the day. There is ample evidence that this is a political myth in the (late modern) perspectival sense of a 'belief held widely'—if weakly, vaguely, or diffusely—'by members of the political community' called 'the United States of America'. Moreover what we know about the patterns of debate and discussion among senators even makes the narrative implicit in this picture of Senate deliberation a strong candidate for political mythhood in the (perversely modern) sense of a 'mistake made routinely by members of the political culture'. Yet the behavioral and verbal myths interact in significant ways to give us the very Senate that we Americans love to scorn and respect in almost the same breath.

Our lore and textbooks about U.S. government agree that Congress, especially the Senate, is a deliberative body. The sheer existence of such an epithet unto chant is a nearly infallible mark of myth. So strongly, in fact, does the persistence of such a pat phrase evidence the presence of one or more associated myths that any citations for its occurrence usually seem superfluous. As with many myths, consequently, we may say that the myth of Senate deliberation is so widespread that the very language tells its existence, by sustaining the cliché. At times, in fact, rhetoric textbooks or even newsmagazines tell us the meaning of this formula by relating how some great speech by Henry Clay, Daniel Webster, Hubert Humphrey, or other rapturous orator led the way toward landmark legislation.

What brings all this to mind is the way in which several months reverberated with newspaper and television compendiums of this mythic account of Senate deliberation—and some other standard but telling tales of U.S. politics—in connection with congressional debates over approval for the Bush war against Saddam Hussein in the Persian Gulf. To hear both participants and commentators tell of those debates, they worked as in the words of Donald Kingsbury: "in a back and forth ritual" on the way to some political equivalent of "poetry." The many exchanges on the Senate floor helped to refine not just the positions and reasons of individual senators but also the positions and reasons of the Senate as an institution. Such deliberations can look confusing and disorderly, but they follow logics of learning through challenges and replies that eventually lend a measure of wisdom to decisions by the institution. (And since the war turned out so well, you observe with a full measure of irony but only a little of sarcasm, surely later events have fortified this verbal myth of Senate wisdom through deliberation.)

We know, however, that we can rely on many a historian to debunk any such case in point as far more complicated—or interest oriented or pressure politicked or otherwise determined—than the mythical account of primarily (let alone purely) persuasive discourse would imply. We can expect political scientists without number to add that the volume of Senate work is too huge for genuine deliberation on the floor, that committees do most congressional business, that senators seldom have time even to stay on the floor and hear speeches by their colleagues, that they vote according to simple cues from powerful politicians (or senior staffers or public pollsters) rather than complex speeches from eloquent colleagues, and so on and on. Moreover we can always find a journalist, columnist, or other paid political analyst to sneer truthfully that Senate speeches have become primarily a species of posturing for the media—making at most a minor contribution to "the political spectacle" in (or of) the United States.[19] We may not think daily about these alternate accounts, but we do not find it hard to acknowledge that they tend to override the lore of legislative deliberation. (Please remember that the overriding is itself a mythic move, arising from other standard stories of big organizations, interest politics, and the like.)

For a first stab at these mythic matters, we can set aside for now the admittedly legitimate question of whether a deliberative Congress or Senate is likely to prove good for U.S. government, particularly in matters of war. More than a few partisans of presidential decision hold that our late modern conditions generally require for international relations far greater dispatch, secrecy, univocality, and the like than either house of Congress could achieve even in the absence of genuine deliberation—which is bound to be slow, public, equivocal (or at least plurivocal), and so on. A more adequate assessment of the myth of Senate deliberation would need to address such issues far more directly and extensively than seems desirable here.

Mythically, though, the clincher might be what we know firsthand, from viewing C-SPAN (or CNN or PBS) and listening to National Public Radio. Regular watchers of C-SPAN might estimate that many another issue to reach the Senate floor elicits (similarly modest) forms and degrees of deliberative oratory. Ordinary, infrequent watchers may be pardoned, furthermore, for disputing the recurrent declarations (by members and commentators alike) that framed the congressional proceedings in both houses as "historic deliberation" on the Gulf war. Media commentators to the contrary notwithstanding, in fact, seldom did we witness interactive exchanges or progressions when the Senate debated to war or not to war.[20] Rarely did we encounter the kinds of conversations through oratory that have a question-and-answer equivalent in many Senate hearings—hearings that often merit the resonant epithet *deliberative*.[21] To many viewers, even modest forms of deliberation surely seemed missing for the most part, and there was ample reason to suspect that some of the apparent instances of deliberative exchange amounted only to posturing for the cameras and microphones. Thus the celebration of a revival in Senate deliberation could seem to stem from the fact that even a few genuine exchanges occurred—or from the bare possibility that a few senators and their constituents learned a little more than usual from the "debates on the floor."

Deliberation in the proper primary sense is a collective-unto-communal learning through oratory, discussion, or conversation.[22] The structure of the word suggests that deliberative interaction in public dialogue gradually converges on truths, insights, or agreements. This was part of Aristotle's reason in his *Rhetoric* to contrast deliberative with forensic and epideictic oratory. There he holds that deliberation addresses the future and commits its participants to action. Forensic speech makes cases to judge the past, and epideictic oratory praises or blames aspects of the present. Accordingly the historical etymology of deliberation yields a Ciceronian republican position that such properly reflective commitment to concerted action is what can keep a community free.[23] Then de-liberation would be of-liberation. It would be what frees us or in what our shared freedom consists.

Yet a tropal deconstruction of deliberation might well etymologize the word more imaginatively, to appreciate its mythic resonance with the Western proclivity to talk about persuasion as a force or pressure that moves us in particular directions. Then persuasive deliberation is the impulse that moves its participants into or out of specific positions.[24] In deliberation, consequently, we take the exchanges of argument and reflection to be constraining or coercive. In deliberation, we might say, the considerations adduced on all sides serve more or less to force the parties toward positions capable of accommodating the diverse truths of many perspectives. In these ways, the deliberative sense of truth is interest or perspective oriented, so that deliberation de-liberates by taking away liberty, just as a deicer takes away ice or a deformer takes away form. Before deliberating together, each of us might be free to go our separate ways in speech and experience; after deliberating, each of us hears and says too much with the others to stay free for talking and acting idiosyncratically or independently.

Deliberation in a liberal democratic republic can be appreciated as a dialogue between these liberating and constraining dynamics. In this respect we may say that each deliberation constructs, comprises, or at least requires a public. This sense of *public* is at once more humble but less vacuous than America's largely liberal sense of the *public sector* for government activity. Each deliberation constitutes a particular space or distinctive place of ongoing exchange in argument. There the claims, styles, stories, or many other commitments of the speakers and listeners configure the conditions and courses of their interactions. Thus the deliberations take on specific shapes, creating possibilities in some directions and limiting them in others.

In debating whether to embark soon on a Gulf war, the rituals of discussion that the senators (and the representatives) followed did begin to configure a public place (topos) or thing (res—whence res publica) for themselves and others in their polity. Some prowar Republicans, for instance, felt constrained to rebut the appeals from the antiwar Democrats to let the trade sanctions work as originally projected. And some Democrats felt required to address the Republican reply that the coalition enforcing the sanctions against Iraq could not remain intact for long. According to the kinds of considerations cleverly celebrated by William H. Riker in *The Art of Political Manipulation*, the senators were constructing through their strategic words and gestures a particular force field of politics that had to limit one another's options in some significant ways.[25] So we may say that the Senate at least began to provide the edges or outline of deliberation in addressing the Gulf war.

To deconstruct deliberation as de-liberation is especially helpful for regarding rituals as mythic arguments. On one side, the modern prejudice against ritual, tradition, and related accoutrements of premodern life inclines us to portray them as overly static, repetitive, and unreflective. This is the side of modernity that wants arguments to proceed unfettered in a free marketplace of ideas. And in this light, we moderns worry that rites and rituals tend to constrain us unduly. We fear that rituals tend to be literally de-liberating or even enslaving. On another side, however, the modern world wants the facts to "speak for themselves" and "compel the assent of reasonable people." Likewise, it seeks logics and rationales that can "convince" doubters, literally "conquering" them and dispelling their hesitations or reservations.

Yet deliberation is more than constraining interaction in speech. Deliberation also involves the characters whom we can call *deliberators.* They are 'speakers who listen and learn' from the experiences and insights of other speakers. After only a few minutes, however, any interloper could notice that Senate speeches about authorizing the Gulf war spoke far less to colleagues on the Senate floor than to constituents in our networked world. This alone leaves the historical suggestions of an incremental—let alone a radical—return to past days of Senate deliberation more than a little dubious. And we can say this without impugning the quality of contributions by individual senators. Speech by speech, most of us found the discourse informed and intelligent, if seldom imaginative. But the question is whether the senators' scant shuttle of point-counterpoint, consideration and response, actually helped the Senate to learn, precisely in the collegial fashion of republican deliberation. Even were such learning hard in principle to discern, and therefore good in principle to downplay in assessing deliberation, the pervasive observation might easily be that we viewers witnessed little specifically collective deliberation. Instead we heard one individual senator after another claim to be voting after days of intense personal reflection. At most, then, celebrants of renewed Senate deliberation might only invoke the oxymoronic notion of "individual deliberation."

Oxy-Moron

Look behind that bush for it is not a bush. Contradictions do not perplex the logician. They arise because there are more rules to an open game than can be known.
—Donald Kingsbury[26]

As a rhetorical aside, let us notice that to call the notion of individual deliberation *oxymoronic* is not to say that the alleged "contradiction in terms" must make the claim confused, incoherent, or incorrect—let alone literally unintelligible, as some misguided literalists like to imply. Rather the trope of oxymoron warns and intrigues us with the possibility that familiar, conventional meanings cannot be at issue. And it delights us with the promise that two or more meanings of the component terms will twist around to comment on one another. Often the tone is sardonic ("military intelligence" or "creative imitation"), but on occasion our oxymorons turn toward the subtly dialectical ("concrete universal") or the outright inscrutable ("subjective objectivity")—and far be it from me to suggest that these are the same. How other than by oxymorons, after all, can we fully express temporality ("future past" or "past future"), challenge limits ("living dead" or "thinking machine"), acknowledge apocalypse ("survivable missiles" or "proven deterrence"), and project epiphanies ("the multiple self" or "the decentered state").

Consequently oxymoron becomes a mark of myth. At least, this is its signal role in our distinctively late or postmodern times—as we try to talk about our experiences of what comes after the newest, what is more reasonable than rationality, more effective than efficiency, more virtuous than the good, more ethical than morality, and so on. For us moderns, who know that *modernity* is as up to date as can be, *postmodernity* is itself an oxymoron. Still we can recognize that the prime domains of oxymoron in postmodernity include theology and science fiction—widely identified as two of our most mythic literatures.[27]

The tropal and mythic point, therefore, is mainly that individual deliberation is an oxymoronic offshoot of the "decentered subject" in postmodern times. Individual deliberation regards the senator as a collection of disparate voices (or reasons or inclinations or even selves). For the senator, thinking becomes reconceived (in the phrase of Hannah Arendt) as "a dialogue between me and myself." So individual deliberation treats the senator's singularity as a unique and dynamic multiplicity. By envisioning a collectivity in conversation among its components, the postmodern oxymoron of individual deliberation can imply a search for personal community that may generate decisions and commitments (in the form of votes or policies or positions or actions) but should not end in dogmas or determinisms. As the deconstructivists might add, if the rhetoricians had not already said it, this is why an oxymoron is not simply a contradiction or any other kind of error, pure and simple: neither an oxymoron nor a metaphor nor a proposition nor a decision can be strictly univocal. To interpret an oxymoron as merely a contradiction in terms (or to treat a decision as wholly a declaration in terms) is not so much wrong as it is inadvisable. But then this is hardly news, because the lesson of myth for the literalistic times of modernity is often a corrective reminder of polysemy and ambiguity.

Right-You-All

> *Thus the tradition is not clear in the minds of men, however clear it is upon paper. . . . The law is what is read, not what is written.*
> —Donald Kingsbury[28]

To return to the mythic point, though, the Senate's war debate did not seem deliberative—in either the primary (soberly republican) sense or the secondary (playfully deconstructive) sense—because the senators did not speak principally to listen and learn from one another. Instead they spoke to (warn) Saddam Hussein: do not mistake democratic debate for incapacitating disagreement, the senators said, do not doubt America's resolve! And especially they spoke to (warm) the folks back home, the people ritually and therefore mythically responsible for the keys to reelection or the presidency: here is your chance to take pride in a conscientious, reflective, farsighted statesman—each senator proclaimed—for I approach this historic vote mindful that war is hell and hopeful that sanctions will work, with some personal tie to our troops, with a fundamental principle to note in passing, and above all a shared commitment to support our soldiers in the desert. But where, we may wonder, beyond individual agonizing, was the deliberation in that?

The doubt compounds itself when we notice that the Senate debate over the Gulf war showed little convergence of any kind that we might regard as institutional consensus. In Western civilization, at least, truly deliberative oratory (as analyzed from Aristotle onward) tries to drive toward substantial agreement among the debaters. For that reason, late modern tongues incline to talk of such deliberation in terms of *discussion* rather than *debate* (which we regard as more oriented toward conflict and victory) or *oratory* (which we relegate to one-sided speech by a focal person who tries to sway an audience in no position to speak back or among itself in comparable ways). Some might say that the two political parties each developed a consensus, because the eventual votes in the Senate did not deviate greatly from party-line ballots. Yet the express reasoning was so various on each side that deliberative progress toward agreement was difficult to discern even within the parties taken singly. (Moreover the questions put to vote engaged only obliquely the centrally debated issue of whether to war soon against Saddam Hussein's Iraq or to give the economic sanctions considerably more time to work.)

Even so, I want to suggest, the ritual dynamics of speech enforced by the Senate's rules still encouraged and even amounted to genuine, full-fledged, collective deliberation. I have in mind *the rituals of public deliberation expressed in Senate rules*. Thus the senators stood instructed (as usual) not to turn their remarks to potential listeners beyond the chamber. Given the penchant of senators for playing through the cameras and microphones to audiences beyond the chamber, this made the resulting two rituals of proper address seem especially formal in the modern sense of 'artificial, contrived, or even irrelevant to the detailed conduct of business'. As already mentioned, when a senator directed remarks to the Senate's presiding officer ("Mister President, we must all agree . . .") or to the senators assembled ("My distinguished colleagues in this great deliberative body, we have all seen"), the contents often spoke instead to electoral constituents, coalition countries, administration officials, or enemy leaders. Nevertheless the rituals themselves spun a story of senators talking persuasively to one another—in search of wise judgments about what had happened, why, and how to respond. And following their own forms, the senators sometimes slipped into sustained moments of actual deliberation—perhaps by accident as far as the individuals were concerned but very much by design in terms of the institution and its rituals for deliberation. A number of senators, for example, sounded as though they learned and were moved through particular exchanges with senators Sam Nunn (D-Ga.) and Bob Dole (R-Kans.).

The same pattern took shape for the Senate's rules of comity in addressing other senators as individuals or groups. As the senators sometimes needed reminding during their debate over the Gulf war, their rules prohibit personal attacks that impugn the integrity or standing of other senators. Moreover Senate traditions strongly encourage speakers to go out of their way to praise colleagues. (Rules of the House of Representatives outlaw ad hominem attacks and personally disparaging remarks, and they surfaced several times in the House debate over the Gulf war. But the far larger number of House members necessitates such strict time limits for floor debate that they have little opportunity for irrelevant flattery of colleagues and even less for authentic practices of deliberation. Since 1994, especially, a few members have been managing to find plenty of time for personal attacks on their colleagues, even aside from the personal orders of the day, where the only audience is a modest viewership on C-SPAN. Not surprisingly, the comity and the credibility of that House seem to be suffering in consequence.)

At least three rituals result from the Senate's rules of comity. They surfaced frequently in the Senate's talk on the floor about the Gulf war. Again they often came across to casual listeners as mere forms, so lacking in sincerity and vitality of performance as to mock the institution and its dedication to deliberation. But, again, the point about rituals as myths is that they still told senators and observers stories of genuine deliberation that spoke persuasively to some senators in ways evident from their conduct on the floor (and later).

One ritual of comity in Senate conversations is to *personalize the discourse* by connecting issues and positions to their expositors in the Senate. By extension, this ritual encourages senators seldom to mention their colleagues without putting elaborate and colorful epithets before, after, or in the place of the referents' proper names. By synecdochic enactment, this ritual often encompasses the senators' states, families, interests, associations, and other related entities. ("My dear, eminent friend from the Citrus State surely has a most courageous son, to serve so cheerfully—as he has related—with our other heroic soldiers in this generous Shield in the Desert; yet I ask my esteemed colleague: how many of America's best youth will it take for us to keep playing policeman for the whole world?" I exaggerate, of course, to make the point.) The Senate is famous for such flowery talk. Nonetheless this ritual of personal and complimentary address might be said to start as a simple exaggeration of a sound principle (and practice) commonplace in persuasive communication among people: to show interest in the personal details of conversants is to establish conditions conducive to effective and constructive exchange on both sides.

Are such remarks nearly empty forms? I suspect that this becomes less and less the case for senators, ordinary or wise. If nothing else, the convention requires senators to rehearse these telling phrases so often and with such wit that they assume the poetic flow of epithets. And what are epithets—except mythic monikers that admit of immense repetition, variation, and creativity in use? As poets, dramatists, and anthropologists know about oral recitation, the aural power of ritual phrases helps to make myths into vivid, living realities. Furthermore the convention provides senators with a shared repertoire of political characterizations that continually remind them of the relevant concerns about the personalities and situations of their legislative colleagues. These concerns seldom surface in press accounts or legislative reports, yet they figure prominently in dynamics of deliberation. Daily practice in shaping these refrains to changing conditions can remold the Senate's sense of its members and itself—flowing subtly into the interactions, spoken and unspoken, that make the Senate what it is at any given time.

But do such remarks relate to the substance of Senate deliberation only distantly, indirectly, and therefore insignificantly? Reading this ritual as a myth of senatorial community, I would say instead that it suggests stories of the deliberators as personally concerned for their colleagues. This is a dimension of political argument crucial to Senate business.[29] Beyond that, it projects tales about how every issue on the Senate agenda *for* deliberation is an important issue *of* deliberation. These are stories of success or failure in seeking out the many diverse interests of senators and speaking well to as many of them as possible. By representational implication, of course, these are equally stories of speaking well to the diverse interests of the senators' constituents.[30] Epithets are a mark of myth, and to make personal shows of concern into ritualistic chants is to weave the distinctive skeins of deliberative talk into the Senate's daily fabric. More than enhancing deliberation in the Senate, the debate over the Gulf war seemed to strain and frazzle that fabric. It produced unusual pressure to talk beyond the forum and colleagues at hand. Senators who earlier resisted televising the body's proceedings worried precisely that the change in primary audience would destroy the chamber's deliberative character. Whether we take the main audience for Senate talk to be the Senate itself or the citizens beyond depends, of course, on whether we favor the more republican mythos of deliberation or the decidedly liberal mythos of representation.

According to the present story of deliberation, please notice, the senators do not "go out of their ways" to invoke mythically the concerns and characteristics of their colleagues. Rather they seize almost every available opportunity to take interest in one another. Thus the Senate ritual of epithetic address jibes with a second ritual of respectful talk and successful deliberation, whereby senators laud their colleagues individually and collectively at nearly every turn in the conversation. These ritual compliments contribute substantively to Senate deliberation because a major challenge for deliberation is to bring people together. The vocal appreciation of the participants' diverse virtues helps to specify how they can fit together into a continuing community of mutual concern. And the ritual of *continual compliments* accomplishes more than a little of this mutual appreciation. This same ritual also discourages the prima donna search for monopolizing the spotlight of public acclaim, a pressing trouble in times when the Senate has become a presidential launching pad of large egos. The Senate ritual of continual compliments replaces deliberation among active participants with posturing before passive spectators, because the ritual compliments encourage a steady and public sharing of credit for cooperative achievements.

A third ritual of comitous and commodious address is to *apologize promptly and profusely* when a senator might be regarded by colleagues as violating Senate rules or rituals. This holds with special force for the body's more-than-perfunctory rituals of comity and proper address. The presiding officer or another senator can sometimes prompt the ritual of apology by general and usually gentle reminders that Senate debate is to remain decorous—precisely in order to become deliberative. Thus the ritual of apology is as much a rite of deliberation as it is an act of contrition. But it discourages waiting for another senator to prompt one's own pledges that any unintended slight to a colleague or to the body as a whole be forgiven as the unfortunate effect of an excess of the passion of the moment on the senator's part. Perhaps because the practice of deliberation depends on skill with words, apologies for undue passion strike me as much more common—in the Gulf war debate and other Senate discussion on the floor—than apologies for careless or imprecise phrasing. Respect for all senators as deliberators seems to discourage the notion that any senator would be clumsy with words. Furthermore regard for the great issues under consideration by these colleagues large in soul, sympathy, and judgment seems to encourage the mythic inference that a standing danger of deliberation on such a high plane is occasionally being carried away by intense enthusiasms. Because these requests for the body's understanding and pardon can often lead into ritual compliments for colleagues and the Senate as an institution, some senators seem to learn to invoke the ritual of apology as one way to create occasions for praising their partners in deliberation.

By a bad but telling pun, the lesson is that comity in the Senate makes each rit-u-al into a public pattern of speech-in-action that says right-you-all (or as the mythic southerner would say, "Right, y'all"). Each enactment of these three rituals affirms that each senator respects the full collection of colleagues and thereby helps to keep the whole body on the right deliberative track. Is it any wonder that the United States associates such conventions of senatorial courtesy with the drawling and drawn-out speech of the South, where I learned the English uses of drawling "you all." Long-serving senators from the Solid South, such as Sam Ervin (D-N.C.) and Ernest Hollings (D-S.C.), may continue to epitomize senatorial comity as a politically righteous comedy of rit-u-al.

De-Bait

> *There were questions upon which no poem budded. Then the*
> *discussion ceased to be formal and debate raged.*
> —Donald Kingsbury[31]

Yet these rituals and their related rules choreograph the Senate's dance of legislation as steps in deliberation far more than debate. In the case at hand, a critic might say that America's incipient war in the Persian Gulf overwhelmed these rituals of deliberation, though it seldom overrode the rules that embody them. Absent the ethos of deliberation, where speakers talk and listen persuasively and progressively to other speakers, the senators left themselves in an oddly fruitless debate.

In the modern sense pertinent to the Senate's exchanges over the pending Gulf war, debate might as well be spelled *de-bait*. It abandons the sweet lure of persuasion in favor of battering opponents and their reasoning with the hardest and sharpest arguments available. Modern debate becomes the battle of words, the combat of arguments, far more than the exchange of views or the conduct of conversations. Modern debate takes away the bait. It does not deal in the persuasive morsels that the deliberative orator uses to attract the attention of listeners, inducing them to bite into the speaker's line of reasoning. Like all persuasive speakers, the deliberator offers bait as incentive to try an argument. The hope, of course, is to hook the audience and reel it in. Senatorial oratory on the Gulf war mostly took away the bait for luring colleagues into agreement. In its place, senators battered one another in hopes of scoring points with constituents far beyond the floor.

Emphasis on congressional debate—with its apparatus of issues, advocates, and judgment by some third party (such as the electorate)—traces to the American ideology of liberalism far more than the American mythology of republicanism. For liberalism, debate in public forums is domesticated warfare in politics, just as exchange in private markets is the civil equivalent of war in economics.[32] The fundamental dynamic of legislation is representation: re-presenting the private interests of individuals and institutions in public venues, so that the politicians and bureaucrats expert in aggregating and negotiating differences in interest can formulate and implement laws to solve collective problems. With the premium on re-presenting social concerns in government, the rites of public speech function mainly to ensure accurate communication between public and private realms. In that light, injunctions to direct talk only to other legislators or to use epithets understandable mainly by insiders must seem perverse impediments to political representation as ample, accurate communication across the divide between government and civil society. If they have a constructive function, such rituals of legislative speech presumably would have to operate to keep internal conditions of the public sphere suitable for receiving or transmitting outside messages with the clarity and force needed for representation.

As far as liberalism is concerned, therefore, the three rituals of congressional address involve mutuality, consensus, or characterization only insofar as these stem from enforcement of some minimal order for what otherwise might become verbal free-for-alls in Congress. Thus a liberal reading of these rituals mainly would discern a legalistic respect for rules of procedure that ensure enough order to conduct the tame combat of debate and negotiation that configures most legislative business, as understood by liberals.[33] Yet as rites of debate, the three rituals of congressional address probably would seem superfluous to maintaining civility these days, and so they would be accounted empty forms that distract attention from the real needs and dynamics at hand.

Modern debate spurns persuasive bait as mere style (a masquerade of pseudo-substance) or as outright manipulation (a power play of sheer deception). So it responds by pitting power against power—according to the liberal and progressive model of countervailing power. And the main dynamic of modern talk in this mode is to de-bait, to take away the bait. Thus modern debate would deny itself the means to engage in bait-and-switch and other smarmy sales techniques thought unsuited to lofty considerations of the public good. Either such debate refuses recourse to any sweet morsels for attracting attention and inducing persuasion, or it sours the bits that it does offer by emphasizing their function as bait. Like so much modern rhetoric, debate in this sense prides itself on spurning the persuasive aspiration to lure and hook an audience, for it regards the aspiration and its devices as perversely manipulative.

The deliberative rejoinder is that declining to work with bait does not eliminate the enterprise of persuasion. Instead it tends to leave political rhetoric unaware of its purposes and unskillful in its operations. To articulate this conceit of persuasion as fishing for agreement, we might say that forgoing the bait leaves us with only the massive commercial network to trap and suffocate the prey, or the quick lance of the tribal hunter to spear it, or the crude paw of the bear to stun it and claw it to land. These are tales of political coercion and force. By contrast, the rituals of deliberation in the U.S. Senate and elsewhere work to keep the stories and characters of public conversation in the mode of adventure, discovery, and persuasion.

Trad(e)-Ition

> *Tradition is a set of solutions for which we have forgotten the problems. Throw away the solution and you get the problem back. Sometimes the problem has mutated or disappeared. Often it is still there as strong as it ever was.*
> —Donald Kingsbury[34]

Myth and satire are the closest of kin. Therefore we should not be surprised that some aspects of the account to this point start to slide almost imperceptibly from mythic characterization and tropal deconstruction into satirical caricature, even parody.[35] Still the implication remains available in both republican and liberal accounts that we might well know too much for the myth of Senate deliberation to stay persuasive—even as many of us who probably ought to know better continue nevertheless to recount and embellish it.

So what's the problem? demands the thoroughly modern multitude. Needing neither hesitation nor qualification, this multitude is ready and eager to embrace the caricature of Senate deliberation—as long as we admit that it is a caricature, an exaggeration, and thus a kind of falsification. In our truly modern times of high science, the multitude knows as a matter of enlightened sensibility that the culturally correct response to the sort of situation exemplified by Senate deliberation is straightforward and emphatic: when they aren't mere ornaments, pretty empty and innocuous, myths become worse than popular mistakes. And then they sink rapidly into disastrous fabrications, systematic falsehoods, even calculated lies—with the manipulative intentions gradually forgotten. Accordingly all the counterconsiderations simply establish that Senate deliberation is in fact a myth, a story widely but mistakenly believed! Perhaps it is at long last a myth ready for effective debunking: many people are starting to be able to see how it is wrong, and the reputation of Congress is sinking miserably low. But it remains a myth nonetheless. As a result, we moderns must stay the course of Science, surmounting one mistake and myth after another, as we ascend peaks of enlightenment scarcely glimpsed by the earlier times and primitive places that have suffered unaware from the benighted politics and epistemology of myth. Or so the conventional wisdom goes, in modern ignorance of its own myths.

Ritually, of course, the scientistic debunking of myths has become so pervasive in our cultures that the modern antimyth is not nearly so much false as it is unfortunate in effect. Let us leave to other times the (plausible) argument that this conceit of transcending myth is among the most ironically characteristic—and tragically foolish—myths of the modern age.[36] The key consideration for now is that this aura of mistake fosters the very distance between current ritual and current myth that encourages us to read the ritual as myth anew. To infer from ritual to myth is to speak persuasively to the pragmatic sensibilities of many (but not all) modernizers and modernists, because it practices suspicion of what we say and privileges surveillance of what we do.

We might also notice in passing the implication that myths may be true as well as false—and in myriad ways.[37] Thus we can appreciate how the modern (anti)myth of mythlessness—that is, the modern myth of enlightenment—is true. And then we can recognize how it reveals the ambition and self-understanding of modern culture, and especially modern science, even though it is false and misleading about the achievements and dynamics of modern civilization.

Already we have glimpsed some dimensions of how the myth of Senate deliberation might be true as well as false. The mention of committees and hearings can suggest—correctly so—that Senate work beyond the floor often achieves the good (and the bad) features of deliberation: detailed (but slow) and cooperative (but convoluted) inquiries (but also controversies) about decisions (or detours) on policies (and priorities) that can be wise (or sophisticated) in pursuing justice (in politics). Few citizens, journalists, or even political scientists have appreciated properly this (displaced) truth to the myth of Senate deliberation. But the ones who have are the ones best attuned to the *rituals of expertise and inquiry* in connection with congressional committees.

Reading (and refining) the political myths from related rituals is a particularly good way to understand the recent path-breaking research on congressional committees by such political scientists as Richard Hall and G. R. Boynton.[38] These scholars attend to the normal transactions of Congress. Thus they explicate the actual patterns of policy making in the Senate and the House of Representatives. An important aspect of such work involves how these patterns differ markedly (but intelligibly) from one committee and subcommittee and period to the next. Yet it also engages how these still comprise *conversations* (to use Boynton's word) that make excellent sense as accounts of congressional deliberations. Much the same goes for the conduct of representational conversations inside, outside, and across congressional committees. And this surfaces prominently in Boynton's pioneering studies of the rituals of expertise and inquiry that configure many a congressional hearing.[39]

Political scientists often take such inquiries to be processual accounts of decision making. The trouble with *good* accounts of decision is that they set out to explain a focal moment but then tend to make it disappear into an encompassing chain or context of connections. Good accounts make strong connections between earlier elements or events and the decision, yet these make the decision seem to have been made before it was previously taken to occur. Like the shared understanding needed for successful communication, this makes a decision seem always already to have happened. In more general terms, of course, this is the West's standard metaphysical trouble with ever-receding origins and endlessly doubted foundations. Both become infinite regressions, and the decision disappears just as the behavior vanishes.

We do better to appreciate accounts of congressional deliberation and debate as postmodern studies of political discourse. They explore how congressional transactions can become traditions of trade— among the members, the committees, the staffs, their publics, and more. Then the currency, the medium of exchange, is language. And the goods become meanings: ideas, decisions, emotions, stories, symbols, arguments, and more. Deliberation, debate, and all other modes of sustained discourse in politics can become traditions of trade. Indeed the Myth and Ritual School may be taken to teach us that all traditions are self-sustaining transactions, exchanges that keep themselves going discursively. They are, in short, trad(e)-itions, and we should investigate them as such.

HERE, WE MAY SAY, IS THE MAIN MORAL (OUT OF MANY) FOR THIS TALE OF RITUAL DE-LIBERATION: WE STAND TO LEARN WELL ABOUT MANY OF OUR MYTHS, ESPECIALLY IN POLITICS, BY RECOGNIZING AND READING THEM IN PART FROM THE RELATED RECURRENT ACTIONS THAT WE MAY REGARD AS THEIR RITUALS. Please appreciate that the technical term for any such moral (as at the end of an Aesop fable) is *epimyth,* which is to say, 'what comes after the myth proper'. Because this is a deconstruction or a dialogue more than a myth, diminishing any narrative suspense that might arise, we need not worry that our lesson was signaled unduly from the start. Nor need we fear that it appears here more as a thesis for argument than as a maxim for memory or a precept for action. It serves these exploratory remarks nonetheless as an epimyth to inform our future action. And if you have entered at all into the dialogue, we might even agree that this can be an appropriate outcome for our deliberation.

10 TURNING STANDS INTO STANCES

A FIGURAL ARGUMENT ABOUT FORMS OF POLITICAL ACTION

Much current political theory escapes our standard categories, corresponding to neither utopia nor ideology, treatise nor history, dialogue nor confession. Two concepts that can clarify current theory are the political stance and the political stand. The stance fits the give and take of ordinary politics, when principle is created by and for compromise. But when compromise is the corruption of principle, a more rigid and lasting posture is called forth. The political stand offers a way of taking responsibility for the world, as well as oneself, without eroding principles.

Form and Content

> *It is immensely moving when a mature man—no matter whether old or young in years—is aware of a responsibility for the consequences of his conduct and really feels such responsibility with heart and soul. He then acts by following an ethic of responsibility and somewhere he reaches the point where he says: "Here I stand; I can do no other." That is something genuinely human and moving. And every one of us who is not spiritually dead must realize the possibility of finding himself at some time in that position. In so far as this is true, an ethic of ultimate ends and an ethic of responsibility are not absolute contrasts but rather supplements, which only in unison constitute a genuine man—a man who can have the "calling for politics."*
> —Max Weber[1]

Echoing the famous declaration of Martin Luther, this familiar passage from "Politics as a Vocation" draws into public affairs that deep-seated spiritual commitment that Weber himself argued to be the mark of religion rather than politics. In this politically ultimate sense, taking a stand probably is not something for all seasons or even many. But it is fitting and perhaps required for times of terrible trouble, when the very possibility of politics seems imperiled. It is the politics for "a polar night of icy darkness and hardness."[2] As such, it is what Weber believed to be the politics appropriate for his times, as it is for many since, because Weber's times are our times. Taking a stand is an important project of political action in our day. Accordingly making a stand is a major form of postmodern political theory.[3] Where such action and theory converge, the stand passes beyond an occasional recourse of regular politics to become the distinctive politics for times of trouble. Thus I argue here that the concept of a political stand has special significance for current politics.

More particularly, my first thesis is that taking a stand is a distinct project of political action. One of its more remarkable features is its emphasis upon theorizing as a mode of action. In turn, articulating stands is a discrete form of political theory: separate not only from ideologies and utopias but also from platforms, commentaries, treatises, and the like.

Often as not, the cutting edge of postmodern politics has been the dagger of the stand, not the broadsword of ideology. This second thesis is not derived from the frequency of the stand in comparison with other projects and forms. Instead it is a claim about the contributions of many leading actors and thinkers in our day. Indeed taking the stand seriously as action means reclassifying some "mere thinkers" in order to give their projects of political action proper recognition.

Many theorists of the late nineteenth and twentieth centuries have seen politics in terms of cultural diremption and decay. Their works demonstrate that stand making and taking are typical of such times. This leads to a third thesis: the stand is part of the politics of turmoil and uncertainty in the West. Of course, not all politics turn toward stands in response to cultural crisis. Nor is this response usually unalloyed. But the stand is common enough during cultural crisis that there is reason to regard it as characteristic of such times of trouble.

Some theorists are convinced that ours is a time of troubled transition. The issue here is not the accuracy of that diagnosis but its current prominence and its significance for the near future. Insofar as stands fit our situation, seen in such apocalyptic terms, preoccupation with stand making and taking will continue in coming years. And that is my fourth claim.

Let me emphasize that not everyone responds to crises of culture by making and taking stands. Even when this is a person's main response, it is usually mixed with others. Certainly what is studied here from the standpoint of stands should be studied from other angles as well. I claim only that this notion can add much to our understanding of politics.

My argument involves various theorists of recent politics. Keeping the argument to an essay (instead of a book) means focusing on only a few figures of special significance and sorting among their projects in a highly schematic and abbreviated way. This leaves lots of room for omission, overemphasis, and other occasions for criticism. But I encourage you to take this limitation as an invitation to join in the argument, furnishing an independent investigation of the forms and projects of current politics. Then, even as you test my claims by your own sense of current conditions, practices, and theories, the concept of political stands will enter the arena of public thought and action. Because my examples must be few and elliptical, I invite you to work through your own, to share my burden of inquiry. For the same reason, my rhetoric is meant to echo that of recent stand takers, to convey the common flavor of their projects. In the end, when this essay encounters deeper questions, those it must confront but cannot answer adequately, we should be well into the discussion I want to begin.

Principle and Compromise

> *Every virtue and every prudent act . . . is founded on*
> *compromise.*
> —Edmund Burke[4]

> *Important principles may and must be inflexible.*
> —Abraham Lincoln[5]

What is the stuff of political stands? When making a stand, what is it of? When taking a stand, what is it on? The standard answer is "principle," and the conventional opposite of standing on principle is compromise. Thus stands and stances differ in their relation to principle and compromise.

Conventional wisdom sees *compromise* as synonymous with *sell-out*.[6] Compromise is called the corruption and destruction of principle, not a responsible route for carrying it into practice. It is conceived as the very opposite not only of standing on principle but of principle per se. These days, "principled compromise" sounds like a contradiction in terms. Little wonder, then, that politicians in particular and politics in general are now held in low regard.

Ordinarily, though, this view misconceives compromise, principle, and politics. Not only are compromise and principle both crucial to politics as usual, but they complement and shade into one another so much as to be almost indistinguishable in some lights.[7] Good but ordinary politics are so thoroughly textured of compromise that standing on principle is either taken as a posturing preliminary to compromise or as an outright obstruction of politics. Henry Fairlie notes, "The politician who says that he is taking a stand on some issue will, if he is wise, cross his fingers, and mutter under his breath that it is only shifting sand on which he has a footing."[8] Because principle and compromise can and must go together in ordinary times, the language and practice of stands should not be a part of everyday politics.

But what are we to call the choice and dynamics of principle in usual politics? I suggest we talk of "taking stances." In the declaration of Martin Luther, *stand* implies a firm, unmoving, enduring commitment. It evokes such phrases as "Custer's last stand," "standing by someone," "standing for something," "standing up to be counted," "standing pat," and so on. But *stance* carries opposite connotations. It is synonymous with *posture*. Stances and postures are temporary; they are either preliminary or intermediary. We talk of the batter's stance at the plate before swinging at the ball or the posture of the dancer at the height of a leap. Stances and postures connote snapshots of action scenes, and they can even imply the artificiality or superficiality of being posed. This is apparent in our related notion of *posturing*. But its recent overtones of insincerity, lack of substance, or even lack of principle disqualify posturing for use here.

Overall, then, ordinary politics are best described in terms of stances or postures. Holding out for a better bargain may look for a while like a stand, but it is only a result of stance strategy.[9] Stands may occur in ordinary politics, but they will almost always be misunderstood and (if of any consequence) deplored. They may look saintly at first but soon seem petty and self-righteous. Yet although they do not belong in politics as usual, stands are mainstays of troubled times.

Thought and Action

> *There are periods in history in which it is not possible to reconcile the hopes of the moment and the needs of the future, when a congruence between one's personal life and the collective direction of all mankind cannot be established without doing violence either to one's existence or to one's understanding. I believe that ours is such a time and that we must learn to live with its irreconcilable conflicts and contradictions.*
> —Robert L. Heilbroner[10]

When institutions are thoroughly corrupt; when terror, resentment, and exploitation are the principles of politics; when criticism and reform are debased, forbidden, or forgotten; when compromise is capitulation, if even conceivable, then ordinary politics are out of the question, and it is time to stand on principle. Heilbroner is hardly alone in regarding our era as one of irreconcilable conflicts and contradictions. Such are times when politics themselves are put in question, when troubles seem so severe that not even revolutions suffice.[11] Then compromise is corrupt or incoherent, and the ethics of politics and religion converge. Tom Paine's era tested political talent and imagination: trying men's courage, conviction, and capacity for action. But what Heilbroner has in mind would truly be times that try men's souls.[12]

The key question in such an era is what consistent moral stand we could recommend to a person of goodwill.[13] How can goodwill be given a concrete shape or program? When the problem is to find any ethical ground at all, it is time to ponder standing pat on whatever principles promise to coalesce into a responsible position.

Whereas days of revolution are haunted by injustice, times of terrible trouble are possessed by it. Then it is almost instinctive to look to your principles, to seek to guard them as they are to guide and guard you. And where evil, apathy, or oppression seem so widespread that revolution becomes immoral or impossible, it is time to worry whether proper principles can be conceived, let alone effected intact. If ordinary politics offer shifting sands, then the winds that rip through times of trouble whip those sands into a single stinging gloom. Fighting loss, some invoke the facility for making and taking stands. This explains and justifies the prominence of stands in hard times. True compromise cannot occur in a world dominated by corruptions and caricatures of politics. Then the challenge is to achieve any plausible and consistent principles. When even extraordinary politics are elusive, stands come into their own.

Times of trouble are marked by what their more perceptive inhabitants see as a radical split between thought and action. Because normal patterns and resources of thought are inadequate for understanding common occurrences or coping with everyday problems, a gulf is opened between practice and theory (as well as between practice and principle). New theories, new patterns of thought must be created to keep open the possibility of controlling life enough to take responsibility for one's own actions. Thus the main part of taking a stand typically turns out to be the theoretical effort of making a stand. Such fusion of theory and practice is one reason that our usual talk of politics should be supplemented with a terminology of stands and stances.

Despite occasional appearances, the language of stands and stances is not common. It is seldom encountered in studies of recent political theory, for it has not been recognized as providing a set of concepts for assessing politics or political theory. Largely this reproduces the current gap between thought and action. We tend to divide political concepts into two compartments: theory and practice. But stands and stances bridge the two.

By stands or stances, I do not mean only theories about the world, visions for it, or techniques of acting in it. Instead I mean their confluence. Stands and stances toward the world include or are informed by theories. But in addition to explicit cognition, let alone highly structured theory, they involve less conscious and less rationalistic components to shape personal relationships to the world. Stands and stances are the patterns of these relationships. On the other hand, they are not merely habitual ways of being in the world, even if habits are grounded in principle. For stands and stances involve not only intellection but also relations to unusual situations. Most important, stands and stances include patterns of action in the world: ways of expressing and effecting theories, moralities, principles, visions, emotions, and the like. Thus they are more than simple techniques for action; they extend to the choice and ordering of ends as well as means. The element of action needs emphasis, since no study examining only theories enunciated in speech or writing can hope to fathom fully what differentiates one stand or stance from another. Not only must proposals for effecting views be studied but also actual deeds, both public and private.

That stands and stances must be described by joining terms of theory and practice suggests that our split between thought and action is wide and deep. This supports a diagnosis of our times as troubled. The gap comes from basic uncertainty about both the proper relationship between thought and action and the ways (whatever their propriety) in which thought and action may be brought into any regular and productive relationship.

In turn, our uncertainty has many sources. Common to all is a tie to our calamitous actions. Evidently neither compromise nor revolution now allows even the greatest skill to transform moral aims into practical realities with sufficient integrity or reliability. In times of trouble, the world seems so warped that any remaining area of action must distort and pervert intention beyond recognition. Yet when few intentions can be projected even approximately intact, the very possibility of action is put in doubt. Thus stand takers believe that routes to political action are practically nonexistent. Worse, such doubt about present practices unsettles categories of thought and standards of judgment, which are supposed to make sense out of the arena of action. The result is serious disruption of ties between thought and action or even thought itself. When action atrophies, true thinking wastes away.[14]

Paradoxically, the gap between thought and action becomes so radical in troubled times that true thinking is made into a kind of action. When thought loses contact with current practices, it loses access to the fresh observations and unexpected experiences that allow it to reform and redirect itself. In bad times, one who really thinks is taking responsibility for self and world in the only way widely available, for few have access to space for constructive political action. In ordinary politics, thinking and acting may be quite distinct; but in the stand taker's attempt to create the extraordinary politics for hard times, they converge. Then to project thought into speech is virtually to act, insofar as action can occur in such severe circumstances. Thus explicit theorizing becomes an arena for scarce action.

This explains why the main part of stand taking typically is the theoretical task of stand making, for taking a stand cannot even begin without new patterns of thought for coming to grips with current perplexities. Indeed, given the dearth of alternate arenas for action, the only practical path to worthy principles is simply to formulate them. In extreme conditions, stand making can be identical to stand taking.

Then the task is truly to think. As Hannah Arendt argued, "This may indeed prevent catastrophes, at least for myself, in the rare moments when the chips are down."[15] Then stands become not just fundamentally but fully defensive and individual. Even when stand taking is not wholly swallowed by stand making, two corollaries arise. First, the political theorists of troubled times may be reckoned among the key actors of the day, for the posturing of ordinary actors may be beside the point. And second, although study of theories cannot complete the study of most stands, it can go far toward a good grasp of their structures and dynamics.

Making and Taking

> *Today's hero is not skeptical, dilettantish, or decadent; he has simply experienced chance, disorder, and failure. . . . He lives at a time when duties and tasks are unclear. He has a sharper sense of human liberty and of the contingency of the future than anyone has ever had before. Taking everything into account, nothing is certain—not victory, which is still so far away, and not other people. Never before have men had such good evidence that the*

> *course of events is full of twists and turns, that much is asked of*
> *daring and that they are alone in the world and before one*
> *another. . . . The contemporary hero is not Lucifer; he is not*
> *even Prometheus; he is man.*
> —Maurice Merleau-Ponty[16]

The stand departs from other forms of theory and projects of action in its characteristics, concerns, connections, and contrasts. Once explained, these areas of departure clarify two lines of convergence between stands and stances.

CHARACTERISTICS OF THE STAND

There are many ways to describe the stand. The characteristics to follow are by no means exhaustive. These seven features are sufficient but not necessary conditions for a theory or course of action to be a stand.

Disillusionment. Almost always, political stands are products of the profound disillusionment common in troubled times. Sometimes stands are not based on disillusionment. But then they are usually romantic, immature, or rooted in misjudgments of the times. Stands not grounded in disillusionment are likely to be evangelical and optimistic in ways that neglect most complications of the human condition. These days, some theorists reject the politics of incremental technique and apocalyptic revolution; they reject not just the Enlightenment but the Modern Age itself; they despair of Western Civilization and perhaps of civilization per se. Failure is feared but so is success; idealism is attacked but so are ideals; optimism is assailed but so is hope.[17]

Yet in a Cartesian dénouement, others become caught up in distrusting their own doubt. Spawned by pervasive disillusionment is an equally pervasive desperation. It lunges after a critical commitment that our disillusionment tends to make into a contradiction in terms. In response, stands defy despair by fixing upon a few principles for a refuge in troubled times and a promise of better things to come. Stands make this possible by accepting disillusionment with all but the most immediate ideals, activities, and individuals. Much disillusionment is accommodated in order to protect against even more. This ethos is readily evident in recent political theory. Among its three most repeated particulars are the next three characteristics of the stand.

Rejection of Rationalism. The stand taker accepts abstract analytical intellection as a proper part of responsible living but rejects the rationalism that would make it into the sole guiding force for human existence. (When the stand taker does not reject rationalism but embraces it, then the usual result is something like the peculiar stand of pluralism explored later.) In this sense, rationalism is the idolization of that analysis upon which the West is founded. It should not be confused with rationalization, its specifically late or postmodern form. In premodern times of trouble, stand takers renounced versions of rationalism peculiar to the times. But in our times, to reject rationalism is to renounce the modern autonomization of reason and the subsequent threat to rationalize all aspects of life.

After Weber's image of the iron cage, rationalization is portrayed as the antinomy of freedom and the epitome of superficiality. The modern confidence in automatic mechanisms of regulation or progress has collapsed, and the postmodern observer sees instead only accident or perverse control. To keep rationality within proper bounds, other faculties are revived if not exalted. Will, imagination, and emotion re-emerge to qualify intellect. We try to rediscover the virtues of habit and tradition. In response to the acid or arid criticality encouraged by rationalism, the stand taker seeks a solid ground of commitment for digging in and establishing roots to resist troubles. For us, this may mean repudiating the modern worship of science and technology. But with Weber, one can stand on at least some of the virtues and projects of such science and still reject rationalization itself.

Rejection of Impersonal Equality. Most who feel forced to take a stand see recent corruption at least partly as the reduction of human possibility to a very low and common denominator. Thus some castigate mass society as the unrestricted reach of system, closure, and sameness. Then stands are understood to rescue persons increasingly deprived of individuality. Given extreme threats to personal integrity, concern with the individual easily becomes concern with the self. In a way, stand taking tries to protect the self first and foremost, for otherwise there may be too few critics left to give visions of better conduct and communities a chance to stay alive in such corrupt conditions. An obvious danger is lapsing into some sort of narcissism.[18] But if our times are deeply troubled, then protecting the integrity of the self may indeed be our main moral challenge. Further, true stand takers reject mass society to promote the principle of individuality for all, not merely for themselves.

Rejection of Ordinary and Large-Scale Politics. The stand taker rejects large-scale political enterprises for the same reasons as ordinary political compromises: they seem futile; worse, they spread rather than constrict violence, corruption, and fear. Many think that the overreaching of revolutionary politics has caused the last several centuries to go astray. Arthur Koestler's *Darkness at Noon* makes the old revolutionary call to "arise, ye wretched of the earth" into a sharp malapropism to say as much: "awry, ye wretched of the earth."[19] The repeated perversion of revolutions suggests that large-scale politics are easily derailed to destroy rather than renew. More generally, stand takers see overblown ambitions behind twentieth-century corruptions. Perhaps politics are always a dirty business, but even stand takers who agree will insist that politics in their day are fully and unnecessarily filthy. To promote large-scale collective tasks is to prompt atrocity and disaster.

As stand takers assess them, political actors in times of trouble possess almost no capacity to encourage events in desirable directions. Considerable disillusionment comes from the repeated collapse of collective projects and the miscarriage of adventurous ideals.[20] Political stands often arise from the conviction that cultivating sweeping political aims through present action is courting moral suicide. Yet for all this, stand takers typically refuse to reject politics per se and remain committed to a peculiar kind of action. It is meant to have a large impact, but only as an indirect result of deeds severely restricted in immediate import. Otherwise, risks cannot be kept within reasonable bounds.

Insistence on Personal Responsibility. Stands are not based on an ethic of absolute ends, if by that is meant an indifference to the consequences of holding fast to personal principles. With Weber, stand takers see stands as the only way to exercise personal responsibility in hard times. Stands embody a belief that, for the time being, purity of principle is the only real route to responsibility for the consequences of personal conduct. To take a stand is not to withdraw wholly from politics, let alone the world. Stands seek neither cynical avoidance of responsibility nor hermetic restriction of it to oneself. The very notion of responsibility verges on incoherence when the world is ignored in favor of concentration solely on oneself, and stand takers know this. Probably their main problem, then, is finding a formula for responsibility beyond the self—but without becoming corrupted and without contributing to any politics and world that are fundamentally corrupt. How can they be involved without being implicated?

Insistence on Limited Politics. Generally stand taking responds to the problem of personal responsibility by trying to create small-scale politics of severely limited ends and means. It tries to be constructive, for stand takers typically regard slipping into defeatist stances as a major temptation of the times. Lately this temptation is sometimes said to be compounded by attractions of nihilism.[21] Indeed avoiding nihilism has been a central impulse toward stand taking. Although stands are never strictly defensive, their constructive aspects exist beside their deeply defensive purposes, for the possibility of constructive action depends on protecting individual stand takers.

Beyond that, direct efforts seldom extend further than small groups of friends. Stand takers regard overextension as another great danger of political endeavor in hard times. What result are largely personalistic politics. These are very limited politics, providing little more than small arenas of direct action, even while protecting actors and deeds from being engulfed by threats of the day. Although stand takers want to extend effective action as far as possible, they worry about overextension to the point of coaching against getting their hopes up and letting their guards down. Some stands are even predicated upon suspicion of their own, perhaps apparent, success. Accordingly limited politics lead to highly limited projects of action.

Insistence on Limited Action. Providing positive projects of action while also protecting stand takers means limiting both the scope and nature of action. Four forms of limited action dominate recent stand taking. In order of increasing severity, they may be described as reductions of action to personal example, to speech, to theory, and to thought. The first reduction, of action to personal example, is the main (and often the only) mode of overt, positive endeavor readily recognized by stand takers as action. The effects of good examples of personal conduct can reach beyond close associates but seldom directly and thus seldom forcefully. Even so, their effects should not be underestimated. For as Weber observed of charisma, we often emulate exemplary patterns of conduct. Even when the positive effects fall far short of full success, personal example often remains the only mode of action that avoids implicating stand takers in the corruption everywhere about them. Nor is it strictly self-oriented, since it seriously intends a principled influence on the lives and politics of others. Such personal projects draw together the purposes in politics, ethics, economics, religion, and other spheres. Because their point is to provide examples of the whole, well-rounded, responsible person, stands try to overcome the compartmentalization of late modern life. In part, to take a stand is to try to stand out as an example to others.

The three reductions of action to speech, theory, and thought echo my earlier claims about the reduction of stand taking to stand making. All are justified by the absence of any more overt, intrusive, or active ways to influence the course of human events. Other ways, although more easily recognized as action, seem to stand takers to be too vulnerable to miscarriage and corruption. Likely they will not only fail but fail disastrously. They require accommodations that jeopardize integrity and yet offer no real prospects of success. Indeed conceptions of action proposed by recent theorists come close to reducing all action to speech, theory, or thought.[22] These reductions reflect recent perversions of action that try to push beyond these limits. We know few instances of unequivocally successful action that transcends them. To protect capacities for future action, stands tend to reduce all current action to criticizing, creating visions of a better world, and communicating those views. As Arendt suggested, stand takers often insist that the best available acts are those that set examples of excellence in theorizing.

CONCERNS OF THE STAND

From these characteristics of the stand, at least four main concerns are evident. They deserve separate discussion.

Praxis. Almost obsessively, stand takers are fascinated by problematics of theory and practice, which tie closely to the problematics of critical commitment just noted. Ceaseless discussions of proper participants, purposes, premises, and strategies of action signal deep doubt about whether theory and practice can be well connected.

As a result, there has been a revival of thought about politics and action. The last century has seen many attempts, at least in theory, to return politics to the center of reflection and direction in human affairs. Recent theory has replaced other symbolic forms (especially society and economy) with politics as the category of totality: the sphere responsible for comprehending and coordinating all other domains of understanding and endeavor. But such theory has not been matched in practice, where economy and society remain entrenched in areas formerly or at least properly political. This split between theory and practice is behind the recent renaissance in political theory but has also held it back from the full flowering it desires. And political stands have become important precisely because few thorough thinkers now have much confidence in the coherence of large-scale, active connections between theory and practice.

Community. In rejecting large-scale endeavors and impersonal associations, stand takers seek to protect and revitalize individuals (especially themselves). But they typically recognize that recovering lasting individuality requires overcoming the loneliness, the lack of intimate connection and cooperation, that erodes the security needed for full independence. For this reason stand takers often cultivate a keen concern for community, seeing it as the one soil rich enough for viable individuality to take root and flourish. However abstract their principles of justice, they do directly engage the world in this context of community. Here stand takers assume much of their burden of responsibility for others. Their visions of alternate politics for the future usually emphasize close communities. In addition, their interim actions are typically predicated on the presence of small communities of colleagues or converts. They provide protected spaces for the limited politics meant to last out hard times. Thus concern for individuality becomes concern for community.

Communication. The importance of the stand-taking concern with communication is evident from the reductions of action to speech, theory, or thought. (After all, even thought requires contact with others to be independent and effective.) This significance is suggested also by the stand-taking concern with community, since "the precondition of community is communication."[23] A focus on communication is evident in the increasing study of political language, which now seems to be leading political theory into perhaps the most intense interest in rhetoric since the Renaissance.[24] Such concern for political language and rhetoric is common in times of trouble and might even be among their distinguishing marks. In the nineteenth century this concern turned back on itself to produce systematic studies of historical sources and structures of human thinking. In Hegel's hands these studies led to the phenomenology of mind, and in Mannheim's to the sociology of knowledge. Thus does the stand's concern with communication modulate into its concern with the origins and natures of human knowing.

Epistemology. In the unsettled conditions of troubled times, self-conscious stand takers are almost inevitably drawn to issues of epistemology. To ask where to stand leads to asking how to stand and on what. Eventually such questions lead us to wonder what standing is. By that point we are well within the sticky web of the study of knowing. Thus not all stand-taking interest in epistemology comes from current conflicts over the status of political theory in an era of political science. Many deplore that "the contemporary literature on political theory advises us . . . to approach political theory as though it existed within the philosophical framework of the problem of knowledge or as though it were a subcategory of the dispute over scientific methodology."[25] To the extent that this is true, it becomes more understandable and defensible when the vantage of stands is taken into account. In hard times corruption makes not only action and thought but even perception suspect. What should be done is hard to specify—at least partly because what can be known is unclear. What ordinarily would be problems of politics are pushed back into epistemology. Politics comes to lean on epistemology to an extraordinary degree, which leads political theory to do likewise.

Linking great political theory with drastic political change has become commonplace, but linking both with epistemology is every bit as justified. Plato and Aristotle, Hobbes and Locke, Kant and Hegel, Marx and Mill: all interwove theories of acting with theories of knowing. Political theory and epistemology converge in crisis, because the conditions that unsettle the one also unsettle the other. Intertwinings of epistemology and politics are yet another respect in which theory can be considered action in bad times. Seeing our times as troubled times, the current concern for epistemology makes sense, even as it may also draw us away from concrete responsibilities into absorption with abstract conjectures.

CONNECTIONS OF THE STAND

The main connections of the stand are plainly implicit in its concerns and characteristics. The first connection is to catastrophes and corruptions of the times. Recent atrocities and disasters include clusters of world wars and imperialism, attempted genocides, and successful fratricides. Ours is the century of totalitarianism, mass society, pollution, nuclear proliferation, and the population explosion. In the face of such threats, politics appear to have gone wrong or been inadequate. Thus a further connection is to that complicated shift in sensibilities associated with various existentialisms. These decry our problems but refuse to leap to large-scale, collectivist solutions. Instead they focus upon individual responsibility for coping with corruption and making sense out of absurdity. Their injunctions to action flirt with nihilism, utopianism, and ideology, but mostly they pull back toward a few principles for guiding individual action. Certainly existentialists themselves embrace exemplary action.

The connections to religion and depth psychology have structures similar to that of existentialism. All three usually reject rationalism. All three try to attend to the individual in all aspects and responsibilities, and they are heavily involved in the epistemological struggles of our times. All three seek a basis for critical commitment and action to withstand the temptations and threats about us. Recent stand taking draws deeply from these sources, as evidenced by its political symbolism. Prometheus and Faust are largely left behind. As Albert Camus's characters suggest, stands respond to our troubled times after the fashion of Sisyphus or the Stranger. And there is some of these in the stand taker. But more apt is Camus's figure of the Rebel. For what could be more reminiscent of stand takers than the short description, injunction, and prophecy that conclude the instruction of the Rebel?

> Each of us tells the other that he is not a God; this is the end of romanticism. At this moment, when each of us must fit an arrow to his bow and enter the lists anew, to reconquer, within history and in spite of it, that which he owns already, the thin yield of his fields, the brief love of this earth, at this moment when at last a man is born, it is time to forsake our age and its adolescent furies. The bow bends; the wood complains. At the moment of supreme tension, there will leap into flight an unswerving arrow, a shaft that is inflexible and free.[26]

Inflexible and free, so stand takers would leap into unswerving flight in our times of supreme tension. The Rebel is a stand taker's text.

Equally apt as symbols of the stand are images in Heilbroner's *Inquiry into the Human Prospect*. As a response to bad times, Heilbroner appeals to the model of the monastery. With overtones of a religiously grounded fortress against decline and corruption, this model stands well for stand taking, especially its concern for community and its small-scale action by example and neighborhood assistance.[27] Even more evocative is Heilbroner's symbol of the stand taker as an Atlas waiting out troubled times.

> The question, then, is how we are to summon up the will to survive—not perhaps in the distant future, where survival will call on those deep sources of imagined human unity, but in the present and near-term future. . . . At this last moment of reflection another figure from Greek mythology comes to mind. It is that of Atlas, bearing with endless perseverance the weight of the heavens in his hands. If mankind is to rescue life, it must first preserve the very will to live, and thereby rescue the future from the angry condemnation of the present. The spirit of conquest and aspiration will not provide the inspiration it needs for the task. It is the example of Atlas, resolutely bearing his burden, that provides the strength we seek. If, within us, the spirit of Atlas falters, there perishes the determination to preserve humanity at all cost and any cost, forever.[28]

To conjoin Camus and Heilbroner is to see the Rebel as Atlas and vice versa. What results is the ultimate symbol of the stand taker as proposed by both Weber and Merleau-Ponty: the symbol is man. This is because the ultimate challenge in times of trouble is to withstand all the forces that would lessen individuals by tempting them to more or by terrorizing them to nothing. Whether or not stand takers believe with William Faulkner that man will prevail, their task is to ensure, at the least, that man will endure.

CONTRASTS WITH THE STAND

Considered as a form of political theory, the stand differs from such other forms as the treatise, dialogue, and history in having a project of action to propose. As a highly personal form, it often converges with the essay, yet the essay also tends to avoid projecting a course of action. This personal orientation gives the stand some resemblance to the confession, after the fashion of Augustine or even Rousseau, but the stand is less concerned to declare deficiencies and more directed toward articulating principles for conduct than is the typical confession. Of course, political theory takes many other forms, any of which can at times be amalgamated to the stand, considered as a form.

The two forms of political theory most like the stand are those that most obviously follow it in combining a form for theory with a project for action: the ideology and the utopia. Much has already been done to contrast the stand with the ideology. The stand is usually more cautious, self-doubting, and defensive; the ideology is usually adventurous, rationalist or even "scientific," and offensive. The stand emphasizes small-scale action by individuals or close communities; the ideology emphasizes large-scale action by movements or masses. The stand is a few principles for endurance; the ideology is a vast program for progress or even revolution. According to this specific, historically restricted conception of ideology, the main instances would include modern liberalism, socialism, and conservatism.[29] An important political development of our times is the frustration and fragmentation of such ideologies. In picking up their pieces, many postmodern people put them back together more as stands than as ideologies. As argued later by example, many current projects now classified as liberalisms, socialisms, or conservatisms are better viewed as attempts at personal stands than programmatic ideologies.

To contrast the stand and the utopia is more difficult since the stand usually includes a utopian vision, however vague. Actually there are two contrasts: between the stand and the modern utopia, and also between the stand and the classical utopia.[30] All utopian projects offer concrete visions of alternate ways of life. But the modern utopia is distinctive in two respects. First, it insists on a vision of the good life, so that it is always a utopia. Second, it insists on a confident, even programmatic, expectation that its vision will be realized, often in the relatively near future. Thus despite its smaller concern with precisely how to get from here to there, the modern utopia converges with the modern ideology. They are close enough that contrasts with the stand are the same, with one qualification. Stands are usually less concrete and detailed in their visions of alternatives than are modern utopias. Stands echo the caution sounded by late modern ideologies, from Hegel on, which doubts the possibility of being specific about what will or can happen in the future.[31]

The classical utopian vision gives a critical comparison for current culture. It is not a program to be realized, and it does not pretend to be the good society. Thus the classical utopia is more a thought experiment than an action project. That is why it is named after nowhere. The stand's vision usually has the same purpose of critical comparison with present conditions; indeed its abstraction preempts other purposes. Hence it is usually less specific than the vision of the classical utopia. But the basic difference goes deeper to the very idea of taking a stand. As Peter Euben has written, "Given that utopian means no place, it suggests that standing no place, i.e., adopting no stance or standpoint, is utopian, coming from nowhere."[32] Even when reducing action to theory or thought, the stand presents itself as a project of action, not merely as an exercise in thought. And thus, even when it involves utopian visions, it cannot be reduced to them alone. While stand takers experiment in thought, they cling in practice to the principles that make up their stands.

CONVERGENCE OF STANDS AND STANCES

In general, the stand is appropriate for extraordinary politics, while the stance finds its home in ordinary politics. Nevertheless they converge in two ways. First, the stand is designed to be enduring but not eternal. It is grounded in the distinction between ordinary and extraordinary politics, and that means it must, however implicitly, look toward a return to ordinary politics. The stand is designed to make man endure until hard times have passed and better days are at hand. By projection, it works to make itself into a stance at the proper point in history. Hence it must continually reconsider its justification, in the hope that it may have succeeded in working itself out of its job. In the interim the stand must try to keep a certain flexibility. This is a flexibility less of principle than of mind: a quality of self-criticism to be kept in careful control, lest it undermine the stand itself. In this first respect, the stand/stance distinction remains important, although subtly less dramatic than may be implied by previous parts of this argument.

Second, the stand and the stance can converge by virtue of a paradoxical possibility: some stands can be stances. Two examples come readily to mind. One is the stand based upon systematic criticism and pluralism. Its main principle is a firm commitment to the priority of ordinary politics, as understood by pluralism. Rules and processes are what count, with less attention to products and substance. In a sense, this stand refuses to accept any substantive principles as a firm-enough grounding. But what has been said about troubled times implies that this stand tends to undermine itself. Survival in such times apparently requires some substantive principles for self-definition, let alone for defining responsibilities to others. This stand's peculiar lack of concrete content makes it inordinately difficult to sustain. At best, its ambition to avoid substantive principles is practically bound to fail, with some of its concrete products—not its processes—coming to be its real basis as a stand.

The other is the stand that offers itself as a sort of superstance. It insists on shifting relentlessly from stance to stance. This is a kind of "ironism."[33] To stand on pluralism is to avoid all concrete and substantive principles in favor of a particular set of abstract and procedural ones, but to stand on ironism is to reject all principles save those that specify the distrust of principle. Whereas the pluralist stand emphasizes the partial validity of at least most available positions, the ironist stand stresses the partial error of all available positions (save itself, perhaps). While the stand of pluralism parcels stances to the political field at one per person per situation, ironism runs the ironists themselves through diverse stances within each situation.

For ironists the world is so corrupt that all principles, stances, and commitments can (and practically must) be assumed to contain some seeds of corruption. Hence they seek to endure untainted by staying one step ahead of temptation, switching from stance to stance before the seeds of corruption can flower for them. By this principle of unceasing movement among principles, ironists strive to keep alive relatively worthy examples, to remain able to act in at least limited ways, and to sustain the possibility of some better form of life in the future. Accordingly, the ironists' symbolic embodiment would be Proteus, steadfast only in continual change. Probably no more apparent antinomy to Atlas could be imagined. And yet, in a curious way, protean ironists can indeed count as stand takers. As for all other stands, the purpose of ironism is to allow individuals to withstand torturous times while still taking responsibility. Hence ironism may be the most extreme stand: a last possible defense against trouble but still a stand.[34]

Being and Doing

One of the most serious questions arising from the disappointing and tragic events of this century is how man—not merely man generically, but every individual human being—can participate in history.
—Glenn Tinder[35]

Today, on one side many people are fiercely determined to transform society through action; on the other side, the number of failed plans and the scale of political violence in recent times have brought many others to a state of political despair. Civility is an effort to stand clear of both extremes, and neither to count on historical transformation nor to fall into political despondency.
—Glenn Tinder[36]

Current stands span the standard political spectrum. Here I identify some clear candidates for study in light of the concept, highlighting a few special features in each case. Let me begin with Glenn Tinder. Since his "civility" is proposed self-consciously as a stand, it easily sustains the full list of characteristics, concerns, connections, and contrasts of the stand. Tinder divides civility into three main principles: historical autonomy, comprehensive communality, and exemplary action.

Historical autonomy involves "standing off from history." It despairs of ideologies, groups, and leaders; it demands that the person maintain doubt and distance from the mainstreams of history, without withdrawing from responsibility and participation. "One cultivates civility when the primary question in every historical situation is not 'How can such and such an historical goal be reached?' but rather, 'How should I bear myself?' "[37] Recognize limits, but act nonetheless.

Comprehensive communality involves availability, an unreserved attentiveness and readiness to respond to others. "Such attentiveness expresses a concern for all human experience, an unwillingness that anything should remain unheard or unknown." Yet "only a few of the most prominent political and cultural leaders can speak to all mankind; many people may feel that they have no opportunities to speak seriously at all—not even to those to whom they are closest. Hence all that can be asked of most of us is that we be prepared to respond to our 'neighbor'—to the one whom we happen to encounter in a situation with communal possibilities—and in responding to speak of the concerns of mankind." This is not to pull away from principles or autonomy. Instead "comprehensive attentiveness and availability engage one in a universal relationship which precludes total absorption in any particular relationship; in this way they dissolve ideologies and group demands."[38]

Tinder's idea of exemplary action is much the same as mine. He explains that "although civility expresses a dislike of action, it is not simply a form of inaction. . . . Responsibility in the absence of community entails action. The problem is to find a formula for action that is congruent with autonomy." The solution is to "carry out those acts which [one] believes would be historically beneficial if all, or at least all in some particular class to which [one] belongs, were [one] to carry them out. Adhering to such a standard expresses a responsibility toward all human beings. At the same time it permits autonomy."[39] Tinder's exemplary action epitomizes Weber's ethic of absolute ends. The actual consequences of action are subordinated to the hypothetical results that would occur if the examples were followed by most people. Not all exemplary action need downgrade actual effects, but Tinder's fuses insistence on responsibility with absolution for the actual results of standing on principle. A better merging of Weber's ordinarily opposite ethics to withstand troubled times could hardly be concocted.

Clearly Tinder's stand of civility arises from an analysis of our conditions as hard times. Indeed Tinder tends to read this into the very nature of politics and history.[40] Many stand takers do this, for it provides a way to slide between stands and stances. Thus the hope, humility, and responsibility without illusions at the center of civility may slip easily into willingness to compromise under favorable conditions. Such resonance with pluralism points to other key aspects of Tinder's stand. Tinder connects civility with virtues of liberalism, forging the fragments of that ideology into a postmodern stand. This is especially true of his treatment of tolerance and individual autonomy.[41] Liberalism is peculiarly vulnerable to the shift from ideology to stand because of how it enjoys presenting itself as the enemy of ideologies. But connections common for stands are clear in the case of civility, for Tinder is explicit in erecting his stand upon perspectives and principles drawn from religion and existentialism. In these respects and others, Tinder's civility shows itself to be a stand in the wake of liberalism.

Stand taking is apparent also in the afterglows of socialism and conservatism. Robert Heilbroner affords a socialist example. Since he is a source of my definition, there should be no doubt that his diagnosis of our times falls under the category of troubled times. Already quoted are his concerns for formulating a stand on the principles of Atlas. One root of that stand reaches into ancient stoicism (thereby suggesting yet another, much earlier stand in times of trouble). But its other main root is unquestionably nourished by democratic socialism. This is obvious from Heilbroner's earlier work, but it is plain enough in justifying that stand for our times.[42]

Still Heilbroner parts with ambition, collectivism, rationalism, and other mainstays of socialism in favor of an emphasis on personal responsibility for human survival. With all stand takers, he knows that "it is one thing to appraise matters of life and death by the principles of rational self-interest and quite another *to take responsibility for our choice.*" To be sure, "there are moral dilemmas to be faced even if one takes one's stand on the 'survivalist' principles." But this "essential commitment to life's continuance gives us the moral authority to take measures, perhaps very harsh measures, whose justification cannot be found in the precepts of rationality, but must be sought in the unbearable anguish we feel if we imagine ourselves as the executioners of mankind." As he says, this principle is grounded in religion, and it contrasts instructively with Tinder's considerably more cautious conception of action. But they agree that "to accept the limitation of our ability, both as individuals and as a collectivity, seems to be the most difficult idea that Promethean man must learn. But learn it he must and learn it he will. The only question is whether the teacher will be history or ourselves."[43]

If anything, modern conservatism is even more anti–ideological than liberalism. This leaves postmodern conservatism ever on the verge of easing from an ideology into a stand. Peter Berger has made that move. His "conservative humanism" concedes that bad times call for adjustments, and his assessments of current conditions portray us in troubled times, so that his stand is far from always with the status quo. In Berger's own words, "Our time is full of visions of the future, loudly and arrogantly proclaimed. Moral self-righteousness is evenly distributed throughout the political spectrum. They all tell us so confidently where it's at today and where, if only they have their way, it will be tomorrow. Yet in fact they know so very little, all these self-confident prophets of doom and salvation."[44]

Berger finds all other ideologies dated and perverse.[45] But while his brand of conservatism contains some time-honored principles of that ideology, it fits as well or better the contours of a stand. For Berger, "a conservative accepts the messiness of history and is suspicious of the idea of progress. . . . A conservative is skeptical of innovation. He is doubly skeptical of violent innovation. . . . A conservative accepts human beings as they are" and "values order, continuity, and triviality in social life. . . . A conservative is skeptical of grand intellectual designs for the improvement of society" and "of 'movements.' . . . A conservative is inclined to leave people alone." Berger eschews political programs because they must inspire masses of people; he would address individuals. And nowhere is his stand clearer than in its "very simple political maxims: Learn how to refuse the existing orthodoxies. Learn also how to refuse the would-be orthodoxies of tomorrow. Participate in the lives of others, but think your own thoughts. Accept 'alienation'—it is the price of freedom. Learn how to stand apart."[46]

Berger's interest in religion and the sociology of knowledge, two connections common among stand takers, is well known. His concerns for community and action are equally evident. His turn toward a stand surfaces in his insistence that "it is necessary to cultivate the quiet art of disbelief. It is necessary to act quietly and disbelievingly, out of that compassion which is the only credible motive to any actions to change the world." For few "visions survive a single generation. Few historical actions lead to the intended consequences. This insight need not be paralyzing. Political morality does not demand visions or certainties, only that we act as best we can. The best political morality is informed by the heavy knowledge of the past. Its fruits are humility and compassion."[47] Celebrating humility, compassion, independent action, restrained responsibility, and the rest, Berger both sings the praises of ordinary politics and yet shapes the principles of autonomy for periods when politics as usual break down or get abandoned. A full-scale study of Berger's work (especially his "political morality") would show the stand at least as prominent in his project as the standard forms of ideology, social science, or critique.

Modern ideologies have not disappeared altogether, so that self-professed liberals, socialists, and conservatives today include some ideologists. An easy source of American examples is the neoconservative ideology of classical liberalism. But some neoconservatives are better seen as stand takers. In addition to Berger, they include Robert Nisbet and Garry Wills. Even George Will may be migrating in this direction.[48]

Such stress upon ingredients of stands is scattered throughout the work of recent political theorists. Previous citations suggest some ways in which Hannah Arendt was a stand taker.[49] The same holds for Camus and Merleau-Ponty. All came to be uncomfortable with any ideology, even the ones with which they started. In this they repeated the political pattern of Weber, finding in our iron-cage conditions the call to take a stand. Just as Weber's two late essays, "Politics as a Vocation" and "Science as a Vocation," combined to state his stand, so Arendt, Camus, and Merleau-Ponty became increasingly specific about the stand side of their thought and action. In all these cases, the commitment to define what Merleau-Ponty termed "a new humanism" signaled a turn toward the stand.

Sheldon Wolin and John Schaar may fit this mold. Both argue the inadequacy of ideologies in form, content, and project, whatever their location from left to right. But neither proposes a blueprint for an alternative, and both are cautious in their visions for the future. They prize the individual but criticize individualism; they praise community but only on a small scale. Inspired to some extent by stoicism, Schaar counsels against hope but for patience and irony. "Hopeful people, when hope is too often defeated, frequently turn spoiled and bitter; or, what is equally debilitating, vacillate between hope and despair. Sustained struggle is more likely to spring from an outlook that catches up both of the opposites and transforms them into something different from each. I have no name for this outlook, but I am pretty sure that its chief ingredients are patience and irony."[50]

Wolin treats political theory as a vocation, a project of exemplary action in our times of trouble.[51] Moreover he argues that theorists in other times have taken this stand, thereby creating an epic tradition of political theory pursued as political action. "The phrase 'epic tradition' refers to a type of political theory which is inspired mainly by the hope of achieving a great and memorable deed through the medium of thought. Other aims that it may have, such as contributing to the existing state of knowledge, formulating a system of logically consistent propositions, or establishing a set of hypotheses for scientific investigation, are distinctly secondary."[52] In this context, Wolin mentions not only Achilles but also Plato to exemplify the glorious political actor. And Wolin's own theory seems to strive for that aim.[53] If we ask what Schaar and Wolin are trying to accomplish in their theory, the best single answer may be "a stand."

The same might even be said for some of the Frankfurt School. Martin Jay's book on the dialectical imagination of its early members emphasizes their criticism of ideologies, including the Marxism with which they began.[54] It traces their preoccupation with praxis, which arose from distress at recent revolution and despair about the appearance of some true agent of change. It even notes their "cosmic irony," their penchant for future visions almost too abstract to be utopian, and their focus upon Critical Theory as our closest possible approximation to responsible political action. Thus the works of Walter Benjamin, Max Horkheimer, Theodor Adorno, and Herbert Marcuse may be plumbed from perspectives of the stand. There are few plainer examples of the stand than Marcuse's "Great Refusal."[55] And there are few harder indictments of the twentieth century as an interim of irreconcilable conflicts and contradictions than these thinkers provide. Even later members (like Jürgen Habermas) may be turning toward stands. They seek no new ideologies but concentrate on Critical Theory as a kind of action, and they express concerns with praxis and communication. Indeed some lean toward the extreme, unstable stand of ironism.

Certainly there are other prominent theorists of our times whose work eludes standard categories for political forms and projects. Leo Strauss, Michael Polanyi, and Eric Voegelin come quickly to mind. But they are only a few on the list of possible stand makers and takers. Even the work of Henry Kariel (who stresses continual movement, open systems, and redefinition of self) can be explicated in terms of taking a stand. In Kariel's case, of course, the stand must be pretty peculiar to be capable of incorporating his repeated stress upon keeping open not just options but principles. Yet it is this very feature that calls to mind ironism, that most paradoxical of stands. Especially in promoting "experimental action," Kariel seems to call for the strategy of Proteus in withstanding troubled times.[56]

Still we need not confine the concept of the stand to our own period. We should expect some stands in all times of civilizational turmoil—and especially when prospects for constructive, at least partially controlled change seem poor. The key is not so much a period's objective character as its subjective perception on the part of individual thinkers and actors. This determines whether to turn away from utopias, ideologies, stances, or other projects, and toward some stand—as well as what the stand will be. But, of course, the validity and viability of a project depend in important ways on how accurately we assess the objective ethos of the times.

Fire and Rain

> *I've seen fire and I've seen rain.*
> *I've seen sunny days that I thought would never end.*
> *I've seen lonely times when I could not find a friend.*
> *But I always thought that I'd see you again.*
> *Look down upon me, Jesus, you've got to help me take a stand.*

You've just got to see me through another day.
My body's aching and my time is at hand.
And I won't make it any other way.
—James Taylor[57]

    The issue here is how to understand current political forms and projects, especially among political theorists. I argue that diagnosing contemporary conditions as troubled times encourages taking political stands, that many twentieth-century theorists make that diagnosis, and that their projects are often better interpreted as stands than otherwise. The issue here is not whether ours are times of trouble, for that has been assumed more than argued. Still it must claim a few words in closing. Plainly I do think that there is some reason to interpret our times as times of trouble, which means that there is now much to recommend making and taking stands. And if this is true, not all the outstanding political actors of our day are revolutionaries or great practitioners of ordinary politics. Stand-taking theorists, whose exemplary action may be more in tune with the times, deserve serious consideration as some of our greatest political figures. When we see among the glorious political actors of the past not only Achilles but also Plato, Aristotle in addition to Alexander, and More as well as Henry VIII, we are reminded that this judgment is far from unprecedented, let alone undue.

It follows also that we may expect the making and taking of stands to continue to comprise a significant part of political theory and practice in years ahead. Of course, we should expect different degrees of awareness in doing so. In fact, some of the most fascinating cases are middle ones, where individuals do not set out to take stands, but explicitly eschew other options, and end up enunciating or embracing a few basic principles as protection against corruption and irresponsibility.

Political theory is only one arena among many in which a small community may be sought and a protected space for exemplary action found. After all, there are a number of other forums that can provide a suitable space to stand. Among the most obvious are literature and art, which can contribute exemplary action for close colleagues and converts, plus modes of communication for reaching others.[58] Another is the religious communalism of our times, which should serve as a reminder of the sphere Weber originally intended for ethics of absolute ends. Indeed interactions among political and religious movements of late signal this possibility even without Weber's nudge.[59] In these and other places, stands will be made. Even when outside ordinary politics, they will tend to be, in a significant sense, political stands. For in the well-known words of Thomas Mann, "in our time the destiny of man presents its meaning in political terms."

To stand times of trouble, there are few substitutes for holding fast to the most fundamental principles of responsibility. When old institutions and hopes collapse, the fires and rains of trouble rage unabated, and the time comes to make a stand or be swept away. In the winds that blow then, only the protection of the strongest principles and the firmest friends can suffice. Only they can afford a sheltered space to survive the storm. And only there can we stand upright.

NOTES

INDEX

NOTES

Cited among these notes are various unpublished papers provided to me by the authors. I wish to thank them for their generosity.

Introduction

1. Lionel Trilling, "George Orwell and the Politics of Truth," pp. 343–57, in Irving Howe, ed., *Orwell's Nineteen Eighty-Four*, 2d ed. (New York: Harcourt Brace Jovanovich, 1982), 344.

2. Jorge Luis Borges, *Seven Nights*, trans. E. Weinberger (London: Faber and Faber, 1986), 13.

1. Returning Pluralism to Political Science

1. Quoted in Laurence J. Peter, *Peter's Quotations* (New York: Bantam, 1977), 374.

2. See John S. Nelson, "Natures and Futures for Political Theory," pp. 3–24, in John S. Nelson, ed., *What Should Political Theory Be Now?* (Albany: State University of New York Press, 1983).

3. See Frederika Randall, "Why Scholars Become Storytellers," *New York Times Book Review*, January 29, 1984, pp. 1, 31; Allan Megill and John S. Nelson, "Academics Meet to Talk About Making Their Talk Understandable," *Des Moines Register*, March 25, 1984, op-ed sec., p. 3; Ellen K. Coughlin, "Finding the Message in the Medium: The Rhetoric of Scholarly Research," *Chronicle of Higher Education*, April 11, 1984, pp. 1, 9; Herbert W. Simons, "Chronicle and Critique of a Conference," *Quarterly Journal of Speech* 71 (February 1985): 52–64; John R. Lyne, "Rhetorics of Inquiry," *Quarterly Journal of Speech* 71, (February 1985): 65–73; Karen J. Winkler, "Questioning the Science in Social Science, Scholars Signal a 'Turn to Interpretation,' " *Chronicle of Higher Education*, June 26, 1985, pp. 5–6.

4. My efforts directed toward the twilight zone between abstract philosophy of science and detailed design of research include "The Ideological Connection, Parts I and II," *Theory and Society* 4 (fall–winter 1977): 421–48, 573–90, and "Education for Politics: Rethinking Research on Political Socialization," pp. 413–78, in Nelson, *What Should Political Theory Be Now?*

5. Early studies of tropes in inquiry include Stephen Pepper, *World Hypotheses* (Berkeley: University of California Press, 1942); Hayden White, *Metahistory* (Baltimore: Johns Hopkins University Press, 1973), and *Tropics of Discourse* (Baltimore: Johns Hopkins University Press, 1978). Also see John S. Nelson: "Review Essay on *Metahistory* by Hayden White," *History and Theory* 14 (1975): 74–91, and "Tropal History and the Social Sciences," *History and Theory* 19 (1980): 80–101.

234

6. See Everett Mendelsohn and Yehuda Elkana, eds., *Sciences and Cultures* (Boston: D. Reidel, 1981).

7. See John S. Nelson, "Account and Acknowledge, or Represent and Control? On Postmodern Politics and Economics of Collective Responsibility," *Accounting, Organizations, and Society* 18 (February–April 1993): 207–29.

8. See John S. Nelson, "Irony and Autonomy: How and Why to Read John Gunnell," *Tradition, Interpretation, and Science* (Albany: State University of New York Press, 1986), 1–20.

9. See John S. Nelson, "Political Theory as Political Rhetoric," pp. 169–240, and "Education for Politics" in Nelson, *What Should Political Theory Be Now?*

10. See John S. Nelson and Allan Megill, "Rhetoric of Inquiry: Projects and Prospects," *Quarterly Journal of Speech* 72 (February 1986): 20–37; John S. Nelson, Allan Megill, and D. N. McCloskey, eds., *The Rhetoric of the Human Sciences* (Madison: University of Wisconsin Press, 1987).

11. Randolph Bourne, *Youth and Life* (1913), quoted in John Gross, ed., *The Oxford Book of Aphorisms* (Oxford, England: Oxford University Press, 1983), 249.

12. See John S. Nelson, Allan Megill, and D. N. McCloskey, "Rhetoric of Inquiry," pp. 3–18, in Nelson, Megill, and McCloskey, *Rhetoric of the Human Sciences*.

13. In addition to works cited in notes 2 and 9, see W. J. T. Mitchell, ed., "The Politics of Interpretation," *Critical Inquiry* 9 (September 1982): 1–278; Daniel Bell, ed., "New Directions in Modern Thought," *Partisan Review* 51 (1984): 215–300; Ralph Cohen, ed., "Interpretation and Culture," *New Literary History* 17 (winter 1986): 183–390; Ralph Cohen, ed., "Philosophy of Science and Literary Theory," *New Literary History* 17 (autumn 1985): 1–171.

14. See John S. Nelson, "Political Foundations for Rhetoric of Inquiry," pp. 258–89, in Herbert W. Simons, ed., *The Rhetorical Turn* (Chicago: University of Chicago Press, 1990).

15. On sociology, see Robert W. Friedrichs, *A Sociology of Sociology* (New York: Free Press, 1970); and Alvin W. Gouldner, *The Coming Crisis of Western Sociology* (New York: Avon, 1970). On economics, see George J. Stigler, *The Economist as Preacher* (Chicago: University of Chicago Press, 1982); and D. N. McCloskey, *The Rhetoric of Economics* (Madison: University of Wisconsin Press, 1985). On historiography, see J. H. Hexter, *On Historians* (Cambridge, Mass.: Harvard University Press, 1979); and Dominick LaCapra and Steven L. Kaplan, eds., *Modern European Intellectual History* (Ithaca, N.Y.: Cornell University Press, 1982). On psychology, see Richard Nisbet and Lee Ross, *Human Inference* (Englewood Cliffs, N.J.: Prentice-Hall, 1980); and Donal E. Carlston, "Turning Psychology on Itself: The Rhetoric of Psychology and the Psychology of Rhetoric," pp. 145–62, in Nelson, Megill, and McCloskey, *Rhetoric of the Human Sciences*. On anthropology, see Dell Hymes, ed., *Reinventing Anthropology* (New York: Random House, 1969); and Renato Rosaldo, "Where Objectivity Lies: The Rhetoric of Anthropology," pp. 87–110, in Nelson, Megill, and McCloskey, *Rhetoric of the Human Sciences*. On political science, see David M.

Ricci, *The Tragedy of Political Science* (New Haven, Conn.: Yale University Press, 1984); and John G. Gunnell, *Between Philosophy and Politics* (Amherst: University of Massachusetts Press, 1986). On reflexive social science in general, see Gareth Morgan, ed., *Beyond Method* (Newbury Park, Calif.: Sage, 1983).

16. See Nelson, Megill, and McCloskey, *Rhetoric of the Human Sciences*.

17. See Stephen Toulmin, *The Uses of Argument* (New York: Cambridge University Press, 1964), and *Human Understanding* (Princeton, N.J.: Princeton University Press, 1972).

18. See John S. Nelson, "Toltechs, Aztechs, and the Art of the Possible: Parenthetic Comments on the Political Through Language and Aesthetics," *Polity* 8 (fall 1975): 80–116, and "Seven Rhetorics of Inquiry: A Provocation," pp. 407–34, in Nelson, Megill, and McCloskey, *Rhetoric of the Human Sciences*.

19. See Glenn Tinder, *Community* (Baton Rouge: Louisiana State University Press, 1980); Nelson, "Natures and Futures for Political Theory" and "Political Theory as Political Rhetoric" in Nelson, *What Should Political Theory Be Now?*

20. Alexis de Tocqueville, quoted in Peter, *Peter's Quotations*, 224.

21. See Nelson, "Political Theory as Political Rhetoric" Nelson, *What Should Political Theory Be Now?*

22. See John S. Nelson, "Beyond an Old Divide: Rediscovering Humanities in Political Science," *Social Education* 49 (September–October 1985): 433–34.

23. See William T. Bluhm et al., "Political Science and the Humanities: A Report of the American Political Science Association," *PS* 18 (spring 1985): 247–59.

24. Johann Wolfgang von Goethe, quoted in W. H. Auden and Louis Kronenberger, eds., *The Viking Book of Aphorisms* (New York: Penguin, 1962), 252.

25. Coughlin, "Finding the Message," 1.

26. See Bruno Latour and Steve Woolgar, *Laboratory Life* (Princeton, N.J.: Princeton University Press, 1986); Bruno Latour, *Science in Action* (Cambridge, Mass.: Harvard University Press, 1987).

27. See W. Phillips Shively, ed., *The Research Process in Political Science* (Itasca, Ill.: F. E. Peacock, 1984); M. Patricia Golden, ed., *The Research Experience* (Itasca, Ill.: F. E. Peacock, 1976); Elinor Ostrom, ed., *Strategies of Political Inquiry* (Newbury Park, Calif.: Sage, 1982); Judith A. Gillespie and Dina A. Zinnes, eds., *Missing Elements in Political Inquiry* (Newbury Park, Calif.: Sage, 1982); Herbert B. Asher et al., eds., *Theory-Building and Data Analysis in the Social Sciences* (Knoxville: University of Tennessee Press, 1984); Phillip E. Hammond, ed., *Sociologists at Work* (Garden City, N.Y.: Doubleday, 1964).

28. See John S. Nelson, "Stories of Science and Politics: Some Rhetorics of Political Research," pp. 198–220, in Nelson, Megill, and McCloskey, *Rhetoric of the Human Sciences*.

29. See W. J. T. Mitchell, ed., "On Narrative," *Critical Inquiry* 7 (autumn 1980): 5–236.

30. See Michael Calvin McGee and John S. Nelson, "Narrative Reason in Public Argument," *Journal of Communication* 35 (autumn 1985): 139–55.

31. See David R. Hiley, James F. Bohman, and Richard Shusterman, eds.,

The Interpretive Turn (Ithaca, N.Y.: Cornell University Press, 1991); Nelson, "Political Foundations for Rhetoric of Inquiry" in Simons, *Rhetorical Turn.*

32. See Aristotle, *Rhetoric* and *Poetics,* trans. W. Rhys Roberts and Ingram Bywater, ed. Friedrich Somlsen (New York: Random House, 1954). Also see Kenneth Burke, *A Grammar of Motives* (Berkeley: University of California Press, 1945), *Language as Symbolic Action* (Berkeley: University of California Press, 1966), *The Philosophy of Literary Form,* 3d ed. (Berkeley: University of California Press, 1973, and *A Rhetoric of Motives* (Berkeley: University of California Press, 1950). See Wayne C. Booth, *Modern Dogma and the Rhetoric of Assent* (Chicago: University of Chicago Press, 1974), *The Rhetoric of Fiction* (Chicago: University of Chicago Press, 1961), and *A Rhetoric of Irony* (Chicago: University of Chicago Press, 1974). Also see White, *Metahistory* and *Tropics of Discourse.*

33. See Paul F. Kress, "Against Epistemology: Apostate Musings," *Journal of Politics* 41 (May 1979): 526–42; Daniel R. Sabia Jr., "Comment on Paul Kress's 'Against Epistemology,' " *Journal of Politics* 42 (November 1980): 1154; Lawrence A. Scaff, "Bringing Politics Back In," *Journal of Politics* 42 (November 1980): 1155–59; Eugene F. Miller, "Epistemology and Political Inquiry: Comment on Kress' 'Against Epistemology,' " *Journal of Politics* 42 (November 1980): 1160–67; Paul Kress, "Reply to Commentaries on 'Against Epistemology," *Journal of Politics* 42 (November 1980): 1168–69; Jane Flax, "Why Epistemology Matters: A Reply to Kress," *Journal of Politics* 43 (November 1981): 1006–24; Paul Kress, "Rejoinder to Flax," *Journal of Politics* 43 (November 1981): 1025–28. Also see many of the essays in Nelson, *What Should Political Theory Be Now?*

34. See Richard Ashcraft, "On the Problem of Methodology and the Nature of Political Theory," *Political Theory* 3 (February 1975): 5–25, and "Political Theory and the Problem of Ideology," *Journal of Politics* 42 (August 1980): 687–705; David V. J. Bell, *Power, Influence, and Authority* (New York: Oxford University Press, 1975); William T. Bluhm, *Theories of the Political System* (Englewood Cliffs, N.J.: Prentice-Hall, 1965); Pierre Bourdieu, *Outline of a Theory of Practice,* trans. Richard Nice (Cambridge, England: Cambridge University Press, 1977); Richard H. Brown, *A Poetic for Sociology* (New York: Cambridge University Press, 1977); William E. Connolly, *The Terms of Political Discourse* (Lexington, Mass.: Heath, 1974), and *Appearance and Reality* (Amherst: University of Massachusetts Press, 1981); John Danford, *Wittgenstein and Political Philosophy* (Chicago: University of Chicago Press, 1978); Maria Falco, ed., *Through the Looking-Glass* (Washington, D.C.: University Press of America, 1979); Paul K. Feyerabend, *Against Method* (Atlantic Highlands, N.J.: Humanities Press, 1975); Jørgen Habermas, *The Theory of Communicative Action,* trans. Thomas McCarthy (Boston: Beacon, 1981); Thomas S. Kuhn, *The Structure of Scientific Revolutions* (Chicago: University of Chicago Press, 1970); Harold D. Lasswell, *Politics* (New York: World, 1958); Harold D. Lasswell and Abraham D. Kaplan, *Power and Society* (New Haven, Conn.: Yale University Press, 1950); Alasdair MacIntyre, *After Virtue,* 2d ed. (Notre Dame, Ind.: University of Notre Dame Press, 1984); Hanna Fenichel Pitkin, *Wittgenstein and Justice* (Berkeley: Univer-

sity of California Press, 1972); Paul Ricoeur, *The Rule of Metaphor,* trans. Robert Czerny (Toronto: University of Toronto Press, 1977); Stanley Rosen, *Nihilism* (New Haven, Conn.: Yale University Press, 1969); Roberto Mangabeira Unger, *Knowledge and Politics* (New York: Free Press, 1975); Ludgwig Wittgenstein, *Philosophical Investigations,* 3d ed., ed. and trans. G. E. M. Anscombe (New York: Macmillan, 1958); Ellen Meiksens Wood, *Mind and Politics* (Berkeley: University of California Press, 1972).

35. See J. G. A. Pocock, "Political Theory, History, and Myth: A Salute to John Gunnell," *Annals of Scholarship* 1 (fall 1980): 3–25; John G. Gunnell, "Method, Methodology, and the Search for Traditions in the History of Political Theory: A Reply to Pocock's Salute," *Annals of Scholarship* 1(fall 1980): 26–56; J. G. A. Pocock, "Intentions, Traditions and Methods: Some Sounds on a Fog-Horn," *Annals of Scholarship* 1 (fall 1980): 57–62.

36. See Stanley Cavell, *The Claim of Reason* (New York: Oxford University Press, 1979); MacIntyre, *After Virtue;* Robert Nozick, *Philosophical Explanations* (Cambridge, Mass.: Harvard University Press, 1981); Richard Rorty, *Philosophy and the Mirror of Nature* (Princeton, N.J.: Princeton University Press, 1979).

37. See Jonathan Culler, *Structuralist Poetics* (Ithaca, N.Y.: Cornell University Press, 1976); Paul de Man, *Allegories of Reading* (New Haven, Conn.: Yale University Press, 1978); Jacques Derrida, *Of Grammatology,* trans. Gayatri Chakravorty Spivak (Baltimore: Johns Hopkins University Press, 1976), and *Writing and Difference,* trans. Alan Blass, (Chicago: University of Chicago Press, 1978); Northrop Frye, *Anatomy of Criticism* (Princeton, N.J.: Princeton University Press, 1957); Geoffrey H. Hartman, *The Fate of Reading* (Chicago: University of Chicago Press, 1975); E. D. Hirsch Jr., *Validity in Interpretation* (New Haven, Conn.: Yale University Press, 1967); Fredric Jameson, *The Political Unconscious* (Ithaca, N.Y.: Cornell University Press, 1981); Edward Said, *Beginnings* (New York: Basic, 1975).

38. See Max Black, *Models and Metaphors* (Ithaca, N.Y.: Cornell University Press, 1962), *The Importance of Language* (Ithaca, N.Y.: Cornell University Press, 1962), *The Labyrinth of Language* (New York: Praeger, 1968), and *Margins of Precision* (Ithaca, N.Y.: Cornell University Press, 1970). Also see Paul Ziff, *Semantic Analysis* (Ithaca, N.Y.: Cornell University Press, 1960), *Philosophic Turnings* (Ithaca, N.Y.: Cornell University Press, 1966), and *Understanding Understanding* (Ithaca, N.Y.: Cornell University Press, 1972).

39. See Robert L. Scott, "On Viewing Rhetoric as Epistemic," *Central States Speech Journal* 18 (February 1967): 9–17; Michael C. Leff, "In Search of Ariadne's Thread: A Review of the Recent Literature on Rhetorical Theory," *Central States Speech Journal* 29 (summer 1978): 73–91.

40. See Paul N. Campbell, "Poetic-Rhetorical, Philosophical, and Scientific Discourse," *Philosophy and Rhetoric* 6 (winter 1973): 1–29; James Benjamin, "On Symbological Hierarchies," *Philosophy and Rhetoric* 8 (summer 1975): 165–71; Richard M. Weaver, *The Ethics of Rhetoric* (Chicago: Regnery, 1953). On the traditional contrast between rhetoric and either logic or philosophy, see Jerrold E. Seigel, *Rhetoric and Philosophy in Renaissance Humanism* (Princeton, N.J.:

Princeton University Press, 1968); Albert William Levi, *Humanism and Politics* (Bloomington: Indiana University Press, 1969); Nancy S. Struever, *The Language of History in the Renaissance* (Princeton, N.J.: Princeton University Press, 1974); Linda Gardiner Janik, "Lorenzo Valla: The Primacy of Rhetoric and the Demoralization of History," *History and Theory* 12 (1973): 389–404; James Stephens, "Rhetorical Problems in Renaissance Science," *Philosophy and Rhetoric* 8 (fall 1975): 213–29; Lawrence J. Johnson, "The 'Linguistic Imperialism' of Lorenzo Valla and the Renaissance Humanists," *Interpretation* 7 (September 1978): 29–49; Rainer Weiss, "The Humanist Rediscovery of Rhetoric as Philosophy: Giovanni Viovano Pontano's Aegidius," *Philosophy and Rhetoric* 13 (winter 1980): 25–42; Ernesto Grassi, "Can Rhetoric Provide a New Basis for Philosophizing? The Humanist Tradition, Parts I and II," *Philosophy and Rhetoric* 11 (winter–spring 1978): 1–18, 75–97, and "Italian Humanism and Heidegger's Thesis of the End of Philosophy," *Philosophy and Rhetoric* 13 (spring 1980): 79–98.

41. Abraham Kaplan, *The Conduct of Inquiry* (Scranton, Pa.: Chandler, 1964).

42. See Pepper, *World Hypotheses;* Burke, "Four Master Tropes," *A Grammar of Motives,* 503–17; Frye, *Anatomy of Criticism;* White, *Metahistory;* W. J. T. Mitchell, ed., "Metaphor," *Critical Inquiry* 5 (autumn 1978): 3–200; Ralph Cohen, ed., "Narrative Analysis and Interpretation," *New Literary History* 13 (winter 1982): 179–339. Also see Nelson, "Review Essay on *Metahistory*" and "Tropal History and the Social Sciences."

43. See Bluhm et al., "Political Science and the Humanities"; Nelson, "Beyond an Old Divide."

44. See Bryan S. Green, *Literary Methods and Sociological Theory* (Chicago: University of Chicago Press, 1988).

45. Oliver Sacks, quoted in Walter Clemons, "Listening to the Lost: Case Histories by an Unusual Doctor Become Literary Art," *Newsweek,* August 20, 1984, p. 70. See Charles Bazerman and James Paradis, eds., *Textual Dynamics of the Professions* (Madison: University of Wisconsin Press, 1991).

46. See Herbert W. Simons, ed., *Rhetoric in the Human Sciences* (Newbury Park, Calif.: Sage, 1989); Jack Selzer, ed., *Understanding Scientific Prose* (Madison: University of Wisconsin Press, 1993).

47. See D. N. McCloskey, *The Rhetoric of Economics* (Madison: University of Wisconsin Press, 1985), *The Writing of Economics* (New York: Macmillan, 1987), *If You're So Smart* (Chicago: University of Chicago Press, 1990), *Knowledge and Persuasion in Economics* (New York: Cambridge University Press, 1993), and *The Vices of Economists, the Virtues of the Bourgeoisie* (Amsterdam: Amsterdam University Press, 1996). Also see Arjo Klamer, D. N. McCloskey, and Robert M. Solow, eds., *The Consequences of Economic Rhetoric* (New York: Cambridge University Press, 1988); Marianne A. Ferber and Julie A. Nelson, eds., *Beyond Economic Man* (Chicago: University of Chicago Press, 1993). An economist who practices rhetoric of inquiry within his economics is Albert O. Hirschman, *Exit, Voice, and Loyalty* (Cambridge, Mass.: Harvard University Press, 1970), *The Passions and the Interests* (Princeton, N.J.: Princeton University

Press, 1977), *The Rhetoric of Reaction* (Cambridge, Mass.: Harvard University Press, 1981), and *Shifting Involvements* (Princeton, N.J.: Princeton University Press, 1982).

48. See James Boyd White, *The Legal Imagination* (Chicago: University of Chicago Press, 1973), *When Words Lose Their Meaning* (Chicago: University of Chicago Press, 1984), *Heracles' Bow* (Madison: University of Wisconsin Press, 1985), and *Justice as Translation* (Chicago: University of Chicago Press, 1990). Also see John S. Nelson, "When Words Gain Their Meanings," *Rhetoric Society Quarterly* 21 (summer 1991): 22–37.

49. See James Clifford and George E. Marcus, eds., *Writing Culture* (Berkeley: University of California Press, 1986); Clifford Geertz, *Works and Lives* (Palo Alto, Calif.: Stanford University Press, 1988); Paul Hernadi, ed., *The Rhetoric of Interpretation and the Interpretation of Rhetoric* (Durham, N.C.: Duke University Press, 1989).

50. See Robert von Hallberg, ed., "Canons," *Critical Inquiry* 10 (September 1983): iii–223; W. J. T. Mitchell, ed., "More on Canons," *Critical Inquiry* 10 (March 1984): 462–542.

51. See Ralph Cohen, ed., "On Conventions: I," *New Literary History* 13 (autumn 1981): 1–177.

52. See Ralph Cohen, ed., "On Conventions: II," *New Literary History* 14 (winter 1983): 225–407.

53. See John G. Gunnell, *Political Theory* (Cambridge, Mass.: Winthrop, 1979).

54. T. S. Eliot, quoted in Bernard Darwin, ed., *The Oxford Dictionary of Quotations*, corrected 3d ed. (Oxford, England: Oxford University Press, 1980), 205.

55. See Nelson, "The Ideological Connection, I–II."

56. See G. R. Boynton, "Telling a Good Story: Models of Argument, Models of Understanding in the Senate Agriculture Committee," pp. 429–38, in Joseph W. Wenzel, ed., *Argument and Critical Practices* (Annandale, Va.: Speech Communication Association, 1987), "Conversations about Governing," pp. 167–74, in Bruce E. Gronbeck, ed., *Spheres of Argument* (Annandale, Va.: Speech Communication Association, 1989), "Ideas and Action: A Cognitive Model of the Senate Agriculture Committee," *Political Behavior* 12 (June 1990): 181–213, and "When Senators and Publics Meet at the Senate Environmental Protection Subcommittee," *Discourse and Society* 2 (April 1991): 131–55. Also see Milton Lodge and Kathleen McGraw, eds., *Political Judgment* (Ann Arbor: University of Michigan Press, 1995).

57. See Glenn Tinder, *Tolerance* (Amherst: University of Massachusetts Press, 1975); John L. Sullivan, James Piereson, and George E. Marcus, "An Alternative Conceptualization of Political Tolerance: Illusory Increases, 1950s–1970s," *American Political Science Review* 73 (September 1979): 781–94.

58. See Dan D. Nimmo and Keith R. Sanders, eds., *Handbook of Political Communication* (Newbury Park, Calif.: Sage, 1981); Nelson, "Education for Politics" in Nelson, *What Should Political Theory Be Now?*

59. See Michael Calvin McGee, "The Ideograph: A Link Between Rhetoric

and Ideology," *Quarterly Journal of Speech* 66 (February 1980): 1–16, "The Origins of 'Liberty': A Feminization of Power," *Communication Monographs* 47 (March 1980): 25–45, and "An Essay on the Flip Side of Privacy," pp. 105–15, in David Zarefsky, Malcolm O. Sillars, and Jack Rhodes, eds., *Argument in Transition* (Annandale, Va.: Speech Communication Association, 1983). Also see John Louis Lucaites, "Substantive and Regulative Functions of Ideographs: 'Liberty,' 'Order,' and 'Public Trust' in Eighteenth-Century Anglo-Whiggism," pp. 285–304, in Zarefsky, Sillars, and Rhodes, *Argument in Transition;* Celeste Michelle Condit and John Louis Lucaites, *Crafting Equality* (Chicago: University of Chicago Press, 1993).

60. See Murray Edelman, *The Symbolic Uses of Politics* (Urbana: University of Illinois Press, 1985), and *Constructing the Political Spectacle* (Chicago: University of Chicago Press, 1988). Also see Charles D. Elder and Roger W. Cobb, *The Uses of Political Symbols* (New York: Longman, 1983).

61. See Ferber and Nelson, *Beyond Economic Man.*

62. See Charles Jencks, *What Is Postmodernism?* (New York: St. Martin's, 1986); John Fiske, *Reading the Popular* (Boston: Unwin Hyman, 1989); Jim Collins, *Architectures of Excess* (New York: Routledge, 1995).

63. See Hannah Arendt, *On Revolution* (New York: Viking, 1963); Nelson, "Political Foundations for Rhetoric of Inquiry," in Simons, *Rhetorical Turn.*

64. See Burke, "Four Master Tropes."

65. See Roman Jakobson, *Language in Literature* (Cambridge, Mass.: Belknap Press, 1987); Richard H. Brown, *A Poetic for Sociology* (Chicago: University of Chicago Press, 1977).

66. See Max Black, "Metaphor," *Models and Metaphors* (Ithaca, N.Y.: Cornell University Press, 1962), 25–47. This has been a trouble for even the best philosophers of metaphor: see Monroe Beardsley, "The Metaphorical Twist," *Philosophy and Phenomenological Research* 22 (March 1962): 293–307; Douglas Berggren, "The Use and Abuse of Metaphor, Parts I and II," *Review of Metaphysics* 26 (December 1962 and March 1963): 237–258, 450–72, and "From Myth to Metaphor," *Monist* 50 (October 1966): 530–52; Colin M. Turbayne, *The Myth of Metaphor* (New Haven, Conn.: Yale University Press, 1962); Philip Wheelwright, *Metaphor and Reality* (Bloomington: Indiana University Press, 1962); Martin Foss, *Symbol and Metaphor in Human Experience* (Lincoln: University of Nebraska Press, 1949); Earl R. MacCormac, "The Language Machine and Metaphor," *Philosophy of the Social Sciences* 2 (December 1972): 277–89, "Metaphor Revisited," *Journal of Aesthetics and Art Criticism* 30 (winter 1971): 239–50, and *Metaphor and Myth in Science and Religion* (Durham, N.C.: Duke University Press, 1976); Ina Loewenberg, "Truth and Consequences of Metaphors," *Philosophy and Rhetoric* 6 (winter 1973): 30–46; Walker Percy, "Metaphor as Mistake," *Sewanee Review* 66 (winter 1958); 79–99.

67. George A. Kennedy, *New Testament Interpretation Through Rhetorical Criticism* (Chapel Hill: University of North Carolina Press, 1984), 26–29.

68. See Richard A. Lanham, *A Handlist of Rhetorical Terms* (Berkeley: University of California Press, 1968); Arthur Quinn, *Figures of Speech* (Berkeley: University of California Press, 1986).

69. See de Man, *Allegories of Reading*. Also see Jacques Derrida, "White Metaphor: Metaphor in the Text of Philosophy," *New Literary History* 6 (autumn 1974): 5–74, *Dissemination*, trans. Barbara Johnson (Chicago: University of Chicago Press, 1981), and *Writing and Difference.*

70. See William Corlett, *Community Without Unity* (Durham, N.C.: Duke University Press, 1989); Diane Rubenstein: "Food for Thought: Metonymy in the Late Foucault," *Philosophy and Social Criticism* 12 (1987): 83–101, "Hate Boat: Greenpeace, National Identity, and Nuclear Criticism," pp. 231–55, in James Der Derian and Michael Shapiro, eds., *International/Intertextual Relations* (Lexington, Mass.: Heath, 1989), "The Mirror of Reproduction," *Political Theory* 17 (November 1989): 582–606, "The Anxiety of Affluence: Baudrillard and Science Fiction of the Reagan Era," pp. 73–94, in William Stearns, ed., *Baudrillard in the Mountains* (New York: St. Martin's, 1990), and "This Is Not a President: Baudrillard, Bush and Enchanted Simulation," *The Hysterical Male* (New York: St. Martin's Press, 1991), 253–65; Michael J. Shapiro: "The Rhetoric of Social Science: The Political Responsibilities of the Scholar," pp. 363–80, in Nelson, Megill, and McCloskey, *Rhetoric of the Human Sciences,* and "Representing World Politics: The Sport/War Intertext," pp. 69–96, in Der Derian and Shapiro, *International/Intertextual Relations.*

71. Michael Pollan, *Second Nature* (New York: Dell, 1991), 286.

2. Returning History to Political Science

1. Michel Foucault, *Discipline and Punish,* trans. Alan Sheridan (New York: Random House, 1977), 215.

2. On Western and especially modern epistemology as visual, see Richard Rorty, *Philosophy and the Mirror of Nature* (Princeton, N.J.: Princeton University Press, 1979), 16–60; Michael Calvin McGee and John S. Nelson, "Narrative Reason in Public Argument," *Journal of Communication* 35 (autumn 1985): 139–55. Also see Martin Jay, *Downcast Eyes: The Denigration of Vision in Twentieth-Century French Thought* (Berkeley: University of California Press, 1993), and *Vision in Context: Historical and Contemporary Perspectives on Sight* (New York: Routledge, 1996).

3. See John S. Nelson, "Commerce Among the Archipelagos: Rhetoric of Inquiry as a Practice of Coherent Education," pp. 78–100, in L. Robert Stevens, G. L. Seligmann, and Julian Long, eds., *The Core and the Canon* (Denton: University of North Texas Press, 1993).

4. See John S. Nelson, "Political Foundations for Rhetoric of Inquiry," pp. 258–89, in Herbert W. Simons, ed., *The Rhetorical Turn* (Chicago: University of Chicago Press, 1990).

5. See Paul K. Feyerabend, *Against Method* (Atlantic Highlands, N.J.: Humanities Press, 1975), and *Science in a Free Society* (London: New Left Books, 1978).

6. Wendell Berry, *Standing by Words* (San Francisco: North Point Press, 1983), 14.

7. Foucault, *Discipline and Punish*, 137.

8. See Hannah Arendt, *On Revolution* (New York: Viking, 1963), 139–215; Berry, *Standing by Words*, 3–23; Edward Shils, *Tradition* (Chicago: University of Chicago Press, 1981); Garry Wills, *Confessions of a Conservative* (Garden City, N.Y.: Doubleday, 1979), 209–31.

9. See Max Weber, *From Max Weber*, ed. and trans. H. H. Gerth and C. Wright Mills (New York: Oxford University Press, 1946), *Max Weber on Law in Economy and Society*, ed. Max Rheinstein, trans. Edward Shils and Max Reinstein (New York: Simon & Schuster, 1954), *On Charisma and Institution Building*, ed. S. N. Eisenstadt (Chicago: University of Chicago Press, 1968), and *Weber*, ed. W. G. Runciman, trans. E. Matthews (Cambridge, England: Cambridge University Press, 1978).

10. Foucault, *Discipline and Punish*, 209.

11. Ibid.

12. Berry, *Standing by Words*, 47.

13. See John S. Nelson, "Natures and Futures for Political Theory," pp. 3–24, in John S. Nelson, ed., *What Should Political Theory Be Now?* (Albany: State University of New York Press, 1983), 17–19.

14. See Harold Rosenberg, *The Anxious Object* (New York: Horizon Press, 1964), 227–55; Arendt, *On Revolution*, 217–85. Also see Robert Jay Lifton, "Protean Man," *Partisan Review* 35 (winter 1968): 13–27.

15. Philip Rieff, *Fellow Teachers* (New York: Harper & Row, 1972), 185–86.

16. See John S. Nelson and Allan Megill, "Rhetoric of Inquiry: Projects and Prospects," *Quarterly Journal of Speech* 72 (February 1986): 20–37; John S. Nelson, Allan Megill, and D. N. McCloskey, eds., *The Rhetoric of the Human Sciences* (Madison: University of Wisconsin Press, 1987).

17. Foucault, *Discipline and Punish*, 187.

18. See Berry, *Standing by Words*, 70. On the marginality of political theory to political science, see Nelson, "Natures and Futures for Political Theory" in Nelson, *What Should Political Theory Be Now?*; Robert Booth Fowler, "Does Political Theory Have a Future?" pp. 549–80, in Nelson, *What Should Political Theory Be Now?* On the advantages of marginality for inquiry both historical and rhetorical, see Wendell Berry, *The Unsettling of America* (San Francisco: Sierra Club Books, 1977), 170–223; Robert Hariman, "Status, Marginality, and Rhetorical Theory," *Quarterly Journal of Speech* 72 (February 1986): 38–54.

19. See also Renato Rosaldo, "Where Objectivity Lies: The Rhetoric of Anthropology," pp. 87–110, in Nelson, Megill, and McCloskey, *Rhetoric of the Human Sciences*; Paul Hernadi, "Literary Interpretation and the Rhetoric of the Human Sciences," pp. 263–75, in Nelson, Megill, and McCloskey, *Rhetoric of the Human Sciences*.

20. John G. Gunnell, "Interpretation and the History of Political Theory: Apology and Epistemology," *American Political Science Review* 76 (June 1982): 317–27, "Political Theory: The Evolution of a Subfield," pp. 3–45, in Ada W. Finifter, ed., *Political Science: The State of the Discipline* (Washington, D.C.: American Political Science Association, 1983), and "In Search of the Political

Object: Beyond Methodology and Transcendentalism," pp. 25–52, in Nelson, *What Should Political Theory Be Now?*

Also see Kathleen Toth, "The Art of Tradition," *Annals of Scholarship* 3 (1984): 65–91; John G. Gunnell, "Between Philosophy and Political Theory: Thinking on the Cusp," *Annals of Scholarship* 3 (1984): 93–101.

21. See Arjo Klamer, D. N. McCloskey, and Robert M. Solow, eds., *The Consequences of Economic Rhetoric* (New York: Cambridge University Press, 1988); James H. Nichols Jr. and Colin Wright, eds., *From Political Economy to Economics . . . And Back?* (San Francisco: Institute for Contemporary Studies Press, 1990).

22. See Richard J. Bernstein: *The Restructuring of Social and Political Theory* (Philadelphia: University of Pennsylvania Press, 1976), *Beyond Objectivism and Relativism* (Philadelphia: University of Pennsylvania Press, 1983), and *The New Constellation* (Cambridge, Mass.: MIT Press, 1991).

23. Berry, *Standing by Words*, 14.

24. Albert Somit and Joseph Tanenhaus, *The Development of Political Science* (Boston: Allyn and Bacon, 1967). I am not inclined to count the most likely counterexample: David M. Ricci, *The Tragedy of Political Science* (New Haven, Conn.: Yale University Press, 1984). As an indictment of the discipline for increasing irrelevance to politics, Ricci's book better fits the mold of transformational history discussed in connection with David Easton and John Gunnell. Through the American Political Science Association, Gunnell and others did mount a 1985 panel discussion of the book, but the mainstreams of the discipline show no signs of taking its arguments seriously. As an Israeli political theorist, moreover, Ricci remains doubly outside the discipline's core of American behavioralism. The other candidate is Raymond Seidelman, *Disenchanted Realists* (Albany: State University of New York Press, 1985). Yet it has received little notice.

25. See Terence Ball, *Political Theory and Praxis* (Minneapolis: University of Minnesota Press, 1977), *Idioms of Inquiry: Critique and Renewal in Political Science* (Albany: State University of New York Press, 1987), *Conceptual Change and the Constitution* (Lawrence: University Press of Kansas, 1988), and *Reappraising Political Theory* (New York: Oxford University Press, 1995). Also see Terence Ball, James Farr, and Russell L. Hanson, eds., *Political Innovation and Conceptual Change* (New York: Cambridge University Press, 1989).

26. Thomas S. Kuhn, *The Structure of Scientific Revolutions* (Chicago: University of Chicago Press, 1970), 136–43.

27. Typical of introductory methods texts is Alan C. Isaak, *Scope and Methods of Political Science*, 2d ed. (Homewood, Ill.: Dorsey Press, 1975), 31–43. But many texts lack even a chapter on disciplinary history. See Dickinson McGaw and George Watson, *Political and Social Inquiry* (New York: Wiley, 1976).

28. John S. Dryzek and Stephen T. Leonard, "History and Discipline in Political Science," *American Political Science Review* 82 (December 1988): 1245–46. I thank John G. Gunnell for suggesting that I clarify the relationship between my essay and that of Dryzek and Leonard, because we mostly agree.

29. Ibid., 1254, 1258.

30. Kuhn, *Structure of Scientific Revolutions*, 10–22.

31. See John S. Nelson, "Once More on Kuhn," *Political Methodology* 1 (spring 1974): 73–104.

32. See Charles J. Helm, "The Undisciplined 'Discipline': Searching for the Founders of Political Science," *Social Science Quarterly* 65 (December 1984): 1112–18; Heinz Eulau, "The Greening of Political Science: Where It Is At," *Social Science Quarterly* 65 (December 1984): 1119–28; Charles J. Helm, "Political Theory and the Structure of Political Science: Reviewing Some Issues," *Social Science Quarterly* 66 (June 1985): 461–63.

33. See Charles Bazerman, "Codifying the Social Scientific Style: The APA Publication Manual as a Behaviorist Rhetoric," pp. 125–44, in Nelson, Megill, and McCloskey, *Rhetoric of the Human Sciences*.

34. See David Easton, *The Political System* (New York: Knopf, 1953); John G. Gunnell, *Between Philosophy and Politics* (Amherst: University of Massachusetts Press, 1986), and *The Descent of Political Theory* (Chicago: University of Chicago Press, 1993); William H. Riker, "Political Theory and the Art of Heresthetics," pp. 47–67, in Finifter, *Political Science*.

35. See John G. Gunnell, *Political Theory* (Cambridge, Mass.: Winthrop, 1979), *Between Philosophy and Politics*, and *Descent of Political Theory*. Also see J. G. A. Pocock, "Political Theory, History, and Myth: A Salute to John Gunnell," *Annals of Scholarship* 1 (fall 1980): 3–25; John G. Gunnell, "Method, Methodology, and the Search for Traditions in the History of Political Theory: A Reply to Pocock's Salute," *Annals of Scholarship* 1 (fall 1980): 26–56; J. G. A. Pocock, "Intentions, Traditions and Methods: Some Sounds on a Foghorn," *Annals of Scholarship* 1 (fall 1980): 57–62; John S. Nelson, ed., *Tradition, Interpretation, and Science* (Albany: State University of New York Press, 1986).

36. See Paul F. Kress, "Self, System, and Significance: Reflections on the Political Science of Professor Easton," *Ethics* 77 (October 1966): 1–13; John S. Nelson, "Education for Politics," pp. 413–78, in Nelson, *What Should Political Theory Be Now?* 417–33.

37. See John S. Nelson, "Review Essay on *Metahistory* by Hayden White," *History and Theory* 14 (1975): 74–91.

38. See John G. Gunnell, *Philosophy, Science, and Political Inquiry* (Morristown, N.J.: General Learning Press, 1975), and "Realizing Theory: The Philosophy of Science Revisited," *Journal of Politics* 57 (November 1995): 923–40. Also see J. Donald Moon, "The Logic of Political Inquiry: A Synthesis of Opposed Perspectives," pp. 131–228, in vol. 1 of Fred I. Greenstein and Nelson W. Polsby, eds., *Handbook of Political Science* (Reading, Mass.: Addison-Wesley, 1975).

39. See Georg Simmel, *The Sociology of Georg Simmel*, ed. and trans. Kurt H. Wolff (New York: Free Press, 1950), 402–408.

40. Wolf Lepenies and Peter Weingart, "Introduction," pp. ix–xx, in Loren Graham, Wolf Lepenies, and Peter Weingart, eds., *Functions and Uses of Disciplinary Histories* (Boston: D. Reidel, 1983), xiii.

41. See Nelson, "Education for Politics" in Nelson, *What Should Political Theory Be Now?*
42. See Nelson, *Tradition, Interpretation, and Science.*
43. Berry, *Standing by Words,* 14.
44. See Charles J. Helm, "The History of the Social Sciences: 'Presentism' with a Friendly Face," paper for the North American Society for Social Philosophy, annual meeting of the American Political Science Association, Chicago, 1983. On the natural sciences, see Graham, Lepenies, and Weingart, *Functions and Uses of Disciplinary Histories.*
45. Lepenies and Weingart, "Introduction," xv.
46. Ibid., xii.
47. Ibid.

3. Turning Underground into Approved Rhetorics

1. See Stanley Fish, "Comments from Outside Economics," pp. 21–30, in Arjo Klamer, D. N. McCloskey, and Robert M. Solow, eds., *The Consequences of Economic Rhetoric* (New York: Cambridge University Press, 1988).
2. W. H. Auden, "Shorts II," *Collected Poems,* ed. Edward Mendelsohn (New York: Random House, 1976), 639; see Michael Walzer, "Philosophy and Democracy," pp. 75–99, in John S. Nelson, ed., *What Should Political Theory Be Now?* (Albany: State University of New York Press, 1983), 79.
3. See D. N. McCloskey, *The Rhetoric of Economics* (Madison: University of Wisconsin Press, 1985); John S. Nelson, Allan Megill, and D. N. McCloskey, eds., *The Rhetoric of the Human Sciences* (Madison: University of Wisconsin Press, 1987).
4. See Richard H. Brown, *A Poetic for Sociology* (New York: Cambridge University Press, 1977); D. N. McCloskey et al., "Argumentation in Special Fields," pp. 170–284, in David Zarefsky, Malcolm O. Sillars, and Jack Rhodes, eds., *Argument in Transition* (Annandale, Va.: Speech Communication Association, 1983).
5. See John S. Nelson and Allan Megill, "Rhetoric of Inquiry: Projects and Prospects," *Quarterly Journal of Speech* 72 (February 1986): 20–37. Also see Herbert W. Simons, ed., *Rhetoric in the Human Sciences* (Newbury Park, Calif.: Sage, 1989), and *The Rhetorical Turn* (Chicago: University of Chicago Press, 1990). As I have been arguing, of course, the social sciences share many rhetorical concerns with the humanities: see William T. Bluhm et al., "Political Science and the Humanities: A Report of the American Political Science Association," *PS* 18 (spring 1985): 247–59; John S. Nelson, "Beyond an Old Divide: Rediscovering Humanities in Political Science," *Social Education* 49 (September–October 1985): 433–34.
6. See John S. Nelson, "Political Theory as Political Rhetoric," pp. 169–240, in Nelson, *What Should Political Theory Be Now?*
7. See Richard H. Brown, *Society as Text* (Chicago: University of Chicago Press, 1987); John S. Nelson, "Stories of Science and Politics: Some Rhetorics

of Political Research," pp. 198–220, in Nelson, Megill, and McCloskey, *Rhetoric of the Human Sciences.*

8. See Michael C. Leff, "Modern Sophistic and the Unity of Rhetoric," pp. 19–37, in Nelson, Megill, and McCloskey, *Rhetoric of the Human Sciences.* Also see George A. Kennedy, *New Testament Interpretation Through Rhetorical Criticism* (Chapel Hill: University of North Carolina Press, 1984).

9. See Donal Carlston, "Turning Psychology on Itself: The Rhetoric of Psychology and the Psychology of Rhetoric," pp. 145–62, in Nelson, Megill, and McCloskey, *Rhetoric of the Human Sciences.*

10. See D. N. McCloskey and John S. Nelson, "The Rhetoric of Political Economy," pp. 155–74, in James H. Nichols Jr. and Colin Wright, eds., *From Political Economy to Economics . . . And Back?* (San Francisco: Institute for Contemporary Studies Press, 1990).

11. See Michael J. Shapiro, "The Rhetoric of Social Science: The Political Responsibilities of the Scholar," pp. 363–80, in Nelson, Megill, and McCloskey, *Rhetoric of the Human Sciences;* John S. Nelson, "Political Foundations for Rhetoric of Inquiry," pp. 258–89, in Simons, *Rhetorical Turn.*

12. See Walter Fisher, *Human Communication as Narrative* (Columbia: University of South Carolina Press, 1986); Michael Calvin McGee and John S. Nelson, "Narrative Reason in Public Argument," *Journal of Communication* 35 (autumn 1985): 139–55.

13. On mathematics and statistics see Philip J. Davis and Reuben Hersh, *The Mathematical Experience* (Boston: Houghton-Mifflin, 1981), and *Descartes' Dream* (New York: Harcourt Brace Jovanovich, 1986). Also see Ted Porter, *The Rise of Statistical Thinking, 1820–1900* (Princeton, N.J.: Princeton University Press, 1986). On physics see Norwood Russell Hanson, *Patterns of Discovery* (Cambridge, England: Cambridge University Press, 1965); Paul K. Feyerabend, *Against Method* (Atlantic Highlands, N.J.: Humanities Press, 1975); Heinz R. Pagels, *The Cosmic Code* (New York: Simon & Schuster, 1982).

14. On biology see Horace Freeland Judson, *The Eighth Day of Creation* (New York: Simon & Schuster, 1980; John Lyne and Henry R. Howe, "Punctuated Equilibria: Rhetorical Dynamics of a Scientific Controversy," *Quarterly Journal of Speech* 72 (May 1986): 132–47; John Lyne, "Learning the lessons of Lysenko: Biology, Politics, and Rhetoric in Historical Controversy," pp. 507–12, in Joseph W. Wenzel, ed., *Argument and Critical Practices* (Annandale, Va.: Speech Communication Association, 1987); John Angus Campbell, "Charles Darwin: Rhetorician of Science," pp. 69–86, in Nelson, Megill, and McCloskey, *Rhetoric of the Human Sciences,* and "Science, Imagination, and Metaphor: The Case of British Empiricism from Bacon to Blake," pp. 499–506, in Wenzel, *Argument and Critical Practices;* Alan G. Gross, "A Tale Twice Told: The Rhetoric of Discovery in the Case of DNA," pp. 491–98, in Wenzel, *Argument and Critical Practices;* David J. Depew and Bruce H. Weber, *Darwinism Evolving* (Cambridge, Mass.: MIT Press, 1995). On geology see John McPhee, *Basin and Range* (New York: Farrar, Straus and Giroux, 1981), *In Suspect Terrain* (New York: Farrar, Straus and Giroux, 1983), and *Rising from the Plains* (New York: Farrar, Straus and Giroux, 1986). On biology and geology see Stephen Jay Gould, *Ontogeny and Philogeny* (Cam-

bridge, Mass.: Harvard University Press, 1977), *Ever Since Darwin* (New York: Norton, 1977), *The Panda's Thumb* (New York: Norton, 1980), *Hen's Teeth and Toes* (New York: Norton, 1983), *The Flamingo's Smile* (New York: Norton, 1985), *Time's Arrow, Time's Cycle* (Cambridge, Mass.: Harvard University Press, 1987), and *Wonderful Life* (New York: Norton, 1989).

15. See Herbert A. Simon, *The Sciences of the Artificial*, 2d ed. (Cambridge, Mass.: MIT Press, 1981), *Models of Thought* (New Haven, Conn.: Yale University Press, 1979), and *Reason in Human Affairs* (Palo Alto, Calif.: Stanford University Press, 1983). Given the emergent concern of artificial intelligence and cognitive science with communication, there needs to be much greater interaction between these fields of research, which have thus far been pursued almost entirely in ignorance of each other.

16. On women's studies see Jean Bethke Elshtain, "Feminist Political Rhetoric and Women's Studies," pp. 319–40, in Nelson, Megill, and McCloskey, *Rhetoric of the Human Sciences*, and *Power Trips and Other Journeys* (Madison: University of Wisconsin Press, 1989). Also see Mary E. Hawkesworth, *Beyond Oppression* (New York: Continuum, 1990). I know of no similar attention to the rhetoric of research in American studies, African American studies, and global studies.

17. See John S. Nelson, "Education for Politics: Rethinking Research on Political Socialization," pp. 413–78, in Nelson, *What Should Political Theory Be Now?*

18. James A. Stimson, "Pursuing Belief Structure: A Research Narrative," pp. 75–87, in W. Phillips Shively, ed., *The Research Process in Political Science* (Itasca, Ill.: F. E. Peacock, 1984), 85.

19. See James A. Stimson, "Belief Systems: Constraint, Complexity, and the 1972 Election," *American Journal of Political Science* 19 (May 1975); 393–417, reprinted in Shively, *Research Process in Political Science*, 53–75.

20. See Ralph Cohen, ed., two special issues: "On Convention," *New Literary History* 13 (autumn 1981): 1–177, and 14 (winter 1983): 225–407.

21. See John S. Nelson, Allen Megill, and D. N. McCloskey, "Rhetoric of Inquiry," pp. 3–18, and Nelson, "Seven Rhetorics of Inquiry: A Provocation," pp. 407–34, in Nelson, Megill, and McCloskey, *Rhetoric of the Human Sciences*. For other purposes we might call them myths: see John S. Nelson, "Destroying Political Theory in Order to Save It (Or, John Gunnell Turns on the Western Tradition)," pp. 281–318, in John S. Nelson, ed., *Tradition, Interpretation, and Science* (Albany: State University of New York Press, 1986).

22. See Charles Bazerman, "Codifying the Social Scientific Style: The APA Publication Manual as a Behaviorist Rhetoric," pp. 125–44, in Nelson, Megill, and McCloskey, *Rhetoric of the Human Sciences*.

23. For an argument against such honorific uses of *science* and *scientific*, see D. N. McCloskey, "The Literary Character of Economics," *Daedalus* 113 (summer 1984): 97–119.

24. See Donald D. Searing, "Values in Empirical Research: A Behaviorist Response," *Midwest Journal of Political Science* 14 (February 1970): 71–104.

25. See John G. Gunnell, *Philosophy, Science, and Political Inquiry* (Morris-

town, N.J.: General Learning Press, 1975), and *Between Philosophy and Politics* (Amherst: University of Massachusetts Press, 1986). Also see Nelson, *Tradition, Interpretation, and Science.*

26. See Christopher H. Achen, "Toward Theories of Data: The State of Political Methodology," pp. 69–93, in Ada W. Finifter, ed., *Political Science: The State of the Discipline* (Washington, D.C.: American Political Science Association, 1983).

27. See David M. Ricci, *The Tragedy of Political Science* (New Haven, Conn.: Yale University Press, 1984); Raymond Seidelman, *Disenchanted Realists* (Albany: State University of New York Press, 1985).

28. See John S. Nelson, "Natures and Futures for Political Theory," pp. 3–24, in Nelson, *What Should Political Theory Be Now?*

29. See W. Lance Bennett, *The Political Mind and the Political Environment* (Lexington, Mass.: Heath, 1975); John C. Wahlke, "Prebehavioralism in Political Science," *American Political Science Review* 73 (March 1979): 9–31.

30. See John S. Nelson, "Once More on Kuhn," *Political Methodology* 1 (spring 1974); 73–104.

31. See Frank T. Denton, "Econometric Data Mining as an Industry," *Review of Economics and Statistics* 67 (August 1985): 124–27.

32. See Philip L. Beardsley, "Substantive Significance Versus Quantitative Rigor in Political Inquiry: Are the Two Compatible?" *International Interactions* 1 (1984): 27–40; Frank T. Denton, "The Significance of Significance: Rhetorical Aspects of Statistical Hypothesis Testing in Economics," pp. 163–83, in Klamer, McCloskey, and Solow, *Consequences of Economic Rhetoric.* Also see D. N. McCloskey, "Why Economic Historians Should Stop Relying on Statistical Tests of Significance and Lead Economists and Historians into the Promised Land," *Newsletter of the Cliometrics Society* 2 (December 1986): 5–7, and "The Rhetoric of Significance Tests," pp. 154–73, in McCloskey, *Rhetoric of Economics.*

33. See William H. Panning, "What Does It Take to Have a Theory? Principles in Political Science," pp. 479–511, in Nelson, *What Should Political Theory Be Now?*

34. See John S. Nelson, "The Ideological Connection, Parts I and II," *Theory and Society* 4 (fall-winter 1977): 421–48, 573–90.

35. See John S. Nelson, "Accidents, Laws, and Philosophic Flaws: Behavioral Explanation in Dahl and Dahrendorf," *Comparative Politics* 7 (April 1975): 435–57.

36. See Thomas S. Kuhn, *The Structure of Scientific Revolutions* (Chicago: University of Chicago Press, 1970).

37. See George Devereux, *From Anxiety to Method in the Behavioral Sciences* (The Hague: Mouton, 1967); Robert Jay Lifton, ed., *Explorations in Psychohistory* (New York: Simon & Shuster, 1974); Rosalie H. Wax, *Doing Fieldwork* (Chicago: University of Chicago Press, 1971); Michael Clarke, "Survival in the Field: Implications of Personal Experience in Fieldwork," *Theory and Society* 2 (spring 1975): 95–123; Robert A. LeVine, "Knowledge and Fallibility in An-

thropological Field Research," pp. 172–93, in Marilynn B. Brewer and Barry E. Collins, eds., *Scientific Inquiry and the Social Sciences* (San Francisco: Jossey-Bass, 1981).

38. See M. Donald Hancock, "Comparative Public Policy: An Assessment," pp. 283–308, in Finifter, *Political Science*.

39. See Clifford Geertz, *The Interpretation of Cultures* (New York: Basic, 1973), and *Local Knowledge* (New York: Basic, 1983).

40. Daniel Webster, Quoted in W. H. Auden and Louis Kronenberger, eds., *The Viking Book of Aphorisms* (New York: Penguin, 1962), 67.

41. See Bazerman, "Codifying the Social Scientific Style" in Nelson, Megill, and McCloskey, *Rhetoric of the Human Sciences*.

42. See Seymour Martin Lipset, ed., *Politics and the Social Sciences* (New York: Oxford University Press, 1969); Alan C. Isaak, *Scope and Methods of Political Science*, 2d ed. (Homewood, Ill.: Dorsey, 1975); M. Margaret Conway and Frank B. Feigert, *Political Analysis*, 2d ed. (Boston: Allyn & Bacon, 1976); William A. Welsh, *Studying Politics* (New York: Praeger, 1973); W. Phillips Shively, *The Craft of Political Research* (Englewood Cliffs, N.J.: Prentice-Hall, 1974); Dickinson McGaw and George Watson, *Political and Social Inquiry* (New York: Wiley, 1976); Kenneth R. Hoover, *The Elements of Social Scientific Thinking* (New York: St. Martin's, 1976).

43. See Jonathan Potter and Michael Mulkay, "Scientists' Interview Talk: Interviews as a Technique for Revealing Participants' Interpretive Practices," pp. 247–71, in Michael Brenner, Jennifer Brown, and David Canter, eds., *The Research Interview,* (New York: Academic Press, 1985). The University of Kentucky's oral history archive for political science can be a telling resource in this connection.

44. For one among many examples see Bruno Latour and Steve Woolgar, *Laboratory Life* (Princeton, N.J.: Princeton University Press, 1986).

45. See Paul de Man, *Allegories of Reading* (New Haven, Conn.: Yale University Press, 1979).

46. See Nelson, "Accidents, Laws, and Philosophic Flaws," 448–54.

47. Horace Freeland Judson, "Coming Attractions," *New York Times Book Review,* April 21, 1985, p. 32.

48. See Bernard Crick, *In Defense of Politics* (Baltimore, Penguin, 1962); Charles A. McCoy and John Playford, eds., *Apolitical Politics* (New York: Crowell, 1967); Philip Green and Sanford Levinson, *Power and Community* (New York: Random House, 1969).

49. Marquess of Halifax, *Moral Thoughts and Reflections,* late-seventeenth century; quoted in John Gross, ed., *The Oxford Book of Aphorisms* (Oxford, England: Oxford University Press, 1983), 215.

50. St. Augustine, *The Confessions of St. Augustine,* trans. John K. Ryan (Garden City, N.Y.: Doubleday, 1960).

51. See Susan T. Fiske and Shelley E. Taylor, *Social Cognition,* 2d ed. (New York: McGraw-Hill, 1991); Milton Lodge and Kathleen McGraw, eds., *Political Judgment* (Ann Arbor: University of Michigan Press, 1995).

52. See James D. Watson, *The Double Helix* (New York, New American Library, 1968).

53. Charles Lave and James March, *An Introduction to Models in the Social Sciences* (New York: Harper & Row, 1975; Richard Fenno, *Home Style* (Boston: Little, Brown, 1978); Judith A. Gillespie and Dina A. Zinnes, eds., *Missing Elements in Political Inquiry* (Newbury Park, Calif.: Sage, 1982); Elinor Ostrom, ed., *Strategies of Political Inquiry* (Newbury Park, Calif.: Sage, 1982); see note 18 for full publication information about Shively's book. At times, the *American Journal of Political Science* has identified such articles by publishing them in a specially marked section at the end of the issue. Ten early articles from the workshop section appear along with four additional chapters in Herbert B. Asher et al., eds., *Theory-Building and Data Analysis in the Social Sciences* (Knoxville: University of Tennessee Press, 1984).

54. Phillip E. Hammond, ed., *Sociologists at Work* (Garden City, N.Y.: Doubleday, 1964); C. Wright Mills, *The Sociological Imagination* (New York: Oxford University Press, 1969); M. Patricia Golden, ed., *The Research Experience* (Itasca, Ill.: F. E. Peacock, 1976).

55. David Easton, "The New Revolution in Political Science," *American Political Science Review* 63 (December 1969): 1051–61; Gabriel Almond and Stephen Genco, "Clouds, Clocks, and the Study of Politics," *World Politics* 29 (July 1977): 489–522; William Riker, "Political Theory and the Art of Heresthetics," pp. 47–67, in Finifter, *Political Science;* see note 29 for a full citation of the Wahlke piece and note 26 for a full citation of Achen's. Perhaps I should add that the immediate sequel to the Riker essay was his presidential address to the American Political Science Association: "The Heresthetics of Constitution Making: The Presidency in 1787, with Comments on Determinism and Rational Choice," *American Political Science Review* 78 (March 1984): 1–16.

56. Benjamin Franklin, *Poor Richard's Almanac,* 1738; quoted in John Bartlett, ed., *Bartlett's Familiar Quotations,* 14th ed. (Boston: Little, Brown, 1968), 422b.

4. Overturning Argument in Political Science

1. Amelie Oksenberg Rorty, "Experiments in Philosophic Genre: Descartes' *Meditations,*" *Critical Inquiry* 9 (March 1983): 545–64. The quotation comes from page 545, and all the section titles in this chapter come from page 555 of the same essay.

2. Ibid., 550.

3. On theory, see John G. Gunnell, *Philosophy, Science, and Political Inquiry* (Morristown, N.J.: General Learning Press, 1975), "Philosophy and Political Theory," *Government and Opposition* 14 (spring 1979): 198–216, "Political Science and the Poverty of Theory," pp. 92–110, in Maria J. Falco, ed., *Through the Looking-Glass* (Washington, D.C.: University Press of America, 1979), *The Descent of Political Theory* (Chicago: University of Chicago Press, 1993), and "Realizing Theory: The Philosophy of Science Revisited," *Journal of Politics* 57

(November 1995): 923–40. Also see John S. Nelson, "Education for Politics: Rethinking Research on Political Socialization," pp. 413–78, in John S. Nelson, ed., *What Should Political Theory Be Now?* (Albany: State University of New York Press, 1983), 456–67.

On method, see Sheldon S. Wolin, "Political Theory as a Vocation," *American Political Science Review* 63 (December 1969): 1062–82, "History and Theory: Methodism *Redivivus*," pp. 43–67, in John S. Nelson, ed., *Tradition, Interpretation, and Science* (Albany: State University of New York Press, 1986). Also see John G. Gunnell, "Method, Methodology, and the Search for Traditions in the History of Political Theory," *Annals of Scholarship* 1 (fall 1980): 26–56, and "In Search of the Political Object: Beyond Methodology and Transcendentalism," pp. 25–52, in Nelson, *What Should Political Theory Be Now?*

On models, see Marshall Spector, "Models and Theories," *British Journal for the Philosophy of Science* 16 (August 1965): 121–42; Paul F. Kress, "On Validating Simulation, with Special Attention to Simulation of International Relations," *International Interactions* 1 (1974): 41–50; Philip C. Wall, "How Scientific Are Political Science Models?" *Political Methodology* 1 (summer 1974): 83–118.

On logic, see John S. Nelson, "The Ideological Connection, Parts I and II," *Theory and Society* 4 (fall–winter 1977): 426–36. On testing, see William H. Panning, "What Does It Take to Have a Theory? Principles in Political Science," pp. 479–511, in Nelson, *What Should Political Theory Be Now?* 479–84. On evidence, see John G. Gunnell, "Social Science and Political Reality: The Problem of Explanation," *Social Research* 35 (spring 1968): 159–201, and "Philosophy and Political Science: Some Persistent Problems," *Polity* 9 (spring 1977): 344–55.

On objectivity, see Thomas A. Spragens Jr., *The Dilemma of Contemporary Political Theory* (New York: Dunellen, 1973); Hans Skjervheim, "Objectivism and the Study of Man, Parts I–II," *Inquiry* 17 (summer–autumn 1974): 213–40, 265–302; Edward B. Portis, "Political Action and Social Science: Max Weber's Two Arguments for Objectivity," *Polity* 12 (spring 1980): 409–27; John S. Nelson, "Political Theory as Political Rhetoric," pp. 169–240, in Nelson, *What Should Political Theory Be Now?* 190–91, 197ff, and 220ff.

4. See John G. Gunnell, "Social Scientific Knowledge and Policy Decisions: A Critique of the Intellectualistic Model," pp. 29–38, in Phillip M. Gregg, ed.,*Problems of Theory in Policy Analysis* (Lexington, Mass.: Heath, 1976), "Encounters of a Third Kind: The Alienation of Theory in American Political Science," *American Journal of Politics* 25 (August 1981): 440–61, and *Between Philosophy and Politics* (Amherst: University of Massachusetts Press, 1986).

5. See Bernard Crick, *In Defense of Politics* (Baltimore: Penguin, 1962); Charles A. McCoy and John Playford, eds., *Apolitical Politics* (New York: Crowell, 1967); Philip Green and Sanford Levinson, eds., *Power and Community* (New York: Random House, 1969).

6. See G. R. Boynton, *Mathematical Thinking about Politics* (New York: Longman, 1980). The book's title reflects its emphasis on formal and especially

mathematical studies of politics. But its issues and examples explain how political science slights studies of government because it has little sense of how to conduct them.

7. See Nelson, "Education for Politics," in Nelson, *What Should Political Theory Be Now?* 456–67.

8. See David M. Ricci, *The Tragedy of Political Science* (New Haven, Conn.: Yale University Press, 1984); Raymond Seidelman, *Disenchanted Realists* (Albany: State University of New York Press, 1985); Gabriel A. Almond, "Separate Tables: Schools and Sects in Political Science," *PS*, 21 (fall 1988): 828–42.

9. See Charles W. Anderson, "Political Theory and Political Science: The Rediscovery and Reinterpretation of the Pragmatic Tradition," pp. 390–409, in Nelson, *What Should Political Theory Be Now?*

10. Rorty, "Experiments in Philosophic Genre," 550.

11. Condorcet's paradox and other parts of analytical theory identify some troubles in the liberal democratic theory of representation. For reflections on troubles of democracy as the starting point for political theorizing, see John Dunn, *Western Political Theory in the Face of the Future* (Cambridge, England: Cambridge University Press, 1979). For related troubles of representation, see Hanna Fenichel Pitkin, *The Concept of Representation* (Berkeley: University of California Press, 1967); Nancy L. Schwartz, *The Blue Guitar* (Chicago: University of Chicago Press, 1988); Michael J. Shapiro, *The Politics of Representation* (Madison: University of Wisconsin Press, 1988); Hans Kellner, *Language and Historical Representation* (Madison: University of Wisconsin Press, 1989); Harry Redner, *A New Science of Representation* (Boulder, Colo.: Westview, 1994); Elaine Scarry, *Resisting Representation* (New York: Oxford University Press, 1994); Richard Harvey Brown, ed., *Postmodern Representations* (Urbana: University of Illinois Press, 1995); Brian Seitz, *The Trace of Political Representation* (Albany: State University of New York Press, 1995).

12. See David Easton, *A Framework for Political Analysis* (Englewood Cliffs, N.J.: Prentice-Hall, 1965); Paul F. Kress, "Self, System, and Significance: Reflections on Professor Easton's Political Science," *Ethics* 77 (October 1966): 1–13. Also see John G. Gunnell, "The Idea of the Conceptual Framework: A Philosophical Critique," *Journal of Comparative Administration* 1 (August 1969): 140–76, and "Deduction, Explanation, and Social Scientific Inquiry," *American Political Science Review* 63 (December 1969): 1233–46. And see John S. Nelson, "Accidents, Laws, and Philosophic Flaws: Behavioral Explanation in Dahl and Dahrendorf," *Comparative Politics* 7 (April 1975): 435–57, and "Education for Politics," pp. 417–28, in Nelson, *What Should Political Theory Be Now?* Not all systems theories lack political substance. For example, Morton A. Kaplan's continues in subtle but important ways to influence research in international relations: *System and Process in International Politics* (New York: Wiley, 1957).

13. See Nelson, "Education for Politics," in Nelson, *What Should Political Theory Be Now?* 428–33.

14. See G. R. Boynton, "Linking Problem Definition and Research Activi-

ties: Using Formal Languages," pp. 43–60, in Judith A. Gillespie and Dina A. Zinnes, eds., *Missing Elements in Political Inquiry* (Newbury Park, Calif.: Sage, 1982).

15. See Heinz Eulau, *The Behavioral Persuasion in Politics* (Palo Alto, Calif.: Stanford University Press, 1963); and Heinz Eulau, ed., *Behavioralism in Political Science* (New York: Atherton, 1969).

16. See Heinz Eulau, *Micro-Macro Political Analysis* (Chicago: Aldine, 1969).

17. See John C. Wahlke, "Prebehavioralism in Political Science," *American Political Science Review* 73 (March 1979): 9–31.

18. See Nelson, "Education for Politics," in Nelson, *What Should Political Theory Be Now?* 475–76.

19. See Nelson: "Accidents, Laws, and Philosophic Flaws" and "The Ideological Connection." Also see Panning, "What Does It Take to Have a Theory?" in Nelson, *What Should Political Theory Be Now?*

20. See Sheldon S. Wolin, "Political Theory as a Vocation," and "Paradigms and Political Theories," pp. 125–52, in Preston King and Bhikhu C. Parekh, eds., *Politics and Experience* (Cambridge, England: Cambridge University Press, 1968).

21. See Paul F. Kress, "Against Epistemology: Apostate Musings," *Journal of Politics* 41 (May 1979): 526–42.

22. See John H. Schaar, "The American Biases of American Political Science," paper prepared for the annual meeting of the American Political Science Association, Washington, D.C., 1968; Green and Levinson, *Power and Community.*

23. See Garry Wills, *Nixon Agonistes* (Boston: Houghton Mifflin, 1969); Theodore R. Lowi, *The End of Liberalism,* 2d ed. (New York: Norton, 1979); H. Mark Roelofs, *Ideology and Myth in American Politics* (Boston: Little, Brown, 1976); Samuel H. Beer, "In Search of a New Public Philosophy," pp. 5–44, in Anthony King, ed., *The New American Political System* (Washington, D.C.: American Enterprise Institute, 1978).

24. See Michael S. Lewis-Beck and Tom W. Rice, "Government Growth in the United States," *Journal of Politics* 47 (February 1985): 2–30.

25. See Henry Fairlie, "In Search of a President," *Washington Post,* May 23, 1976, p. C1, and "The Politician's Art," *Harper's Magazine,* December 1977, pp. 33–46, 123–24; Garry Wills, *Confessions of a Conservative* (New York: Penguin, 1979), 80–105.

26. See G. R. Boynton, "Three (Short) Essays in Democratic Theory," unpublished paper.

27. See Robert A. Dahl, *A Preface to Democratic Theory* (Chicago: University of Chicago Press, 1956), *After the Revolution?* (New Haven, Conn.: Yale University Press, 1970), and *Polyarchy* (New Haven, Conn.: Yale University Press, 1971). Also see Charles Lindblom, *The Intelligence of Democracy* (New Haven, Conn.: Yale University Press, 1965), and *Politics and Markets* (New York: Basic, 1977). And see Harry Redner, *An Heretical Heir of the Enlightenment* (Boulder, Colo.: Westview, 1993).

28. See William H. Riker, *Liberalism Against Populism* (San Francisco: W. H. Freeman, 1982).

29. See Gabriel A. Almond and Sidney Verba, *The Civic Culture* (Boston: Little, Brown, 1963); Sidney Verba and Lucian W. Pye, eds., *The Citizen and Politics* (Stamford, Conn.: Greylock, 1978); Gabriel A. Almond and Sidney Verba, eds., *The Civic Culture Revisited* (Boston: Little, Brown, 1980).

30. See Peter Bachrach, *The Theory of Democratic Elitism* (Boston: Little, Brown, 1967); William E. Connolly, ed., *The Bias of Pluralism* (New York, Atherton, 1969).

31. See Robert A. Dahl, *Who Governs?* (New Haven, Conn.: Yale University Press, 1961); Nelson W. Polsby, *Community Power and Political Theory* (New Haven, Conn.: Yale University Press, 1963).

32. See Nelson, "Education for Politics," in Nelson, *What Should Political Theory Be Now?* 439–56 and 467–73.

33. Michael Walzer, *Radical Principles* (New York: Basic, 1980), 4.

34. See Nelson, "Political Theory as Political Rhetoric," in Nelson, *What Should Political Theory Be Now?* esp. pp. 204–14.

35. See J. Roland Pennock and John W. Chapman, eds., *Nomos X: Representation* (New York: Atherton, 1968); A. H. Birch, *Representation* (New York: Praeger, 1971).

36. Theodore Sturgeon, quoted in Frederik Pohl, *The Way the Future Was* (New York: Ballantine, 1978), 19.

37. See William T. Bluhm et al., "Political Science and the Humanities: A Report of the American Political Science Association," *PS* 18 (spring 1985): 247–59.

38. Rorty, "Experiments in Philosophic Genre," 551.

39. This notion is interesting to compare with the closely related but far from identical inclination of J. Donald Moon, "The Logic of Political Inquiry: A Synthesis of Opposed Perspectives," pp. 131–228, in vol. 1 of Fred I. Greenstein and Nelson W. Polsby, eds., *Handbook of Political Science* (Reading, Mass.: Addison-Wesley, 1975), "Interpretation, Theory, and Human Emancipation," pp. 149–78, in Elinor Ostrom, ed., *Strategies of Political Inquiry* (Newbury Park, Calif.: Sage, 1982), and "The Problem of Reflexivity in Theory Building," pp. 253–59, in Gillespie and Zinnes, *Missing Elements in Political Inquiry.*

40. Among myriad examples, see Thomas C. Schelling, *Arms and Influence* (New Haven, Conn.: Yale University Press, 1966), and "Dynamic Models of Segregation," *Journal of Mathematical Sociology* 1 (July 1971), 143–86; Robert Axelrod, "The Emergence of Cooperation among Egoists," *American Political Science Review* 75 (June 1981): 306–18, and *The Evolution of Cooperation* (New York: Basic, 1984); Russell Hardin, *Collective Action* (Baltimore: Johns Hopkins University Press, 1982); William H. Panning, "Uncertainty and Political Participation," *Political Behavior* 4 (spring 1982): 69–81, and "Rational Choice and Congressional Norms," *Western Political Quarterly* 35 (June 1982): 193–203.

41. See William H. Riker, *The Art of Political Manipulation* (New Haven, Conn.: Yale University Press, 1982), and "The Heresthetics of Constitution

Making: The Presidency in 1787, with Comments on Determinism and Rational Choice," *American Political Science Review* 78 (March 1984): 1–16. Also see Hayward R. Alker Jr., "The Dialectical Logic of Thucydides' Melian Dialogue," *American Political Science Review* 82 (September 1988): 805–20.

42. See Peter Winch, *The Idea of a Social Science* (New York: Humanities Press, 1958); A. R. Louch, *Explanation and Human Action* (Berkeley: University of California Press, 1966); Charles Taylor, "Interpretation and the Sciences of Man," *Review of Metaphysics* 25 (September 1971): 3–51; Hanna Fenichel Pitkin, *Wittgenstein and Justice* (Berkeley: University of California Press, 1972). For surveys of such projects, see Richard J. Bernstein, *Praxis and Action* (Philadelphia: University of Pennsylvania Press, 1971), *The Restructuring of Social and Political Theory* (Philadelphia: University of Pennsylvania Press, 1976), and *The New Constellation* (Cambridge, Mass.: MIT Press, 1991). Also see Fred R. Dallmayr and Thomas A. McCarthy, eds., *Understanding and Social Inquiry* (Notre Dame, Ind.: University of Notre Dame Press, 1977), 159–88.

43. See Hans-Georg Gadamer, *Truth and Method,* ed. Garret Barden and John Cumming (New York: Seabury Press, 1960, 1975); Richard Rorty, *Philosophy and the Mirror of Nature* (Princeton, N.J.: Princeton University Press, 1979); Michael J. Shapiro, *Language and Political Understanding* (New Haven, Conn.: Yale University Press, 1981); Richard J. Bernstein, *Beyond Objectivism and Relativism* (Philadelphia: University of Pennsylvania Press, 1983), 109–69.

44. See Hannah Arendt, "History and Immorality," *Partisan Review* 24 (winter 1957): 11–35, and *The Human Condition* (Chicago: University of Chicago Press, 1958), esp. pp. 175–247; Kurt Wolff, "On the Significance of Hannah Arendt's *The Human Condition* for Sociology," *Inquiry* 4 (1961): 67–106; Pitkin, *Wittgenstein and Justice,* esp. pp. 241–63.

45. See John S. Nelson, "Stories of Science and Politics: Some Rhetorics of Political Research," pp. 198–220, in John S. Nelson, Allan Megill, and D. N. McCloskey, eds., *The Rhetoric of the Human Sciences* (Madison: University of Wisconsin Press, 1987), and "Commerce Among the Archipelagos: Rhetoric of Inquiry as a Practice of Coherent Education," pp. 78–100, in L. Robert Stevens, G. L. Seligmann, and Julian Long, eds., *The Core and the Canon* (Denton: University of North Texas Press, 1993).

46. On three modes of social science, see Terrence E. Cook, *Criteria of Social Scientific Knowledge: Interpretation, Prediction, Praxis* (Lanham, Md.: Rowman and Littlefield, 1994).

47. See D. N. McCloskey, "The Literary Character of Economics," *Daedalus* 113 (summer 1984): 97–119.

48. Rorty, "Experiments in Philosophic Genre," 550–51.

49. See John Rawls, *A Theory of Justice* (Cambridge, Mass.: Harvard University Press, 1971); Robert Nozick, *Anarchy, State, and Utopia* (New York: Basic, 1974).

50. See Herbert A. Simon, *The Sciences of the Artificial* (Cambridge, Mass.: MIT Press, 1969), and "The Behavioral and Social Sciences," *Science* 209 (July 1980): 72–78. Also see James G. March, "What Administrative Reorganization

Tells Us About Governing," *American Political Science Review* 77 (June 1983): 281–96; and James G. March and Johan P. Olsen, *Ambiguity and Choice in Organizations*, 2d ed. (Bergen, Norway: Universitetsforlaget, 1979).

51. See G. R. Boynton, "On Getting from Here to There: Reflections on Two Paragraphs and Other Things," pp. 29–68, in Ostrom, *Strategies of Political Inquiry*, "Ideas and Action: A Cognitive Model of the Senate Agriculture Committee," *Political Behavior* 12 (June 1990): 181–213, and "Computational Modeling: A Computational Model of a Survey Respondent," pp. 229–48, in Milton Lodge and Kathleen M. McGraw, eds., *Political Judgment* (Ann Arbor: University of Michigan Press, 1995).

52. Early classics of rational choice theory include Anthony Downs, *An Economic Theory of Democracy* (New York: Harper & Row, 1957); James M. Buchanan and Gordon Tullock, *The Calculus of Consent* (Ann Arbor: University of Michigan Press, 1962); Mancur Olson, *The Logic of Collective Action* (New York: Schocken Books, 1965). Also see D. N. McCloskey and John S. Nelson, "The Rhetoric of Political Economy," pp. 155–74, in James H. Nichols Jr. and Colin Wright, eds., *From Political Economy to Economics . . . And Back?* (San Francisco: Institute for Contemporary Studies Press, 1990).

53. See John S. Nelson, "Meaning and Measurement Across Paradigms," paper prepared for the annual meeting of the American Political Science Association, Washington, D.C., 1977, pp. 16–22.

54. See William H. Riker, "Political Theory and the Art of Heresthetics," pp. 47–67, in Ada W. Finifter, ed., *Political Science: The State of the Discipline* (Washington, D.C.: American Political Science Association, 1983). Also see William H. Panning, "Formal Models of Legislative Processes," *Legislative Studies Quarterly* 8 (August 1983): 427–55; Ronald J. Terchek, "Positive Political Theory and Heresthetics," *Political Science Reviewer* 8 (1983): 43–66.

55. See Panning, "Formal Models of Legislative Processes," 442–45, and "What Does It Take to Have a Theory?" in Nelson, *What Should Political Theory Be Now?* 491–93.

56. See D. N. McCloskey, "Notes on the Character of Argument in Modern Economics," pp. 170–87, in David Zarefsky, Malcolm O. Sillars, and Jack Rhodes, eds., *Argument in Transition* (Annandale, Va.: Speech Communication Association, 1983), see esp. pp. 173–76.

57. See Nelson, "The Ideological Connection."

58. See Nelson, "Education for Politics," in Nelson, *What Should Political Theory Be Now?* 443–56, and "Political Theory as Political Rhetoric," in Nelson, *What Should Political Theory Be Now?* 193–204.

59. See James G. March, "How We Talk and How We Act: Administrative Theory and Administrative Life," seventh David D. Henry Lecture, University of Illinois at Urbana, 1980, "Decision-Making Perspective: Decision in Organizations and Theories of Choice," pp. 205–48, in Andrew H. Van de Ven and William F. Joyce, eds., *Perspectives on Organization Design and Behavior* (New York: Wiley, 1981), "Theories of Choice and Making Decisions," *Society* 20 (November–December 1982): 29–39, and "Organizations, Leaders, and Po-

etry" and "Theories of Choice and the Making of Decisions," Ida Beam Lectures, University of Iowa, Iowa City, 1983.

60. Multiple rationalities mean many principles of reasoning. See Boynton, "On Getting from Here to There" in Ostrom, *Strategies of Political Inquiry*; Panning, "What Does It Take to Have a Theory?" in Nelson, *What Should Political Theory Be Now?* 490–507. Also see Nelson, "Meaning and Measurement Across Paradigms."

61. See Panning, "Formal Models of Legislative Processes," 438ff.

62. See Dina A. Zinnes and Robnert G. Muncaster, "Fitting Versus Testing," Triple-I [Illinois, Indiana, and Iowa] Seminar on Complex Systems, Urbana, Ill., 1985.

63. See Steve Fuller, "How Economists Defeated Political Scientists at Their Own Game," *Philosophy, Rhetoric, and the End of Knowledge* (Madison: University of Wisconsin Press, 1993), 126–33.

64. See D. N. McCloskey, *The Rhetoric of Economics* (Madison: University of Wisconsin Press, 1985), *If You're So Smart*, (Chicago: University of Chicago Press, 1990), and *Knowledge and Persuasion in Economics* (New York: Cambridge University Press, 1993). Also see McCloskey and Nelson, "The Rhetoric of Political Economy," in Nichols and Wright, *From Political Economy to Economics*.

65. Riker, "Political Theory and the Art of Heresthetics," in Finifter, *Political Science*, 59.

66. Ibid., 66.

67. Ibid., 60ff.

68. See Nelson, "Political Theory as Political Rhetoric," in Nelson, *What Should Political Theory Be Now?* 171–93.

69. Paul Ricoeur, *The Rule of Metaphor*, trans. Robert Czerny (Toronto: University of Toronto Press, 1977).

70. See Riker, "Political Theory and the Art of Heresthetics," in Finifter, *Political Science*, 61–62.

71. See David Zarefsky, "Moral Argument in Political History: The Case of the Lincoln-Douglas Debates," pp. 201–12, in Zarefsky, Sillars, and Rhodes, *Argument in Transition*.

72. See William H. Riker, *The Strategy of Rhetoric* (New Haven, Conn.: Yale University Press, 1996).

73. Rorty, "Experiments in Philosophic Genre," 552.

74. See Gunnell, *Philosophy, Science, and Political Inquiry*, 177–229; John S. Nelson, "Destroying Political Theory in Order to Save It," pp. 281–318, in Nelson, *Tradition, Interpretation, and Science*.

75. For an example of how befuddling distinctions between direct and indirect observation can be, see Dickinson McGaw and George Watson, *Political and Social Inquiry* (New York: Wiley, 1976), 10–11, 113–15, 122–23, and 140–44. For troubles with this type of distinction, see J. L. Austin, *Sense and Sensibilia* (Oxford, England: Oxford University Press, 1962), 19; Rorty, *Philosophy and the Mirror of Nature*, 31 and 50.

76. The journal *Political Methodology* apparently intends to include refine-

ment of statistics and research design, substantive demonstrations of them, *and* theories of inquiry. But its articles fall almost exclusively into the first two categories.

77. See Christopher H. Achen, "Toward Theories of Data: The State of Political Methodology," pp. 69–93, in Finifter, *Political Science*.

78. See Ian Hacking, *The Emergence of Probability* (Cambridge, England: Cambridge University Press, 1975), 35ff; Thomas S. Kuhn, *The Essential Tension* (Chicago: University of Chicago Press, 1978), 31–65.

79. See McCloskey, "The Literary Character of Economics," 106–8.

80. See Karl R. Popper, *Conjectures and Refutations* (New York: Harper & Row, 1963). Also see Imre Lakatos, *The Methodology of Scientific Research Programmes* (Cambridge, England: Cambridge University Press, 1978); Paul K. Feyerabend, *Against Method* (Atlantic Highlands, N.J.: Humanities Press, 1975).

81. See McCloskey, *Rhetoric of Economics*; John S. Nelson and Allan Megill, "Rhetoric of Inquiry: Projects and Prospects," *Quarterly Journal of Speech* 72 (February 1986): 20–37; John S. Nelson, "Seven Rhetorics of Inquiry: A Provocation," pp. 407–43, in Nelson, Megill, and McCloskey, *Rhetoric of the Human Sciences*.

82. See Harold D. Lasswell, *Psychopathology and Politics* (New York: Viking, 1930), and *Power and Personality* (New York: Viking, 1948). Also see Robert E. Lane, *Political Life* (New York: Free Press, 1959), *Political Ideology* (New York: Free Press, 1962), *Political Thinking and Consciousness* (Chicago: Markham, 1969), and *Political Man* (New York: Free Press, 1972).

83. A clever defense of one kind of "humanistic" and clinical evidence appears in George Devereux, *From Anxiety to Method in the Behavioral Sciences* (The Hague: Mouton, 1967). For a persuasive case on behalf of another sort of clinical data, see Erik Erikson, "The Nature of Clinical Evidence," *Insight and Responsibility* (New York, Norton, 1964), 47–80, and "On the Nature of Psychohistorical Evidence: In Search of Gandhi," pp. 42–77, in Robert Jay Lifton, ed., *Explorations in Psychohistory* (New York, Simon & Schuster, 1974).

84. Rorty, "Experiments in Philosophic Genre," 564.

85. See Nelson, "Stories of Science and Politics," in Nelson, Megill, and McCloskey, *Rhetoric of the Human Sciences*.

86. See Fuller, *Philosophy, Rhetoric, and the End of Knowledge*; Charles Alan Taylor, *Defining Science: A Rhetoric of Demarcation* (Madison: University of Wisconsin Press, 1996).

87. See John S. Nelson, "Beyond an Old Divide: Rediscovering Humanities in Political Science," *Social Education* 49 (September–October 1985): 433–34.

88. See John S. Nelson, "Tropal History and the Social Sciences," *History and Theory* 19 (1980): 89ff.

5. Returning Argument to Political Inquiry

1. Russell Hoban, *Pilgermann*, quoted by David Lehman in "Pilgrim's Progress," *Newsweek*, May 30, 1983, p. 92.

2. See Hannah Arendt, *The Human Condition* (Chicago: University of Chicago Press, 1958). Also see John G. Gunnell, "Political Inquiry and the Concept of Action: A Phenomenological Analysis," pp. 197–275, in vol. 2 of Maurice Natanson, ed., *Phenomenology and the Social Sciences*, (Evanston, Ill.: Northwestern University Press, 1973), and "Political Science and the Theory of Action: Prolegomena," *Political Theory* 7 (February 1979): 75–100.

3. In this general regard it resembles accounts by Richard J. Bernstein, *Praxis and Action* (Philadelphia: University of Pennsylvania Press, 1971), *The Restructuring of Social and Political Theory* (Philadelphia: University of Pennsylvania Press, 1976), and *Beyond Objectivism and Relativism* (Philadelphia: University of Pennsylvania Press, 1983).

4. Oscar Wilde, quoted in Laurence J. Peter, ed., *Peter's Quotations* (New York: Bantam, 1977), 23.

5. For a pertinent tale about the study and conception of argument in another social science, see Michael Billig, *Arguing and Thinking* (Cambridge, England: Cambridge University Press, 1989).

6. Useful works on behavioralism are far too numerous to itemize completely in a single note. Among the pieces I find especially helpful are Heinz Eulau, *The Behavioral Persuasion in Politics* (Palo Alto, Calif.: Stanford University Press, 1963); Heinz Eulau, ed., *Behavioralism in Political Science* (New York: Atherton, 1969); George J. Graham, Jr., and George W. Carey, eds., *The Postbehavioral Era* (New York: McKay, 1972); John G. Gunnell, *Philosophy, Science, and Political Inquiry* (Morristown, N.J.: General Learning Press, 1975); Charles A. McCoy and John Playford, eds., *Apolitical Politics* (New York: Crowell, 1967); Thomas A. Spragens Jr., *The Dilemma of Contemporary Political Theory* (New York: Dunellen, 1973). Also see John S. Nelson, "Natures and Futures for Political Theory," pp. 3–24, in John S. Nelson, ed., *What Should Political Theory Be Now?* (Albany: State University of New York Press, 1983), 8–15; John S. Nelson, ed., *Tradition, Interpretation, and Science* (Albany: State University of New York Press, 1986).

7. Important works on rational choice approaches to politics also are too many to cite here, but I especially recommend James J. Buchanan and Gordon Tullock, *The Calculus of Consent* (Ann Arbor: University of Michigan Press, 1962); Maria J. Falco, ed., *Through the Looking-Glass* (Washington, D.C.: University Press of America, 1979); Carl J. Friedrich, ed., *Nomos VII: Rational Decision* (New York: Atherton, 1964); William H. Riker, *The Art of Political Manipulation* (New Haven, Conn.: Yale University Press, 1982); Donald P. Green, *Pathologies of Rational Choice Theory* (New Haven, Conn.: Yale University Press, 1994); Emily I. Hauptmann, *Putting Choice Before Democracy* (Albany: State University of New York Press, 1996).

8. See Philip L. Beardsley, "Substantive Significance Versus Quantitative Rigor in Political Inquiry: Are the Two Compatible?" *International Interactions* 1 (1974): 27–40, and *Redefining Rigor* (Newbury Park, Calif.: Sage, 1980). Also see John S. Nelson, "Education for Politics: Rethinking Research on Political Socialization," pp. 413–78, in Nelson, *What Should Political Theory Be Now?*

9. La Rochefoucauld, quoted in W. H. Auden and Louis Kronenberger, eds., *The Viking Book of Aphorisms* (New York: Penguin, 1962), 252.

10. See J. L. Austin, *Sense and Sensibilia* (Oxford, England: Oxford University Press, 1962), 19, 31, and 50; Richard Rorty, *Philosophy and the Mirror of Nature* (Princeton, N.J.: Princeton University Press, 1979), esp. pp. 17–69.

11. See Gunnell, *Philosophy, Science, and Political Inquiry*; John S. Nelson, "Accidents, Laws, and Philosophic Flaws: Behavioral Explanation in Dahl and Dahrendorf," *Comparative Politics* 7 (April 1975): 435–57.

12. Gabriel A. Almond, "Political Theory and Political Science," *American Political Science Review* 60 (December 1966): 869–79; Gabriel A. Almond and Stephen J. Genco, "Clouds, Clocks, and the Study of Politics," *World Politics* 29 (July 1977): 489–522.

13. David Easton, "The New Revolution in Political Science," *American Political Science Review* 63 (December 1969): 1051–61.

14. John C. Wahkle, "Prebehavioralism in Political Science," *American Political Science Review* 73 (March 1979): 9–31.

15. See Nelson, "Education for Politics," in Nelson, *What Should Political Theory Be Now?* 460–62.

16. See Terrence E. Cook, *The Great Alternatives of Social Thought* (Lanham, Md.: Rowman and Littlefield, 1991).

17. Leonard Louis Levinson, quoted in Peter, *Peter's Quotations*, 477.

18. See Thomas S. Kuhn, *The Structure of Scientific Revolutions* (Chicago: University of Chicago Press, 1970); Imre Lakatos and Alan Musgrave, eds., *Criticism and the Growth of Knowledge* (Cambridge, England: Cambridge University Press, 1970).

19. See Ada W. Finifter, ed., *Political Science: The State of the Discipline* (Washington, D.C.: American Political Science Association, 1983); Ada W. Finifter, ed., *Political Science: The State of the Discipline II* (Washington, D.C.: American Political Science Association, 1993).

20. See John S. Nelson, "The Ideological Connection, Parts I and II," *Theory and Society* 4 (fall–winter 1977): 421–48, 573–90.

21. Michael S. Lewis-Beck, "What Political Theory Is," draft, September 1980, pp. 2 and 3. See Michael Lewis-Beck, *Applied Regression* (Newbury Park, Calif.: Sage, 1980).

22. See Marshall Spector, "Models and Theories," *British Journal for the Philosophy of Science* 16 (August 1965): 121–42; Paul F. Kress, "On Validating Simulation, with Special Attention to Simulation of International Politics," *International Interactions* 1 (1974): 41–50; Philip C. Wall, "How Scientific Are Political Science Models?" *Political Methodology* 1 (summer 1974): 83–118.

23. See John G. Gunnell, "The Idea of the Conceptual Framework: A Philosophical Critique," *Journal of Comparative Administration* 1 (August 1969): 140–76.

24. See Beardsley, "Substantive Significance Versus Quantitative Rigor"; Frank T. Denton, "The Significance of Significance: Rhetorical Aspects of Statistical Hypothesis Testing in Economics," pp. 163–83, in Arjo Klamer, D. N.

McCloskey, and Robert M. Solow, eds., *The Consequences of Economic Rhetoric* (New York: Cambridge University Press, 1988); D. N. McCloskey, "The Rhetoric of Significance Tests," *The Rhetoric of Economics* (Madison: University of Wisconsin Press, 1985), 154–73.

25. Christopher H. Achen, "Toward Theories of Political Data," pp. 69–93, in Finifter, *Political Science*. Also see Christopher H. Achen, *Interpreting and Using Regression* (Newbury Park, Calif.: Sage, 1981).

26. Lewis Namier, *Personalities and Powers*, 1955, quoted in John Gross, ed., *The Oxford Book of Aphorisms* (Oxford, England: Oxford University Press, 1983) 236.

27. William H. Riker, "Political Theory and the Art of Heresthetics," pp. 47–67, in Finifter, *Political Science*, 47.

28. William H. Panning, "Formal Models of Legislative Processes," *Legislative Studies Quarterly* 8 (August 1983): 427, 441–42.

29. William H. Panning, "What Does It Take to Have a Theory? Principles in Political Science," pp. 479–511, in Nelson, *What Should Political Theory Be Now?* 490.

30. See Panning, "Formal Models of Legislative Processes,"442–45. Also see Panning, "What Does It Take to Have a Theory?" in Nelson, *What Should Political Theory Be Now?* 489–507; Nelson, "Political Theory as Political Rhetoric," pp. 169–240, in Nelson, *What Should Political Theory Be Now?* 193–204.

31. See Ellen Meiksins Wood, *Mind and Politics* (Berkeley: University of California Press, 1972); Roberto Mangabeira Unger, *Knowledge and Politics* (New York: Free Press, 1975); Charles E. Lindblom, *Politics and Markets* (New York: Basic, 1977).

32. See Panning, "What Does It Take to Have a Theory?" in Nelson, *What Should Political Theory Be Now?* 491–93; Riker, "Political Theory and the Art of Heresthetics," in Finifter, *Political Science*, 47–55.

33. See John S. Nelson, "Meaning and Measurement Across Paradigms," paper prepared for the annual meeting of the American Political Science Association, Washington, D.C., 1977, pp. 15–22.

34. See Riker, "Political Theory and the Art of Heresthetics," in Finifter, *Political Science*, 55–65; Panning, "What Does It Take to Have a Theory?" in Nelson, *What Should Political Theory Be Now?* 501–507; Panning, "Formal Models of Legislative Processes," 28–30. Riker proposes a discipline of "heresthetics" to study the strategy of decision; more specifically, it is to explore the origin and manipulation of preferences and alternatives. As I argue elsewhere, notwithstanding Riker's argument to the contrary, this may be regarded as an important part of the discipline of rhetoric. Relatedly Panning's proposals too are closely linked to inquiry into processes of persuasion and other modes of influence.

35. Friedrich Nietzsche, "On Truth and Falsity in Their Extramoral Sense," pp. 1–13, in Warren Shibles, ed., *Essays on Metaphor* (Whitewater, Wisc.: Language Press, 1972), 5.

36. See Michael Calvin McGee, "The Ideograph: A Link Between Rhetoric

and Ideology," *Quarterly Journal of Speech* 66 (February 1980), 1–16; Michael Calvin McGee and John S. Nelson, "Narrative Reason in Public Argument," *Journal of Communication* 35 (autumn 1985): 139–55; Charles Willard, *Argumentation and the Social Grounds of Knowledge* (University: University of Alabama Press, 1983).

37. See Ludwig Wittgenstein, *Philosophical Investigations*, 3d ed., trans. G. E. M. Anscombe (New York: Macmillan, 1958); Friedrich Waismann, *How I See Philosophy*, ed. Rom Harre (New York: St. Martin's, 1968); Hanna Fenichel Pitkin, *Wittgenstein and Justice* (Berkeley: University of California Press, 1973); Stanley Cavell, *The Claim of Reason* (New York: Oxford University Press, 1979).

38. See Paul Ricoeur, *The Rule of Metaphor*, trans. Robert Czerny (Toronto: University of Toronto Press, 1977); Andrew Ortony, ed., *Metaphor and Thought* (Cambridge, England: Cambridge University Press, 1979); Mark Johnson, ed., *Philosophical Perspectives on Metaphor* (Minneapolis: University of Minnesota Press, 1981).

39. See Earl R. MacCormac, *Metaphor and Myth in Science and Religion* (Durham, N.C.: Duke University Press, 1976); Nelson, "Meaning and Measurement Across Paradigms."

40. See Stephen C. Pepper, *World Hypotheses* (Berkeley: University of California Press, 1942); Hayden White, *Metahistory* (Baltimore: Johns Hopkins University Press, 1973). Also see John S. Nelson, "Review Essay [on *Metahistory*]," *History and Theory* 14 (1975): 74–91, and "Tropal History and the Social Sciences," *History and Theory* 19 (1980): 80–101.

41. See George Lakoff and Mark Johnson, *Metaphors We Live By* (Chicago: University of Chicago Press, 1980).

42. My favorite such text for teaching undergraduates is full of these examples: Howard Kahane, *Logic and Contemporary Rhetoric*, 4th ed. (Belmont, Calif.: Wadsworth, 1984).

43. See Nietzsche, "On Truth and Falsity" in Shibles, *Essays on Metaphor*; Paul de Man, "Nietzsche's Theory of Rhetoric," *Symposium* 28 (spring 1974): 33–51, and *Allegories of Reading* (New Haven, Conn.: Yale University Press, 1979).

44. A fine exploration of argumentative traps is Gabriel Stolzenberg, "Can an Inquiry into the Foundations of Mathematics Tell Us Anything Interesting About Mind?" pp. 221–69, in George A. Miller and Elizabeth Lenneberg, eds., *Psychology and Biology of Language and Thought* (New York: Academic Press, 1978). Such traps of argument may call to mind the traps of gumption, value, and truth surveyed by Robert M. Pirsig in *Zen and the Art of Motorcycle Maintenance* (New York: Bantam, 1974), 298–318. Although not exactly the same, Pirsig's traps do relate closely to the ones that beset many inquiries in the university, which Pirsig tellingly terms "the Church of Reason."

45. See Thomas S. Kuhn, *The Essential Tension* (Chicago: University of Chicago Press, 1977); Paul K. Feyerabend, *Against Method* (Atlantic Highlands, N.J.: Humanities Press, 1975).

46. See Nelson, "Meaning and Measurement Across Paradigms."

6. Turning Politics into Words

1. Antoine de Saint-Exupéry, *The Little Prince*, trans. Katherine Woods (New York: Harcourt, Brace and World, 1943), 67.

2. Both remarks appear in H. J. Jackson, "Coleridge, Etymology and Etymologic," *Journal of the History of Ideas* 44 (January–March 1983): 75. As Jackson explains, Coleridge often used and defended a distinctively etymological method of argument. In doing so Coleridge seems to have conceived his etymology as historical. Few of us would regard many of his word histories as decently accurate, but the key point is that most of us would recognize his principles of "etymologic" as decisively poetic and rhetorical. They are principles of intertwined invention-and-evidence for arguments far beyond the histories of words in some narrow sense. Thus they anticipate what I term *imaginative etymology*.

3. See John S. Nelson, "Ironic Politics," doctoral dissertation, University of North Carolina, Department of Political Science, Chapel Hill, N.C., 1977.

4. See Ursula K. Le Guin, *The Dispossessed* (New York: Harper & Row, 1974); J. Roland Pennock and John W. Chapman, eds., *Nomos XXI: Compromise in Ethics, Law, and Politics* (New York: New York University Press, 1979).

5. Works that make this (imaginative) etymological move are legion. See Carl J. Friedrich, ed., *Nomos II: Community* (New York: Atherton, 1959); Fred R. Dallmayr, ed., *From Contract to Community* (New York: Marcel Dekker, 1978); Glenn Tinder, *Community* (Baton Rouge: Louisiana State University Press, 1980).

6. See D. N. McCloskey, *The Rhetoric of Economics* (Madison: University of Wisconsin Press, 1985), esp. pp. 54–68, *If You're So Smart* (Chicago: University of Chicago Press, 1990), and *Knowledge and Persuasion in Economics* (New York: Cambridge University Press, 1994).

7. See Arjo Klamer, D. N. McCloskey, and Robert W. Solow, eds., *The Consequences of Economic Rhetoric* (New York: Cambridge University Press, 1988); Marianne A. Ferber and Julie A. Nelson, *Beyond Economic Man* (Chicago: University of Chicago Press, 1993).

8. See Ludwig Wittgenstein, *Philosophical Investigations*, 3d ed., trans. G. E. M. Anscombe (New York: Macmillan, 1958); W. V. O. Quine, *Word and Object* (Cambridge, Mass.: MIT Press, 1960).

9. See Jonathan Culler, *Structuralist Poetics* (Ithaca, N.Y.: Cornell University Press, 1975).

10. In my home field of political theory, see Quentin Skinner, "Meaning and Understanding in the History of Ideas," *History and Theory* 8 (1969): 3–53, "Conventions and the Understanding of Speech Acts," *Philosophical Quarterly* 21 (April 1970): . 113–38, " 'Social Meaning' and the Explanation of Social Actions," pp. 136–57, in Peter Laslett and W. G. Runciman, eds., *Philosophy, Politics, and Society (Fourth Series)* (Oxford, England, Basil Blackwell, 1972), and "Some Problems in the Analysis of Political Thought and Action," *Political Theory* 2 (August 1974): 277–303. Also see J. G. A. Pocock, *Politics, Language, and Time* (New York: Atheneum, 1972).

264

Notes to Pages 122-26Notes to Pages 122–26

11. For the new history of political theory, see J. G. A. Pocock, *The Ancient Constitution and the Feudal Law* (New York: Norton, 1967), and *The Machiavellian Moment* (Princeton, N.J.: Princeton University Press, 1975); Quentin Skinner, *The Foundations of Modern Political Thought*, 2 vols. (Cambridge, England: Cambridge University Press, 1978); John Dunn, *The Political Thought of John Locke* (Cambridge, England: Cambridge University Press, 1969), and *Political Obligation in Its Historical Context* (Cambridge, England: Cambridge University Press, 1980); Richard Ashcraft, *Revolutionary Politics and Locke's Two Treatises of Government* (Princeton, N.J.: Princeton University Press, 1986); Terence Ball, *Reappraising Political Theory* (Oxford, England: Oxford University Press, 1995). The new-historical emphasis on Locke, the American Founders, and what Pocock calls "the Atlantic Republican tradition" arises from appreciating specifically political intelligence (within popular contexts of history) on the part of works often called *political philosophy* but easily condemned as incoherent philosophically. These have a poetic political power that modernist analytical philosophy cannot parse.

12. See Thomas Dumm, *Democracy and Punishment* (Madison: University of Wisconsin Press, 1987); Stephen A. Tyler, *The Unspeakable* (Madison: University of Wisconsin Press, 1987).

13. J. L. Austin, "A Plea for Excuses," *Philosophical Papers* (Oxford, England: Oxford University Press, 1961).

14. See Stanley Cavell, *Must We Mean What We Say?* (Cambridge, England: Cambridge University Press, 1976), *The Claim of Reason* (New York: Oxford University Press, 1979), *Themes out of School* (Chicago: University of Chicago Press, 1984), *In Quest of the Ordinary* (Chicago: University of Chicago Press, 1988), *This New Yet Unapproachable America* (Albuquerque, N.M.: Living Batch Press, 1989), *Conditions Handsome and Unhandsome* (Chicago: University of Chicago Press, 1990), *A Pitch of Philosophy* (Cambridge, Mass.: Harvard University Press, 1994), and *Philosophical Passages* (Cambridge, Mass.: Blackwell, 1995). Also see John Hollander, "Stanley Cavell and *The Claim of Reason*," *Critical Inquiry* 6 (summer 1980): 575–88; Michael Fischer, *Stanley Cavell and Literary Skepticism* (Chicago: University of Chicago Press, 1989); Richard Fleming and Michael Payne, eds., *The Senses of Stanley Cavell* (Lewisburg, Pa.: Bucknell University Press, 1989).

15. See Norwood Russell Hanson, *Patterns of Discovery* (New York: Cambridge University Press, 1965).

16. See John S. Nelson, "Political Myth Making for Postmoderns," pp. 175–83, in Bruce E. Gronbeck, ed., *Spheres of Argument* (Annandale, Va.: Speech Communication Association, 1989).

17. William and Mary Morris, *Dictionary of Word and Phrase Origins*, 2d ed. (New York: Harper & Row, 1977).

18. See Marshall McLuhan, *Understanding Media* (New York: McGraw-Hill, 1964); Stewart Brand, *The Media Lab* (New York: Viking, 1987).

19. See Raymond Williams, "Distance," *Raymond Williams on Television* (London: Routledge, 1989), 13–21.

20. See William H. Riker, "Preface," *The Art of Political Manipulation* (New Haven, Conn.: Yale University Press, 1986), ix–xi.

21. See William H. Riker, "Political Theory and the Art of Heresthetics," pp. 47–67, in Ada W. Finifter, ed., *Political Science: The State of the Discipline* (Washington, D.C.: American Political Science Association, 1983), and "The Heresthetics of Constitution Making," *American Political Science Review* 78 (March 1984): 1–16.

22. See William H. Riker, *The Strategy of Rhetoric* (New Haven, Conn.: Yale University Press, 1996).

23. See Sigmund Freud, *The Ego and the Id*, ed. James Strachey, trans. Joan Riviere (New York: Norton, 1960), and *Beyond the Pleasure Principle*, ed. and trans. James Strachey (New York: Norton, 1961). Also see Hannah Arendt, *The Origins of Totalitarianism*, 4th ed. (New York: Harcourt Brace Jovanovich, 1973).

24. Raymond Williams, *Keywords*, rev. ed. (New York: Oxford University Press, 1985), 15–16.

25. See Marlena Corcoran, "The Nature of the Subject," Symposium on Kant 200, Project on Rhetoric of Inquiry, Iowa City, 1990.

26. See William E. Connolly, *The Terms of Political Discourse* (Lexington, Mass.: Heath, 1974).

27. See Giambattista Vico, *The New Science of Giambattista Vico*, unabridged trans. of 3d ed., Thomas Goddard Bergin and Max Harold Fisch (1744; Ithaca, N.Y.: Cornell University Press, 1976), and *On the Study Methods of Our Time*, trans. Elio Gianturco, (1709; Indianapolis: Bobbs-Merrill, 1965).

28. See Lawrence Weschler, *The Passion of Poland* (New York: Pantheon, 1984).

29. Soren Kierkegaard, *The Concept of Irony, with Constant Reference to Socrates*, trans. Lee M. Capel (Bloomington: Indiana University Press, 1965), 47.

30. See Michael J. Shapiro, "The Rhetoric of Social Science: The Political Responsibilities of the Scholar," pp. 363–80, in John S. Nelson, Allan Megill, and D. N. McCloskey, eds., *The Rhetoric of the Human Sciences* (Madison: University of Wisconsin Press, 1987), esp. 370–75.

31. See William Corlett, *Community Without Unity* (Durham, N.C.: Duke University Press, 1989).

32. See Jacques Derrida, *Writing and Difference*, trans. Alan Bass (Chicago: University of Chicago Press, 1978), *Dissemination*, trans. Barbara Johnson (Chicago: University of Chicago Press, (1981), and *Positions*, trans. Alan Bass (Chicago: University of Chicago Press, 1981).

33. See John S. Nelson, "Political Theory as Political Rhetoric," pp. 169–240, in John S. Nelson, ed., *What Should Political Theory Be Now?* (Albany: State University of New York Press, 1983).

34. All the quotations used here appear in John Gross, ed., *The Oxford Book of Aphorisms* (Oxford, England: Oxford University Press, 1983) 280–84.

35. See Paul Hernadi, "The Erotics of Retrospection: History Telling, Audience Response, and the Strategies of Desire," *New Literary History* 12 (winter

1981): 243–52; N. Katherine Hayles, "Eroticism in Language, or Argument Is Not All," symposium on the Rhetoric of the Disciplines: Next Steps, Project on Rhetoric of Inquiry, Iowa City, 1988.

36. See Michael Walzer, *Obligations* (Cambridge, Mass.: Harvard University Press, 1970).

37. See Hayden White, *Metahistory* (Baltimore: Johns Hopkins University Press, 1973), and *Tropics of Discourse* (Baltimore: Johns Hopkins University, 1987), esp. pp. 230–60. Also see John S. Nelson, "Tropal History and the Social Sciences," *History and Theory* 19 (1980): 80–101.

38. Thomas Hobbes, *Leviathan*, ed. Michael Oakeshott (1651; New York: Collier, 1962).

39. See Hanna Fenichel Pitkin, *The Concept of Representation* (Berkeley: University of California Press, 1967), and *Wittgenstein and Justice* (Berkeley: University of California Press, 1972); Harry Redner, "Representation and the Crisis of Postmodernism," *PS* 20 (summer 1987): 673–79.

40. Hannah Arendt, *On Revolution* (New York: Viking, 1963); Williams, *Key Words*.

41. Hobbes, *Leviathan*, 125–26; see Hannah Arendt, "Tradition and the Modern Age," *Between Past and Future* (New York: Viking, 1968), 17–40; Richard Sennett, *Authority* (New York: Knopf, 1980).

42. See Philip L. Bearsley, "Substantive Significance Versus Quantitative Rigor in Political Inquiry: Are the Two Compatible?" *International Interactions* 1 (1984): 27–40; D. N. McCloskey, "Why Economic Historians Should Stop Relying on Statistical Tests of Significance, and Lead Economists and Historians into the Promised Land," *Newsletter of the Cliometrics Society* 2 (December 1986): 5–7, and "The Rhetoric of Significance Tests," *Rhetoric of Economics*, 154–73; Frank T. Denton, "The Significance of Significance: Rhetorical Aspects of Statistical Hypothesis Testing in Economics," pp. 163–83, in Klamer, McCloskey, and Solow, *Consequences of Economic Rhetoric*.

43. See Philip E. Converse, "The Nature of Belief Systems in Mass Publics," pp. 206–62, in David Apter, ed., *Ideology and Discontent* (New York: Free Press, 1964).

44. See John S. Nelson, "The Ideological Connection, Parts I and II," *Theory and Society* 4 (fall–winter 1977): 421–48, 573–90.

7. Turning Ideologies into Myths

1. Leonard Cohen, "Everybody Knows," *Leonard Cohen Anthology* (New York: Amsco Music, 1991), 198–205.

2. Mere figures of speech always, of course, turn out to be and do so much more than we usually recognize. See Richard A. Lanham, *A Handlist of Rhetorical Terms*, 2d ed. (Berkeley: University of California Press, 1991); Arthur Quinn, *Figures of Speech* (Berkeley, University of California Press, 1986).

3. See Friedrich Nietzsche, *Friedrich Nietzsche on Rhetoric and Language*, eds. and trans. Sander L. Gilman, Carole Blair, and David J. Parent (New York, Oxford University Press, 1989).

4. See Hayden White, *Metahistory* (Baltimore: Johns Hopkins University Press, 1973), and *Tropics of Discourse* (Baltimore: Johns Hopkins University Press, 1978); John S. Nelson, "Tropal History and the Social Sciences," *History and Theory* 19 (1980): 80–101.

5. See John S. Nelson and G. R. Boynton, *Video Rhetorics* (Urbana: University of Illinois Press, 1997). Also see Bruce E. Gronbeck, "Mythic Portraiture in the 1988 Iowa Presidential Caucus Bio-Ads," *American Behavioral Scientist* 32 (March–April 1989): 351–64, "Negative Narratives in 1988 Presidential Campaign Ads," *Quarterly Journal of Speech* 78 (August 1992): 333–46, and "Negative Political Ads and American Self Images," pp. 60–81, in Arthur H. Miller and Bruce E. Gronbeck, eds., *Presidential Campaigns and American Self-Images* (Boulder, Colo.: Westview, 1994).

6. See Michael Paul Rogin, *Ronald Reagan, the Movie* (Berkeley: University of California Press, 1987); Garry Wills, *Reagan's America* (New York Penguin, 1988). Also see Bruno Bettelheim, "The Art of Moving Pictures: Man, Superman, and Myth," *Harper's Magazine*, October 1981, pp. 80–83.

7. See Murray Edelman, *Constructing the Political Spectacle* (Chicago: University of Chicago Press, 1988); James W. Carey, ed., *Media, Myths, and Narratives* (Newbury Park, Calif.: Sage, 1988).

8. See James Oliver Robertson, *American Myth, American Reality* (New York: Hill and Wang, 1980).

9. See Roland Barthes, *Mythologies*, trans. Annette Lavers (New York: Hill and Wang, 1972), and *The Eiffel Tower and Other Mythologies*, trans. Richard Howard (New York: Hill and Wang, 1979).

10. Samuel Butler, *Notebooks: Music, Pictures, and Books*, quoted in John Bartlett, ed., *Bartlett's Familiar Quotations*, 14th ed. (Boston: Little, Brown, 1968), 756b.

11. See Aristotle, *Rhetoric* and *Poetics*, ed. Friedrich Solmsen, trans. W. Rhys Roberts and Ingram Bywater (New York: Random House, 1954), *On Rhetoric*, trans. George A. Kennedy (New York: Oxford University Press, 1992).

12. See Ludwig Wittgenstein, *Philosophical Investigations*, 3d ed., trans. G. E. M. Anscombe (New York, Macmillan, 1958).

13. See Kenneth Burke, *A Grammar of Motives* (Berkeley: University of California Press, 1945), 503–17.

14. See John S. Nelson, "Natures and Futures for Political Theory," pp. 3–24, in John S. Nelson, ed., *What Should Political Theory Be Now?* (Albany: State University of New York Press, 1983), 17–19.

15. John Ayto, *Dictionary of Word Origins* (New York, Arcade, 1980), 208.

16. See D. N. McCloskey and John S. Nelson, "The Rhetoric of Political Economy," pp. 155–74, in James H. Nichols Jr. and Colins Wright, eds., *From Political Economy to Economics . . . And Back?* (San Francisco: Institute for Contemporary Studies Press, 1990).

17. See Alasdair MacIntyre, *After Virtue*, 2d ed. (Notre Dame, Ind.: University of Notre Dame Press, 1984), 22–34.

18. Kenneth Burke is the twentieth-century master of rhetoric as identifica-

tion (rather than persuasion). See *A Grammar of Motives; A Rhetoric of Motives* (Berkeley: University of California Press, 1950); and *Language as Symbolic Action* (Berkeley: University of California Press, 1966).

19. This is precisely Hegel's sense of *Sittlichkeit* as the ethics that account properly for rituals, institutions, and other communal aspects of good living—by contrast with *Moralität* as the agonal morality for individuals acute in conscience and rationality.

20. See Wayne C. Booth, *The Company We Keep* (Berkeley: University of California Press, 1988); John Gardner, *The Art of Fiction* (New York: Knopf, 1983).

21. Ayto, *Dictionary of Word Origins*, 328.

22. See Richard Brown, *Society as Text* (Chicago: University of Chicago Press, 1987), 64–79; John S. Nelson, "Seven Rhetorics of Inquiry," pp. 409–34, in John S. Nelson, Allan Megill, and D. N. McCloskey, eds., *The Rhetoric of the Human Sciences* (Madison: University of Wisconsin Press, 1987), 423–25.

23. See Stephen E. Toulmin, *The Uses of Argument* (Cambridge, England: Cambridge University Press, 1964), 94–145.

24. George A. Kennedy, *New Testament Interpretation Through Rhetorical Criticism* (Chapel Hill: University of North Carolina Press, 1984), 15.

25. See Robert Hariman, *Political Style* (Chicago: University of Chicago Press, 1995).

26. See Rene Wellek and Austin Warren, *Theory of Literature*, 3d ed. (New York: Harcourt, Brace and World, 1956). This is *not* what Ruskin lambasted in these terms in his third volume on *Modern Painters*, 1888, but his bent against emotion is much the same: "All violent feelings . . . produce in us a falseness in all our impressions of external things, which I would generally characterize as the 'Pathetic Fallacy.' "

27. See John S. Nelson, "A Turn Toward Rhetoric," *North Dakota Quarterly* 56 (summer 1988): 53–59.

28. Johann Wolfgang von Goethe, quoted in Laurence J. Peter, *Peter's Quotations* (New York: Bantam, 1977), 384.

29. Lee C. McDonald, "Myth, Politics, and Political Science," *Western Political Quarterly* 22 (March 1969): 141.

30. See Michael Calvin McGee and John S. Nelson, "Narrative Reason in Public Argument," *Journal of Communication* 35 (autumn 1985): 151–55.

31. See Claude Lévi-Strauss, *Myth and Meaning* (New York: Schocken Books, 1978), 44–54.

32. See John S. Nelson, "Commerce Among the Archipelagos: Rhetoric of Inquiry as a Practice of Coherent Education," pp. 78–100, in L. Robert Stevens, G. L. Seligmann, and Julian Long, eds., *The Core and the Canon* (Denton: University of North Texas Press, 1993).

33. See John S. Nelson, "Political Myth Making for Postmoderns," pp. 175–83, in Bruce E. Gronbeck, ed., *Spheres of Argument*, (Annandale, Va.: Speech Communication Association, 1989).

34. George Bernard Shaw, quoted in Peter, *Peter's Quotations*, 478; Jonathan Swift, "Letter to a Young Clergyman," January 9, 1720; Arthur Schopenhauer,

quoted in W. H. Auden and Louis Kronenberger, *The Viking Book of Aphorisms* (New York: Penguin,1966), 276; J. Robert Oppenheimer, quoted in Peter, *Peter's Quotations*, 478–79.

35. See Hannah Arendt, *The Human Condition* (Chicago: University of Chicago Press, 1958).

36. See Nelson, "Commerce Among the Archipelagos," in Stevens, Seligmann, and Long, *The Core and the Canon*. Also see Hariman, "In Oratory as in Life: Civic Performance in Cicero's Republican Style," *Political Style*, 95–140.

37. See Hannah Arendt, "Thinking and Moral Considerations," *Social Research* 38 (autumn 1971): 417–46; J. Glenn Gray, "The Winds of Thought," *Social Research* 44 (spring 1977): 44–62.

38. See Susan Sontag, "Writing Itself: On Roland Barthes," *New Yorker*, April 26, 1982, pp. 122–41.

39. Edmund Burke, First Letter on a Regicide Peace, 1796; quoted in Bernard Darwin, ed., *The Oxford Dictionary of Quotations*, corrected 3d ed. (Oxford, England: Oxford University Press, 1980), 112.

40. See Louis Hartz, *The Liberal Tradition in America* (New York: Harcourt, Brace and World, 1955); Herbert G. Reid, ed., *Up the Mainstream* (New York: McKay, 1974); Robert D. Holsworth and J. Harry Wray, *American Politics and Everyday Life*, 2d ed. (New York: Wiley, 1987).

41. See John S. Nelson, "Political Foundations for Rhetoric of Inquiry," pp. 258–89, in Herbert W. Simons, ed., *The Rhetorical Turn*, (Chicago: University of Chicago Press, 1990).

42. See Roberto Mangabeira Unger, *Knowledge and Politics* (New York: Free Press, 1975); Ellen Meiksins Wood, *Mind and Politics* (Berkeley: University of California Press, 1972).

43. See Norberto Bobbio, *The Future of Democracy*, ed. Richard Bellamy, trans. Roger Griffin (Minneapolis: University of Minnesota Press, 1987).

44. See Robert N. Bellah et al., *Habits of the Heart* (Berkeley: University of California Press, 1985).

8. Turning Governments Every Which Way but Loose

1. Percy Bysshe Shelley, *A Defense of Poetry*, 1821; quoted in John Bartlett, ed., *Bartlett's Familiar Quotations*, 14th ed. (Boston: Little, Brown, 1968), 573a.

2. See Hannah Arendt, *The Human Condition* (Chicago: University of Chicago Press, 1958).

3. On community, see Milton Mayer, "Community, Anyone?" *Center* 8 (September–October 1975): 2–6. On reciprocal giving, see William Corlett, *Community Without Unity* (Durham, N.C.: Duke University Press, 1989). On the sending of messages, see John Durham Peters, "John Locke, the Individual, and the Origin of Communication," *Quarterly Journal of Speech* 75 (November 1989): 387–99.

4. See Murray Edelman, *From Art to Politics* (Chicago: University of Chicago Press, 1995).

5. Katha Pollitt, "Metaphors of Women," *Atlantic Monthly*, February 1981, p. 43. The second stanza adds a fifth line in the version republished in Pollitt's *Antarctic Traveller* (New York: Knopf, 1982), 53: "A toothache. A lost twin." Also see Katha Pollitt, *Reasonable Creatures* (New York: Knopf, 1995).

6. See Max Black, "Metaphor," *Models and Metaphors* (Ithaca, N.Y.: Cornell University Press, 1962), 25–47.

7. See Thomas S. Kuhn, *The Structure of Scientific Revolutions* (Chicago: University of Chicago Press, 1970).

8. See Michel Foucault, *Discipline and Punish,* trans. Alan Sheridan (New York: Random House, 1977), and *Thomas L. Dumm: Democracy and Punishment* (Madison: University of Wisconsin Press, 1987); Jonathan Simon, *Poor Discipline* (Chicago: University of Chicago Press, 1993).

9. See Les Levidow and Kevin Robins, eds., *Cyborg Worlds* (London: Free Association Books, 1989); Donna Haraway, *Simians, Cyborgs, and Women* (New York: Routledge, 1991).

10. Stewart Brand, *The Media Lab* (New York: Viking, 1987), 228.

11. Ibid.

12. See Murray Edelman, *Constructing the Political Spectacle* (Chicago: University of Chicago Press, 1988), 12–36.

13. See Edelman, *Constructing the Political Spectacle*, 90–102; W. Lance Bennett, *News: The Politics of Illusion*, 2d ed. (New York: Longman, 1988), 35–51; Dan Nimmo and James E. Combs, *Mediated Political Realities*, 2d ed. (New York: Longman, 1990), 14–17. Also see David S. Broder, "The Story That Still Nags Me," *Washington Monthly*, February 1987, p. 30: "It is not an accident that we refer to 'news stories' as the basic ingredient of the news. Reporters are essentially storytellers in the narrative tradition. Whether we acknowledge it or not, we constantly devise the scripts we think appropriate for the events we cover."

14. The very name of "news" tells us as much. See Broder, "The Story That Still Nags Me," p. 32: "Freshness and surprise are built into the definition of news; the unusual, the unexpected and, best of all, the unprecedented are what we seek."

15. See Renata Adler, "Two Trials, Part I," *New Yorker*, June 16, 1986, p. 50; Robert M. Entman, *Democracy Without Citizens* (New York: Oxford University Press, 1988), 30–38; Bennett, *News*, 105–44.

16. See interview of Milan Kundera, "When There Is No Word for 'Home': An Interview by Jane Kramer," *New York Times Book Review* April 29, 1984, p. 46.

17. See Bennett, *News*, 26–35; Edelman, *Constructing the Political Spectacle*, 90–102. Also see John Updike, "At the Hairy Edge of the Possible," *New Yorker*, June 3, 1991, p. 104: "Ours is an age of personalities and interviews, of interest in people rather than abstractions like life and time and liberty and fortune. Personalities contrived by the procedures of media publicity pique the human curiosity once satisfied by the daily intercourse of the village and the city neighborhood."

18. See W. Lance Bennett, "Where Have All the Issues Gone?" Sixth Sum-

mer Conference on Argumentation, Alta, Utah, 1989. Also see Bennett, *News*, xi.

19. See Edelman, *Constructing the Political Spectacle*, 37–65; Dan Nimmo and James E. Combs, *Subliminal Politics* (Englewood Cliffs, N.J.: Prentice-Hall, 1980), 61–92; Jeffrey Tullis, *The Rhetorical Presidency* (Princeton, N.J.: Princeton University Press, 1988); Stephen J. Wayne and Clyde Wilcox, eds., *The Quest for National Office* (New York: St. Martin's, 1992).

20. Elizabeth Drew, "Letter from Washington: July 31, 1989," *New Yorker* July 31, 1989, p. 76.

21. See Elizabeth Drew, "Letter from Washington: November 21, 1990," *New Yorker*, December 3, 1990, p. 182.

22. See James W. Carey, ed., *Media, Myths, and Narratives* (Newbury Park, Calif.: Sage, 1988).

23. See James Oliver Robertson, *American Myth, American Reality* (New York: Hill and Wang, 1980); John S. Nelson, "Political Myth Making for Postmoderns," pp. 175–83, in Bruce E. Gronbeck, ed., *Spheres of Argument* (Annandale, Va.: Speech Communication Association, 1989).

24. See George Lakoff and Mark Johnson, *Metaphors We Live By* (Chicago: University of Chicago Press, 1980). For a more overt (but less adequate) argument about our specifically political metaphors, see George Lakoff, "Metaphor and War: The Metaphor System Used to Justify War in the Gulf," essay disseminated by author on computer diskettes, December 31, 1990.

25. See G. R. Boynton and Milton G. Lodge, "Voter's Images of Candidates," pp. 176–89, in Arthur H. Miller and Bruce E. Gronbeck, eds., *Presidential Campaigns and American Self-Images*, (Boulder, Colo.: Westview, 1994).

26. See Doris A. Graber, *Processing the News*, 2d ed. (New York: Longman, 1988); Shanto Iyengar and Donald R. Kinder, *News That Matters* (Chicago: University of Chicago Press, 1987).

27. This paragraph owes much to conversations with G. R. Boynton, though he should not be held accountable for its connections to myth.

28. Poul Anderson, *Orion Shall Rise* (New York: Simon & Schuster, 1983), 292.

29. For two case studies in recent political myth making, see John S. Nelson, "Orwell's Political Myths and Ours," pp. 11–44, in Robert L. Savage, James E. Combs, and Dan D. Nimmo, eds., *The Orwellian Moment* (Fayetteville: University of Arkansas Press, 1989) ; Barbara J. Hill and John S. Nelson, "Facing the Holocaust: Robert Arneson's Ceramic Myth of Postmodern Catastrophe," pp. 189–209, in Robert Hobbs and Fredrick Woodard, eds., *Human Rights/Human Wrongs* (Seattle: University of Washington Press, 1986).

30. See Ronald Berkman and Laura W. Kitch, *Politics in the Media Age* (New York: McGraw-Hill, 1986); Charles Press and Kenneth Verburg, *American Politicians and Journalists* (Glenview, Ill.: Scott, Foresman, 1988).

31. On all these matters, see Jean Baudrillard, *In the Shadow of the Silent Majorities*, trans. Paul Foss, John Johnston, and Paul Patton (New York: Semiotext(e), 1983); Edelman, *Constructing the Political Spectacle*.

32. Anderson, *Orion Shall Rise*, 191.

33. The great exception is my Iowa colleague G. R. Boynton, whom I thank for innumerable conversations that weave in and out of this essay—no doubt to his persistent and (partly?) justified dissatisfaction.

34. See Elisabeth Noelle-Neumann, "The Spiral of Silence: A Theory of Public Opinion," *Journal of Communication* 24 (1974): . 43–51, and "Turbulences in the Climate of Opinion," *Public Opinion Quarterly* 41 (1977): 143–58. Also see Benjamin Ginsberg, *The Captive Public* (New York: Basic, 1986); Frank Louis Rusciano, *Isolation and Paradox* (New York: Greenwood, 1989).

35. See Jim Collins, *Uncommon Cultures* (New York: Routledge, 1989).

36. Here the kinds of investigations encouraged by such "new historians of political theory" as Quentin Skinner, J. G. A. Pocock, John Dunn, and Richard Ashcraft can be highly informative.

37. Anderson, *Orion Shall Rise*, 268.

38. See the political prisoner's mad lament in Arthur Koestler, *Darkness at Noon*, trans. Daphne Hardy (New York: Macmillan, 1941).

39. For a bill of particulars, see Robert L. Heilbroner, *An Inquiry into the Human Prospect*, rev. ed. (New York: Norton, 1980).

40. On other troubles for late-modern sciences of politics with counterfactual conditionals, see John S. Nelson, "Accidents, Laws, and Philosophical Flaws: Behavioral Explanation in Dahl and Dahrendorf," *Comparative Politics* 7 (April 1975): 435–57.

41. See Nelson, "Political Myth Making for Postmoderns," Gronbeck, *Spheres of Argument*.

42. See Wendell Berry, *The Unsettling of America* (San Francisco: Sierra Club Books, 1977).

43. See John S. Nelson, Allan Megill, and D. N. McCloskey, eds., *The Rhetoric of the Human Sciences* (Madison: University of Wisconsin Press, 1987).

44. Anderson, *Orion Shall Rise*, 267.

45. "The Talk of the Town," *New Yorker,* August 27, 1990, p. 27:

> In a way, the Gulf crisis is beginning to feel a little like two of our other current problems—the savings-and-loan crisis and the budget crisis. And, in fact, all three have a common source: a decade's obliviousness of the minimum requirements of governance itself. In the case of the budget crisis, the claims of supply-side advocates that cutting tax rates would actually increase federal revenues always constituted an iffy proposition (George Bush himself famously dismissed such assertions as "voodoo economics" during the 1980 primaries), and matters weren't likely to be helped any by huge increases in defense spending. Plenty of people were pointing out the growing inconsistencies, but nobody in government was paying them any mind. Nor was there a lack of whistle-blowers warning of impending disaster in the case of the savings-and-loan crisis; it was just that the prevailing ethos insisted on the self-evident benefits of deregulation and the magical propensities of the unfettered marketplace. In both cases, a refusal to govern—to plan and to

monitor and to respond appropriately—was government policy throughout the decade.

46. Ibid., 28.

47. See Jean Baudrillard, *Seduction,* trans. Brian Singer (New York: St. Martin's, 1990), *Simulations,* trans. Paul Foss, Paul Patton, and Philip Beitchman (New York: Semiotext(e), 1983), *The Evil Demon of Images* (Sydney: Power Institute of Fine Arts, 1987), and *The Ecstasy of Communication,* ed. Sylvere Lotringer, trans. Bernard and Caroline Schutze (New York: Semiotext(e), 1988). Also see Guy Debord, *Society of the Spectacle* (Detroit: Black and Red, 1977).

48. See Edelman, *Constructing the Political Spectacle.*

49. See Hanna Fenichel Pitkin, *Fortune Is a Woman* (Berkeley: University of California Press, 1984).

50. See Aldo Leopold, *A Sand County Almanac, with Essays on Conservation from Round River* (New York: Ballantine, 1966); Michael Pollan, *Second Nature* (New York: Dell, 1991).

51. See Susan Sontag, *Illness as Metaphor* (New York: Farrar, Straus and Giroux, 1978), and *AIDS and Its Metaphors* (New York: Farrar, Straus and Giroux, 1988).

9. Turning Deliberations into Debates

1. Ramsey Campbell, *The Hungry Moon* (New York: Tom Doherty Associates, 1986), 45.

2. Jane Ellen Harrison, *Themis,* 2d ed. (Cleveland, Ohio: World, 1927), 378.

3. William Doty, *Mythography* (University: University of Alabama Press, 1986), 73.

4. Edmund R. Leach, *Political Systems of Highland Burma* (Cambridge, Mass.: Harvard University Press, 1954), 14.

5. Henry Tudor, *Political Myth* (New York: Praeger, 1971), 11.

6. Roland Barthes, *Mythologies,* trans. Annette Lavers (New York: Hill and Wang, 1972, and *The Eiffel Tower, and Other Mythologies* trans. Richard Howard (New York: Hill and Wang, 1972).

7. On modern separations between thought and action, theory and practice, see John S. Nelson, "Toltechs, Aztechs, and the Art of the Possible: Parenthetic Comments on the Political Through Language and Aesthetics," *Polity* 8 (fall 1975): 80–116.

8. See John S. Nelson, "Political Myth Making for Postmoderns," pp. 175–83, in Bruce E. Gronbeck, ed., *Spheres of Argument* (Annandale, Va.: Speech Communication Association, 1989).

9. Lest I start new myth(take)s here, like H. L. Mencken writing about the origins of bathroom fixtures, let me add that I know next to nothing about Druid beliefs. For the moment, at least, I lack the interest that would get me to a library to find out more. Instead I simply invent beliefs of the kinds that

the Myth and Ritual School might attribute to the Druids for the purpose of explaining the continuing rituals—of mistletoe kissing, salt shouldering, and three-speaking—that Ramsey Campbell traces to the Druids.

10. For a different account of three-thinking, though, see John S. Nelson, "Ironic Politics," doctoral dissertation, Department of Political Science, University of North Carolina, Chapel Hill, 1977, 232–317. And to make three, cognitive scientists surely would want to talk in this same connection about information and attention span. On elective affinity and prefigured memory, see Hayden White, *Metahistory* (Baltimore: Johns Hopkins University Press, 1973). Also see John S. Nelson, "Review Essay on *Metahistory* by Hayden White," *History and Theory* 14 (1975): 74–91, and "Tropal History and the Social Sciences," *History and Theory* 19 (1980): 80–101.

11. George W. S. Trow, "Annals of Discourse: The Harvard Black Rock Forest," *New Yorker*, June 11, 1984, p. 46.

12. See Lee C. McDonald, "Myth, Politics, and Political Science," *Western Political Quarterly* 22 (March 1969): 141–50.

13. See Stanley Cavell, "Recounting Gains, Showing Losses (A Reading of *The Winter's Tale*)," *In Quest of the Ordinary* (Chicago: University of Chicago Press, 1988), 76–101. Also see Cavell on "natural conventions" in *The Claim of Reason* (New York: Oxford University Press, 1979).

14. Samuel R. Delany plays with these mythic phenomena in his Neveryon series: *Tales of Neveryon*, 3d ed. (Hanover, N.H.: University Press of New England and Middletown, Conn: Wesleyan University Press, 1993), *Neveryóna*, 3d ed. (Hanover, N.H.: University Press of New England and Middletown, Conn.: Wesleyan University Press, 1993), *Flight from Neveryon*, 3d ed. (Hanover, N.H.: University Press of New England and Middletown, Conn.: Wesleyan University Press, 1994), and *Return to Neveryon*, 3d ed. (Hanover, N.H.: University Press of New England and Middletown, Conn.: Wesleyan University Press, 1994).

15. l appropriate this terminology from Roland Barthes ("Myth Today," *Mythologies*, 109–59), who faulted bourgeois ideology for its political myth-making but enjoyed similar performances in reflecting brilliantly—if iconically—on "The World of Wrestling" (15–25), "The Face of Garbo" (56–57), "Striptease" (84–87), and the like.

16. Donald Kingsbury, *Courtship Rite* (New York: Pocket Books, 1982), 121.

17. See Henry Fairlie, "In Search of a President," Washington Post Syndicate, May 23, 1976, and "The Politician's Art," *Harper's Magazine*, December 1977, pp. 33–46 and 123–24.

18. Kingsbury, *Courtship Rite*, 290.

19. See Murray Edelman, *Constructing the Political Spectacle* (Chicago: University of Chicago Press, 1988).

20. See E. J. Dionne, "Foolishness Falls Victim to War Debate as Eloquence Escalates," *Washington Post*, January 12, 1991, pp. A8 and A14.

21. See G. R. Boynton, "Telling a Good Story: Models of Argument, Models of Understanding in the Senate Agriculture Committee," pp. 429–38, in

Joseph W. Wenzel, ed., *Argument and Critical Practices* (Annandale, Va.: Speech Communication Association, 1987), and "When Publics and Senators Meet at the Senate Environmental Protection Subcommittee," *Discourse and Society* 2 (April 1991): 131–55.

22. See James S. Fishkin, *Democracy and Deliberation* (New Haven, Conn.: Yale University Press, 1991); Carlos Santiago Nino, *The Constitution of Deliberative Democracy* (New Haven, Conn.: Yale University Press, 1996); Michael Sandel, *Democracy's Discontent* (Cambridge, Mass.: Harvard University Press, 1996).

23. See John Ayto, *Dictionary of Word Origins* (New York: Arcade, 1980), 162. Also see Marcus Tullius Cicero, *On the Commonwealth*, trans. George Holland Sabine and Stanley Barney Smith (Indianapolis, Ind.: Bobbs-Merrill, 1929), *Basic Works of Cicero*, ed. Moses Hadas (New York: Random House, 1951). On the consequent connection between promises (as commitments for action into the future) and freedom, see Ursula K. Le Guin, *The Dispossessed* (New York: Avon, 1974), 197–99.

24. See Steven Mailloux, *Rhetorical Power* (Ithaca, N.Y.: Cornell University Press, 1989).

25. William H. Riker, *The Art of Political Manipulation* (New Haven, Conn.: Yale University Press, 1982).

26. Kingsbury, *Courtship Rite*, 36.

27. On how the two meet, see Alexei and Cory Panshin, *The World Beyond the Hill* (Los Angeles: Jeremy P. Tarcher, 1989).

28. Kingsbury, *Courtship Rite*, 356.

29. Note the accounts of such senatorial talk in Christopher Matthews, *Hardball* (New York: Harper & Row, 1988); Robert Caro, *The Years of Lyndon Johnson: Means of Ascent* (New York: Knopf, 1990).

30. Thus it echoes the Jean-Jacques Rousseau plot in *The Social Contract* (trans. G. D. H. Cole [New York: Random House, 1933]) for democratic deliberation.

31. Kingsbury, *Courtship Rite*, 289.

32. See John S. Nelson, *Cowboy Politics*, forthcoming.

33. See Judith N. Shklar, *Legalism* (Cambridge, Mass.: Harvard University Press, 1964).

34. Kingsbury, *Courtship Rite*, 179.

35. See David Worcester, *The Art of Satire* (New York: Russell and Russell, 1940); Robert C. Elliott, *The Power of Satire* (Princeton, N.J.: Princeton University Press, 1973). Many commentators on postmodernism take one of its characteristic ploys to be parody.

36. See John S. Nelson, "Orwell's Political Myths and Ours," pp. 11–44, in Robert L. Savage, James E. Combs, and Dan D. Nimmo, eds., *The Orwellian Moment* (Fayetteville: University of Arkansas Press, 1989), and "Political Myth Making for Postmoderns." Also see Barbara J. Hill and John S. Nelson, "Facing the Holocaust: Robert Arneson's Ceramic Myth of Postmodern Catastrophe," pp. 189–209, in Robert Hobbes and Frederick Woodard, eds., *Human*

Rights/Human Wrongs (Seattle: University of Washington Press, 1986). Though his arguments at times become confused on this point, also see Doty, "The Functional Contexts and Truths of Myths and Rituals," *Mythography*, 60–65.

37. See Frederick Ferré, "Hope and Myth in a World of Scarcity," *Georgia Review* 32 (fall 1978): 553–70, and "Limits, Myths, and Morals," *Georgia Review* 34 (fall 1980): 481–94. Also see Doty, "Mythic Dimensions of Our Decentered Cosmos," *Mythography*, 245–48.

38. See Richard L. Hall, "Participation and Purpose in Committee Decision Making," *American Political Science Review* 81 (March 1987): . 105–28; Richard L. Hall and C. Lawrence Evans, "The Power of Subcommittees," *Journal of Politics* 52 (May 1990): 335–55; and Richard L. Hall and Frank W. Wayman, "Buying Time: Moneyed Interests and the Mobilization of Bias in Congressional Committees," *American Political Science Review* 84 (September 1990): 797–820. Also see G. R. Boynton, "Conversations About Governing," pp. 167–74, in Bruce E. Gronbeck, ed., *Spheres of Argument* (Annandale, Va.: Speech Communication Association, 1989), and "Ideas and Action: A Cognitive Model of the Senate Agriculture Committee," *Political Behavior* 12 (June 1990): 181–213.

39. See Boynton, "Telling a Good Story" and "When Senators and Publics Meet."

10. Turning Stands into Stances

1. Max Weber, "Politics as a Vocation," pp. 77–128, in H. H. Gerth and C. Wright Mills, eds. and trans., *From Max Weber* (New York: Oxford University Press, 1946), 127.

2. Ibid., 128.

3. The idea of our times as a postmodern period is specified and defended in John S. Nelson, "Political Theory as Political Rhetoric," pp. 169–240, in John S. Nelson, ed., *What Should Political Theory Be Now?* (Albany: State University of New York Press, 1983); "Seven Rhetorics of Inquiry: A Provocation," pp. 407–34, in John S. Nelson, Allan Megill, and D. N. McCloskey, eds., *The Rhetoric of the Human Sciences* (Madison: University of Wisconsin Press, 1987); and "Commerce Among the Archipelagos: Rhetoric of Inquiry as a Practice of Coherent Education," pp. 78–100, in L. Robert Stevens, G. L. Seligmann, and Julian Long, eds., *The Core and the Canon* (Denton: University of North Texas Press, 1993. Also see Hannah Arendt, "Tradition and the Modern Age," *Between Past and Future* (New York: Viking, 1968), 17–40.

4. Edmund Burke, "Second Speech on Conciliation with America," 1775.

5. Abraham Lincoln, last public address, Washington, D.C., 1865.

6. See Joseph Tussman, *Obligation and the Body Politic* (New York: Oxford University Press, 1960), 104–21.

7. Plainly, there is more to be said about the relationship between compromise and principle, but that leads beyond my immediate argument here.

8. Henry Fairlie, "The Politician's Art," *Harper's Magazine*, December 1977, p. 44.

9. See Garry Wills, "Feminists and Other Useful Fanatics," *Harper's Magazine*, June 1976, pp. 35–42.

10. Robert L. Heilbroner, *An Inquiry into the Human Prospect* (New York: Norton, 1975), 167–68.

11. Detailed comparison of revolutionary strategies and times with stands and times of trouble is another topic that this essay can only skirt.

12. There is a fine point of history and politics in the masculinist terminology of the stand makers and takers. They celebrate "man" and "humanist" values of the West in ways out of step with the largely later feminism of talk that strives for gender neutrality. To neuter their words would be anachronistic and could be to alter their politics. For feminist doubts about stand making and taking, see Ursula K. Le Guin, "Hier Steh' Ich," *Wild Angels* (Santa Barbara, Calif.: Capra Press, 1975), 20.

13. Heilbroner, *An Inquiry*, 167.

14. See Hannah Arendt, "Thinking and Moral Considerations," *Social Research* 38 (autumn 1971): 417–46; John S. Nelson, "Toltechs, Aztechs, and the Art of the Possible," *Polity* 8 (fall 1975): 80–116; Gerald Sykes, *The Cool Millennium* (Englewood Cliffs, N.J.: Prentice-Hall, 1967).

15. Arendt, "Thinking and Moral Considerations," 446.

16. Maurice Merleau-Ponty, *Sense and Nonsense*, trans. Hubert L. Dreyfus and Patricia A. Dreyfus (Evanston, Ill.: Northwestern University Press, 1964), 186–87.

17. See Judith N. Shklar, "Subversive Genealogies," *Daedalus* 101 (winter 1972): 134: "The contents of Pandora's jar are scattered among men—sorrow, disease, and misery. Only hope does not escape, because Zeus prevents it from leaving the jar. Even hope is denied men." Or John H. Schaar, "Power and Purity," *American Review* 19 (January 1974): 178: "The right reading of the story of Pandora's box is not that hope was released after all the other evils so that they might be endurable. Rather, hope was the last of the evils."

18. See Henry Malcolm, *Generation of Narcissus* (Boston: Little, Brown, 1971); Jim Hougan, *Decadence* (New York: Morrow, 1976); Christopher Lasch, *The Culture of Narcissism* (New York: Norton, 1978).

19. Arthur Koestler, *Darkness at Noon*, trans. Daphne Hardy (New York: Macmillan, 1941), 98.

20. See Richard Crossman, ed., *The God That Failed* (New York: Bantam, 1949); Judith N. Shklar, *After Utopia* (Princeton, N.J.: Princeton University Press, 1957).

21. See Hannah Arendt, *The Origins of Totalitarianism*, 4th ed. (New York: Harcourt Brace Jovanovich, 1973); Michael Polanyi, *Beyond Nihilism* (Cambridge, England: Cambridge University Press, 1960); John S. Nelson, "Ironic Politics," doctoral dissertation, University of North Carolina, Department of Political Science, Chapel Hill, N.C., 1977.

22. Nelson, "Ironic Politics," 685–702, 710–14.

23. Milton Mayer, "Community Anyone?" *Center Magazine* 8 (September–October 1975): 4.

278

24. See Nelson, "Political Theory as Political Rhetoric," in Nelson, *What Should Political Theory Be Now?*

25. Richard Ashcraft, "On the Problem of Methodology and the Nature of Political Theory," *Political Theory* 3 (February 1975): 16. See Paul F. Kress, "Against Epistemology: Apostate Musings," *Journal of Politics* 41 (May 1979): 526–42.

26. Albert Camus, *The Rebel*, trans. Anthony Bower (New York: Random House, 1954), 306.

27. Heilbroner, *An Inquiry*, 161–62.

28. Ibid., 143–44.

29. See Willard A. Mullins, "On the Concept of Ideology in Political Science," *American Political Science Review* 66 (June 1972): 498–510; John S. Nelson, "Ashcraft's Problem of Ideology," *Journal of Politics* 42 (August 1980): 709–15.

30. Judith N. Shklar, "The Political Theory of Utopia," pp. 101–15, in Frank E. Manuel, ed., *Utopias and Utopian Thought* (Boston: Beacon, 1965).

31. Of late, almost the only concrete, detailed, yet credible, projections of other ways of life have not been ideologies or utopias but dystopias.

32. J. Peter Euben, "Politics, Piety, and Professing," paper prepared for the annual meeting of the American Political Science Association, Washington, D.C., 1977, p. 25.

33. Nelson, "Ironic Politics," 14–43.

34. See Robert Jay Lifton, "Protean Man," *Partisan Review* 35 (Winter 1968): 13–27; Richard Rorty, *Contingency, Irony, and Solidarity* (Cambridge, England: Cambridge University Press, 1989).

35. Glenn Tinder, "Transcending Tragedy: The Idea of Civility," *American Political Science Review* 68 (June 1974): 547.

36. Glenn Tinder, "In Defense of Pure Tolerance," *Polity* 6 (summer 1974): 465.

37. Tinder, "Transcending Tragedy," 551, 553.

38. Ibid., 554, 555.

39. Ibid., 555.

40. See Glenn Tinder, *The Crisis of Political Imagination* (New York: Scribner's, 1964), *Political Thinking* (Boston: Little, Brown, 1979), *Community* (Baton Rouge: Louisiana State University Press, 1980), and *Against Fate* (Notre Dame, Ind.: University of Notre Dame Press, 1981).

41. See Glenn Tinder, *Tolerance* (Amherst: University of Massachusetts Press, 1975).

42. See Robert L. Heilbroner, *The Making of Economic Society* (Englewood Cliffs, N.J.: Prentice-Hall, 1962), *The Great Ascent* (New York: Harper & Row, 1963), and "A Radical View of Socialism," *Social Research* 39 (spring 1972): 1–15.

43. Heilbroner, *An Inquiry*, 74, 168.

44. Peter L. Berger, *Pyramids of Sacrifice* (New York: Basic, 1974), 231. See Peter L. Berger and Richard J. Neuhaus, *Movement and Revolution* (Garden

City, N.Y.: Doubleday, 1970); Peter L. Berger, Brigitte Berger, and Hansfried Kellner, *The Homeless Mind* (New York: Random House, 1973).

45. Berger, *Pyramids of Sacrifice*, 198–228.

46. Berger and Neuhaus, *Movement and Revolution*, 20–30.

47. Berger, *Pyramids of Sacrifice*, 231.

48. See Garry Wills, *Nixon Agonistes* (Boston: Houghton Mifflin, 1969), *Inventing America* (New York: Random House, 1978), *Confessions of a Conservative* (New York: Penguin, 1979), *Lead Time* (Garden City, N.Y.: Doubleday, 1983), *Explaining America* (Garden City, N.Y.: Doubleday, 1981), *Cincinnatus: George Washington and the Enlightenment* (Garden City, N.Y.: Doubleday, 1984), and *Lincoln at Gettysburg* (New York: Simon & Schuster, 1992). See George F. Will, *Statecraft as Soulcraft* (New York: Simon & Schuster, 1983), and *Restoration* (New York: Free Press, 1992).

49. See John S. Nelson, "Politics and Truth: Arendt's Problematic," *American Journal of Political Science* 22 (May 1978): 270–301.

50. Schaar, "Power and Purity," 178.

51. See Sheldon S. Wolin, "Political Theory as a Vocation," *American Political Science Review* 63 (December 1969): 1062–82.

52. Sheldon S. Wolin, *Hobbes and the Epic Tradition of Political Theory* (Los Angeles: University of California Press, 1970), 4.

53. See Sheldon S. Wolin, *Politics and Vision* (Boston: Little, Brown, 1960), and *The Presence of the Past* (Baltimore: Johns Hopkins University Press, 1989).

54. See Martin Jay, *The Dialectical Imagination* (Boston: Little, Brown, 1973).

55. See Herbert Marcuse, *One-Dimensional Man* (Boston: Beacon, 1964).

56. See Henry S. Kariel, "Expanding the Political Present," *American Political Science Review* 63 (September 1969): 768–76, *Open Systems* (Itasca, Ill: Peacock, 1969), "Creating Political Reality," *American Political Science Review* 64 (December 1970): 1088–98, *Saving Appearances* (Belmont, Calif.: Duxbury Press, 1972), *Beyond Liberalism: Where Relations Grow* (San Francisco: Chandler and Sharp, 1977), and *The Desperate Politics of Postmodernism* (Amherst: University of Massachusetts Press, 1989). Also see Nelson, "Ironic Politics," 837–42.

57. James Taylor, "Fire and Rain," *James Taylor* (New York: Amsco Music, 1971).

58. See Murray Edelman, "Antidotes," *Constructing the Political Spectacle* (Chicago: University of Chicago Press, 1988), 126–30.

59. See Robert D. Holsworth, *Let Your Life Speak* (Madison: University of Wisconsin Press, 1989); J. Patrick Dobel, *Compromise and Political Action* (Savage, Md.: Rowman and Littlefield, 1990).

INDEX

Abduction, 53–54, 128, 186
Abstraction, xvi, 5, 7, 15, 18–23, 27, 31, 43, 45, 61, 84, 159, 165, 212–13, 221–22, 227
Achen, Christopher, 67–68, 70
Achilles, 227, 229
Action, xviii–xix, 11, 19, 27–29, 48, 56, 72–74, 85–86, 89, 91–93, 99, 102, 104, 110, 135, 142, 144–46, 150–52, 156, 159, 161, 163, 180–86, 191, 193–94, 203–30
Ad hoc hypothesizing, 57, 76–77
Administration, 55, 130, 148, 161
Adorno, Theodor, 228
Aestheticism, 145–46
Aesthetics, xvii, 6, 24, 127–28, 132; of inquiry, xvi, 96, 131, 133
African American studies, 50
Aggregate data, 11, 96
Alexander the Great, 229
Almond, Gabriel, 66, 76, 82
Alternate rhetorics, 52–54, 58, 61, 64, 71
Ambition, 38, 40, 48, 75, 101, 185, 202, 214, 225
American studies, 50
Analogy, 136–38
Analysis, xix, 25, 117, 127, 136–37, 183–86, 213
Analytical theories, 16, 75, 87–92, 96
Anderson, Poul, 160, 162, 166, 170
Anecdotes. *See* Stories
Anomalies. *See* Aporia; Paradox
Anthropology, xiv, xvii, 4–5, 7, 25, 44, 54, 78, 86, 180, 197; of inquiry, 7, 58, 96
Aphorism, xix, 131
Apologies, 198
Aporia, 58–59, 65, 70, 130, 154, 210
Apostrophe, 29
Approved or official rhetorics, 12–14, 23, 27, 51–71
Archaeology, xviii, 183; of inquiry, 122
Architecture, 30
Archives, 11
Area studies, 24, 54, 78

Arendt, Hannah, 37, 83, 86, 126, 132, 145–46, 193, 211, 216, 226–27
Argument, xv, xvii–xix, 5, 7, 9–11, 17–18, 25, 27–30, 44, 49, 51, 56, 72–98, 99–114, 118–19, 122, 135–49, 163, 168, 181, 191–92, 197, 199, 203, 207; definition of, 114; detours of, xix, 27, 111–13; repressions of, 70; tokens of, xix, 27, 99, 106, 111–13; traps of, xix, 27, 111–14, 262; tropes of (*see* Tropes)
Aristotle, xix, 18, 31, 91, 104, 136–37, 140, 143–44, 147, 190, 194, 218, 229
Artificial intelligence, 50, 125, 163, 167–68
Arts, xiv–xviii, 6, 48, 84, 229
Association, 42, 55, 57, 67, 103, 135, 161, 167, 196
Assumptions, xv, xviii, 5, 20, 25–26, 73, 81–82, 84, 88–89, 97, 101–2, 108–9, 181
Atlas, 219–20, 222, 224
Auden, W. H., 48
Audiences, xv, xviii, 7, 14, 18–19, 25, 29, 31, 92, 96, 104, 120, 124, 137–39, 141–43, 195–201
Augustine, 62, 104, 220
Austin, J. L., 122
Authority, 11, 29, 38, 97, 104, 129, 132, 167, 171, 225
Authorization, 32
Ayto, John, 138–39

Barthes, Roland, 181
Baudelaire, Charles, 131
Baudrillard, Jean, 171
Beauty, 141, 145–46
Behavior(al)ism, 18, 24–25, 42, 57, 66, 74–88, 100–4, 110, 117, 144, 159, 182, 203
Benjamin, Walter, 228
Bentham, Jeremy, 34
Berger, Peter L., 225–26
Bernstein, Richard J., 40
Berry, Wendell, 36–38, 40, 44
Biology, xiv, 29, 50, 62–63, 87

Index

100–4, 119, 125, 132, 143, 177, 209, 212, 214, 220, 227, 229, 277
Rhetoric, xiii–xvii, 5–8, 16, 19, 22, 40, 48–49, 51, 86, 121, 126, 36–137, 217; as discipline or tradition, xv–xvi, 23, 25, 31–32, 34, 48–49, 67–68, 144, 171–72; as epistemic, 22, 26, 60; as political science, 10, 91–92; definition of, xv, xvii, 9–10, 91–92, 181; of inquiry, xiv–xviii, 4–9, 38–39, 43, 45, 47–50, 55–71, 87, 97–98, 111–14, 120–21, 134, 202; theories of, 21, 25, 49, 162–63, 168
Rhetoric of political inquiry, xviii, 3–33
Rhythms, 131, 145, 153, 157, 171, 173, 182
Rieff, Philip, 38
Rights, 11, 140, 147–48, 160–61, 164–66
Riker, William, 41–42, 66–68, 70, 77, 82, 88, 90–92, 126, 192
Rituals, xiv, 94, 143, 173, 180–204, 210, 213
Rochefoucauld, 102
Roosevelt, Franklin, 147
Rorty, Amelie Oksenberg, 72–73, 75, 84, 87, 92, 97
Rorty, Richard, 21
Rouechè, Burton, 60
Rousseau, Jean-Jacques, 220
Rubinstein, Diane, 32
Rules, xv, 4, 6–8, 12, 18, 85, 94, 117, 139, 155, 169, 175, 193, 196, 198–200, 222. *See also* Regulation

Sacks, Oliver, 24
Saint-Exupéry, Antoine de, 117
Samuelson, Robert, 60
Satire, 201
Satisficing, 89
Schaar, John, 227
Schopenhauer, Arthur, 145
Schrag, Calvin, 21
Science fiction, 155, 193
Sciences, xiv–xvii, 3, 6, 19–20, 45, 131, 170, 178, 213; definition of, xvii, 98, 123
Seduction, 171–72
Sellars, Wilfrid, 21
Semiotics, 117
Sennett, Richard, 132
Service, xiii, 36, 89, 161
Setting. *See* Occasion

Shaftesbury, Lord, 124
Shapiro, Michael J., 32, 129
Shaw, George Bernard, 145
Shelley, Percy Bysshe, 150, 153
Shils, Edward, 37
Shively, W. Phillips, 65
Simmel, Georg, 43
Simon, Herbert A., 77, 88–89
Sisyphus, 218
Situation. *See* Occasion
Skepticism, 75–84, 96, 118, 211–12, 223, 226
Social sciences, xiv–xviii, 4, 8, 11, 17–20, 23–25, 35, 39, 44–45, 48–51, 64, 66, 69, 72–75, 84–87, 95–98, 101, 118–23, 126–27, 131, 133, 144, 154, 226, 245
Social studies of science, 58
Socialism, 155, 160–61, 167, 171, 220, 224–26
Society, 8, 37–38, 50, 54, 84–86, 104, 127–28, 136, 151, 155–57, 161, 163, 167, 170, 216, 223; civil, 151–52, 162, 200; mass, 146, 162, 165–68, 177, 213, 218, 220, 226
Sociobiology, 103–4
Sociology, xvii, 4–5, 7, 29, 74, 77, 89, 102, 144; of inquiry, xvi, 7, 13–15, 58–59, 87, 96, 217, 226
Sontag, Susan, 177
Sophists, 10, 91
Sovereignty, 129, 149, 160–61, 164–66, 169–70, 173
Speaker, 29, 39, 138–43, 188–92, 199
Specialization, xiii, 8, 35, 45, 73–74, 215
Spectacle, 171, 175, 189, 198
Speculation, xv, 5, 41, 43, 74, 77, 96, 101, 104
Speech act theory, 32
Stances, xix, 29, 160, 190, 198, 205–30; definition of, 208
Standards, 17–22, 26–27, 92, 95–97, 128, 150, 161, 163–64
Stands, xix, 160, 205–230; definition of, 208
State of nature, 147, 161
States. *See* Government
Station, 161
Statistical significance, 53, 107, 133
Statistics, 4, 11, 15, 41, 50, 52, 55–57, 66, 68, 73, 78, 80, 92, 94–95, 99–100, 102–7, 112–14, 127–28

RHETORIC OF THE HUMAN SCIENCES

Lying Down Together: Law, Metaphor,
and Theology
Milner S. Ball

Shaping Written Knowledge: The Genre and
Activity of the Experimental Article in Science
Charles Bazerman

Textual Dynamics of the Professions: Historical
and Contemporary Studies of Writing in
Professional Communities
Charles Bazerman and James Paradis, editors

Politics and Ambiguity
William E. Connolly

The Rhetoric of Reason: Writing and the
Attractions of Argument
James Crosswhite

Philosophy, Rhetoric, and the End of Knowledge:
The Coming of Science and Technology Studies
Steve Fuller

Machiavelli and the History of Prudence
Eugene Garver

Language and Historical Representation: Getting
the Story Crooked
Hans Kellner

The Rhetoric of Economics
Donald N. McCloskey

The Rhetoric of Economics, Second Edition
Deirdre N. McCloskey

Therapeutic Discourse and Socratic Dialogue:
A Cultural Critique
Tullio Maranhão

The Rhetoric of the Human Sciences: Language and
Argument in Scholarship and Public Affairs
*John S. Nelson, Allan Megill, and
Donald N. McCloskey, editors*

Tropes of Politics: Science, Theory, Rhetoric, Action
John S. Nelson

What's Left? The Ecole Normale Supérieure and
the Right
Diane Rubenstein

Understanding Scientific Prose
Jack Selzer, editor

The Politics of Representation: Writing Practices in
Biography, Photography, and Policy Analysis
Michael J. Shapiro

The Legacy of Kenneth Burke
Herbert Simons and Trevor Melia, editors

The Unspeakable: Discourse, Dialogue, and
Rhetoric in the Postmodern World
Stephen A. Tyler

Heracles' Bow: Essays on the Rhetoric and the
Poetics of the Law
James Boyd White